Shanghai's metropolitan heart crowds the banks of the Huangpu River. [Staffan Holgersson]

INTRODUCTION

herever you are, however you came to pick up this book, first be confident that your interest in China is entirely justified. What's difficult to understand is how anyone could not be attracted by its endless intrigues. China presents innumerable, simultaneous layers of thought-provoking spectacle, contrasts that won't be explained away quickly. Its images render us breathless, and stay in memory.

For starters, it's huge. Trace the Chinese border with a moving finger and consider the implied complexity of the culture. Born on the outside of the border, you would call yourself one of many diverse nationalities: Vietnamese or Afghan, Korean or Indian, Russian or Lao, Pakistani or Burmese. Born on the inside of the line, you will consider yourself part of China. The Chinese call their homeland the "Middle Kingdom", which does indeed imply that everywhere else is peripheral. When you stand astride a ruined section of the Great Wall—imagine one foot is in barbarian terrain, the other within the boundaries of civilization.

So many other nations have tried, and eventually given up on the experiment of drawing lines on the map to create giant, culturally unified, geographically contiguous blocks. Rulers from ancient Persia through Rome to the defunct USSR have learned over the millennia that sustained political unity is impossible, and that cultural unity cannot be enforced. In stark contrast, the Chinese have collected their own data and come to the opposite conclusion: that sustained political and cultural unity is a prerequisite for survival.

The theory certainly makes for more interesting travel. To explore the diverse landscapes that China's borders embrace leads to marvelling at the power exerted by the essence of Chinese identity. From the deep woods where tall, sauerkraut-eating northeasterners tell tales of tigers; to the arid southwest where the only item on the menu, day in and day out, is mutton; from the wet wharves of the shrewd, stocky fish-eating Cantonese to the misty river-laced mountains of Guilin; from the rugged cliffs of Chongqing teeming with tough, fire-eating longshoremen to Beijing's wide boulevards plied by articulate, earthy, intellectuals; or the super-slick city streets of the sophisticated Shanghainese, sporting elegant coiffures, shod in Italian sandals, quaffing cappuccino. China's central government over the centuries has contended with regionalist tendencies by touting the benefits of an ideal great nation, and keeping all regions in tribute with divide-and-conquer tactics.

Numerous minority groups help compose the Chinese cultural identity. [Wong How Man]

*A Formula 1 Jaguar roars round the Shanghai International Circuit, opened in 2004,
the year that F1 racing debuted in China (the final year of Hongkong & Shanghai
Banking Corporation's sponsorship of the Jaguar Team, an eight-year run). [Ford-Jaguar]*

Though China amazes by spanning so much space, more intriguing is how it encompasses time. China's history books refer to 5,000 years of heritage, during which time the key pattern repeats: territory consolidates so unification can be rightly imposed, then preserved, then cyclically, tragically disturbed, and finally heroically restored. (For a contemporary, accessible reference, has anyone seen the 2003 Zhang Yimou film called *Hero*?) Cultural identity looks back, and looks forward at the same time. In China even as the conventional view of history is measured in millennia rather than centuries, so time proceeds in a fashion that is cyclic, not linear, and which refers always powerfully back to the past.

Visiting China reveals a paradox of time, where every economic and social system of the past 1,000 years is still in practice, where villages built around a well hum along just hours outside a city where people ride a magnetic levitation train to the airport.

· The way the Chinese project their culture into both of time's horizons—forward and back—began long ago. Confucius, a powerfully respected thinker in 500 BCE and still so today, declared the ancients and ancestors as exemplars of virtue, and called for the wise governance practised by the Duke of Chou to be reinstated. In other words, 2,500 years ago, a prophet urging regression found a receptive audience. Confucius's teachings survived the purges, the book-burnings and the scholars-being-buried-alive unpleasantness through the ages. All along then, the Chinese have resonated with a call to restore the good old days.

In the 1920s, 2,000 years later, an astute novelist and essayist on Chinese identity, society and politics—that darling of the early Communist Party, Lu Xun—had his archetypal character repeat, in fatalistic explanation for all manner of unfortunate, brutal phenomena, "*Conglai ruci*—it has always been this way".

Lineage is everything, the longer, clearer, and more illustrious the better. Even in the present, Chinese art historians stubbornly exclude all foreign influence from the "pure" line of China's visual artistic tradition while Chinese archaeologists sweat to extend the continuity of Chinese civilization as far back, and over as wide a range, as possible.

Yet despite this allegiance to lineage, here are all these people walking around with cell phones, knocking down historically significant courtyards and erecting skyscrapers, starting Internet companies and going to work at laboratories to map genomes. Growing numbers of Chinese are drinking coffee instead of tea, popping Contac instead of downing a medicinal tonic and choosing Christianity to Buddhism.

What is this place—repository of ancient wisdom, site of ancient monuments; a gentle and meditative place where people accept fate and expect the resolution of conflict over time, if at all?

Or rather, perhaps, China may be the most aggressive part of our own world— the booming powerhouse ready to discard its past, positioned to take charge of our destiny as well as its own. China's political system periodically has no use whatsoever for its own past, and every use in the book for hard foreign money and all the foreign technology that can be put to work for the good of China. It is indeed the Middle Kingdom: a land of people on bicycles and of people who drive like tomorrow never comes, never so much as glancing into the next lane or the rear view mirror.

This dichotomy is pervasive. There are plastic signs in fast-food primary colours, and battered wooden posts pointing to clan villages. In rural villages life goes on largely unmediated by technology. Dinner cooks in a wood-fired wok and water is pulled up from a well. Goats are herded and latrines are dug.

At the same time, China's cities move quickly. Shanghai makes Manhattan seem asleep on its feet. Beijing keeps planning for the future, institutionalizing its participation and even leadership in multilateral organizations. Can China turn back to its inward-looking vision of a nation referring first and foremost to stability, based on a model of its past, while simultaneously adopting transparency, automation, and an economic system that calls for a dialectic? As in Marx—where dialectic calls for constant change. Where the founder of the current political state—Mao Zedong—

called for ceaseless revolution? If, as Bill Joy states, there are three forces: Man, Nature and Technology, how do the Chinese triangulate? If there are two approaches to social structure—open and closed, Western and Eastern—and China sees itself as open *to* the West, then how does China view the idea of being open *like* the West? (If this intrigues you, read Jonathan Spence, Lu Xun and contemporary reportage.)

What year is it in China now? In our own land apparently it is 2008 CE? Though I suggest we spend a moment understanding how it may also be, as the Chinese calendar suggests, 4705.

Four thousand seven hundred and five years ago, a man named Fu Xi set out an agricultural almanac based on yin and yang theory—a cyclic theory of energy. It began with nine representations of the interplay between two primary forces, yin and yang, which determines all that happens. Active yang energy rises, builds, peaks, deteriorates, falls, while nurturing yin gains, consolidates, fatigues, is overwhelmed. In other words, spring overtakes winter, waxes to summer, is outlasted by the call to fruition called autumn. Autumn deepens, hardens stubbornly to winter's deep hibernation, and then surrenders in turn and in time to gathering heat.

The endless interplay of yin and yang were further mapped in 64 permutations of combining energy ranging from *qian*—all active—to *kun*—all passive. Codified later by Taoist theory, commented on by the originally skeptical Confucius into the fourth of his Four Classics, the *Book of Changes* (we call it the *I Ching*), the theory of yin and yang is the foundation of Chinese medicine, feng shui, and in a broad sense the entire psychic underpinnings of what we could call "an Asian sensibility". The Asian view of time takes life's course as cyclic, not linear; takes negative space as essential; takes the body's energy as sacred, and the ideas of fate and free will as equally valid, coexistent.

Those 64 hexagrams were rearranged by King Wen into an order that Leibniz credits as the inspiration for binary code, which Watson and Crick referred to in organizing the molecular structure of DNA, and Carl Jung consulted as a tool for divining the machinations of the subconscious.

What could be more ancient than an agricultural almanac? What could be more modern than the tool used to crack the underpinning codes of computer science, bioengineering and psychology?

At once esoteric and practical, ancient and modern, the yin and yang theory is quintessentially Chinese. It leads us to view things in ways that, for Western minds,

A smiling vision of Shanghai—yesterday, today, or tomorrow? [Anthony Cassidy]

are more grounded in history, more ambiguous. Here are a few examples for your coming trip to China. As you travel, ask yourself what year it is:

In the Banpo Neolithic village just outside Xi'an, it is the present day, meeting explanatory text first drafted in the cautiously revealing early 1980s, as we study moat-encircled life in a matriarchal village circa 4600 BCE.

Fifty kilometres away at the Terracotta warriors, it is at the same time 212 CE (when the warriors were made); 1982 (when the big quonset hut that shelters pit No 2 was first opened), and six years behind whatever year it is in Beijing currently (check the local fashions and music).

Everyone will tell you that conservative Tianjin is 60 kilometres southeast and 20 years behind Beijing. Although by now, it may be 30 years behind Beijing.

In Beijing, it is the waxing era of nationalistic prestige, nearly 60 years into a stable reign. It may be just a matter of months before it hosts the 2008 Olympics, or it may be a replay of 1792, in the Qing reign of the Qianlong emperor: China, secure with its huge and growing trade surplus, told the British envoy that though they were happy to keep exporting, there was nothing they could imagine wanting to import. Or are we watching the continued unfolding of a world power, peaking—the Yuan under Kublai Khan? The early Ming circa 1400, prospering through trade, launching its magnificent fleet under Zheng He, who explored India and Africa, who circled the Cape of Good Hope 60 years before Vasco deGama? If so, should we expect a coming replay of the late Ming, when the emperor burned all the ships and shut the country down to foreigners?

Guangzhou is both Hong Kong in 1978, still waiting for its skyscrapers, and Hong Kong in 2024, fast forwarded, gone-to-seed, sleazy and hardcore. Everyone has evolved, or devolved—it's hard to say—into a masterfully focused, archetypal trader of wares. Life follows the primal beat: eat, buy low, sell high, sleep, repeat.

Shanghai in 1999, in its optimistic flush of starlit glamour, felt for all the world like Hong Kong in 1991. By 2005, Shanghai took on the energy of Hong Kong's manic, hell-for-leather boom time—early 1997. In the minds of the city's architectural planners, the time is whenever the cartoon called *The Jetsons* takes place. Gaze at the skyline and try to deny that those purple neon lit overpasses, those studiously futuristic skyscrapers, that 400kph magnetic levitation train were not envisioned as a frame for the cruising of shapely personal spacecraft. For us, it is contemporary and familiar: Western architecture and urban parkland with benches. Coffee shops, ice cream, Mister Donut!

Guilin suspends in a mist-shrouded mythical era, except the hawkers of pirated Hollywood DVDs, not yet released to theatres in America. Is it next week already?

Building an understanding of China requires a framework of some kind. Try the following: yin representing the weight of the reflective past, yang portraying the busy, technology-laden future; yin for ancient temples and world monuments, yang for skyscrapers and maglev trains; yin for China's spiritual traditions, yang for China's materialistic culture; yin for Asia, yang for West. Have some fun as you contemplate that the 64 hexagrams may represent some substantive, ineffably revealing code. (Ask Leibniz, Jung, Confucius, or Crick & Watson.)

The world isn't ever black or white, modern or ancient, open or closed, moving forward or moving back. It's never simple or stable. In fact it is not linear, but it can be described at any point as one of 64 permutations of yin and yang, on its way to a different one of the 64 moments. Nowhere is this fact more obvious than in multi-layered, multi-temporal China.

Janet Carmosky studied Chinese history at the University of Pennsylvania, then spent two long, wild decades living and doing business in China while also serving as daughter-in-law to the Zhang clan. She has a decent grasp of the cyclic nature of time.

Ming Pao Daily, 16 October 2003. A historic day, as China's first spaceman
Yang Liwei lands safely after 21 hours in orbit. China is continuing to develop
and broaden its space programme. [Ming Pao Daily]

Shanghai's skyline seems to change on an almost weekly basis. The image above shows a view of Pudong from the Bund, looking across to the site of the new Shanghai World Financial Center, completed in summer 2008. Towering over the Jin Mao Building, at 492 metres it is China's tallest building. [Superview rendering image courtesy of Kohn Pedersen Fox Associates and the Mori Building Co. Ltd.]

BEIJING'S OLYMPIAN ARCHITECTURAL FEAT
—By *Paul Mooney*

I n its preparations to host the 2008 Olympic Games, Beijing underwent one of the most ambitious urban makeovers the world has ever seen. The transformation extended from state-of-the-art athletic facilities to fast-rising residential and business districts, high-tech transportation networks and the renewal of historical sites, significantly remaking the layout of a city that has not changed much since imperial times.

Organizers say the scale and complexity of the Olympic projects was unprecedented. Beijing officials, aware of the international spotlight that would be turned on the city as a result of the Games, turned to the leading names in international architecture to give the city a modern look. A consortium led by Swiss-based Herzog & de Meuron Architekten of Switzerland built the US$500 million main arena for the Olympic Games, with a design that looks like a giant bird's nest. The National Stadium, made of interlocking bands of grey steel covered with a transparent membrane and a retractable roof, can accommodate 100,000 spectators.

Meanwhile, an Australian-Chinese consortium led by Sydney firm PTW Architects Australia designed the US$100 million National Aquatics Center. The company's amazing Watercube (H2O3) design is made from a state-of-the-art plastic material designed to react to lighting and projection to create an interesting visual and sensory effect. The box alternates between transparent and translucent.

Beijing airport's new Terminal 3, built to open just in time to greet the Olympic throng, is equipped with state-of-the-art airport technology. Experts describe it as one of the most impressive airport facilities in the world. The Norman Foster-designed terminal, which covers some 1 million square metres, is the biggest in the world, with a larger combined surface area than all five of Heathrow's terminals, and twice as large as Hong Kong's Chek Lap Kok. It also has a 3,800-metre-long by 60-metre-wide runway to accommodate the biggest aircraft in the world, the Airbus A380.

(Preceding pages) *A 2006 view from the top of the Peace Hotel across the Huangpu River to Pudong New Area, the Oriental Pearl TV Tower's architecture dominating the skyline.*

The geometry of the structure was designed to direct the flow of passengers, almost hypnotically, in the right direction. The sweeping shape of the arrival hall, which looks like a modernistic 17th-century train station, reinforces the movement, drawing people inside. The lights in the roof run due north across the north-south axis of the building, serving as a sort of compass, changing some 16 shades along the way, also keeping passengers moving forward.

The designers were asked to make the airport state-of-the-art, but at the same also evoke Chinese traditional culture. Consequently the terminal has a massive sloping gold tiled roof, similar to the colour of the roof tiles at the Forbidden City, which was created to resemble the back of a dragon. The texture of the roof tiles is uneven to give them the look of a dragon's scales, and large red columns reminiscent of imperial architecture grace the structure.

Another exciting development is the high-speed light rail connection that whisks travellers along the 28km stretch between the airport and the Dongzhimen station in less than 20 minutes, making four stops along the way.

Beijing's hosting of the 2008 Olympics sparked a massive urban building effort that cost as much as US$37 billion; the National Aquatics Center, or "Watercube", a model of which is shown above, cost US$100 million alone. [Peter Danford]

Special Topic

The light rail station is linked with Beijing's subway system and so transportation is seamless. Passengers are able to check in for their flight downtown and get rid of their bags before heading out to the airport.

In order to spruce up the city for the Olympics, a number of other dazzling buildings have been built around the Chinese capital. Dutch architect Rem Koolhaas designed the 575,000-square-metre broadcast headquarters for China Central Television (CCTV). The estimated US$750 million complex employs a continuous loop of horizontal and vertical sections rising 230 metres into the sky (see page 81).

Right next door is the glittering Television Cultural Center (TVCC), also designed by the radical Dutch firm OMA. The building, which rises and falls like a mountain wrapped in metal, is home to what has to be one of the world's most stunning hotels: the new 241-room Mandarin Oriental, Beijing with its 21-storey atrium.

Another impressive new place to stay is the sleek Park Hyatt, a 63-storey, 237-room boutique hotel, penthouse and condo residence, and retail complex flanked by two office buildings. Check-in takes place on the 63rd floor, and

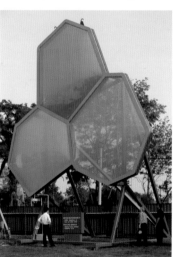

the hotel's rooftop bar, which resembles a huge Chinese lantern, offers wonderful views of the city.

A new major landmark has been created by Paul Andreu of France, the chief architect of Aeroports de Paris, who designed the futuristic National Grand Theatre. Andreu's very controversial design features a titanium and glass dome that appears to float on water, standing over a three-theatre complex.

The Watercube's plastic polygons react to light for interesting optical effects. [Peter Danford]

(Above) *The National Stadium, aka the Bird's Nest. [Peter Danford]*

Visitors to the US$365 million theatre, which opened in December 2007, have to board escalators to travel through the submerged lobby.

But for Beijing the Olympic Games has not been simply about concrete and steel. In the run-up to the Games the government was determined to deal with a problem that most Beijingers talk constantly about: the weather. Officials developed a method they believed could delay or push away rain clouds that might disrupt the Games. Equally difficult, however, has been changing people's behaviour, another stated goal of the Olympic organizers. The city's Communist Party secretary promised to re-educate people who use locally invented profanity to cheer and jeer players at sporting events. To raise Beijing's 'civility' level, the government cracked down on people who use *jingma*, a Chinese phrase loosely translated as 'Beijing cursing'.

A big push was also made to discourage the habit of spitting, which is widespread throughout China. And finally, to start getting people used to the idea of not cutting in line, Wednesdays were declared, 'Stand in line day'. Whether these behavioural lessons bear fruit beyond the 2008 summer Olympics and into the years ahead, only time will tell.

Special Topic

WHAT'S IN A WORD?
OFTEN, A WHOLE CULTURE

Czech proverb that I cannot possibly pronounce declares something like: "To speak another language is to live another life."

There may be sound historical reasons for the Czechs to have mastered more than one tongue, literally to "live another life" under the boot of yet another foreign invader.

But the saying also points to the fascination of learning a new tongue and, above all, of entering its culture. Because culture is where the dictionary ends and where the linguist finds real meaning, crossing over into the life and world of another people.

While this journey is pure enjoyment for some, it becomes a vital necessity if we transpose the task to the field of international relations, where the call for translators, or translation by any means, human or mechanical, is ever more urgent. Here, relations with China and with the Arab world, both with radically different linguistic and cultural characteristics from the West's, are of critical importance.

We can learn words and translations of words, but then there is understanding, which is something else altogether.

An early machine translation expert, Yehoshua Bar-Hillel, pointed out the impossibility of getting a computer translation program to even understand the simple phrase "the box is in the pen." Only our knowledge of dimensions in the world around allows us to find a possible sense in this apparently odd sentence.

Meaning arises from context and, by extension, from the external context of culture. Modern sociolinguistics describes the dynamic relationship between a culture and its language, each shaping the other with endlessly creative vitality.

We experience puzzlement when we find that a culture has no word for something that to us is basic, familiar and an essential part of our reality. What can life be like for the Algonquins, native Americans who have no word for time? Or for Australian aboriginal language speakers who have no word for left or right?

The Australian Law Reform Commission published a report in 1986 that drew attention to the difficulties of interrogating Aboriginal suspects because of the conceptual gaps between English and, for instance, Pitjantjatjara. That tongue has no word for "because," so cause and effect, along with other relational aspects, are conceived and expressed quite differently. Notions of time, place, number and kinship are also far removed from those of a typical English-speaker.

The report points out that, as a result, undue suspicion falls on those unable to give the clear, precise and therefore trustworthy answers much loved of white judges. Not to put too fine a point on it, in a court of law where languages cross such a cultural gap, we can see the huge potential for injustice.

On a larger scale, the potential for huge misunderstanding can arise in diplomatic exchanges. Mistrust arises, especially in politics, when trying to cross an untranslatable gap.

When Jiang Zemin, the Chinese president, visited the United States in 1997, he caused much fuss by suggesting that the idea of democracy originated 2,000 years ago with Chinese philosophers. Liberal American commentators thought this absurd. But as Elvin Geng, a graduate in Asian studies, points out: "The word minzhu first appeared in a classic work called Shuji where it referred to a benevolent 'ruler of the people,' that is, a leader whose legitimacy rests on the people's welfare. In Chinese, the one term can mean 'rule of the people' as well as 'ruler of the people'."

"Both uses of minzhu share the sense that the government ought to meet the needs of the people. This criterion may be fulfilled by an enlightened dictator or a Leninist regime as well as by a U.S.-style constitutional democracy."

The concept of "human rights" equally leads to misunderstanding between China and the West because of the Confucian ideal of natural harmony lingering in the word quan, which can mean both power and rights. According to Geng, "the Chinese do not assume an adversarial relationship between the state and individual—a notion prominent in the Western understanding of rights."

How does one begin to bridge such gaps? To live another life oneself is, yes, at least a step toward international understanding. A colleague who has seen me break into Spanish at book fairs once commented, "You become another person." I like that.

C.J. Moore is the author of In Other Words: A Language Lover's Guide to the Most Intriguing Words Around the World, published by Oxford University Press. "What's in a Word?" first appeared in the International Herald Tribune, January 6, 2005.

Literary Excerpt

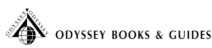

ODYSSEY BOOKS & GUIDES

Odyssey Books & Guides is a division of Airphoto International Ltd.
903 Seaview Commercial Building, 21–24 Connaught Road West, Sheung Wan, Hong Kong
Tel: (852) 2856-3896; Fax: (852) 2565-8004
E-mail: magnus@odysseypublications.com; www.odysseypublications.com

Distribution in the USA by W.W. Norton & Company, Inc., 500 Fifth Avenue, New York, NY 10110, USA
Tel: 800-233-4830; Fax: 800-458-6515; www.wwnorton.com

Distribution in the UK and Europe by Cordee Books and Maps, 3a De Montfort St., Leicester, LE1
7HD, UK   Tel: 0116-254-3579; Fax: 0116-247-1176; www.cordee.co.uk

China—Renaissance of the Middle Kingdom, Ninth Edition

ISBN: 978-962-217-794-9   Library of Congress Catalog Card Number has been requested.
Copyright © 2008, 2006, 2004, 2003 Airphoto International Ltd.
Copyright © 2000, 1999, 1998, 1995, 1994, 1992, 1989 Odyssey Publications Ltd.

Additional text contributions: William Lindesay; Madeleine Lynn, Stephen Hallett and Olivia Walker

Grateful acknowledgment is made to the following authors, publishers and contributors:
University of Hawaii Press for Rickshaw by Lao She, translated by Jean M James © 1979 University of
Hawaii Press and Diary of a Madman and Other Stories by Lu Xun, translated by William A Lyell © 1979
University of Hawaii Press; Stanford University Press for Born Red: A Chronicle of the Cultural
Revolution by Gao Yuan © 1987 by the Board of Trustees of the Leland Stanford Junior University; the
MIT Press for Living Together by Hu Yeh-p'in and Autumn Harvest by Mao Dun, from Straw Sandals:
Chinese Short Stories 1918–1933 by Harold Robert Isaacs © 1974 Massachusetts Institute of Technology;
Random Century Group and Jonathan Cape Publishers for Destination Chungking by Han Suyin ©
1942 Han Suyin; Alfred A Knopf (a division of Random House) for After the Nightmare by Liang Heng
and Judith Shapiro © 1982, 1983, 1984, 1985, 1986 Liang Heng and Judith Shapiro; Hodder &
Stoughton for The Gobi Desert by Mildred Cable ©1943 Mildred Cable; Jeff Hesselwood; Frédérique
Tsaï-Klassen

Editor: Jeremy Tredinnick
Design: Au Yeung Chui Kwai
Map Consultant: Professor Bai Yiliang
Maps: Aubrey Tse, Mark Stroud
Where uncredited, photography is by Magnus Bartlett
Cover photography: Staffan Holgersson (top); Jeremy Tredinnick (bottom)

Production and printing by Twin Age Ltd, Hong Kong
E-mail: twinage@netvigator.com
Manufactured in Hong Kong

*(Pages 4–5) This exquisite example of ceramic roofing is located at the northernmost part of the
Forbidden City adjacent to the Imperial Garden.*

CHINA
RENAISSANCE OF THE
MIDDLE KINGDOM

CHARIS CHAN

REVISED BY
JEREMY TREDINNICK
INTRODUCTION BY
JANET CARMOSKY

*"The use of travelling is to regulate imagination by reality,
and instead of thinking how things may be, to see them as they are."*
—Samuel Johnson (1709–1784)—

Notes to the Reader

*The many contributions to this guide have come from several sources,
and so in deference to those authors' and other contributors' preferences you may find both
English and American spellings employed. In addition, in most cases,
the traditional BC (Before Christ) and AD (Anno Domini) have been replaced with the more
neutral BCE (before the common era) and CE (common area), whereby "common" simply
refers to the most frequently used timeline reference, the Gregorian Calendar.*

CONTENTS

A mythic bronze lion fiercely guards gates within the Summer Palace, Beijing.

TRIP PLANNING

T he standard of travel arrangements in China has improved enormously during the past decade or so. There are comfortable international-standard hotels, new airports and an increasing number of areas open to tourists. China is rapidly developing itself and while open to tourists since 1978, tourism has been developed almost from scratch in a relatively short time. Thus English speakers are still in short supply and guides and hotel staff may not be very fluent. Attitudes to service jobs are improving, but you may still occasionally encounter surly and slow service.

Whether on a group tour or travelling independently, the key word for travelling in China is flexibility. Be prepared for itinerary changes, particularly flight changes and delays. Sometimes plane seats (and even entire cruise ships!) are commandeered by government officials with no advance warning. Bad weather in one area can wreak havoc with plane schedules across the country.

Most tourists in China travel on a package basis, which was once the only way, but the options have multiplied. There was a time when travellers could visit China only on a group tour organized by the state-run tourism agency, China International Travel Service (CITS). Not only are there many kinds of itineraries offered by travel agents and airlines worldwide, but independent travel is common. Either way, careful research and planning beforehand is essential.

This guide has been designed to help you plan your itinerary before you go, and to give you up-to-date information on the most attractive destinations once you get there. It is not comprehensive, but it includes the places most worthwhile to visit as well as a selection of exotic and adventurous expeditions that can be enjoyed either as part of a tour or be undertaken independently. The layout of the book reflects the way in which many people arrange their travel programmes: an itinerary which includes a selection of cities or an extended journey to one or more special regions.

City destinations in this book have been divided into four categories: Cultural Capitals, Cities Traditional and Modern, Cities in a Landscape and World Heritage sites. While there should not be any rules for choosing destinations, picking one from each category will provide the opportunity to see the range and contrasts of Chinese urban life and to gain an insight into the development of China's cultural heritage. The 'Expeditions' chapters cover the other possibilities that can be combined with a 'standard' tour—from the popular Yangzi River cruise to off-the-beaten-track exploration of China's border regions.

PACKAGE TOURS

The organized China tour, with its ready solution to the problems of time, language and money, is a blessing for first-time China travellers. A well-organized tour with a local escort is highly recommended even to those who would arrange their own itinerary elsewhere in the world. People who have lived and worked in China also like the problem-free nature of a tour, since they are all too well aware of what can go wrong in some of China's more far-flung regions. Group tours are definitely the best way to see a lot of China in a short time. Tour operators usually book hotels and Yangzi cruise ships directly and arrange guides, sightseeing, some or all meals and transportation.

As the Chinese open more and more destinations to foreign visitors, independent travellers are finding their options both extended and restricted. There are more places to visit, but there are also more people travelling. The economic reforms since 1978 have meant that ordinary Chinese people now have more money to go sightseeing. This has strained China's transport systems, and the independent traveller often has to fight and cajole his or her way onto a plane, boat or train.

During the boom years of China travel in the mid-1980s, hotels in the larger cities were invariably full to bursting during the popular tourist seasons of spring and autumn. Independent travellers who had not booked in advance found themselves having to sleep on floors or to journey out to dormitory hostels far from the centre of town. Although the supply of hotel rooms in the main cities has increased dramatically in recent years, you may still need to expend time and effort on locating one that suits your pocket and requirements.

On the other hand, hotel tariffs in China are now very competitive; many of them, especially those in cities which have been oversupplied as a result of a construction boom, offer special deals such as discounted weekend rates or winter packages, so it pays to shop around. Travellers now find that it is possible just to turn up at the front desk of a hotel and to negotiate for a room price considerably lower than the advertised rate (unless it is a state-operated hotel where the pricing policy tends to be inflexible).

Booking tickets for long-distance transport has become much easier. Competition between domestic airlines has increased the number of flights and the size of the planes being used. In larger cities the railway stations have special ticket offices for booking sleeping accommodation where some English is spoken, although in smaller towns limited allocations of tickets lead to a thriving black market, and it may be necessary to ask a local ticket agent to handle the purchase for a fee. Advance online ticket

Trip Planning

booking is now possible—visit www.china-train-ticket.com or www.seat61.com/
China.htm for more information. Return tickets are only available on some routes—
more usually you must buy two one-way tickets for each leg. Buying long-distance
bus tickets is rarely a problem due to the increasing number of private services.

The days are gone when Chinese guides insisted on starting sightseeing at 8:00am
sharp and included obligatory factory visits with briefings about the miraculous
production increases under socialism. Today's itineraries are more relaxed and free of
ideology. However, they are still quite strenuous; there is a lot of walking (sometimes
it seems as though every sight in China is at the top of myriad flights of steps!) and a
full programme of sightseeing is planned for every day, often finished off with a Chinese

In the Little Three Gorges area of Wushan County, Sichuan Province, trackers haul
a sampan through the Daning River rapids the traditional way, 1978. [Wong How Man]

opera or dance show in the evening. Shopping is often included in itineraries, as guides urge you to 'keep China green' (with banknotes, that is). *Caveat emptor*, however, as some guides may receive commission from those shops to which they take tourists, and their advice on a 'fair price' may be inflated to cover their commission. Most reputable tour operators prohibit their guides from exacting these sorts of commissions.

If, for reasons of time and convenience, you choose a tour, remember that you can select either a special-interest tour (anything from bicycling to botany) or a series of general tours with a mixture of contrasting destinations. If you have scientific or educational interests, it may be worth contacting the relevant professional or specialist organization in China (whether it is bird-watching or acupuncture) for help with organizing visits to specialist-interest sites or setting up exchange programmes.

Those on a general tour who wish to see an institution or site because of professional interest need not hesitate to ask their tour operator if a visit can be fitted into the schedule within any given city or region. Tour operators, if notified in advance, can pass on the request, apply for admission and make the appointment.

If you do decide to make your own way somewhere while on tour, it is easy to arrange transport (by hiring a taxi from your hotel or more cheaply by stopping vehicles in the street the previous day to negotiate), to use your own maps and the advice of a sympathetic guide. Although many guides are like good shepherds who want to keep their flock together for their own peace of mind, there is usually no problem if you decide to forego a prearranged excursion and go off on your own.

REGIONAL & SELF-PLANNED ITINERARIES

This section has been devised for those choosing a regional tour in China, as well as for those wanting to make their own travel arrangements. Indeed, the word 'expedition' should not discourage the comfort-loving traveller who may think that choosing an adventurous itinerary in China necessitates hardship. Every year, new areas of China that were either closed to foreigners or solely the domain of Chinese-speaking backpackers have been opened up by enterprising travel agents. These agents, in cooperation with the Chinese government, have helped to develop facilities where previously there were none, and they have also urged that more historical and archaeological sites be included on tourist itineraries—sites which once were known only to scholars.

An organized itinerary for adventure travel does not mean that the adventure is lost. Often it can mean that the tourist has more access to little-known places, which would be difficult to visit independently. Perhaps this is best illustrated by the tours to the Yangzi River. The independent traveller has the fun of booking a berth on a regular passenger steamer and travelling downstream in the company of a boat full of Chinese people on their daily business or on holiday themselves. The tourist who chooses to go on a luxury cruise loses this day-to-day contact with ordinary people, but does get the chance to make side-trips and stop at small towns which the scheduled steamer just glides past. As a generalization, one could say that the organized expedition is for those with less time but few financial restrictions, while the independent journey is for those with plenty of time but less cash.

If you decide to travel independently, prepare well by reading widely and by talking extensively to as many experienced China travellers as you can, and consider joining your local China friendship society (search the Internet and you'll find such societies in abundance, some English language sites follow: New Zealand, www.nzchinasociety.org.nz; Australia, www.acbc.com; in the UK try the Society for Anglo-Chinese Understanding, or Great Britain-China Centre, www.gbcc.org.uk; in the US the US-China Peoples Friendship Association, www.uscpfa.org). The Internet can also put you in direct contact with other travellers via the newsgroup *rec.travel.asia* or the China travel mailing list, *The Oriental-List* (pnh@axion.net). Web pages and blogs (Web-logs or online diaries) of independent travellers are another information resource. Overlooked by some independent travellers are the state-owned CITS or CTS, which have offices in many cities, and the user-friendly China National Tourism Authority website (www.cnta.com).

Check up on vaccination requirements, especially if you plan to visit some of the poorer border regions. Unless you are planning to scale a Himalayan peak, you will not need specialist equipment for mountain walking. The best thing you can take to China is a pair of stout walking shoes that are already broken-in; most other daily necessities for budget travelling can easily be bought in department stores throughout the country.

The list of do's and don'ts for independent travel in China will vary according to your age, health, and willingness to pick up some of the Chinese language. Make sure that you buy a phrase book before you go to China, since most people encounter language difficulties. When sightseeing, you can join up with an organized day tour in big cities if getting to the sights beyond the city is not easy or cheap. Going by bus is fun but time-consuming. Meeting up with someone and sharing a taxi for the day can often be the best solution. In fact, it is good to share meals too, since Chinese food is always better when there are a few people eating together.

Local travel agents can also save you time and energy by buying your train tickets for you. Commissions vary according to the agent, the difficulty in obtaining the ticket, and the class of berth chosen—shop around. Often, even when a certain train has been pronounced 'sold out', agents can use their connections and part of the fee you've paid them to get access to other allocations. Some agents have computer terminals for domestic airlines, and can sell you a ticket commission-free. Others will make the trip to the airline offices for you, again for a fee, typically ranging from Rmb50 to Rmb100. Bargain.

Above all, China travellers who go it alone should be models of patience, tolerance and forbearance in adversity. The Chinese have never admired people who lose their temper easily. There is a Chinese saying that you should be able to 'hold

Trip Planning

A pilgrim stands at the gilded entrance to the main hall of Songzhanling Monastery near Zhongdian, Yunnan Province. [Jeremy Tredinnick]

a boat in your stomach', the English equivalent of which is 'turn the other cheek'! Common problems on China expeditions range from no hot water to occasional power failures. If minor discomforts are going to cause you to lose your cool, then avoid travelling outside of the main cities in China. Bear in mind that travel in China has been known to test the patience of sages.

There are many off-the-beaten-track destinations in China waiting to be explored. Increasingly, there are also programmes that incorporate some adventurous activity like mountaineering and trekking. The Expeditions section of this book will point you to those areas that offer something more challenging than the standard China tour. The list is by no means comprehensive, but it does cover more exotic—as well as some of the most popular—destinations in the remote regions and in a few of the most scenic provinces.

If you decide to travel without arrangements set up in advance, in spite of the great leaps forward in China's travel services be prepared to spend frustrating hours chasing after plane and train tickets, especially at peak times: Chinese New Year, May to June and September to October. All transportation in China is invariably crowded and tickets are at a premium. Beware of touts selling train tickets—sometimes they are fake. With these provisos in mind, you will find most Chinese to be friendly and helpful, although often with limited English.

Naxi musicians tuning up for an impromptu concert, Lijiang, Yunnan.

FACTS FOR THE TRAVELLER
VISAS

All foreign travellers planning to visit China require a valid visa. China offers a number of different visa options including group visas (for travel groups) and individual visas issued for single, double and multiple entries (note: travellers visiting China as members of a tourist group can do so with an individual visa). The requirements for obtaining a China visa include passport validity of **at least six months after the date of your departure from China and one full, blank page for the China visa stamp.** Visas are issued by Chinese embassies and consulates abroad—many travel companies and independent visa service companies can do this on your behalf (you should obtain your visa at least 14 days prior to your departure). Applicants need to fill out a China visa application form and provide one photograph.

A China visa is normally issued with a validity of 30 days after your date of entry with its overall validity good for a period of three months from the date of issue. Double and multiple entry visas can be good from three to six months depending on your choice when applying. A group visa is a manifest on which passport details of the group members are listed (**there must be at least five persons to constitute a group**). **The group must enter and exit China by the same mode of transport.** "Landing Visas" (or "Visas on Arrival") can be obtained at some international airports and train stations (eg. Shenzhen) in China (this is subject to change) but it should be noted that EU (European Union) **passport holders of British Nationality are not eligible for a landing visa.**

If you are visiting Hong Kong prior to your entry into China you can obtain a China visa in as little as half a day (express service). The offices of CITS and CTS as well as many Hong Kong travel companies and visa services can obtain visas for travellers. It should be noted, however, that there are hefty surcharges for weekend and public holiday processing (normally two to three times the cost).

Visa extensions, valid for 30 days, are granted instantly at Public Security Bureaux (PSB, *Gongan Ju*) in most cities and towns. Application should be made no sooner than four days before the expiry of the current visa or extension. The number of extensions varies for different countries, for example US-passport holders are permitted only one extension. Generally the maximum number of extensions is three, though the last one may be difficult to obtain. Unextendable double-entry tourist visas are also available, as well as multiple-entry business visas.

Tourist visas give access to almost all open cities and regions, but some minority areas are only open with the acquisition of an additional permit from the PSB, and a special fee must be paid before the purchase of a bus or plane ticket to Lhasa is permitted. Some short trips from Hong Kong and Macau to neighbouring cities are possible with a limited visa granted at the border.

CUSTOMS

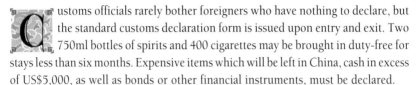

ustoms officials rarely bother foreigners who have nothing to declare, but the standard customs declaration form is issued upon entry and exit. Two 750ml bottles of spirits and 400 cigarettes may be brought in duty-free for stays less than six months. Expensive items which will be left in China, cash in excess of US$5,000, as well as bonds or other financial instruments, must be declared.

The export of antiques is controlled. It is forbidden to export any artefacts made earlier than 1795, unless they are common, such as Han dynasty coins. Most antiques sold in Friendship Stores or curio shops are not very old and many are fake. As long as they carry a red wax seal or a paper label indicating that the authorities approve, you may take them out of China. You should keep your sales receipts in case the customs officers ask to see them. Generally speaking, you will have no trouble taking out other old artefacts which you may have bought in a market—but if any question arises, the decision is left to the discretion of the customs officer on duty.

MONEY

RENMINBI

Chinese currency is called *renminbi* (meaning 'people's currency') and is abbreviated to Rmb. The standard unit is *yuan* (referred to as *kuai* in everyday speech). The yuan or *kuai* is divided into 10 *jiao* (referred to as *mao*) or 100 *fen*. Ten *fen* make one *mao* and 10 *mao* make one *kuai*. Yuan (*kuai*) and *jiao* (*mao*) are available in note forms, one *kuai* and five *mao* denominations appear as coins, and *fen* as small coins. Although it is now possible to exchange Rmb to hard currency outside China, export of more than Rmb6,000 is illegal, and it is better to reconvert within China. All Renminbi may be converted back to foreign currency if the bearer still holds the original exchange receipts, within six months of the original conversion. Renminbi to foreign currency exchange may be done at Bank of China offices at international airports in China and at Bank of China branches in Hong Kong. Conversion to foreign currencies can also be made at most of Hong Kong's many money changers.

FOREIGN CURRENCY

There is no limit to the amount of foreign currency you can bring into China, but you must declare any amount exceeding US$5,000. All prominent freely negotiable currencies can be exchanged at branches of the Bank of China, in hotels and stores. The yuan currently trades at about Rmb 7.3 to the dollar (inevitably this figure fluctuates, so always check just before your trip).

TRAVELLER'S CHEQUES AND CREDIT CARDS

International Visa and Mastercard credit/ATM cards are now widely accepted by many shops and restaurants. Visa and Mastercard signs may indicate, however, the acceptance of Chinese versions only. Foreigners can get cash using an international card from the Bank of China ATMs as well as Industrial and Commercial Bank of China ATMs throughout larger cities. In smaller cities, you often have to go to the main branch. Stickers on an ATM such as Cirrus, Mastercard, and Visa indicate that the machine accepts international cards. Cash can be drawn over the counter at larger branches of the Bank of China for a commission of 4 per cent, but the process can be slow and unreliable. The minimum withdrawal is usually Rmb1,200. Traveller's cheques can be easily exchanged at hotels, so are often preferred by package-tour travellers on tight tour itineraries.

TIPPING

Tipping is a Western practice and not a Chinese one, but is gaining popularity with tour guides, tour-bus drivers and bellhops (tipping was once illegal in proudly communist China, but no longer). However, unless someone offers exceptional service, there is no need to tip; whether to do so is up to individual discretion.

HEALTH

The Chinese authorities ask those who are unfit because of 'mental illness, contagious or serious chronic disease, disability, pregnancy, senility or physical handicap' not to take a China tour. Experience has shown this to be sound advice. A tour that is exhausting but stimulating for the fit becomes a gruelling experience for those who are not.

If you do become ill in China, you will be taken to the local hospital and given the best treatment available (not always of a standard that Westerners are used to) and you will be put in a private room if possible. Costs—particularly of medicines—are high, so it is important to invest in some form of health insurance before visiting China. You may not be released until the bill is paid.

Repainting a section of the Forbidden City, the Imperial Palace of both Ming and Qing dynasties.

There are no mandatory vaccination requirements, although there may be a health form to fill out on arrival unless you are carrying a well-stamped International Certificate of Vaccination. Make sure your basic immunisations are up to date: polio, diphtheria and tetanus. Vaccination against hepatitis A is recommended, as well as the following, although the need may vary according to time of year and which part of China to be visited: meningococcal meningitis, cholera, hepatitis A (as mentioned) and B, and Japanese B encephalitis. There are two different prophylactic regimens against malaria depending on the part of China to be visited, but each must be begun one week before entering the affected area and continued for four weeks afterwards. To check on the latest recommendations, contact your nearest specialist travel clinic or tropical medicine hospital—family doctors are sometimes not entirely up to date. Plan well ahead: it is unwise to take some of these inoculations together, and some require multiple shots spread across a three-month period or more. They can also be very expensive.

The most common ailments contracted by tourists in China are upper respiratory infections and chest colds. In the north, places like Beijing are extremely dry and cold in the winter, and it is sensible to wrap up warmly and drink lots of fluids. Visitors are often surprised by the tendency of the Chinese to dress much more heavily than seems necessary during the transitional seasons of fall and spring. The Chinese believe that keeping warm is the key to staying healthy at these times.

Drink only boiled water while you are in China; hotel rooms are normally supplied with thermos flasks of boiled water—both hot and cold—which are replenished daily, or they will provide mineral or distilled water in the mini-bar. If eating at street stalls, make sure the food is freshly cooked.

Remember to frequently wash your hands especially before eating, and to peel all fruit. Avoid eating raw vegetables unless you are in an upmarket restaurant.

Standards of sanitation lag behind those in the West. However, the advent of SARS has served to make the central government highly conscious of the need to educate the Chinese public about basic hygiene and to significantly improve its monitoring of infectious diseases and disclosure thereof.

CLIMATE AND CLOTHING

Within the nearly 10 million square kilometres (four million square miles) of China's vast territory it is hardly surprising to find immense variations in climate. Even generalizations about relatively small areas are difficult because of the effects of altitude and other local conditions. Before deciding on the best season to take a tour, it is worth checking carefully the weather conditions of each city on the itinerary. Of course, if you choose the most attractive season to visit a city, you also choose the time when tourist spots and hotels are most crowded.

North: (including northeastern China (Manchuria), Inner Mongolia, Hebei, Henan, Shandong and Shanxi) Northern China is distinguished by cold, dry winters and long, hot summers. Spring and autumn tend to be the best times to visit (although they are shorter in duration). Winter temperatures average below 0°C (32°F) in most areas but conditions are generally dry and clear. Summer maximums can reach 38°C (100°F) with high humidity. More than 80 per cent of the annual precipitation falls between May and September. Spring is marked by strong winds with dust (from the Gobi Desert) that sometimes clouds the atmosphere.

Central China: (including the Yangzi River Valley, the provinces of Hubei, Hunan, Jiangsu, Zhejiang, and the Shanghai Municipality) Long hot and humid summers, short cool winters occasioned by outbreaks of cold air from the north. Summer temperatures (June through September) are consistently in the upper 20s C to low 30s C (80s–90s F) while during the short winter they average between 5–9°C (43–48°F). Spring and autumn are the best times to visit. Rain can fall throughout the year but like most of China is most frequent in the summer months. Coastal areas (Hangzhou and Shanghai) are sometimes threatened by typhoons.

Southern China: (including Fujian, Guangdong, Guangxi, Sichuan and Guizhou) Subtropical climate conditions with long, hot summers (in the low 30s or low 90s F) and short, mild winters (between 10–16°C or 50–62°F). Rain falls throughout the year and typhoons can occur from June through October.

Frontier Regions: (including Tibet, Yunnan and Xinjiang) The vast northwest and southwest border regions are influenced by elevation as most of these areas exceed 5,000 feet (1,524 metres) above sea level. The immense alpine plateau of Tibet is subject to dry conditions for most of the year punctuated by periods of rain during the summer months. Xinjiang, in the far northwest, is ringed by towering mountains shutting it off from most rain-bearing weather systems; as a result it is mostly vast tracts of desert. Yunnan, in the eastern foothills of the Himalayas but in a southerly situation, has a mild microclimate. Kunming, its capital, is called "the City of Eternal Spring".

Apart from midsummer, when virtually everywhere open to foreign tourists is hot, most tour itineraries lead the tourist through several different weather zones. But people who decide to travel with several complete changes of wardrobe may find themselves with crippling excess baggage charges—the Chinese tend to be strict

Facts for the Traveller

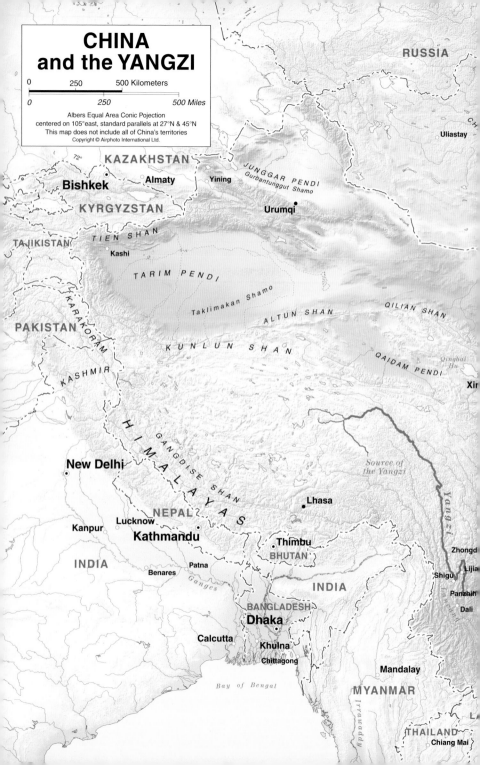

CHINA
and the YANGZI

0   250   500 Kilometers

0   250   500 Miles

Albers Equal Area Conic Pojection
centered on 105°east, standard parallels at 27°N & 45°N
This map does not include all of China's territories
Copyright © Airphoto International Ltd.

RUSSIA

Uliastay

KAZAKHSTAN

72°

Almaty

Yining

JUNGGAR PENDI
Gurbantunggut Shamo

Bishkek

KYRGYZSTAN

Urumqi

TIEN SHAN

TAJIKISTAN

Kashi

TARIM PENDI

Taklimakan Shamo

ALTUN SHAN

QILIAN SHAN

KARAKORAM

PAKISTAN

KUNLUN SHAN

QAIDAM PENDI

Qinghai
Hu

Xir

KASHMIR

HIMALAYAS

GANGDISE SHAN

Source of
the Yangzi

New Delhi

Lhasa

Yangzi

NEPAL

Kanpur

Lucknow

Kathmandu

Thimbu

BHUTAN

Zhongd

Shigu   Lijia

INDIA

Benares

Patna

Ganges

INDIA

Panzhih

Dali

BANGLADESH

Dhaka

Calcutta

Khulna

Chittagong

Mandalay

MYANMAR

Bay of Bengal

Irrawaddy

La

THAILAND

Chiang Mai

about their 20-kilogramme (44-1b) baggage allowance for air travellers. A more practical policy would be to plan on wearing layers that can be removed or added to as the weather dictates.

While visitors to China of 10 years ago constantly remarked on the predominance of 'Mao' suits in blue (known to the Chinese as 'Zhongshan' suits) and green uniforms, the Chinese now wear whatever they can put their hands on. At first liberalization was greeted with the desire, especially among younger people, to wear the most strident colours possible, but now fashions have settled down to parallel those of Hong Kong and the West, with platform shoes just as high and skirts just as short. Even uniforms have brightened up, hotel staff sometimes appearing in turquoise, and railway staff in mushroom-coloured suits with yellow and red piping. In the larger cities, foreign visitors can also wear what they please, although a suit or dress is recommended for those attending business meetings. In remoter areas, and particularly in the Muslim regions of the north and northwest, women should be more conservative, covering themselves to wrist and ankle. Wherever you go, stout comfortable shoes are essential as there is always a lot of walking.

Winter in the far northwest, the northeast and in Tibet demands very heavy clothing—thermal underwear, thick coats, sweaters, lined boots, gloves, and some form of headgear as protection against the biting wind. Hotels and tour buses are usually well-heated, while museums, offices and even some theatres and restaurants are not.

For summer anywhere in China keep clothes as light as possible—many of the places you visit will not be air-conditioned. You may be sightseeing during the heat of the day, so take plenty of protection against the sun, particularly if you are planning to visit Tibet or Xinjiang, where sunglasses are a must. A light raincoat is a wise addition to your luggage at any time.

You need a few changes of clothing since hotel laundry is not cheap here, and it's sometimes cheaper to buy new clothes in China. Dry cleaning is possible, although it may be wiser to wait until you are home to get your most treasured clothes cleaned.

WHAT'S AVAILABLE
FOOD, DRINK AND TOBACCO

China has more than 600 breweries, and 51 of the top 60 have formed joint ventures to produce lager, or light beer. Foreign brewers such as Heineken, Carlsberg and Budweiser all have factories in the mainland while Miller pulled out. A surprisingly wide choice of wines and spirits is available, even in medium-sized cities in the hinterland. Whiskies and brandies have become popular with China's nouveaux riches, and are marketed aggressively. As for wines, there are some quite drinkable locally made ones available such as Grace Vineyards, Dragon Seal and Great Wall. Foreign cigarettes are available everywhere, at a much cheaper price than back home. Conclusion: unless your taste for a toddy or smoke is extremely unusual, then use your baggage allowance to pack something else. Sachets of instant coffee are easy to find, a perfect complement to the thermos flasks of freshly boiled water which are always available. Inexpensive yet decent ground Yunnan coffee can now be found in shops around China. For those who like chocolate, Cadbury's, Mars and Nestlé operate in China and their goodies are easy to find in provincial capitals.

FILM AND VIDEO

Fuji and Kodak locally manufacture basic grade colour films—Fujicolor and Kodacolor—in China. They import and distribute better emulsions, including Fuji Super HG and Gold, but Reala is difficult to find. As for transparency films, Fujichrome Sensia, Provia and Velvia can be found in many cities, as can Kodak's positive films. Always check the 'process before' date when you buy, and buy from a department store or specialist shop. Each traveller is allowed to import 72 rolls of film and 3,000 feet of movie film. Videocameras and cassettes are widely available throughout the country. Batteries are readily available, both Western and local name-brands. Flashcards or memory sticks are gaining popularity and can be found in the bigger metropoli, as can Internet services to upload your photos/movies to your website or remote host. However, you should prearrange such a website or data host prior to arrival. Otherwise most computer service centres can transfer your files to CD-Rom for a fee should you find your storage medium is filling rather quickly. In remote regions, it is best to bring more video cassettes than you think you'll need, or extra-large capacity storage devices. For battery recharging, see Electrical Applicances on the next page.

MEDICINE AND TOILETRIES

Naturally, one should bring any prescribed medicine and a small first aid kit with a few painkillers and elastoplasts, and maybe a broad spectrum of antibiotics if one plans to go into the countryside, merely for convenience. Some books advise travellers to bring toiletries. No need, as increasing numbers of Western brandnames are available for toothpaste, soap, shampoo, razors and blades, toilet paper, tissues, sanitary towels and tampons—you'll find many Western brands even in the smallest of cities in the far west. Travellers may wish to bring condoms or other birth control devices with them, as quality and availability can vary.

THE CHINA GUIDE

The China Guide
Web: www.TheChinaGuide.com
E-mail: tour@thechinaguide.com; Office phone: (86) 13552363179
Address: Jianguomenwai Diplomatic Compound, Beijing, China

Destination Guide

www.TheChinaGuide.com is an interactive destination guide to China of interest to those traveling on a tour or independently. Experience the sites through 360-degree virtual tours, hear some useful Chinese words, explore the cuisine and check out some off-the-beaten-track places we recommend.

Travel Services

The China Guide is a full service Western managed travel agency based in Beijing. We can arrange custom private tour itineraries for small or large groups. We also handle train tickets, domestic air tickets and show tickets.

Build Your Own Tour

Build and price your private tour on the fly. Instant quotes from our database. Images throughout the itinerary show you where you're going.

Electrical Appliances

Voltage may vary slightly from region to region, but it is within the 220–240V range. Some travellers have reported their laptop keyboards and printers being damaged by surges in current. Wall sockets in China are sometimes US (two flat pins), occasionally European (two round pins) in format, or most commonly three flat pins in an angled arrangement. Many sockets are designed to take two or three of these formats, and adapters are widely available. Nonetheless, to be sure, take an international plug kit and determine if your battery charger for your laptop computer, electric razor or MP3 player are 110 or 220 before arrival. If need be, buy a portable voltage converter, which may be heavy, but worthwhile.

Reading Material

Bring along some relevant books to read, since the travel experience can be vastly enhanced by knowing more about the history and culture of any country visited—this applies particularly to China; some suggestions can be found on page 389.

For more current information, the *Asian Wall Street Journal* and the *International Herald Tribune* are widely available for international news. *China Daily*, launched in 1981, is the only national daily English language newspaper in China. It is distributed free in some hotels, on many flights, and is also on sale in other locations. Although controlled by the government, the paper's information can be helpful in discerning the current direction of the political wind, and provides updates on international sports and world news events. On Sunday, China Daily publishes *Business Weekly*, a round-up of the week's top China business news items.

For entertainment listings and a more objective view of life for foreigners in China, look for *That's China, That's Beijing, That's Shanghai*, and *That's Guangzhou* in the respective cities, and *Time Out*. These monthly magazines are on the cutting edge of what's hot and what's cool in China's large urban areas, including dining, music, art, and other trends. Also helpful is *City Weekend*, published as a national edition with local listings in the largest cities. Every Friday in Beijing, China Daily publishes *Beijing Weekend*, a sanitized listing of Chinese cultural events. *Shanghai Star* is published fortnightly in that city, in English. Beijing Youth Daily publishes an English newspaper every Friday featuring events and cultural news, *Beijing Today*.

In Hong Kong, the *South China Morning Post* and *The Standard* serve English readers. For entertainment listings, the magazines *HK* and *BC* are both distributed free at bars and restaurants in Central, Wanchai, and Causeway Bay, and hit the streets weekly and fortnightly, respectively.

Facts for the Traveller

GETTING TO CHINA

By air the main international gateways to China are Beijing, Shanghai, Guangzhou (Canton), Hong Kong and Macau, and all are excellently connected with cities across the country. Onward connections from Hong Kong to other Chinese cities (which under the 'one country, two systems' policy are still treated as international flights) tend to be more expensive than those from neighbouring Guangzhou or Shenzhen. Several other cities have connections to neighbouring Asian countries, including: Changchun (Seoul, Vladivostok), Chengdu (Bangkok, Singapore), Chongqing (Bangkok, Nagoya), Dalian (Fukuoka, Hiroshima, Osaka, Pyongyang, Seoul, Tokyo), Guilin (Fukuoka), Harbin (Blagoveschensk, Khabarovsk, Niigata, Seoul, Vladivostok), Hohhot (Ulaan Baatar), Kunming (Bangkok, Chiang Mai, Kuala Lumpur, Osaka, Rangoon, Singapore, Vientiane), Lhasa (Kathmandu), Nanning (Hanoi), Qingdao (Fukuoka, Osaka, Seoul, Singapore), Shantou (Bangkok), Shenyang (Irkutsk, Khabarovsk, Osaka, Sapporo, Seoul), Shenzhen (Manila), Tianjin (Irkutsk, Nagoya, Novosibirsk, Osaka, Seoul), Urumqi (Almaty, Bishkek, Islamabad, Moscow, Novosibirsk, Sharjah), Wuhan (Fukuoka), Xiamen (Kuala Lumpur, Manila, Osaka, Penang, Singapore), Xi'an (Fukuoka, Hiroshima, Nagoya, Niigata, Osaka), Xishuangbanna (Bangkok), and Yantai (Seoul).

There are other points of entry by rail, by road, and by sea. A relatively recent addition to the rail routes from Moscow via Ulaan Baatar or Harbin is the link from Almaty in Kazakhstan to Urumqi. There are also rail links from Vietnam's Hanoi to Kunming in Yunnan Province, and Nanning in Guangxi. There are direct train connections from Kowloon, in Hong Kong, to Guangzhou, Shanghai and Beijing. The most impressive entrance by road is on the sinuous and spectacular Karakoram Highway over the Karakoram and Pamir ranges from Pakistan to Xinjiang's ancient market town of Kashgar. There are also land routes from Almaty to Urumqi, from Bishkek in Kyrgyzstan to Kashgar, across the Mongolian border at Dzamin Uüd, and from Laos into Yunnan. As of 1998 overland travel can be arranged, with special permission, from Myanmar to China through the border crossing at Ruili in Yunnan province. There are sea links from Osaka, Yokohama and Nagasaki to Shanghai, from Kobe and Inchon (South Korea) to Tianjin, and from Inchon to Weihaiwei (Shandong Province). There are sea links between Macau, Hong Kong, the Pearl River and coastal ports using hydrofoils, catamarans, hovercraft and steamers, although schedules are being cut back due to the increase in direct high-speed and sleeper buses, and the increase in domestic flights.

TRANSPORTATION

Joining a tour saves you the trouble of making your own arrangements for transport. The local Chinese travel service is responsible for selecting the date, time and type of transport, making reservations, seeing to the neccessary security clearances, and ensuring that luggage gets from the hotel on to the appropriate train or plane. What is left for the tourists is to pay their own excess baggage charges. Most foreign tourists travel the long distances between China's larger cities by air, and the shorter inter-city distances by train.

AIR TRAVEL

China continues to open its airways to foreigners. Its first open-skies agreement was signed with Thailand in 2004, and increasing numbers of foreign carriers are permitted to fly not only directly to China's second tier cities, but also to use China's airports as entrepots to other international destinations. China's own airline industry is also expanding, with airlines flying domestic and international routes such as Beijing-based Air China, acting as the nation's flag bearer; Shanghai-based China Eastern; and Guangzhou-based China Southern, the nation's largest airline. The latter two are publicly listed on the New York Stock Exchange, reflecting a push towards modernizing both the airlines' fleets and their methods of service; Air China is now listed on the London and Hong Kong Exchanges. Although still not comparable in service to the world's foremost carriers, China's airlines now boast excellent safety records and some of the most modern fleets in the world. Indeed, service on some domestic routes is superior to many domestic American carriers.

Chinese airlines are now Boeing's and Airbus's top customers. China ranks second only to the United States in the size of its domestic air route network and it is the fastest growing air network in the world.

China is also continuing a programme of new airport construction. Beijing and Shanghai both opened new international airports in recent years with Beijing serving millions of visitors during the 2008 Olympic Games while Shanghai's Pudong International Airport awaits the thronging masses expected for World Expo 2010. (*See* Practical Information for a list of airlines serving China.)

THE MAGLEV LINK

Where the new-age area of Pudong meets the sea, its sophisticated international airport is now linked to the city's metro system by the Maglev railway—with a top speed of 430 kilometres (267 miles) per hour. Pudong Airport is expected to be one

The Maglev briefly reaches a top speed of 430 kilometres (267 miles) per hour, and links Pudong to Shanghai's Pudong International Airport in only eight minutes. [Peter Danford]

of Asia's busiest hubs by 2010—the year of the World Expo in Shanghai, with an anticipated annual capacity of 50 million passengers, many of whom will be using the world's first commercial magnetic-levitation train. The inaugural journey was made on New Year's Eve, 2002, just two years after the inception of the project—with German Chancellor Gerhard Schroeder and Chinese Premier Zhu Rongji on board. Siemens and Thyssen Krupp, of Germany, have spent decades and billions of dollars developing the system and providing the trains and the stations for the Chinese engineered track. Each train is designed to carry 600 passengers on a cushion of magnetism a few millimetres from the track. The 66-kilometre journey between the airport and the Long Yang Lu Metro station takes about eight minutes. By May 2005 the number of passengers exceeded three million.

A second Maglev link is planned, which will connect Shanghai with Hangzhou in Zhejiang Province, although radiation concerns are proving problematic, with conflict over the buffer distance between the rail track and local housing. If and when it is built, it will be 170 kilometres in length and is scheduled for completion in time for Shanghai's 2010 World Expo.

Cook's Far Eastern Traveller's Gazette, *April–June 1937. [Thomas Cook Archives]*

A LIBERATED WOMAN

O ne day as Wang Ta-pao's wife returned from a meeting of the Farmers' Committee she said, "I have something I want to tell you."

Wang supposed that it was some committee business or else fresh news of the victories of the Red Army and he replied in good spirits, "Please go ahead and tell me."

"What I have to say is very simple," she began. "During the last ten years you have not treated me badly. And of course, as you yourself know, my behaviour toward you has been correct. You have looked after me and I have done a lot of work for you. In the first place, I have managed your home, and in the second place, I have borne you two sons. But now I want to leave you, and I am preparing to go tomorrow with Comrade Chen to register."

Wang Ta-pao listened in stupefaction, his heart beating furiously. The veins stood out on his reddening face.

"You can't do that!" he stammered out miserably.

"Why can't I? Do you think we are still living in the times of the landed gentry? Don't forget that this is the Soviet age. You must be more careful what you say."

She was right. Wang Ta-pao could not oppose her. He hesitated a while and then bethought himself to say, "Why do you want to leave me?"

"For no very important reason," she replied, reddening. "Only—well— I feel that living with Comrade Chen would be better than with you. The Soviet allows this. You mustn't be cross with me about it. If you feel bad about losing me, remember we can still see each other always at work . . . dear Comrade Wang."

She left him rather cheerfully and busied herself in packing up her things.

Hu Yepin, 'Living Together', 1930.

The poet was executed by Nationalists in 1931 because of leftist politics. Hu was married to celebrated author Ding Ling.

TRAINS

Most foreign tourists enjoy China's long-distance train trips. 'Soft Class'—popular with most foreigners—combines comfort with efficiency. Clean, white embroidered seat covers, an endless supply of hot water, effective heating in winter, and dining cars with adequate Chinese meals (beer and bottled drinks are available) are a comfort while watching China's diverse countryside speed by. Overnight passengers are comfortably housed in four-bunk compartments or two-bunk compartments. Each car has basic washing and toilet facilities. Need to get somewhere on time? Chinese trains are well reputed for their punctuality.

TAXIS

In all tourist cities, taxis cruise the streets looking for fares. Larger, more expensive taxis tend to queue up outside hotels, but a cheaper one can be had at the roadside by flagging it down yourself. Always get a cab that has a meter and make sure the driver uses it. Exceptions include: hiring a car and driver for a specific block of time with the price agreed upon in advance; in some small cities the cabs may not have meters and a deal must be struck with the driver—before starting, to avoid getting ripped off. Railway stations, airports and bus stations often have drivers waiting to make a fast buck sans meter. Again, take a short walk to the roadside where you can hail a cab whose driver is willing to use his meter. The smallest of towns will have various motorized transport available, and it is sometimes necessary to haggle about the price. If you cannot speak Chinese, write figures down.

PUBLIC TRANSPORT

Travelling on city buses often involves more than a little push and shove, although the pressure on many routes has been relieved by the arrival of private minibuses running on the same routes for a slightly higher fare. Many larger cities in China now have air-conditioned buses (especially welcome during the hot, humid summers) and underground train systems such as Beijing, Shanghai and Guangzhou.

City maps are given away free at many hotels; maps with marked routes are sold at railway stations, book stores and from street vendors—only the bigger cities have maps with Roman characters. Fares for most journeys are a flat rate, but increase beyond a certain distance. Passengers need to wave a number of fingers to show the number of tickets needed, and to be able to say the name of their destination or have the Chinese characters to show the driver.

COMMUNICATIONS

hina continues to rapidly develop its international communications systems: long-distance telephone calls, faxes and e-mail are widely available in all cities and most towns. IP cards are also available for cheap long-distance calls. Many hotel business centres will offer, to guests and walk-ins, Internet access, e-mail and facsimile services—albeit for excessively high rates. More and more hotels, even small ones, now offer broadband in their rooms as well. Dial-up Internet access numbers, without prepaid cards or registration, can be obtained from hotel concierges.

Internet cafés can usually be found even in very small, out of the way cities. Laptop-toting travellers can buy an inexpensive card (about 30 yuan) for unlimited dial-up for 30 days.

Airmail letters and cards do reach their destinations, although they may take some time. If you are sending any large purchases home, bear in mind that while shipping costs are average, crating charges are high, and the crate may not arrive for many months. Small boxes sent by seamail are often the best solution. Post office staff must be able to examine the contents before a package is sealed.

Looking out from the Peace Hotel across the Huangpu River, the Oriental Pearl TV Tower dominates the Pudong New Area skyline, Shanghai.

COSTS

esterners visiting China are travelling halfway across the world from whichever quadrant they may come from. The chief component of the travel budget is therefore the return airfare. A lack of direct flights to most of China's metropolises previously made it difficult to get to China. Connections from large Western gateways such as London, Vancouver and Sydney once dominated with frequent flights and competitive fares. However new direct international routes from a greater variety of departure points to a growing number of Chinese

Gold Kaiyuan coin. Diameter 2.3cm. Excavated from Hejia village, Xi'an, 1970. [National Museum of Shaanxi History]

cities have opened up the market to competition, which is heating up the industry to the benefit of all travellers. Hong Kong—with its abundance of China-oriented travel agencies and quasi-official Chinese organizations authorized to issue visas—while still an extremely convenient entry point, is offset by the expense of staying there for a few days.

Tour prices vary widely, depending on the destinations and length of stay. Very roughly, for a 'classic' 14-day tour covering Beijing, Xi'an, Shanghai, Suzhou, Guilin and Guangzhou, count on a ground price averaging US$250–300 (£125–150) a day, exclusive of airfares to and from your point of entry and departure, whichever city that may be. This gives you first-class accommodation, meals, all internal transfers and excursions to the most notable sights in each city. Prices vary according to the time of year and are highest in May, June, September and October; they are lowest from December through March. The longer your stay the lower the average price per day, but the more remote destinations can appear to be disproportionately more expensive. Sipping coffee, the visitor to Lhasa is unlikely to spare a thought for the enormous expense of supplying it to a few hotels in Tibet, just so that tourists may order their favourite brew at breakfast. Costs are high as much because of the special effort involved in providing tourist facilities in those places as because of their distance from, say, Beijing or Shanghai.

Even if you are backpacking, sleep in dormitories and travel 'hard class', don't expect China to be a bargain in Asia travel terms, although it remains cheap enough compared to travel in Europe or North America. Daily costs are often triple those of neighbours such as India or Nepal.

Facts for the Traveller

CHINA TRAVEL TODAY   —by *Madeleine Lynn*

The first handful of Western tourists allowed into China in 1978 were grateful simply for the privilege of entering the country at all. Thus they were willing to put up with dismal Soviet-style hotels, bad service and itineraries that were arbitrarily changed from day to day. As many of them agreed, visiting China was an educational experience that they wouldn't have missed, but hardly a vacation. Today not only has China tourism changed beyond recognition, but in many ways so has China itself.

With the disintegration of communism worldwide, China is one of the few countries left proudly to call itself socialist. But to cope with the changing times China has its own unique ideology: 'socialism with Chinese characteristics'. This useful phrase means that any changes, no matter how drastic, can still come under the label of socialism, Chinese style. In reality the country is evolving from a totally planned economy where all land and property was owned by the state, to a partially free market system. More and more state enterprises are being privatized, and those which remain in state hands are expected to turn a profit—an unsettlingly revolutionary idea for many of them. The slogan of the Mao era, 'Serve the people', has been replaced by 'To get rich is glorious', uttered by the late paramount leader Deng Xiaoping himself.

Many have taken him at his word and a new class of entrepreneurs has grown up. Thus for locals and tourists alike, Chinese cities are more colourful and interesting now. The streets are alive with small private restaurants, markets and shops, most of which stay open till late, seven days a week. At night, street stalls selling noodles and other snacks do a brisk business under precariously swinging electric bulbs or by the light of paraffin lamps; by day, tourists are besieged by hawkers selling souvenirs, often handmade. Not only the streets, but the people too have a new look. Gone is the sombre uniform of green Mao suit and short pudding-basin haircut for men and women alike. Imported fashions and imitations of them are everywhere, and clothing for women has become at least as diaphanous and abbreviated as in the West.

With the opening up of the country, tourism facilities, communications and transport have improved beyond measure. Large cities now offer a wide choice of international-standard hotels, many of them as extravagantly luxurious as the best five-star properties anywhere in the world. If you crave Western food, they offer everything from haute cuisine to hamburgers. McDonald's and other fast food-chains have come to the larger cities and are very popular among local Chinese.

In the early 1980s, travellers to China were quite cut off from the outside world. Today they can return to their hotels to watch CNN or the BBC, and call, e-mail or fax home. Urban Chinese hooking up to the Internet to send e-mail and surf the Web are no longer required to sign a declaration guaranteeing that the technology will not be used to subvert the government. Home telephones are more commonplace, but incredibly, as of August 2007 China had more than 515 million mobile-phone users—far more than the US.

New roads have cut travel times to such famous sites as the Great Wall outside Beijing and the Terracotta Army excavation near Xi'an. Comfortable, air-conditioned tour buses have also made the journeys more pleasant. Airports are being upgraded, new ones built and the old Soviet planes have been replaced, for the most part, with the latest American and European aircraft. However, the expansion still cannot keep pace with the ever-increasing demand, particularly since the new affluence and freedom to travel has brought a surge of domestic tourism. Thus travellers can still be hindered by delays and difficulties in getting tickets.

One way to avoid this is to travel off season, during the winter months. The cold weather is compensated for by the delight of having sites like the Great Wall almost to yourself, empty of throngs of other tourists. Lhasa, though cold, boasts brilliant sunshine, deep blue skies and the unforgettable sight of hundreds of Tibetans on winter pilgrimage. Southern China is quite mild throughout the year, while Kunming in Yunnan is known as the 'City of Eternal Spring' because of its pleasant weather year-round. Indeed, China is so vast that it would take many visits to fully explore its wide variety of landscape, ethnic groups and the innumerable historical sites. As transport and accommodation improves and as more areas are opened up for tourists, it is becoming easier (though still an adventure!) to visit remote regions.

Often when people think of China's scenery, they visualize the strangely-shaped mountains of Guilin or the humpbacked bridges and canals of the area around Shanghai, which inspired the popular blue-and-white willow pattern on Chinese porcelain. Yet there is so much more for the intrepid traveller to explore, from the deserts of Gansu and Xinjiang to the wooded mountains of Sichuan. The Three Gorges of the Yangzi River, long famous for their beauty and historical and cultural associations, have been irrevocably altered by the completion of the Three Gorges Dam. However, the gorges can still be travelled in style on a variety of comfortable, international-standard cruise ships.

These days natural scenery vies with man-made entertainments. The large numbers of Asian tourists plus the phenomenal growth of domestic tourism has led to the creation of numerous golf courses (over 40 in Guangdong Province alone and many around the Beijing area), theme parks and funfairs. At one time all of China rose and went to bed with the sun. Now the cities offer not only traditional entertainment such as Chinese opera and acrobats, but also nightclubs, discos and bars, particularly in the many joint venture hotels. Although most Westerners (and many young Chinese) find the screeching falsettoes of Chinese opera to be a hard taste to acquire, everyone will enjoy the spectacular costumes and the more 'acrobatic' or 'martial' operas. Look out for any opera that features the Monkey King; it will definitely have its share of fighting and also humour. In Beijing there are often shows made up of short extracts from a variety of the more action-filled and accessible dramas.

Although over 90 per cent of the population are from the majority Han Chinese group, China has 56 ethnic groups altogether. Even in Xi'an, the heartland of China, there is a sizeable community of about 60,000 Hui people, Muslims who came to Xi'an along the Silk Road many centuries ago. As you wander through the market bazaar in Kashgar, a trading post on the Silk Road to Afghanistan, it is easy to forget you are in China and imagine yourself in a Turkish bazaar. Yunnan and Guizhou provinces in the southwest have magnificent rugged scenery and a host of different minority groups, many of whom still wear traditional costumes and make exquisite embroidery and hand-dyed textiles. Guizhou, a province still largely undiscovered by tourists, celebrates nearly 1,000 minority festivals a year. The sight of Miao girls in their festival finery, with their elaborate, top-heavy silver headdresses, is a feast for photographers. Then there is the chance to stay in a yurt (felt tent) on the grasslands of Inner Mongolia, touristy but fun... The list goes on and on.

Interior courtyard of the Imperial Vault of Heaven, part of the Temple of Heaven Complex, see page 353.

Most tourists naturally focus on China's historical sites, relics of a civilization that boasts of having written records that go back well over 2,000 years. During the Cultural Revolution (1966–76) there was a backlash against everything old and therefore 'feudal' and 'backward'. Temples were destroyed or turned into warehouses, books were burned—incalculable damage was done. Yet today, the Chinese value their heritage again. China's museums, though full of treasures, used to be dusty, uncared-for places with few, if any, English captions. Today, some of them have been totally revamped and rival museums anywhere in the world for their layout and presentation. What's more, many artefacts that were previously not on show because of lack of space are now on display in several museums, such as the beautiful Shaanxi Provincial Museum in Xi'an and the Shanghai Museum, which house world-class collections. Those revisiting China will be surprised to find how many new things there are to see. The Chinese continue to excavate in Xi'an and at other tomb sites around the country and to open areas and mount new exhibits, such as hitherto closed halls and pavilions in Beijing's Forbidden City and Summer Palace.

The communists imagined that with the advent of socialism, religion, that 'opium of the masses,' would gradually disappear. During the Cultural Revolution the

The Bund at night is a shining memorial to Shanghai's heady early 20th-century heyday.
[Jeremy Tredinnick]

process was forcibly hurried along. Temples were closed and monks sent to the countryside to work the fields. After the fall of the Gang of Four in 1976 many temples were opened, largely for the benefit of foreign tourists. Usually manned by a mere handful of elderly monks, they were ghostly museums rather than places of worship. Today, however, much to the consternation of the Communist Party, Buddhist and Daoist (Taoist) temples, Islamic mosques, and Protestant and Catholic churches are all flourishing. The temples are full of worshippers and local sightseers, old and young, and many have been lavishly restored with the help of donations from at home and abroad. New ones are also being built; is this what they mean by socialism with Chinese characteristics? In the past Chinese were reluctant to debate questions like these because of possible repercussions. While political discussions with foreigners are no longer taboo, today most people are simply not very interested. To quote Deng again: 'Who cares if a cat is black or white, as long as it catches mice?' After the suffering and loss of life caused by the endless ideological campaigns since 1949, and the unrest of 1989, the majority of people just want to get on with their private lives and stay away from political issues. The perennial questions you will be asked are ones which may seem rather bad mannered to a Westerner, but which are the Chinese equivalent of inquiring about the weather: what is your salary, the price of all your possessions from your watch to your home, your age and, depending on how old you are, the ages of your parents, and the number and ages of your children and grandchildren. All Han Chinese are supposed to have only one child, though farmers may have two, so many are envious of Westerners' freedom in this regard.

When dealing with problems, always remember that the concept of 'saving face' is very important. An angry head-on confrontation with someone will only embarrass them and make them 'lose face' (particularly if you loudly prove that they are in the wrong). Someone who has been made to 'lose face' usually reacts by being as unhelpful as possible. Negotiating anything in China, from an important business deal to changing a plane ticket, is nearly always best accomplished by using a combination of patience, politeness and good humour. Never bribe. What may seem like simple problems often take a long time to untangle. Save your temper for important battles and lose it only as a last resort! If you are travelling with a group, it is often best to channel all complaints through the tour escort.

Traditional Chinese good manners demand that the speaker should constantly belittle himself and praise the other person. Thus Chinese will often tell you that they speak bad English, that the food they are about to serve you is terrible, and that their country is poor and backward. An American was aghast when the doctor about to operate on her for acute appendicitis started apologising for his 'lack of experience' and 'poor skills'. She was finally persuaded to remain on the operating table by a Chinese who whispered that this was merely the very senior and highly-qualified doctor's way of being polite. These humble phrases are forms only; you are not expected to take them too seriously nor to answer by agreeing with them! Bear in mind that most Chinese are intensely patriotic; they may criticise China themselves but understandably do not take kindly to criticism from casual visitors. As a guest it is polite to give the nation's 'face' some respect.

These days, although some areas (mainly the very poorest regions and military sites) are still closed to foreigners, tourists have much more freedom of movement than before. Some of the most rewarding moments of a visit to China are to be found by taking time out from regular sightseeing to wander around the streets. Especially recommended is an early morning visit to one of the many city parks and squares. Those situated by a river or lake are particularly popular (and photogenic), such as along Guilin's Li River or around beautiful West Lake in Hangzhou. Around 6.30am is generally the busiest, although retirees with time on their hands enjoy the parks at all hours of the day. Groups of people perform the stately and graceful *taiji* (t'ai chi) exercises, while sometimes you will be lucky enough to see practisers of sword-play. You may find groups of pensioners waltzing to old familiar tunes, or doing disco-style aerobics to pop songs. It is all for the sake of their health, they solemnly explain. Old men come to meet their friends and air their caged birds. Hanging the cages in the trees, they settle down to games of cards and chess while the birds sing overhead. Other retirees come to parks throughout the day to sing Chinese opera to the accompaniment of the two-stringed *erhu,* or Chinese violin.

Most tourists spend the bulk of their time in China's cities; and in a country where a medium-sized town may have a population of one million inhabitants, it is easy to forget that urbanites are actually a minority here. More than 65 per cent of Chinese live in the countryside, where life for most people is still one of backbreaking manual labour. But even here, life has improved for many, particularly for those living in fertile areas close to large cities. Charge of the land (although not ownership) has been given back to the peasants under the 'individual responsibility system'. After selling a fixed quota of their produce to the state at state prices, they are free to sell the rest as they please. Instead of spending all their time farming, many have started cottage industries such as furniture making or whatever is most profitable. In the prosperous farmlands around Shanghai and Guangzhou, farmers are building modern, two-storey houses, but in many areas village life remains essentially the same as it has been for centuries. A walk off the beaten tourist path into one of China's villages could well be the highlight of your trip. Peasants and water buffalo plough the rice fields, women with babies strapped to their backs beat clothes by the river, while small boys chase flocks of white ducks. Many of the farming implements and houses are exactly the same in style as the models found in Tang tombs dating back over 1,000 years. Villagers are friendly and hospitable and may invite you into their houses for a cup of tea or hot water. In areas where few or no foreigners have been before, be prepared to be surrounded by a sea of curious, but not hostile, faces. Especially in the countryside, a Polaroid picture of a prized child or grandchild is the perfect gift. But expect to be mobbed by the whole village!

To visit China is to visit a whole world in itself. It is a land of tremendous geographical and ethnic diversity, where historical sites spanning 2,000 years and breakneck modernization projects exist side by side. Each person will come back with a different set of favourite memories and images. Will it be the children's faces, the Great Wall, or maybe cormorant fishing on the Li River? Discover China for yourself. As the Chinese say, 'One look is worth a thousand books'.

Shopping on Nanjing Road, Shanghai. [Anthony Cassidy]

SHOPPING IN CHINA

Christie's, the famous auction house, put a 14th century Chinese porcelain jar on the block in 2005, but the bidding escalated to 10 times the expected price. It was sold to an anonymous collector for £15.68 million (US$27.7 million). With a rich heritage of folk art and a revival of many time-honoured traditions, the visitor to China has a wide selection of items to buy. However, it does not have to be expensive. For those interested in folk crafts, the deep indigo-dyed cloth of Guizhou—with its patterns of dragonflies, peonies and frogs—and ceramic rice bowls, medicine jars and casserole dishes made for the country homes of Guangdong Province are inexpensive buys. In Xi'an, brightly coloured children's waistcoats, embroidered and appliquéd with the traditional 'five poisonous creatures', as well as hats and shoes, are widely sold around the sites visited by tourists.

China's Friendship Stores, once the home of the best of Chinese products, but for foreigners only, failed to keep up with the times and most have closed. Now high streets nationwide are crammed with multistorey temples to the gods of shopping and new street markets spring up wherever there's space, open to all. Mainland China has learned from Hong Kong about quality, variety and style, thus improving China's

A Canton grocer's shop, 19th Century, William Prinsep.
[Hongkong and Shanghai Bank Group Archives]

standards overall. However, foreigners' sizes can be difficult to find still, if you see something you like and hesitate then one of the hundreds behind you will snap it up. Silks are one of China's special attractions. Even the most stuffy men have been known to buy silk shirts. Tailoring is easily available if you are in one place for more than a week, but tailors in Hong Kong are even faster—and usually better at interpreting a foreign style. Heavy brocade silks, displayed in swathes of glittering gold, crimson and emerald, are popular with overseas Chinese visitors. A favourite with many shoppers is Shandong silk, woven with bold checks and stripes, which is of a suitable weight for jackets and trousers. Silk scarves are now better designed than in the early 1980s, and cities have excellent selections in their department stores.

For those who enjoy tea and trying out new varieties, a visit to the southern provinces of China affords a chance to taste some of the finest teas available. Excellent Oolong tea is produced in Fujian; Hangzhou is renowned for its Longjing green tea, as is Yunnan for its Pu Er. You can buy teas from all over China in the big cities. The best accompaniment to a fine caddy of tea is a Yixing teapot. Yixing, in Jiangsu Province, has a centuries-old tradition of making unglazed teaware. The unglazed teapots are remarkable for their stylish simplicity of form. Look out for the pumpkin-shaped versions which have a dragon's head on the lid. When the teapot is tilted for pouring, the dragon will stick out its tongue.

China's precious stones can be enjoyed in the form of jewellery or in carved ornaments made from larger pieces of stone. There are excellent precious-stone-carving factories in many Chinese cities where lapidaries with water drills can spend years carving just one work in jade, coral or rose quartz. Some of the carvings are of strange landscapes, others of Taoist immortals, with the texture or markings of the stone cleverly worked into special features. Chinese jewellery can be either extremely unattractive or stunning to the Western eye. Chinese river pearls are very pretty and cost less than cultured pearls. Many shops offer ropes of coral beads, amethysts, pearls and other precious stones. However, there are many fakes, and only the most knowledgeable should buy. Others should shop in Hong Kong Tourism Board-approved stores in Hong Kong.

Embroidery remains one of the most popular purchases for overseas visitors. It is not hard to see why. Few Western countries maintain a tradition of hand-embroidered goods because of the high labour costs, so Chinese embroidery is increasingly sought-after. The shopper can spend a fortune on the double-sided embroidery which is a feature of Suzhou. The embroiderer works both sides to equal perfection and can often cleverly create a front-and-back effect. More everyday items which can also make excellent gifts are hand-embroidered tablecloths, napkins, guest towels, handkerchiefs and aprons.

Many travellers to China like to return home with a painting or a piece of porcelain. A word of warning, however—there are few bargains to be found in the antique shops of China. (You are more likely to find what you are looking for on Hong Kong's Hollywood Road. Occasionally fine pieces of very early Chinese pottery appear in the curio shops in Hong Kong, where a great number of smuggled antiques from illegal mainland digs end up, and it is also possible to find old Chinese paintings.) Beijing has undergone a market boom in recent years and while antiques are not easily found (nor should you be encouraged to purchase them) there are some great buys to be had. The weekend market at Panjiayuan is a most popular outing in Beijing. Thousands of vendors set up temporary stalls and sell everything from Chinese jades, furniture and porcelain to rare books, maps and paintings. Hongqiao and Guwancheng are covered shopping centres, the latter housing scores of small curio shops, while street markets offer the latest in designer apparel and accessories. The famous street market Silk Alley has shut down, but the sellers have moved into a multi-storied building beside the original alley, which is now called Silk Street.

If you are not daunted by the cost of shipping, Chinese carpets and lacquer screens and furniture are of very fine quality. Smaller items which will take up hardly any room in your luggage include cloisonné dishes, sandalwood fans and a seal carved with your name in Chinese.

Minority handicrafts are becoming widely available in big city stores as well as in the shops of the minority regions. You need not go to Yunnan's Stone Forest to buy a Sani cross-stitch satchel, since they can now be found in arts and crafts shops in Beijing, nor to Lhasa for prayer wheels, daggers and turquoise-and-silver jewellery, which are sold in Chengdu. However, it is still true that the best of the minority handicrafts are available in their places of origin. Particular favourites are Tibetan rugs, Mongolian saddle rugs (for their hard wooden saddles), jewellery and clothes from Yunnan, and boots, embroidered caps and daggers from Xinjiang.

It is not only the minorities who have their specialities. The provinces and individual cities are often famous for one particular craft or art. In Fujian, it is lacquerware; Shantou has a tradition of painted porcelain and fine linen sheets with lace-crocheted edging; Shanghai has a wonderful choice of carved wooden chopsticks inlaid with silver filigree; and Sichuan is famous for its bamboo and rattan goods. The list is endless. Ultimately, however, shopping in China is all about finding your own particular treasure.

EATING IN CHINA

long history, vast territory and extensive contact with foreign cultures have all contributed to the evolution of Chinese cooking into one of the world's great culinary traditions. But with regional cuisines of such startling diversity as that of Sichuan, Canton and Shandong, can we really speak of a single 'Chinese cuisine'?

Perhaps the best place to start answering this question is the kitchen. Nearly all Chinese dishes, as opposed to snacks or staple foods, are cooked in a wok (*guo* in Mandarin), a thin-walled, round-bottomed cast-iron pan. Woks can be used for stir frying, deep frying, stewing, steaming and smoking. To conserve both freshness and fuel, most of the ingredients used in Chinese cooking are cut into tiny slices, strips or cubes and cooked as briefly as possible. These principles are almost universal in China proper. Thus what more readily distinguishes regional dishes in China is flavour rather than technique.

There are four primary cuisines in China, corresponding to geographical regions, though many everyday dishes are common to them all, so that the boundaries between the cuisines are often difficult to distinguish, and there can be much nitpicking. The regions are:

• Shandong, the traditional model for Beijing cuisine, is known for its seafood, particularly dried products such as shrimp, scallops and sea cucumber, prepared with salty sauces. (The most famous dish associated with the capital is force-fed fowl, roasted Yangzhou-style, seasoned in a fermented flour sauce and served with cucumber and spring onion on rice pancakes with a dollop of plum sauce—the classic Peking duck.)

• Sichuan, hearty cooking flavoured with an exotic palette of spices: red and black pepper, sesame paste, flower pepper and fermented bean paste, though not all great Sichuan dishes are spicy-hot.

• Canton (in Guangdong Province), with its remarkable range of ingredients (such as dog, snake and salamander) cooked with a light touch, and featuring roast meats, oyster sauce, black beans and shrimp paste.

• Yangzhou (or Huaiyang), little known outside of China, is the general rubric for the cuisine of the lower Yangzi delta, including Shanghai, Suzhou and Hangzhou. Yangzhou dishes make much use of dark vinegar, sugar and rice wine.

The northern regions of China are generally arid, with long, bitterly cold winters. Food in the north used to be severely limited in the winter season. Thus the northern schools of cooking have more limited menus than their southern counterparts. The cuisine of Guangdong Province is widely regarded by the Chinese themselves as the best in China, because of its variety of ingredients and imaginative techniques of cooking. This is not surprising, since the province has a benevolent climate which ensures a long growing season, and an extensive coastline with a tradition of deep-sea fishing. Cantonese cuisine is also, of course, most well known in the West, thanks to the large number of restaurants opened around the world by emigrants from Hong Kong.

Throughout China, rice and wheat (in the form of noodles and steamed and baked bread) constitute the bulk of the diet. Until recently the communist system failed to deliver more than basic nutrition to the Chinese people (and often not even that), so staple starches became the bulk of the meal. Now partial privatization of food production and the release of food markets from state control has largely returned rice to its place as a filler at the end of the meal for many. Tasty, filling dinners which would only a few years ago have been classed as banquets are now commonplace.

As a general rule, rice is served more regularly at meals in the south than in the north of China. The staples for northerners are wheat noodles and steamed breads. In the northeastern provinces (formerly Manchuria), there is a tradition of eating steamed cornflour bread known as *wotou'r*. The breads of China are nothing like the breads of Europe or America, but they should be tried because usually they are delicious. The traditional northern steamed bread bun is called a *mantou* and is often served at breakfast together with rice porridge (*zhou* or *xifan*) and soybean milk (*doujiang*). As a treat, try a steamed bun filled with sweet red bean paste (*hongdoubao*). In Shanghai, bread buns are popular even though the region is in the rice-growing belt. A Shanghainese meal is often served with a *huajuan*, a twisted steamed bread, which is wonderful for mopping up any sauce remaining on the dish. True to their culinary sophistication, the Cantonese prefer a more varied breakfast. *Dim sum* (*dianxin* in Mandarin) consists of an astonishing variety of steamed, fried and baked breakfast snacks. These can be stuffed with sweet or savoury fillings such as lotus seed paste, barbecued pork and shrimps. The traditional Chinese breakfast is perhaps the first meal on which you should try your new-found sense of culinary adventure—that is, if you can just once renounce the coffee, toast and eggs served at most first-class hotels.

Eating in China

The three cardinal virtues by which Chinese food is judged are colour, fragrance and taste (*se xiang wei*). Critics have noted that these categories are purely superficial, and exclude concern with the nutritional value of a dish. This is a philistine view, as the Chinese diet with its emphasis on vegetables, vegetable oils and vegetable protein is an extremely healthy one. The close link between diet and a person's physical well-being is taken for granted by the Chinese. In fact, there is a long established tradition that designates food as either 'heating' or 'cooling'—not according to their literal state but as an indication of their effect on the body. Thus snake and dog meat are eaten by the Cantonese in the winter months because they are 'warming'. When treating patients, Chinese doctors will adopt a holistic approach to healing, and not only prescribe medicine but also advise what foods should be eaten or avoided. Many foods which Westerners regard as strange are delicacies to the Chinese due to their 'strengthening' qualities. Sea slugs and shark's fin are often included in a Chinese banquet not only because they are rare and costly but also because they are 'good for you'. Foreigners usually do not know or are simply unexcited by this approach, but recognition of its background will make you more sympathetic to Chinese culinary idiosyncracies.

The years of the Cultural Revolution (1966–76) did much to damage the tradition of Chinese cuisine. The art of cooking was deemed as bourgeois and decadent as other traditional arts; old master chefs were thrown out of their jobs, and good restaurants were closed down to be replaced by workers' canteens staffed by untrained and unmotivated cooks. Since farms and factories were also in turmoil, there were few incentives and poor facilities to produce or process good ingredients, spices and seasonings.

China has recovered from that decade of culinary puritanism, the impact of the Cultural Revolution has waned. Increasingly, restaurants outside five-star hotels in China are reaching the high standards achieved by chefs in Hong Kong, Taiwan and other overseas Chinese communities such as Singapore, Vancouver and New York. These are subjective comparisons, but overall food quality has indeed improved.

In the past few years, a number of established restaurants dating from pre-communist days have resumed business after refurbishment and are trying to win back their reputation for fine food. Tens of thousands of new restaurants, from hole-in-the-wall canteens to credit-card taking producers of elaborate banquets have also opened up. They are proving immensely popular, not least because the new-found prosperity of local Chinese now enables them to be selective when dining out. Prices rose with inflation but have now levelled out and are even showing signs of decline.

Most tourists still eat in hotel dining rooms where the food can be average to good, depending on the area and the season. Yet hotel dining rooms are not the best introduction to the regional variety of Chinese food. One result of the economic reforms launched some 20 years ago has been the re-emergence of small family-run restaurants, which are restoring a sense of competition and hence quality to cooking in China. These restaurants offer the best value for money, even if the surroundings can be rather basic. You may find yourself perched on a stool under a canvas awning as half the town passes by, but you may also be tasting a family recipe developed over centuries! Do not be too hasty in judging restaurants by their outward appearance. On the other hand, these places may not be very clean and it is as well to bear in mind that hygiene is as important as authenticity.

If you want to eat out on your own, your guide or a local contact may be able to recommend a couple of local restaurants. Ask for their names to be written down in Chinese, along with instructions for the taxi driver. You can also ask for a good selection of local dishes to be written down, also in Chinese characters, to give to the waiter when you arrive. Alternatively, you can take an exploratory walk and look for a local restaurant that is busy—always a good sign—indicate that you want to sit down, then order by looking over the shoulders of other diners and choosing something that looks appetising. Most Chinese will not mind if you act with discreet good humour. Indeed, there is often someone who wants to practise his English by helping you. You may even end up with a conversational companion as well as a meal.

INTERNATIONAL CUISINE

The explosion of international-brand luxury hotels throughout China's major cities has brought with it a diverse range of world-class culinary offerings, from Italian pizzerias and French Cordon Bleu to Mexican taco joints and Spanish tapas bars. The abundance and variety of high-quality international fare across the urban landscape in China today is astonishing—a new middle-class Chinese generation is keen to taste what the world has to offer, and as a result private restaurants are spreading to cater to those who cannot afford the five-star prices. You can eat excellent French cuisine in Lijiang, fine German sausage in Qingdao, and even find wonderful Caribbean-style chicken in Urumqi! But it is fair to say that virtually all Chinese see international food as a mere novelty—if you ask, you will hear a universal response to the question of which cuisine is the best: Chinese, of course!

With its rich heritage and range in flavours, textures and techniques, it is difficult to argue otherwise.

DREAMING AND FOOD

I would like to be that elderly Chinese gentleman.
He wears a gold watch with a gold bracelet,
But a shirt without sleeves or tie.
He has good luck moles on his face, but is not disfigured with fortune.
His wife resembles him, but is still a handsome woman,
She has never bound her feet or her belly.
Some of the party are his children, it seems,
And some his grandchildren;
No generation appears to intimidate another.
He is interested in people, without wanting to convert them or pervert them.
He eats with gusto, but not with lust;
And he drinks, but is not drunk.
He is content with his age, which has always suited him.
When he discusses a dish with the pretty waitress,
It is the dish he discusses, not the waitress.
The table-cloth is not so clean as to show indifference,
Not so dirty as to signify a lack of manners.
He proposes to pay the bill but knows he will not be allowed to.
He walks to the door like a man who doesn't fret about being respected,
    since he is;
A daughter or granddaughter opens the door for him,
And he thanks her.
It has been a satisfying evening. Tomorrow
Will be a satisfying morning. In between he will sleep satisfactorily.
I guess that for him it is peace in his time.
It would be agreeable to be this Chinese gentleman.

D J Enright, *Dreaming in the Shanghai Restaurant*

Poet, novelist and critic, Dennis Joseph Enright (1920–2002) was born in Warwickshire (UK). He taught overseas—mainly in South-Asian universities from 1947 to 1970—before returning to England to work as an editor and director of a publishing house, and accept an Honorary Professorship of Warwick University. Part of a group of poets that became known as "*The Movement*" in the 1950s, his own poetry was straightforward, sometimes ironic and almost in the style of light verse, often dealing with themes of inequality, and filled with wit, compassion and self-mockery.

CHINESE HISTORY: A BRIEF CHRONOLOGY

PREHISTORY

The beginnings of Chinese culture have been traced to Neolithic settlements along the middle Yellow and Wei river valleys in northern China around the fifth millennium BCE, but the earliest of the dynasties mentioned by traditional Chinese texts is the Xia (c. 2205–1766 BCE). The dynasty is said to have been founded by Yu the Great, a king credited with controlling the floods that afflicted the river valleys of China. Recent discoveries of artifacts have shed some light on the probable existence of the Xia dynasty, once thought to be mythical by many scholars.

THE SHANG (c. 1600–1027 BCE)
AND THE WESTERN ZHOU (1027–771 BCE)

The Shang kingdom, which succeeded the Xia, rose in a part of present-day Henan Province, on the edge of the flood plain of the Yellow River. From oracle inscriptions and other relics, archaeologists have pieced together a picture of an aristocratic culture which waged war with the help of horse-drawn chariots and bronze weapons, built cities walled with rammed earth, and made elaborate vessels for use in ancestor worship.

Ancestor worship, including the offering of sacrifices, was entrusted to the king. His ancestors, it was believed, could intercede with the supreme god of Heaven on behalf of their living descendants. Thus the idea that political power sprang from spiritual power developed early on, and became entrenched by the time the Zhou was established. This evolved into the 'Mandate of Heaven,' the theory that a king's right to rule was dependent on his ability to appease Heaven so that the destructive forces of nature—floods, drought or other natural disasters—would not be unleashed upon his subjects. If the king were unjust or immoral, his harmonious relationship with Heaven would be shattered and famine and chaos would follow. Heaven's mandate would be withdrawn and rebellion given legitimacy.

The mandate of heaven was eventually withdrawn from the Shang. Under the new ruling house of Zhou, formerly a vassal of the Shang, a feudal system was developed based on fiefs granted to the kinsmen of the ruler. As its homeland was in the Wei River valley (today's Shaanxi Province) to the west of the Shang domain, the new dynasty relocated the capital to a city near modern Xi'an—hence the name 'Western Zhou'—for the first two and a half centuries of its reign.

CHRONOLOGY OF PERIODS IN CHINESE HISTORY

NEOLITHIC	7000–1600 BCE
SHANG	1600–1027 BCE
WESTERN ZHOU	1027–771 BCE
EASTERN ZHOU	770–256 BCE
SPRING AND AUTUMN	770–476 BCE
WARRING STATES	475–221 BCE
QIN	221–206 BCE
WESTERN (FORMER) HAN	206 BCE–8 CE
XIN	9–24
EASTERN (LATER) HAN	25–220
THREE KINGDOMS	220–265
WESTERN JIN	265–316
EASTERN JIN	317–420
NORTHERN AND SOUTHERN DYNASTIES	386–589
SIXTEEN KINGDOMS	317–439
FORMER ZHAO	304–329
FORMER QIN	351–383
LATER QIN	384–417
NORTHERN WEI	386–534
WESTERN WEI	535–556
NORTHERN ZHOU	557–581
SUI	581–618
TANG	618–907
FIVE DYNASTIES	907–960
LIAO (KHITAN)	916–1125
NORTHERN SONG	960–1127
SOUTHERN SONG	1127–1279
JIN (JURCHEN)	1115–1234
YUAN (MONGOL)	1279–1368
MING	1368–1644
QING (MANCHU)	1644–1911
REPUBLIC OF CHINA	1911–1949
PEOPLE'S REPUBLIC OF CHINA	1949–

SPRING AND AUTUMN ANNALS (770–476 BCE) AND THE WARRING STATES (475–221 BCE)

A long period of prosperity and expansion under the Zhou began unravelling as family ties with the fiefdoms weakened. While nominally acknowledging Zhou sovereignty, feudal states themselves became power centres acquiring their own vassals. In 770 BCE invaders from the northern steppes attacked the capital, forcing the Zhou king to abandon it for a new base at Luoyang to the east. The Eastern Zhou period is conventionally subdivided into two phases—the Spring and Autumn Annals, named after a chronological history covering those years, and the Warring States, a time of escalating disorder and power struggles. Finally, out of all the competing states, three gained ascendancy.

It was against a background of profound turmoil, in the late Spring and Autumn period, that a new intellectual élite emerged. Its most notable member, Confucius (551–479 BCE) sought to remedy the political and social disintegration around him by advancing the ideal of leadership by moral example: he taught that only when a ruler was possessed of virtue would he be able to call forth the good in all men and exercise authority. Confucius' doctrine did not find much favour with the feudal lords of this time, although it was eventually to be elevated to a state philosophy.

THE FIRST EMPIRE, QIN DYNASTY (221–206 BCE)

Of the three states jostling for mastery of the Chinese world in the Warring States period, it was the western state of Qin which finally triumphed as the leading military power. Qin had substantially extended its boundaries by absorbing Shu (modern Sichuan Province) in 316 BCE, and in the following century it consolidated its territorial gains by further annexations.

The Qin conquest brought the whole of China under a centralized monarchy. Zheng, the young ruler of Qin and architect of that unification, took for himself the title of Qin Shi Huangdi—First Qin Emperor. To administer this vast realm, he created a form of political organization which was to endure for some 2,000 years; perhaps the most notable innovation of the Qin was the bureaucratic apparatus that gradually replaced the old feudal structure. The Qin emperor also built a network of roads for the movement of his troops, repaired and reinforced defensive walls along the frontier, unified the writing system, standardized the coinage and codified the law. All this he did in the 11 years of his reign. He wanted to do more, and he wanted to live forever, but immortality eluded him. He died in 210 BCE, during one of his royal tours and was interred in the massive funerary complex which we know today as the "Terracotta Warriors and Horses Dig" located to the east of Xi'an (*see* page 84).

THE EMPIRE CONSOLIDATED: THE HAN DYNASTY (206 BCE–CE 220)

Qin Shi Huangdi's successor, a nephew, did not last long. Rebellion broke out and swept to power the humble founder of the next dynasty, Liu Bang. The first Han emperor, though uneducated himself, wisely recognized the value of learned advisers. During Han rule the influence of Confucian philosophy was revived and knowledge of the sage's works became a qualification for passing imperial examinations. The system of recruiting civil servants by examination started during this period. In theory and occasionally in practice, these competitive examinations offered a measure of social mobility for commoners unavailable within a feudal system.

As well as many advances in agriculture and technology (the magnetic compass and paper were developed during the Han), there were conquests which at one time extended the imperial sphere of influence beyond its original borders to as far as Korea in the northeast, the seaboard in the south and westwards as far as Central Asia. It was during the reign of one Han emperor, Wudi, that expeditions were made far to the west of China's boundaries. In 139 BCE an official, Zhang Qian, was sent on a mission to find allies against the Xiongnu (Hun) horsemen who were a constant threat in the north. His journeys to Central Asia opened up what was to become the Silk Road, along which Buddhism was brought to China in the first century CE.

The Han dynasty covered more than four centuries, with one interruption (CE 9–24), when the Liu dynastic line was broken by a usurper, Wang Meng, a relative of one of the imperial consorts. As the capital of the first continuous period was at Chang'an (modern Xi'an), the 'Former Han' is also designated as 'Western Han'. In the second period, the court being at Luoyang, the years from the restoration of the house of Liu to the end of the dynasty are known as 'Eastern (or Later) Han'.

The relative prosperity and stability of the Han dynasty ushered in a new era in artistic achievement. Archeological excavations of Han period tombs reveal a flowering of the visual arts with exquisite sculpture, lacquerware, textiles, bronze and gold work. Whereas the militarism of the Qin fostered art produced to awe the masses (as seen in the life-size Terracotta Warriors), the works of the Han were delicate and suggest a new level of realism.

ANARCHY AND PARTITION (220–581)

By about the first century CE, the dynasty was in decline as the growth of factions among the imperial family and the intrigues of eunuchs increasingly debilitated the court. When the centre could no longer hold, the empire fell prey to rebels and pretenders to the throne.

Deprived of authority, the last Han emperor ruled only in name. Power was held by a general, Cao Cao, whose son in 221 forced the abdication of the emperor and founded a new dynasty, Wei. Two rival clans set up their own regional regimes—Wu in the east, and Shu Han in the southwest. Known as the Three Kingdoms (220–265), this period was marked by warfare and turmoil.

Wei emerged the strongest of the three, but it was soon toppled by another clan, which established the Western Jin dynasty (265–316). This spell of unification was also brief, however. Subject to invasions by 'barbarians' from beyond its frontiers, the empire fragmented further. In 316 north China was lost to the nomadic Xiongnu, and thereafter, with the flight of the refugee Jin court to the southern city of Nanjing, the Chinese empire was effectively confined to the Yangzi valley. The north was ruled by a series of short-lived non-Chinese dynasties of the Xiongnu, as well as the Mongols and the Toba Tartars. This profusion of reigns came to be known as the 'Sixteen Kingdoms'. From time to time, the rulers in the south made attempts to recover the Chinese heartland, but their forays were resisted.

This state of affairs lasted until 581. By then, the 'barbarians', who had resorted to Chinese methods of government to control their conquered domain, were thoroughly Sinicized. With no experience of agrarian societies, they used the existing administrative apparatus and in the process came to adopt the Chinese way of life themselves.

The period of invasion and instability provided the catalyst by which Buddhism (which had been first introduced into China as early as the first century) began to take root among the masses. The civil turmoil led people to look elsewhere for solace and the promise of rebirth and the chance to attain nirvana (as compared to the harsh reality of life) appealed to the general population. The Turkic Toba people, having defeated the rival ethnic groups, founded the Northern Wei dynasty (386–534) which ruled northern China, and abandoned their own language, customs and even surnames. The Toba Tartars embraced Buddhism and made it the de facto state religion.

It was a general of mixed Chinese and 'barbarian' descent, Yang Jian, who rose to seize power in 581. He usurped the throne and consolidated his position in the north, before crossing the Yangzi and overthrowing the southern ruler. Once again, China was unified. The new dynasty Yang Jian founded was the Sui.

THE SUI DYNASTY (581–618)

This period, though short, accomplished much in establishing an apparatus for government that provided the foundation for the Tang, the next imperial house, to flourish. Yang Jian was extremely frugal; not so his successor, who was enthroned as Yang Di in 605. Yang Di's extravagance included the building of the Grand Canal, a waterway which linked up existing but derelict channels and which, when completed, stretched from Beijing in the north to Hangzhou in the south. Important as it was for integrating the north and south and shipping grain, this transportation project exacted great hardship on countless construction workers and left a legacy of bitterness among Yang Di's subjects. He also launched a series of expensive but futile campaigns against the Koreans. Dissatisfaction flared into revolt, and Yang Di was assassinated in 618.

THE TANG DYNASTY (618–907)

The new dynasty proclaimed on the collapse of the Sui was to usher in what has been called China's Golden Age. The Tang, building on the system of government left by the Sui, created a strong administration with officials recruited by examination to run the ministries, boards and directorates. There was a great expansion of education, and the spread of literacy was facilitated by the invention, some time during the eighth century, of block printing. If there was one cultural achievement to distinguish the Tang above all others, it was literature. The brilliant poetry of Li Bai, Wang Wei, Du Fu and Bai Juyi attests to a glorious flowering of creativity.

In the economic sphere, trade extended as far as India, and the open and outward-looking attitude which characterized the reign of the second Tang emperor, Taizong (627–649), made the capital, Chang'an (present-day Xi'an), a crossroads of foreign merchants, monks and travellers. Embassies arrived from Persia and the Byzantine Empire. Foreigners and their faiths were welcomed, so that the metropolis harboured several non-Chinese communities. When the monk Xuanzang returned from India with Buddhist scriptures in 645, he was received personally by the emperor, who had some years before also granted an audience to a Nestorian priest. Except towards the end of the dynasty, Buddhism enjoyed great favour throughout the empire.

After Emperor Taizong, the court was dominated by a remarkable woman whose rise from concubine to empress was achieved by complex intrigues and utter ruthlessness. As consort to a weak emperor, she ruled behind the scenes, but as Empress Wu Zetian she took the reins of government entirely, and even changed the dynasty's name from Tang to Zhou until she was forced to abdicate at the age of 80.

With the restoration of the Tang after Wu Zetian's death, China was able to enjoy a long period of stability and prosperity. The reign of Emperor Xuanzong, who has been called Minghuang (the Brilliant Emperor), was the high point of the Tang. It was marked by enlightened government and splendid achievements in the arts. But his long reign (712–756) was to end in disaster, when An Lushan, a general of Turkish descent who was in command of the imperial forces in the northeast, launched a rebellion in 755. In the latter part of his reign, Xuanzong had become out of touch with state affairs, having fallen under the influence of a favourite concubine, Yang Guifei, and members of her family. When An Lushan threatened the capital, Xuanzong fled to Sichuan, and en route Yang Guifei was killed. The dynasty survived another 150 years, but after the rebellion—finally suppressed in 763—the Tang never recovered the political control it had previously exercised. Like An Lushan, the commanders of the military regions remained extremely powerful. Separatist tendencies grew and once again the empire fragmented into independent states.

THE FIVE DYNASTIES AND THE TEN KINGDOMS (907–960)

During this period, five brief dynasties held the north of the country. The capital was transferred from Chang'an to Kaifeng in present-day Henan Province. Over the course of half a century, ten other ruling houses controlled various regions of China, two of them 'barbarian'—the Tangut (a people of Tibetan stock) and the Khitan (a tribe from what was later Manchuria). There was an exodus of officials and scholars from the north to the Yangzi valley, where the heritage of Tang culture was preserved. And as borne out by later events, the impulse for unification had not perished either.

THE NORTHERN SONG (960–1127)
AND THE SOUTHERN SONG (1127–1279)

China was brought under one rule again in 960 with the establishment of the Song dynasty. It centred first on Kaifeng and later on Hangzhou, hence the dynasty's division into 'Northern' and 'Southern' phases.

Although the various nomadic races in the north continued to pose a threat, the pacific Song emperors were initially content to appease them. Unlike their predecessors, the Song did not seek to expand their territory beyond the traditional boundaries south of the Yellow River basin. From about 1000 to the end of the Northern phase, peace was maintained. The empire was regulated by an effective civil service, and enjoyed a long period of economic expansion, due in part to fiscal reforms instituted by a brilliant minister, Wang Anshi, which benefited the peasants

Chinese History

and shifted the burden of taxes on to landowners and rich merchants. Under the patronage of a series of able emperors there was another efflorescence of artistic and intellectual activity. Painting, above all, attained an excellence never equalled since.

The peace ended when, under Emperor Huizong (reigned 1100–25), a new threat appeared on the scene—the warlike Jurchen who, like the Khitan, were from Manchuria. Huizong abdicated the throne in favour of his son and fled south, leaving the way open for the Jurchen to invade, lay siege to Kaifeng and establish the Jin dynasty. At various times the exiled Song court in Hangzhou tried, unsuccessfully, to recover their lost territory in the north, but for the most part the two empires co-existed in uneasy truce. In 1147, the Jin themselves were attacked by a new, savage conquering tribe, the Mongols, and destroyed by them in 1234.

Genghiz became Great Khan in 1206 and intensified a campaign of conquest that eventually left the Mongols in control of a large portion of China. National resistance to Genghiz and later to his grandson, Kublai, kept Hangzhou in the hands of the Song until 1276. Just a few years later, pursued by Mongol forces, the last of the fugitive Song court retreated to Fujian and died off the coast in 1279.

THE YUAN DYNASTY (1279–1368)

angzhou, which escaped pillage by the Mongols, deeply impressed Marco Polo, the Venetian traveller and trader who claimed to have served at the court of Kublai Khan. But it was at the site of modern Beijing that Kublai Khan established his winter capital, Khanbaliq. Although Kublai adopted 'Yuan' as his dynastic name, he made sure the Mongols would not be assimilated by the majority Chinese. Different ethnic groups within the empire were formally distinguished, while the southern Chinese (who were suspected of nationalistic sentiments) were relegated to the lowest of four classes. Obviously the Chinese were forbidden to hold any important posts.

Kublai Khan's reign covered the best years of the Yuan dynasty. Contact was made with the Near East and the West, leading to a flow of scientific and cultural information which brought Arab astronomy to China and a Franciscan mission to Khanbaliq. Europe became more aware of Chinese culture from the reports of the Catholic missionaries.

None of the seven emperors after 1294 had the stature of Kublai Khan. With weakening central authority, social unrest and opposition to the alien dynasty increased and the Yuan was overthrown by insurgents led by a former bandit and monk, Zhu Yuanzhang.

THE MING DYNASTY (1368–1644)

Zhu Yuanzhang was from a poor peasant family in the southern province of Anhui, where he originally intended to set up his capital. However, it was decided that the strategically located Nanjing would be more suitable. From the start, the commoner-emperor, who took the title Hongwu, was determined to concentrate power in the person of the sovereign. His long reign (1368–98) was marked by stability at home and successful conquest abroad.

It was the third Ming emperor, Yongle, who moved the capital to Beijing, probably for defensive purposes. Preoccupation with securing the northern border against the Mongols led to a spate of wall and fortification building during the Ming, the most notable project being the eastern section of the Great Wall.

Interest in exploration and navigation also reached new heights at this time. In 1405 Emperor Yongle sent the admiral Zheng He (1371–1435) on the first of seven voyages which reached the shores of Arabia and as far as Timor in the east Indian Ocean. By 1514, the first Portuguese ships had arrived in Guangzhou (Canton), at a time when Chinese policy was unfavourable to foreigners. Although there were specific laws prohibiting Chinese from private trade with foreigners, the Europeans were undeterred. The Portuguese were followed by the Dutch and, in 1637, by the English.

The dynamic rule of Yongle was not repeated by any of his successors. From the beginning of the 16th century, Ming imperial power was on the wane. In a corrupt court, power was increasingly appropriated by eunuchs. The interests of the empire were neglected, even though vast amounts of money were spent on defending the northern frontier. Meanwhile, the Manchus, a northeastern tribe, were consolidating their power. In 1629 the Manchus reached the Great Wall, but were temporarily halted by the barrier. Soon after, the empire was riven by internal insurrections. When Beijing fell to rebels lead by bandit leader Li Zicheng in 1644, the last Ming emperor, Chongzhen, took his own life on Coal Hill, behind the Imperial Palace. One of his generals, Wu Sangui, hoping to enlist the Manchus' help in quelling the rebellion, opened a gate of the Great Wall at Shanhaiguan, and let them in. The Manchus were able to overthrow Li Zicheng and install themselves as China's new rulers without meeting opposition.

THE QING DYNASTY (1644–1911)

The Manchu conquerors—founders of the Qing dynasty, as they called themselves—first pacified the rebellious south and eventually consolidated their empire under three capable rulers: Kangxi (reigned 1662–1722), Yongzheng (1723–35) and Qianlong (1736–95). Kangxi and his successors, unlike the Mongols, adopted

Chinese culture themselves. The Jesuits who were in Beijing in the 18th century represented the empire as prosperous, splendid, powerful and extensive.

This was all to end in the 19th century. The first signs of dynastic degeneration gave the Europeans their opportunity to open an isolationist China to the Western world. After a war (1839–42) fought over the ban of opium imports into China, the British forced the Qing government to ratify a treaty allowing foreign traders access to five ports in China. Five years later, the Taiping Rebellion weakened Qing rule irreparably.

Repeated defeats suffered by the Qing armies on a number of other fronts subjected the empire to near partition by Russia, Germany, Britain, Japan and France. The disintegration reached crisis proportions and inspired a reform movement which advocated the adoption of Western technology and learning for China's rehabilitation. But the rigidly conservative Dowager Empress Cixi, the most powerful figure at court, was inexorably opposed to modernization.

In so staunchly resisting change, the late Qing made change inevitable. The dynasty did not long survive Cixi, who died in 1908. When the Chinese people decided that national salvation could be achieved only by the overthrow of the Qing dynasty, they cast in their lot with a revolutionary movement led by a Western-trained doctor, Sun Yat-sen.

REPUBLIC OF CHINA (1911–1949)

An uprising on 10 October, 1911 in Wuhan sparked unrest throughout central and south China, and within weeks Doctor Sun Yat-sen was declared President of the Republic of China in Nanjing (*see* page 98). Pu Yi, the boy-emperor, formally abdicated in February 1912, ending more than 2,000 years of imperial dynasties in China. Sun's Nationalist Party advocated nationalism, and people's rights and welfare. But with no military backing, he resigned in 1912 and was replaced by Yuan Shikai who proclaimed himself Emperor Hong Xian in 1915. In March 1916 he stepped down and China was torn apart by warlordism.

In July 1921, 13 Marxists, one of them Mao Zedong, met in Shanghai to establish the Chinese Communist Party (*see* page 140). From 1923 to 1927 the Nationalist and Communist parties formed an alliance against warlords in north China, but in 1925 Dr. Sun died. The unity became uneasy with Chiang Kai-shek as its leader, and it fell apart in 1927.

After a series of failed armed uprisings against Chiang, Mao led his followers to Mt Jinggang where he established the first communist guerrilla base. The main Red Army then consolidated forces around Ruijin, Jiangxi, which was declared the Soviet Republic of China. This communist stronghold was encircled by Nationalist forces.

In October 1934, about 100,000 Red Army soldiers began a secret exodus west to break out of the siege and find a new base area. The campaign, which lasted one year, ended 11,000 kilometres (6,837 miles) away in northern Shaanxi Province, and became known as the Long March. Only 30 women joined the march including Mao Zedong's second wife, He Zizhen (who gave birth to a child en route, giving it up to peasants to care for). Less than 4,000 survived, and en route Mao established himself as leader of the Red Army and the Communist Party.

Yan'an became the new red capital while the Nationalists prepared to make further assaults, humiliated by their inability to wipe out Mao's army on its Long March. At the same time the Japanese were taking Chinese territory without opposition from Chiang who considered the 'Japanese a disease of the skin, the communists a disease of the heart'. But in the interests of national unity, his own generals forced him to join the communists and fight the Japanese (*see* page 90). From 1937 to 1945 the Sino-Japanese War raged, and once the aggressors were defeated, civil war, the War of Liberation (1945–1949), erupted. Chiang's routed forces were forced to flee to Taiwan in 1949 with the mainland under communist control.

PEOPLE'S REPUBLIC OF CHINA (1949–)

Mao Zedong proclaimed the founding of the People's Republic of China in Beijing on 1 October, 1949. Land reform was implemented. Government policies were dictated primarily by ideology and often featured extremist campaigns and tumultuous political upheavals, most notably the Anti-Rightist Campaign against the bourgeoisie; a disastrous economic plan dubbed the Great Leap Forward (1958); and the Cultural Revolution (1966–76), which aimed to 'prevent a restoration of capitalism'. Mao died in 1976. In 1978 Deng Xiaoping became leader and orchestrated China's normalization program of reform and opening to the outside world after its long isolation.

Following Deng's death, the pace of reform quickened as the team of President Jiang Zemin and Premier Zhu Rongji, the 'economic czar', took full control. But moves to privatise China's vast state-owned enterprises revealed deep divisions within the Communist Party. Hardliners, frightened of increasing unrest as unemployment rose to about 20 per cent in most cities and the surplus of about 200 million rural labourers, fought to slow the pace. Buffeted by the Asian economic crisis and an over-valued currency, China's economy suffered price deflation and a reduction in trade surpluses and growth rate. In 1999, US$13.3 billion was spent on celebrating the 50th anniversary of the founding of the People's Republic, but the country entered the 21st century set on becoming a superpower.

Chinese History

OLD WAYS DIE HARD

Guo Heizi had a problem. He had married after the one-child policy had begun to be enforced more strictly in the area, and his wife had given birth to a useless girl who would no doubt eventually marry into another family and leave him destitute in his old age. Heizi was so angry that finally the woman conceived again, slipping off to her parents' home in another district to avoid local officials during her pregnancy. She gave birth there, so that not even hospital authorities, who might have forced her to have a late abortion, knew about it. She returned in triumph to the Guos with a three-month-old baby boy.

According to local policies, there was now a fine of 400 yuan to be paid to the xiang Planned Birth Office. Although this was low because the region was poor and the population not as dense as in some areas, Guo Heizi's entire savings amounted to only about 200 yuan, which he turned in. Then officials ordered his relatives to carry his furniture and other possessions to the xiang to make up the rest. But how could they take away the belongings of their own flesh and blood? the peasants asked, still outraged. In fact, they were all filled with rejoicing at the birth of the little boy! Finally the officials came themselves and took everything—beds, wardrobe, even Heizi's household wok. All this had happened just the week before our visit, and now Heizi and his wife were away at her family clan, borrowing the basic necessities until they could get the money to replace them. The child, however, was right here, the peasants volunteered proudly, pushing a shy-looking woman forward from the outer circle of watchers. By the hand she held a fat toddler, naked from the waist down, the evidence of his maleness clear.

In the opinion of the peasants, Heizi had come out of the affair quite all right. After all, the second child had not been a girl, and the fine did not really matter, especially to someone who had little cash and few possessions in the first place. It was worth it. Even in wealthier areas, where the fine was said to be as high as 2,000 yuan, people often preferred to pay; one family was said to have nicknamed their extra son Caidian, "Color TV," for he had cost them just as much as one. All the newlyweds the Guos knew were waiting for boys. The situation was very clear: under the responsibility system, the more labor power you had, the wealthier you would be. As it was being applied in their district, you got more land each time a child was born, but lost some when a girl married off and left you. If you had only a single daughter, you would have to work in the fields for your rice until you died, poor and lonely.

Literary Excerpt

Not everyone had been as fortunate as Heizi, the peasants said. In another village, the Yang clan had consulted fortune-tellers for months in order to find a bride who would produce a boy for one of their sons. They finally found one, and the marriage feast was as lavish as any that had been seen in many years. Even the Guos had been invited, from several li away. All the old customs had been followed. The red-clothed bride had been fetched from her home, with the plaintive, festive sound of the suona horn in accompaniment; in a long train, the relatives carried the new bedding on shoulder poles to the bridegroom's home. There kowtows were made to the images of the ancestors, and a huge banquet was served, for which five pigs were killed. Glutinous rice cakes were consumed in abundance, and rice wine flowed. It was as if the Yangs were already celebrating the birth of the new baby boy.

Perhaps the fortune was poorly told, or perhaps the pregnant young wife encountered a spirit, a peach ghost. The birth was a tragedy.

The baby girl was ignored by her father; the clan spoke of revenge. Some threatened to beat the soothsayer, others to send the woman back to her family. Then, quietly, the problem was resolved. The baby disappeared during the night. The Yangs let it be known that she had been taken away by the same ghosts who had entered her mother and robbed her of the boy that was hers by right.

Then the county officials came and made an investigation. To everyone's surprise, the unfortunate father was taken off to spend a year in prison for murder! It was so unfair, the Guos complained. What else could a man in his position have been expected to do?

Liang Heng and Judith Shapiro, *After the Nightmare*

Liang Heng was born in Changsha, Hunan Province, in 1954, and graduated from the Hunan Teachers' College in 1981. After his marriage to Judith Shapiro, he went to the United States, and earned an M.A. at Columbia University. He founded a Chinese-language quarterly, *The Chinese Intellectual*, for which he is editor-in-chief.

Judith Shapiro has a degree in anthropology from Princeton, an M.A. in comparative literature from University of Illinois at Urbana, and a second M.A. in Asian studies from the University of California at Berkeley. She has taught American literature at Hunan Teachers' College, but now writes about China and works as an interpreter and consultant.

EARLY ARCHAEOLOGICAL TREASURES

Most visitors to China enjoy tours of archaeological sites and museums, but they are often frustrated by the lack of display signs in major foreign languages. The obvious solution is to make sure that you have your guide or interpreter close at hand. However, if you are part of a large group tour, it is sometimes difficult both to hear what is being said and to see what is actually on display. This introduction to early Chinese treasures is designed to help you find your own way around an exhibition or museum, to go at your own pace and to identify what is on display.

China's first known works of art were pottery vessels and carved jade discs, pendants and sceptres, dating from the Neolithic Period (c. 7000–1600 BCE). The pots were made for everyday use and for ritual purposes. The jade pieces were used as ornaments in life as well as in death (it was customary for aristocrats to be buried with their most precious possessions of carved jade). Recovered from tombs, the earliest surviving jade pieces are usually white or yellow; fewer are grey-green. The most finely-carved pieces of early Neolithic jade have been found in the eastern coastal region of China, at excavations in Zhejiang Province. Pottery from the Neolithic Period has been found in many sites throughout China—even as far west as present-day Xinjiang, long considered outside the orbit of primitive Chinese culture.

The painted pottery of the peoples of the Yellow River plain is best known to foreign visitors because of the famous excavation at **Banpo**, just outside the city of Xi'an. Banpo is the site of a large riverside village which, from 4000 to 3000 BCE, had its own kilns producing distinctive decorated pots. The low-temperature fired red clay pots of Banpo are found throughout the Yellow River region, and are collectively known as 'Yangshao ware'. It is relatively easy to identify Yangshao pottery in a museum, since it is unglazed and has rich decorative designs in red, black and occasionally white. Motifs can be bold swirling patterns, faces, fish or bird designs. 'Yangshao ware' is often referred to as Painted Pottery.

In the area around the Shandong peninsula on China's eastern seaboard, a different kind of pottery was produced in Neolithic times. Known as Black Pottery or 'Longshan ware', the pots have a distinctive black surface which has been polished after firing. Black Pottery was wheel-made and, unlike Painted Pottery, has no surface decoration. The potter put all his skill into creating subtle and elaborate shapes. The ritual vessels are paper-thin and are turned in the most elaborate and impractical forms.

A closeup of one of Xi'an's terracotta warriors shows the ancient sculptors' skill in forming the realistic features of the estimated 8,000 human statues. [National Museum of Shaanxi History]

During the Shang dynasty (1766 BCE–1122 BCE), the crafting of ceramic wares was eclipsed by the newly-discovered science of bronze casting. Bronze was more durable than clay and had important military applications. However, the development of bronze was shaped by the potter's skills—the moulds for the cast bronzes were made from clay, and many of the early shapes of Shang bronzes were derived directly from the refined shapes of 'Longshan ware'. This was particularly true of the high-footed, trumpet-mouthed wine goblets known as *gu*, and the bag-legged, tripod wine heaters (the legs billow out like bags full of water) called *li*. Both shapes were to die out as the bronze-cast art evolved away from the traditions of the early potters.

The working of bronze was also influenced by the skills of the jade carver. One of the best-known features of Shang bronze art is the *tao tie*, an animal motif consisting of a monster head, and this pattern is found as early as 3000 BCE, carved on the jade discs of the eastern coastal people. However, the discovery of bronze did not lead to the dying out of jade carving. Because of its translucent hardness, jade continued to be highly prized.

The Shang bronzes are famous for their vigorous shapes and bold designs. They are more like sculptures than decorated vessels. In the *tao tie* examples, a pair of savage eyes stare out of strong, swirling lines. Some vessels were formed in the contours of an animal, others in the mask of a terrified human face. It is not surprising that archaeologists have speculated that some of these ritual vessels were used at human sacrifices. The vessels were also cast in a large variety of shapes, each corresponding to a specific purpose in worship. For example, the *ding*, a rounded cauldron supported by three or four legs, was used for sacrificial food; the *zun*, a tall vase, was employed for offerings of wine.

With the overthrow of the Shang dynasty and the triumph of the Zhou in 1027 BCE, the function of bronze vessels changed. During the rule of the Shang kings, bronze vessels had a religious function and were important in rituals and sacrifices. Under the Zhou rulers, bronze vessels also became symbols of rank and wealth. Zhou dynasty patrons commissioned bronzes of refined shapes with swirling geometric patterns, such as the elegant 'thunder spiral' pattern (*leiwen*). Monster and beast shapes disappeared.

There has been much debate on whether the art of bronze casting evolved spontaneously in China or was transmitted from the ancient cultures of the Near East. Chinese bronzes are unique in incorporating lead in the bronze alloy of copper and tin—a fact that argues for the independent evolution of bronze casting in China.

The addition of lead to the alloy gives the bronze a grey sheen much prized by connoisseurs.

It is from the bronzes of the Shang and Zhou dynasties that the earliest developments of the Chinese language have been studied. Sometimes the Shang and Zhou bronzes were inscribed with the maker's name and perhaps a short description of the occasion on which the new vessel was presented. These

A Tang dynasty jade powder compact, with carved mandarin ducks and lotus motif. [National Museum of Shaanxi History]

inscriptions have provided scholars with valuable material for their researches on ancient script—the bronze vessels are as much historical records as works of art.

Unlike bronze objects, jade did not appear to be used in ancient times for strictly religious purposes. Shang and Zhou jade pieces symbolized power; the jade discs and sceptres were the Chinese equivalent of the European royal sceptre and orb. Yet the Chinese invested the stone with protective qualities which could be said to have a religious significance, and it served an emblematic purpose in burials. The jade disc—or *bi*—was buried with rulers in the belief that it would help ease the passage of the soul to the afterlife.

Most of what is preserved from China's early dynasties has been excavated from tombs. Rulers and nobles of ancient China believed that they would need treasures, servants and animals in the afterlife (a tradition which still persists in contemporary Chinese culture, with the burning of paper money, paper houses and possessions for the dead). During the Shang dynasty, rulers took their wives and servants to the grave with them; in the Zhou dynasty, figurines of people were generally substituted in these rites. The result was that, by the fourth century BCE, the use of tomb figurines was widespread enough for Confucius to declare that the person who initiated the idea of going to the grave with figurines did not deserve to have descendants. In the 1960s, communist textbooks interpreted the comment to mean that Confucius was recommending the older tradition of human sacrifices. But it is clear from the context—and from other chapters—that Confucius had no interest in the possibility of the afterlife and disliked the tradition of tomb figurines as a reminder of earlier practices.

Early Archaeological Treasure

In the third century BCE, Qin Shi Huangdi, China's first emperor, was buried in a tomb guarded by a complete, larger-than-life model army placed in pits nearby. These warriors and horses, excavated just outside Xi'an, are China's most famous archaeological treasure. The Han dynasty historian, Sima Qian, wrote that Qin Shi Huangdi was also buried with fabulous treasures and members of his household. However, the tomb of the emperor has not yet been excavated, and despite being looted in the early years of the Han dynasty, it is widely believed to contain several undisturbed chambers. Archaeologists have made only exploratory digs around the site of the tomb, but they are concerned about the preservation of the contents and the possibility of booby traps—described by Sima Qian as being set up all around the imperial burial chamber. In spite of the mounting evidence about the actual tomb site the Chinese government has decreed that the tomb will not, at this time, be excavated. Concern for the preservation and protection of treasures that might lie within is the overriding factor holding back the excavation of the tomb. Theft of archaeological treasures from dig sites is one of the most worrying problems in regions like Shanxi and Shaanxi (which are cultural cradles of Chinese civilization) and there is a serious lack of resources to enforce greater protection against such losses.

Recently, excavation work has begun on a 131-metre-long horse-chariot chamber of the Xiongjiazhong Tomb near Jingzhou in Hubei Province, a complex dating to the Warring States Period (475–221 BCE), and more than a century older than the Terracotta Warriors. Thought to be the tomb of one of the kings of the State of Chu, the tomb is expected to be made into a museum eventually.

Pottery warrior figure on horseback, Western Han dynasty (206 BCE to 8 CE); unearthed in 1965 at Yangjiawan, Shaanxi province. [National Museum of Shaanxi History]

Tang-dynasty ox-head agate cup, unearthed at Hejia Village, Xi'an.
It was probably imported from Central Asia or Sasanian Iran.
[National Museum of Shaanxi History]

The Han dynasty, which succeeded the short-lived Qin dynasty in 206 BCE, also left a legacy of tomb treasures. However, the Han emperors did not make such elaborate tomb preparations as did the megalomaniac Qin Shi Huangdi. No living household members are believed to have been placed in Han tombs. In the early period of the Han dynasty, known as the Western Han (206 BCE–CE 8), many precious objects were buried in the tombs of rulers and nobles. By the time of the Eastern Han (CE 25–220), this practice was officially prohibited, and—with some exceptions—bronze vessels were replaced by glazed earthenware or lacquerware, and valuable possessions by representational clay sculptures.

Jade burial suits are perhaps the most spectacular objects from early Han tombs. Made of a material that was hard, enduring and thought to be endowed with protective qualities, the jade burial suit was believed to prevent decay. Bodies of high nobles were encased in jade suits and their orifices sealed with jade discs.

One of the finest examples comes from the second-century BCE tomb of Princess Dou Wan in Hebei Province. Also from that tomb is one of the finest small pieces of early Han sculpture yet excavated: a gilt-bronze oil lamp in the shape of a kneeling maid-servant. Its purity of form and the individuality of facial expression make the work a rare treasure amongst tomb figurines.

Han dynasty tomb figurines are of great interest in providing information about daily life at that time. Miniature farms, houses, city gates, animals and utensils as well as models of favourite servants were placed in tombs. The painted bricks of Han tombs also tell much of daily life. They can depict anything from court ladies at leisure, nobles out hunting with their bows and arrows, to kitchen workers preparing a feast. Fragments of woven silk and lacquerware have also been found in many Han tombs. By the Han dynasty, lacquerware had completely replaced bronze vessels as household items, and thus many of the excavated Han tombs have revealed a wealth of red-and-black patterned lacquer boxes and utensils. One of the best exhibitions of Han tomb artefacts is in the Hunan Provincial Museum at Changsha. The museum has the complete collection of the Mawangdui excavation of a first-century BCE (Western Han) noblewoman's tomb.

It was during the Han dynasty that the first contacts were made with Central Asia which would lead to the opening of the trade routes later known as the Silk Road. After the introduction of Buddhism to China in the first century CE, missionaries and pilgrims travelling along the Silk Road to and from India left a rich legacy of religious art in the stretch of land formed by the narrow Gansu corridor and the fringes of the Taklamakan desert in present-day Xinjiang. To express their devoutness, they created, over many centuries, stupendous and beautiful frescoes and statuaries to adorn cave-shrines. Although much of the art was subsequently destroyed, or removed by foreign archaeologists, many frescoes and sculptures remain, the most stunning of which are in the Mogao Caves in Dunhuang. Nineteenth- and early 20th-century explorers and archaeologists also came upon a rich cache of manuscripts and paintings there. Other artefacts, including silk embroidery, jade carvings and pottery, have also been found in and around the cities of the Silk Road, and are displayed in a number of small but interesting museums in this region.

If the later period of the Han dynasty can be remembered by one object, it is surely the Flying Horse unearthed in Gansu Province, now on display in Lanzhou's museum. The small bronze sculpture has a lightness and fluidity of form far removed from the monumental grandeur of the earlier Zhou and Shang bronzes. Its spirited beauty brings to life the values and interests of a society which, without such works of art, may seem remote and alien.

Buddhist banners painted on silk gauze, more than one metre long, depict the life of Buddha, and were acquired by Marc Aurel Stein for the British Museum. He made three expeditions to China (1900–01, 1906–09 and 1913–1916) funded by the Department of Oriental Antiquities of the British Museum in London where the banners remain. More information about Stein's discoveries can be found at the website of the International Dunhuang Project: http://idp.bl.uk/. [William Lindesay]

THE CHINESE ECONOMY

—Paul Mooney and William Lindesay

I t is 8am and Guangzhou's Qingping Market is already bustling as shoppers jostle each other in the narrow streets and pick through produce piled high on wayside stalls. In Shanghai, consumers crowd a department store examining the latest stereo equipment, TVs and home appliances, as their children push forward for a look at hand-held video games from Hong Kong. In Beijing's Zhongguancun 'computer street', a recent graduate buys a PC and plans to hook up to the Internet.

THE IRON RICE BOWL

The first-time visitor to China may take these everyday scenes for granted. Yet all this would have been unthinkable just 20 years ago, when socialism ruled unchallenged. At that time, the sight of a Chinese housewife queueing at sunrise, before the local market opened, to buy the ingredients for her family's dinner, was all too familiar. If she was lucky, she might come away with a scraggy bit of pork and some tired-looking vegetables. Many others often trudged home empty-handed.

The shelves of department stores were usually bare, while shoppers were conspicuous by their absence unless a shipment of coveted goods was expected. Then, crowds of hopeful customers would pile into the store, trying to squeeze their way to the counter before the few television sets or electric fans were sold out.

This was the aftermath of Mao's death and the Cultural Revolution, when the economy was still a slave to the Stalinist principles of central planning, which provided only the barest essentials of life. China, once a great and wealthy empire, found herself among the world's poorest nations. The communists, who won power in 1949, had promised a better future; but the socialist redistribution of wealth failed to deliver a significant improvement in living conditions.

In the early 1950s, though, such grim repercussions did not cloud the vision of China's new leaders as they pressed forward with their national plan. They went ahead with the collectivization of agriculture in the winter of 1955–56, organizing peasant households into co-operatives and turning over to them what had been privately owned property, including the means of production.

This was followed in 1958 by the 'Great Leap Forward', a campaign to accelerate rural and industrial development. A grand vision conceived by Mao, it was a disaster.

Although Shanghai was the first of China's cities to experience an explosion of modern Western building, Beijing has caught up fast.

It involved a nationwide mobilization of the masses, leading to a fever pitch of work. But under pressure to achieve near impossible output targets, farms and factories took to reporting inflated production figures. Much of what was produced was of low quality or useless, particularly the home-made steel from backyard furnaces. By the time the experiment collapsed, huge amounts of labour and raw materials had been wasted. In the ensuing economic havoc and famine, millions of people are believed to have died. One legacy of the first ten years of socialism was the 'People's Commune'. A form of organization intended to bring about social change in the countryside, the commune embraced several thousand households, and took responsibility for all the activities associated with farming, as well as providing security, education, health care, and even permission to have a baby. A commune was subdivided into 'production brigades', a grouping of several hundred households, and below that were the 'teams', made up of between 20 and 30 families.

Industry and commerce also passed into state ownership, and welfare measures were introduced to protect the worker. Most urban residents were assigned to a *danwei* or unit, the place of employment or study, which took care of just about all their basic needs. A worker lived in housing provided by his unit, which also guaranteed a certain level of rations, medical care, pensions and sometimes even schooling. Once attached to a unit, a person usually stayed for life. The trouble was he also lost his freedom of choice of jobs. Still, dismissal was rare, and when the time came for retirement, the job might go to one of his children. It was a cradle-to-grave welfare system which the Chinese themselves called the 'iron rice bowl'.

THE REFORM DECADE

As against these benefits, the existence of the iron rice bowl also crushed incentive. The command economy functioned poorly—the years of apathy, wasted resources, arbitrary pricing and stultifying bureaucracy all added up to inefficient production and low standards of living for peasants and urban residents alike. Within two years of Chairman Mao's death in 1976, capitalism slowly began to poke its head out again.

China is still a predominantly agrarian country, so the shift to a market approach in agriculture had a profound impact on people's lives. Under the responsibility system implemented in 1979, peasant families were allowed to contract land for private farming. Farmers were no longer required to turn all their produce over to the state, but instead had to fulfil a quota and could then sell any surplus in the newly opened free markets for their own profit. Family farming became the norm even though the vast majority of peasants were still tied to collectives.

With these changes, China, which has 22 per cent of the world's population but only seven per cent of its arable land, began to make impressive gains. The gross value of agricultural production almost doubled in the 1980s, and productivity and farm incomes shot up too. The food shortages of the past faded from memory as markets around the country began offering ample supplies of meat, vegetables and fruit. Peasants became the new rich, able to afford new houses and a wide variety of modern comforts. For the first time in the history of China, urban dwellers, who had little opportunity of supplementing their income, began to look on their country cousins with envy. The agricultural reforms paved the way for sustained growth of agricultural output, which generated a surplus of rural savings which was used to boost industrialization. The introduction of the management responsibility system into state-owned enterprises brought market elements into the socialist economy. Enterprises began to enjoy a greater say in their own management, resulting in a new degree of efficency and productivity.

While people were previously unwilling to give up their iron rice bowls, millions, realizing they would never get rich working for the state, set up their own small businesses, becoming a new force in the economy. While state firms cut employment by 159,000 between November 1993 and June 1994, private firms increased it by two million. These entrepreneurs—in the early 1950s Mao labelled them 'capitalist tails that had to be cut off'—are now among the wealthiest people in China.

A provincial newspaper reported in June 1991 that official audits and secret checks had discovered 490 entrepreneurs who had put away more than a million yuan each, an amount that would take the average Chinese factory worker some 800 years to earn. These millionaires had clearly taken to heart one of Deng Xiaoping's utterances—that it was acceptable 'to make some people rich first, so as to lead all the people to wealth'.

Deng recognized that economic reforms could not be carried out in isolation—for China to catch up with the modern industrialized world she would need Western capital and technology. The 'open door' policy, launched in 1979, was designed to attract foreign investment and joint venture projects. And the Special Economic Zones established along the southern coast were intended to be the focus for such investment.

The reform decade of the 1980s saw the economy expand at an average annual rate of about ten per cent, bringing improved living standards and a doubling of consumption. In China's large cities, some 80 per cent of households now owned a colour television set. By 1990, foreign trade had more than tripled, and China had become the world's 13th largest exporter and a main player in the international arena.

Chinese Economy

Renmin Bridge, Guangzhou in 1978, before redevelopment.

CHAOS IN THE MARKETPLACE

The close of the decade, however, saw serious problems emerging. Rapid industrial growth had exacerbated shortages of energy and raw materials, and severely overstretched an outdated infrastructure, particularly the transportation network. The existing railroad and highway systems simply could not keep pace with demand, and telephone services remained among the worst in the world. The shortfall in energy production was forcing many factories to halt work one or two days a week.

There was a panic buying spree in the summer of 1988. For the first time in decades, prices got out of control and inflation reached 30 per cent. An austerity programme was imposed in the same year to cool down the overheated economy. Bonuses, which by then accounted for as much as half of a worker's wage, were temporarily cut in most factories. Reforms were put on hold and in some cases even reversed. But some problems could not be solved by squeezing money out of the economy. The subsequent recession highlighted several areas of discontent. There appeared to be a diminishing number of jobs for young people and prospects were discouraging. Unemployment rose as industries became more capital intensive and arable land shrank. It has been estimated that by 1998 there were already 150 million urban and rural unemployed. The mounting unemployment in the countryside has resulted in a "floating population"—up to 150 million rural workers (overwhelmingly male) who are flooding into large urban centres in search of work. (In September 2007 China's urban unemployment rate was 4 per cent, only 0.1 per cent down from the previous year despite 10 million new jobs being created.)

Consumer demand remained unabated, despite propaganda urging restraint. To the horror of elderly communists, certain wasteful pre-revolutionary customs had been revived. Young urbanites were holding lavish weddings complete with rented Western wedding gowns, while at elaborate funerals, bereaved relatives were choosing burials that used up valuable land instead of opting for cremation as promoted by the state. In the shops, consumers had become more selective—those who considered radios, bicycles and watches luxury items a decade ago now had their eyes set on colour TVs, refrigerators, DVD recorders and home furnishings.

Corruption worsened. Even top communist officials or cadres began to 'xiahai', or jump into the sea of commerce. Some used their influence to set up relatives and friends in profitable private enterprises. The children of powerful cadres—dubbed princelings—became prominent on the boards of various local and foreign companies. Other officials, exploiting privileged access to scarce commodities, snapped them up at low state prices before reselling them on the free market at a premium.

Early morning exercises at the Southeastern Corner Tower, Beijing.
The elderly and middle-aged help preserve traditional values.

Chinese Economy

THE RISE OF CAPITALISM

The growing public revulsion against corruption in high places and a keener awareness of the outside world through the 'open door' added to the pressures that were already building up for a faster pace of reform and greater freedoms.

Nonetheless, China ploughed ahead with its reforms. In the early 1990s, under its trial-and-error policy of 'crossing the river by feeling for the stones', stockmarkets were opened in Shanghai and Shenzhen, and futures trading markets sprang up around the country. A problem arose: conservatives seized on the chaos of the 1989 demonstrations and stepped up their opposition to Deng's reforms. Though he had resigned from official office in 1989, Deng returned to the fore in early 1992, making a quasi-imperial southern journey to rally the support of local leaders. 'There is no need to be afraid of capitalism ... anyone who does not carry out reforms should be forced to step down, no matter who they are,' the then 88-year-old party patriarch warned.

The much heralded appeal worked as local officials took heart from Deng's exhortations to pick up the pace of reform. Hunan Province, the birthplace of Mao and a hotbed of conservatism, is a good example. Heaven is high and the emperor is far away, goes a popular Chinese saying. Yet when the emperor-like leader made a 15-minute whistle stop at Changsha railway station to make a pitch for speedier economic reform, his message was heard loud and clear.

Hunan officials waited on the platform politely as Deng's train pulled out of the station. But as soon as the tiny figure disappeared waving in the distance, they raced back to their offices to rethink their economic plans. By year-end, Hunan's GDP had more than doubled, foreign trade jumped almost 50 per cent and foreign investors, once shunted off to provincial backwaters, were being warmly welcomed to the province by the hundreds. The Hunan experience was repeated all over China.

The Chinese also moved faster with specific steps to promote economic liberalization. Price controls were liberalized. Dozens of inland cities were opened to the outside world and incentives were sweetened for foreign investment. With

The CCTV Headquarters became an icon of modern Beijing's new architectural landscape even before it was finished; beside it stands another avant-garde building, home to the Mandarin Oriental Hotel. [CCTV/OMA Ole Scheeren and Rem Koolhaas image courtesy of OMA]

record amounts of foreign capital pouring into the country, coupled with a sharp rise in investments by local governments and enterprises, the economy began to overheat.

In the summer of 1993, economic czar Zhu Rongji launched a series of austerity measures aimed at reining in runaway economic growth, with limited effect. Despite vowing to tighten credit, the government, worried about killing off state enterprise and unable to pay wages and debts, continued to pour money into this sector.

Inefficient state enterprises remain a significant problem for China's economic planners. State-run factories, which account for the bulk of manufacturing enterprises, continue to be unresponsive to the more sophisticated Chinese consumer; many still turn out shoddy, outdated products which end up unsold, having to be consigned to already large stockpiles of unwanted goods in warehouses.

If no political ideologies were involved, the appalling performance of the state industries would be ample argument in favour of privatization. Official reports say that as many as half are running at a loss and are only kept afloat by government subsidies, which run into tens of billions of yuan each year, accounting for 50 per cent of China's budget deficit. Yet they contribute about 50 per cent of industrial output and provide jobs for some 70 per cent of the nation's labour force. Worried about massive unemployment and the threat of social instability, in 1998 the government nevertheless began to cast off loss-making industries and cut back government staff in earnest.

'We would rather die in dignity than be taken over by a capitalist,' said the managing cadres of the Chongqing No. 6 Radio Factory to the owner of the Restar Group, the most successful electronics operation in the city, who had made an offer to take over the giant state enterprise. The rhetorical news, reminiscent of the Mao era, came as a shock to the city's mayor, Pu Haiqing, who visited the factory himself in February 1997 to speak to its workers. He was surrounded by angry mobs who hadn't seen a wage packet for more than a year. 'We never said that!' they heckled, 'the leading cadres fabricated those quotes.' The workers said that they didn't mind who paid them, just so long as they got paid.

This Chongqing incident shows that politics are still in command in the minds of many provincial officials, and it highlights contradictions which the government's ideologists are having to confront. The conservative 'old guard' point out that privatization of industry is a fundamental contradiction in a communist country: the individual is forbidden to exploit the masses. Interpreted in its strictest form, anyone who employs others to make personal profit, for example an entrepreneur, is exploiting the masses. But what is perfectly clear, not only to city mayors, but also in Beijing, is that the party must deliver the economic goods to remain in power.

Party leaders know that one of the biggest threats to the country's stability comes from unpaid workers in state enterprises. Hence many economists are urging the government to press on with *zhuada fangxiao*, which translates as 'seizing the large and freeing the small'. It is a policy which offers a lifeline to ailing, key state concerns, while giving the private sector considerable room for expansion.

Basically, the *zhuada* head of the policy allows the government to select 1,000 key state enterprises running in the red, and bail them out, while imposing fairly radical management reform upon them. That is the key. After all, who'd have thought in the late 1970s that Deng's reforms would allow for minnow private companies to eventually outperform the state's goliaths. The *fangxiao* tail of the plan allows ailing enterprises to sink or swim—they will receive no state assistance. Thousands of entrepreneurs are taking over loss-making factories and using their free capital to capitalize on manpower.

The criterion that will decide which enterprises are seized and which are freed is strategic: the state will keep defence and infrastructural industries in its pocket— basically heavy and high-tech sectors including military, vehicles, transport and telecommunications—while letting the light-industrial and consumer-goods factories be taken over and flourish in private hands. This enterprise reform indicates the importance attached to adhering to the late paramount leader's greatest legacy: pragmatism, or in simple terms, to use Deng's oft-quoted adage, not being concerned whether the cat is black or white, as long as it catches mice. With the 'old guard' on the wane, China's path is no longer a forked option between the policies of hardliners and reformers, but one between moderate reformers and more radical ones.

In late 2002, Jiang Zemin and the elder generation of leaders stepped out of the spotlight and yielded to Hu Jintao as the nation's new leader, along with a new Politburo, China's top leadership. Jiang had secured quite a legacy for himself: he presided over the return of Hong Kong and Macau to Chinese sovereignty; China was admitted to the World Trade Organization (WTO); Beijing won the right to host the 2008 Olympic Games; and Shanghai won the right to host Expo 2010.

Perhaps the most telling tales of turnaround are ones such as these: in the first half of 2007, China became Australia's largest trading partner, eclipsing Japan which had held that position for 36 years; while an economic study of China by the Organisation for Economic Co-operation and Development in 2005 revealed that the transition from central planning to free market was succeeding and small private enterprises were driving China's economy rather than the state-run sectors. Today, almost every nation is clamouring for China's trade attentions, and this trend is likely to continue for some time.

Chinese Economy

CULTURAL CAPITALS

eaders may be surprised to find that Beijing is not listed first in this section. Rather than listing these capitals based on their cultural significance, a subjective endeavour, they are instead presented chronologically. Note that many of the following cultural capitals are, or are host to, sites of great historical importance—so much so that they have been selected by UNESCO as World Heritage Sites. Readers will find links from Cultural Capitals to the World Heritage section of this guide.

XI'AN

t is said of the famous English translator of Chinese literature, Arthur Waley, that he never wished to visit modern China, so as to keep intact his vision of ancient China—a vision he had built up carefully through his knowledge of classical texts. It is also said that, in his mind's eye, he could take a walk through the Tang dynasty capital of Chang'an—the city known today as Xi'an—and be familiar with all the city districts, their businesses and specialities. In modern Xi'an, the provincial capital of Shaanxi Province, it takes a great feat of the imagination to believe that this dusty, unassuming city was the site of 11 Chinese dynastic capitals, spanning more than a thousand years. But in fact the loess plains around Xi'an and the River Wei, which flows close to Xi'an and empties into the Yellow River, lie at the heart of Chinese civilization and are a continual source of new archaeological discoveries, the most famous of these being the extraordinary terracotta army of the first emperor of China. It is these discoveries which have made—and will continue to make—Xi'an one of the most popular destinations for Western visitors to China today.

ARCHAEOLOGICAL AND IMPERIAL SITES

A site near present-day Xi'an was the early capital of the Zhou dynasty (1027–221 BCE), the great period of bronze culture. However, archaeologists have unearthed even earlier settlements dating back to Neolithic times, as well as the bones of an early *homo erectus*, said to have originated about 800,000 BCE at sites near the modern city. Enthusiasts of early archaeology can visit an excavated Neolithic village at **Banpo**, 11 kilometres (seven miles) east of the city, which is remarkable for its Painted Pottery. More recent archaeological digs have uncovered Zhou sites, the most exciting being that of a Western Zhou (1027–771 BCE) burial chamber at **Zhangjiapo**, south of Xi'an. The chamber yielded two bronze chariots and the remains of six horses, which can now be seen at a small museum west of the city at the village of Doumen.

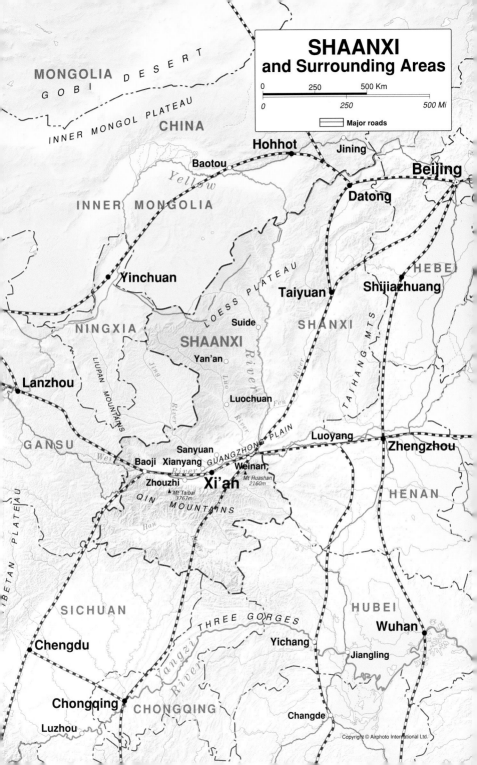

Many Zhou artefacts are in the **Shaanxi Provincial Museum** in Xi'an itself, which should be visited for its fine archaeological exhibits, ranging from Zhou bronzes to Tang coloured porcelain. Formerly located in the Confucian temple, the museum was moved in 1991 into a palatial Tang-style building near the Big Goose Pagoda. The famous 'Forest of Stelae', which formed part of the museum's collection, remains at the old site, which has been renamed the **Forest of Steles Museum**. Stelae are inscribed stone tablets; some in this collection date back to the Tang dynasty, providing a wealth of historical detail for the non-specialist·visitor as well as the scholar. The Forest of Stelae can easily be enjoyed with a well-informed guide and by taking a careful look at the carved illustrations on the stelae—the maps and portraits, for example. Nearby, a new addition to Xi'an's wealth of historical repositories is the **Xian City Museum**, which offers an interesting 'white-glove experience', whereby visitors are able to handle some of the ancient relics on display.

The feudal ruler of the state of Qin, who in 221 BCE conquered his rival kings and unified China, is known as Qin Shi Huangdi, the first emperor of the Qin dynasty. During his reign, he undertook military campaigns to the far corners of the known world, a vast public works programme involving forced labour, the persecution of Confucian scholars, and the burning of books. Jia Yi, a Han dynasty statesman born in 201 BCE, five years after the fall of the Qin dynasty, wrote a famous discourse on the reasons for the rapid overthrow of the Qin. In it he concluded that the mighty Qin fell 'because it failed to rule with humanity and righteousness, and to realize that the power to attack and the power to retain what one has thereby, are not the same'— a very Confucian judgement on Qin despotism. The estimated 8,000 terracotta soldiers and the horses and chariots which lay buried for 2,200 years, guarding the tomb of the first emperor, are a testament to his power and megalomania.

The **Terracotta Army** was discovered in 1974 by peasants digging a well during a drought. The excavation site is in Lintong County, a few miles distant from the actual burial mound of the emperor. Visitors can climb the mound, but the burial chambers have not yet been excavated for fear of damage to the delicate treasures which are thought to lie within. History tells of the tomb being sealed with traps of poisoned arrows to deter violation. However, it is known that the tomb was looted during the Han dynasty, and one wonders how much is left inside. Archaeological work is taking place at the surrounding burial mounds.

Excavation has continued sporadically since the discovery of the Terracotta Army. All three pits are now open. In Pit Number One, which is larger than a football pitch, so far more than 2,000 of the estimated 6,000 warriors and horses have been excavated. Pit Number Three, though small, is thought to be the garrison headquarters of the Qin army. Excavations can be seen proceeding in Pit Number Two, which is believed to represent a Qin period military encampment (the site was opened to the public in October 1994). The soldiers are either standing or kneeling. A selection of the figures is displayed in glass cases, and you can see that each warrior is larger than lifesize, and that hairstyles and details of uniform vary according to rank. The figures were originally painted but the colours have leached away. Wooden implements have also rotted, but the original metal weapons have survived. The arrowheads do indeed have poisoned lead tips. Chariots of bronze with figures cast in bronze have also been unearthed in the vicinity.

For those interested in other Qin excavations, a trip to **Xianyang**, northeast of Xi'an is recommended to see the site of the original Qin capital. Unearthed building materials of the Qin period, as well as a model of the first emperor's palace, are on display in the museum attached to the excavations. The Xianyang Museum, housed in a former Confucian temple, also has an impressive set of several thousand doll-sized painted terracotta figurines of soldiers and horses, dating from the Han dynasty. (*See* also page 322 in the World Heritage section.)

The Qin dynasty lasted 12 years. At its demise, rival armies contended for control of the country, with Liu Bang emerging as the victor. He styled himself Gaozu (High Ancestor) and named his dynasty Han. The name of Han is now synonymous with China itself, Chinese people calling themselves *Han ren* (the Han people). During the first part of the Han reign, known as the Western Han (206 BCE–CE 8), the capital was near modern Xi'an and known as Chang'an.

The **Yangling Tomb**, opened in 1998 to the public, represents one of the most important finds since the discovery of the Terracotta Warriors in 1974. The site lies 10 kilometres from the airport and marks the site of the funerary mound of the Western Han emperor, Jingdi (died 141 BCE). Discovered by accident when the new airport road was being laid in 1990, the site has yielded a treasure trove of magnificent funerary pieces. A site museum exhibits (on two levels) terracotta soldiers (in miniature), earthenware sculptures of domesticated animals, bronze implements, lacquer cases and other artefacts. The underground excavation work, which is still ongoing, is open for public visits, and the nearby tomb of the emperor's wife, Empress Wang, is also now open.

The best collection of Han artefacts is in the Shaanxi Provincial Museum. However, there are also exhibits displayed in a museum at one of the Han tombs in the countryside. This is the **tomb of Huo Qubing**, a young general who served under

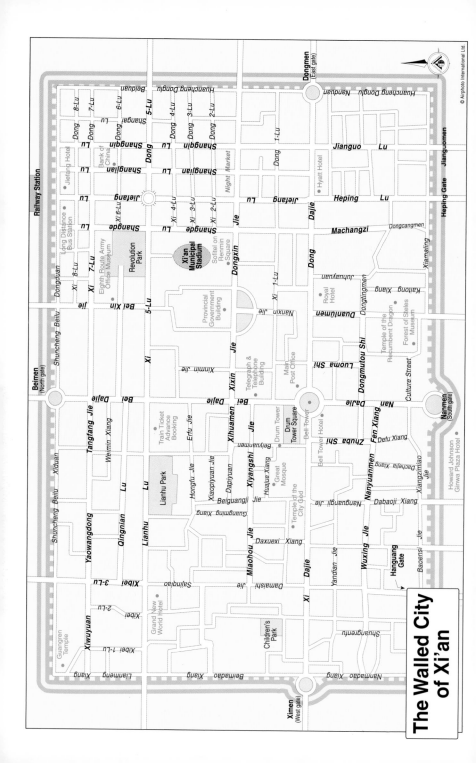

The Walled City of Xi'an

Han Emperor Wudi (reigned 186–140 BCE). It lies to the northwest of Xi'an, close to **Maoling**, the tomb of Emperor Wudi, who ordered it built himself, as a mark of imperial favour. Huo Qubing led six successful campaigns against the nomadic Xiongnu (Huns) from the northern steppes. He died at the age of only 24 from natural causes. To find allies against these nomads, who posed a constant threat to the security of China's northern frontier, Wudi sent his envoy Zhang Qian to Central Asia—and it was as a result of those expeditions that the route to the west was opened up, eventually leading to the establishment of the Silk Road. The general's tomb has wonderful stone sculptures of horses, a tiger, a boar, an elephant and an ox, as well as two strange human figures, possibly depictions of Central Asian gods or demons.

A small museum on site contains bronze articles, including money, agricultural implements and examples of the decorated building materials for which both the Qin and Han were famous.

To the northwest of Xi'an is the site, as yet unexcavated, of the most famous of the **Tang tombs**: that of the first Tang emperor, Taizong (reigned 627–649). However, some satellite tombs have been worked on. The site, known in Chinese as **Zhaoling**, has a small museum with a fine collection of funerary artefacts. Six stone bas-reliefs of horses, which once stood at the entrance to the imperial tomb, reside in the Forest of Steles Museum—four originals with two replicas, while the Museum of the University of Pennsylvania has the remaining two originals.

The other main burial site of the Tang imperial family is to the west of the city, and known as **Qianling**. It is the resting place of the famous Empress Wu Zetian (624–705), the only woman sovereign in Chinese history. She was a concubine of Emperor Taizong and, on his death, flouted convention by marrying his son. Eventually she deposed her own son and usurped the throne. The main tomb of the empress and that of Emperor Gaozong have never been excavated, but of great interest is the excavated tomb of the Princess Yongtai, granddaughter of the Empress Wu, who is said to have been murdered on her grandmother's orders.

The tomb contains reproductions of murals of Tang women in costumes influenced by Central Asian dress (the originals are now protected in the vault of the Shaanxi Provincial Museum). The composition of the murals is light and graceful, with draperies drawn in flowing lines and with figures depicted both in full face and in three-quarter profile. Also in the tomb are paintings of soldiers, grooms with horses, the Tiger of the West and the Dragon of the East. The tomb of the princess's brother, Prince Yide, also a victim of his grandmother's political ambition, is open and has fine paintings showing court attendants and a hunting scene. The nearby

Xi'an

tomb of the Crown Prince Zhanghuai, forced to commit suicide by his mother, the Empress Wu, has a fine mural depicting a polo match. These tombs all show the influence of Central Asia at the court, at a time when trade along the Silk Road was flourishing under the protection of Chinese military outposts.

Close to the excavation of the first emperor's Terracotta Army are the **Huaqing Hot Springs**, originally a Tang dynasty pleasure resort and now still used for bathing. The present buildings are late Qing, and the resort is set against an attractive mountain which is home to several Buddhist and Taoist temples. The resort became famous in recent times as the place where Generalissimo Chiang Kai-shek was captured in his nightshirt by a rebellious young general intent on forcing Chiang into an alliance with the communists against the Japanese. This episode, known as the Xi'an Incident, occurred in 1936 and ended with Chiang's eventual release, his reneging on the promised truce with the communists, and the house arrest of the young general.

Huaqing is also associated with Yang Guifei, the seductive concubine of Emperor Xuanzong (reigned 712–756), who spent several winters here and so enthralled the emperor that he withdrew from his duties at court and nearly lost his throne to rebels. A museum here displays original Tang bathtubs, including a lovely petal-shaped one used by Yang Guifei.

Although the sights mentioned above are located outside Xi'an proper, they are easily accessible. Many tour operators and most of the bigger hotels offer daily tours, either to the east or west of the city. An excursion to the east normally includes the Terracotta Army, Banpo and the Huaqing Hot Springs, while a tour to the west takes you to the tombs of the Han and Tang dynasties.

BUDDHIST TEMPLES

In the Tang dynasty, Chang'an was not only a city of vast wealth but also a prominent religious centre, with Buddhist pilgrims from Central Asia and India arriving to teach and live in the capital. During this period, the monk Xuanzang went to India to bring back Buddhist scriptures for translation. Scholars from Japan and Korea also came to Chang'an to study Buddhism, and much of the temple architecture that survives in Japan today was directly inspired by the buildings of the Tang era.

Sadly, little remains of Tang dynasty architecture in modern Xi'an, or elsewhere in China, because of an extensive religious persecution undertaken by Tang emperor Wuzong in the mid-eighth century. However, many fine Buddhist sites do remain, the most famous of which are the **Big Goose Pagoda** and the **Little Goose Pagoda** in the city centre, both of which formed part of large religious establishments which now no longer exist. The seven-storey Big Goose Pagoda was built in 652 at the request of the pilgrim monk, Xuanzang. It is adjacent to the **Da Ci'en Temple**, of which only a portion remains after the destructions during Wuzong's reign. The Little Goose Pagoda, built in 707, originally had 15 storeys, but the top two storeys collapsed in an earthquake in 1556. Both pagodas are fine examples of Tang masonry, displaying bold, simple lines on a square plan. You can climb to the top of both pagodas through the interior staircases, with the Little Goose Pagoda offering a particularly fine view over the city to the north.

Beyond Xi'an, in the surrounding countryside, are the remains of many Tang temples which were rebuilt in later dynasties. Although they have been in a poor state of repair for years, many of them are being restored, some with the help of funds from Japanese Buddhist foundations.

The **Daxingshan Temple** is a 1950s reconstruction of a famous Sui and Tang temple. It lies in Xinfeng Park, south of Little Goose Pagoda.

Set in pretty countryside, the **Xiangji Temple** is 19 kilometres (12 miles) to the south of Xi'an. It has kept its fine eighth-century, 11-storey pagoda, and is the home of the Pure Land Sect of Buddhism—a sect which has a large following in modern Japan, but in China is nothing more than a part of religious history. Japanese donations have allowed for extensive restoration work. The shop on site sells rubbings including a superb one taken from a Tang carved illustration of the temple.

If time allows, there are other temples to be explored around Xi'an, with the help of a guide, a map and a hired taxi. The **Huayan Temple** is 19 kilometres (12 miles) to the south of Xi'an; **Caotang Temple** is further, some 56 kilometres (35 miles) to the southwest.

A long day trip (approximately 150 kilometres) from Xi'an lies **Famen Temple** (Famensi), probably the most important Tang period Buddhist site in the region. A pagoda and temple ruins were excavated and a secret cache of exquisite gold and silver works unearthed. Famensi was an important site of Buddhist activity during the Tang and was visited on occasion by the imperial family.

CITY SIGHTS

The city of Xi'an as it is laid out today dates from the Ming dynasty, and is much smaller in size than it was in Tang times. You can get an idea of its scale during the Ming by strolling along the ramparts of the **city walls**, which have been renovated in recent years; visitors usually gain access at the South Gate, although several other gates are also open. The wall is open from 7am to 10.30pm and is attractively lit at night. Other Ming sites worth visiting are all easily accessible and within close walking distance of each other: the **Bell Tower**, the **Drum Tower** and the **Great Mosque**. The **Bell Tower** and Drum Tower now face each other across a newly-built square. The bell in question was used to signal the dawn when the city gates opened, and the drum the dusk when they closed. Both towers are open daily. The **Drum Tower** overlooks the main Muslim quarter of the city. Five minutes' walk from the Drum Tower is the **Great Mosque**. The original mosque dates to 743 and was built by Persian merchants who settled in Xi'an during the open era of the Tang dynasty. The mosque was originally located near the Big Wild Goose Pagoda and moved to its current location during the early Ming dynasty (late 14th century). The design of the mosque is unusual, even in China, melding a traditional Chinese temple layout (a Chinese pagoda serves as the minaret) with Arabic and Persian embellishments. The prayer hall includes original 14th century wood carvings and, a more recent addition, all 30 books of the Koran carved by local craftsmen in both Arabic and Chinese scripts mounted on the walls.

There are scores of tourist and handicraft stalls clustering in the area between the Drum Tower and the mosque. Many visitors find it difficult to resist buying a piece or two of local embroidery brought to the city by the peasants from the surrounding countryside. For children, there are wonderful tiger padded shoes, pillows and hats, padded trousers with knee patches of embroidered frogs, and pinafores embroidered with scorpions and spiders to keep evil away from the wearer. If you are offered 'antiques', *caveat emptor*!

(Left) *Delve deeper into this region's rich history with these specialized Odyssey guides.*

(Right) *Big Goose Pagoda, Xi'an.*

LUOYANG

he ancient city of Luoyang, which lies just south of the Yellow River in Henan Province, has a distinguished history as a dynastic capital second only to Xi'an. The Zhou dynasty established its capital here in 1027 BCE, and during the next 2,000 years the city served as the capital of nine dynasties.

Luoyang is best known for the Buddhist carvings of the **Longmen Caves**. Work began on the caves in the fifth century, when the Northern Wei established their capital at Luoyang, and continued until the ninth century, when persecution of the Buddhist faith led to the closure of monasteries and the end of the patronage of Buddhist arts. However, the area around Luoyang is also famous for its rich heritage of archaeological treasures. Significant art works, from Neolithic times until China's early dynasties, have been unearthed in the region and put on display in the **Luoyang Museum** and at the **Henan Museum**. The latter is located in the provincial capital of Zhengzhou; classified as a 'Key' museum (containing national treasures) it is thus a highly desirable destination while en-route to, or coming from Luoyang. For more information visit the impressive **Henan Museum** virtually, at www.chnmus.net.

The modern landscape of Luoyang is heavily marked by industrialization, but the city's gardens are renowned for their peonies ever since their cultivation began under imperial patronage in the Sui and Tang dynasties. A Peony Festival is held each year from April 15 to 25 and the best place to view the peonies is in **Huancheng Park**. The park is also notable for its New Year lantern festival (lantern-making is a traditional craft in Luoyang) as well as the fine wall paintings of two Han tombs, which have been excavated beneath the park gardens and are open to the public.

Luoyang's **East is Red Tractor Factory** was once a tour staple: the bright red tractors were an important symbol of China's reconstruction in the 1960s and the factory, with its model facilities for workers, was once considered a showpiece. Today, tractors are no longer an inevitable part of tour itineraries.

OUTINGS FROM LUOYANG

Thirteen kilometres (eight miles) to the south of Luoyang, on the banks of the River Yi, lie the **Longmen Caves**. The craftsmen actually used the river-side cliffs to create these monumental 1,352 caves with more than 40 pagodas, and some 97,000 statues.

Carving of the caves began in the Northern Wei dynasty, when the Emperor Xiaowen moved his capital to Luoyang in 494. The Wei emperors were devout Buddhists, and they manifested their piety by commissioning the creation of these large-scale shrines. The caves are scattered in various locations, but there are six which are the most frequently visited: the **Binyang**, **Lianhua** and **Guyang** caves of the Northern Wei dynasty, and the three Tang dynasty caves of **Qianxi**, **Fengxian** and the **Ten Thousand Buddhas** (Wanfo Dong). (*See* page 363 in the World Heritage section for more information about the Longmen Grottoes.)

Many of these caves have been badly damaged by earthquakes, water erosion and looters (both Chinese and foreign), but most of what remains is still impressive. The sculptures from the Northern Wei dynasty are highly textured and dynamic in form. They include beautiful flying *apsaras* (Buddhist angels) who float through flower- and cloud-filled skies, trailing fluttering ribbons. In the Sui dynasty carvings, there is a more static feel to the sculptures, whose huge faces and foreshortened limbs create a deliberately imposing effect. In contrast, the Tang sculptures (particularly those in the Fengxian cave) have great freedom of form and a liveliness of expression. The sculptures seem to be independent of the rock face from which they are carved, and the torsos twist and move in dance-like postures.

Slightly more than 10 kilometres (six miles) to the east of Luoyang lies the **White Horse Temple** (Baima Si). This is considered to be one of the earliest Buddhist foundations in China, dating from the first century (Eastern Han dynasty), when the capital was at Luoyang. The surviving temple structures all date from the Ming dynasty, but many of the buildings have the original Han bricks. The temple is now a centre for Chan—better known by its Japanese name, Zen—learning.

A half-day drive southeast from the Longmen Caves, in Dengfeng County, the **Songyue Temple Pagoda** looms on Mount Song. As the earliest surviving brick pagoda in China, it has obvious value as an architectural rarity. It was built around 520, in Indian style, and rises 40 metres (130 feet) in 12 storeys. It was once part of a thriving monastery founded in the Northern Wei dynasty.

Also in Dengfeng County is the **Shaolin Temple**, a place known to all *kungfu* enthusiasts. Set up at the end of the fifth century, Shaolin was the earliest Chan Buddhist temple in China. The style of martial art associated with it was developed by a band of 13 monks at the end of the Sui dynasty. Since 1988 there has been a martial arts training centre attached to the temple.

Eighty kilometres (50 miles) southeast of Luoyang lies the **Gaocheng Observatory**. Built in the Yuan dynasty, it is one of a series established throughout China. An imposing brick structure, it looks like a pyramid with its top chopped off. The Yuan dynasty imperial astronomer, Guo Shoujing, worked here and in 1280 calculated the length of the year to be 365.2425 days—some 300 years before the same calculation was made in the West.

Luoyang

KAIFENG

aifeng, in northeastern Henan Province, was the capital of the Northern Song dynasty (960–1127). Like Xi'an under the Tang emperors, it was the centre of power and learning in a glorious period of Chinese civilization. The city had previously served as the capital of several dynasties before the Song, but today, sadly, little of that imperial heritage has survived. The city has suffered a number of disasters, such as its sacking in 1127 by the Jin Tartars who moved into north China from Manchuria, causing the Song court to flee southwards; another was the deliberate flooding of the city in 1644 by Ming loyalists, desperate to push back the Manchu troops threatening the city. Kaifeng also suffered from periodic floods when the Yellow River—10 kilometres (six miles) to the north—overflowed its banks, so it is perhaps not surprising that the city has never developed into an influential metropolis in recent centuries.

The original city walls still remain, however, revealing that the Song city was laid out in three concentric circles. The city architects of the later Ming dynasty built their cities on a rectangular plan.

Visitors to Kaifeng must include a stop at the Youguo Temple Pagoda, also known as the **Iron Pagoda**, which can be found in the northeastern part of the city. The exterior of the pagoda is inlaid with iron-coloured glazed bricks. Its eaves, pillars and lintels are made from bricks glazed to resemble wood. The bricks have been carved in a very naturalistic style, with motifs of Buddhist immortals, musicians, flowers, plants and animals. Built in 1044 on the site of an earlier wooden pagoda which had been struck by lightning, the tower has an elegant octagonal shape and rises 13 storeys. Its base was badly damaged in a flood in 1841, but its fabric has survived very well. Close to the pagoda stands a small pavilion which shelters a Song dynasty bronze statue of a minor deity. It is considered to be one of the finest surviving masterpieces of Song bronze casting.

The **Xiangguo Monastery**, though founded in the sixth century, didn't come into its own as a centre of Buddhist learning until the Northern Song dynasty. It was completely destroyed by the flooding of the city during 1644 and the present

buildings, close to the city centre, date from the Qing dynasty. One of the temple halls is octagonal, with a small six-sided pavilion rising from the centre of the roof—a curiosity, since temple halls are usually rectangular.

Within the old city walls, **Yuwangtai**— sometimes known as the Old Music Terrace—can also be visited. It is set in landscaped gardens and is named after the legendary Emperor Yu, who tamed a great flood in prehistoric times—an appropriate tribute from a city bedevilled by floodwaters. (The bed of the Yellow River, held between high dykes, is several metres higher than the ground on which the city is built.) More recently, the temple was popular with poets of the Tang dynasty who came here to compose and carouse.

In an attempt to recreate its heyday as the Song capital, the city now boasts a Song dynasty street, lined with buildings in the appropriate style. Kaifeng was the capital of the Northern Song for 167 years.

Northwest of the city, but close to the old walls, is the **Dragon Pavilion** (Long Ting). Set on a series of rising terraces overlooking lakes and gardens, it stands on the site of a Song dynasty imperial palace and park. Like much of Kaifeng, the site was flooded in 1644, and all earlier buildings were lost. Prior to its redevelopment in the Qing dynasty, the site was known simply as Coal Hill. Its present name, Dragon Pavilion, is believed to be derived from the magnificent cube of carved stone which stands inside the pavilion. The four sides of the stone are carved with curling dragons.

Kaifeng has earned some international interest in recent years with its historic ties to Judaism. During the Northern Song, Sephardic traders from the Levant made their way to Kaifeng with some settling and intermarrying with Chinese women. A small but influential community of Chinese Jews was established that flourished through the Qing dynasty. A synagogue existed, as did a Torah. During the 19th century American Christain missionaries converted many of the community and with the upheavals of the 20th century the community faded into obscurity. American Jewish scholars have researched the history of the community and there are stele in the city museum referring to the Jewish presence.

(Above) *A 1663 inscription (fragment) commemorating the rebuilding of the synagogue of Kaifeng.*

(Left) *East Gate of Kaifeng where the synagogue was located. Most Jews lived in the surrounding area. A fascinating read for anyone is* The Jews in China *(see Recommended Reading, page 389).*

NANJING

I n its present form, Nanjing (Nanking) is a Ming dynasty creation. It was the capital of the first Ming ruler, Emperor Zhu Yuanzhang (reigned 1368–98), who called the city Yingtianfu. During his reign he commissioned a magnificent palace as well as a massive city wall, exceeding 32 kilometres (20 miles) around, intersected by 13 gates. In 1421, however, his son, Emperor Yongle (reigned 1402–24), moved the capital north to Beijing, for which he was to implement a design that would eclipse Yingtianfu in grandeur. Nanjing was then given its present name—the Southern Capital.

Unfortunately it has suffered more damage from war and rebellion than Beijing. Even though it is still the proud possessor of drum and bell towers, it has lost sections of the original walls and some of the gates. The Ming palace was destroyed in the 19th century. Nanjing no longer has the air of a proud imperial city, but rather the peaceful atmosphere of a provincial capital overseeing its fertile and wealthy hinterland. Jiangsu Province, of which Nanjing is the capital, is one of China's most prosperous regions and famous for its silk industry.

The location of the city is strikingly attractive, swept on its northern flank by the Yangzi River and surrounded by mountains. The river and mountains have made the city of strategic importance throughout history. It has been the capital of eight dynasties, and the setting of many bloody battles. The Rape of Nanking must be the worst example of these bloodbaths in recent times. In 1937 the Japanese occupied the city in the wake of the fleeing Kuomintang (Nationalist) army, which had made the city its temporary capital after the Japanese conquest of northern China. The occupation was followed by the brutal massacre of an estimated 300,000 people, both soldiers and civilians.

In the 19th century, Nanjing had already experienced tumult, for it served as the centre of a rebel regime which came very close to toppling the ruling Qing dynasty. The rebellion was led by a young scholar named Hong Xiuquan who believed himself to be the younger brother of Jesus Christ. Soon, the revolt—which had originated in the coastal province of Guangdong—turned into a tidal wave and civil war swept across southern China. After declaring the establishment of a new state, the Taiping Heavenly Kingdom, Hong and his followers captured Nanjing in 1853 and proclaimed it as their capital. Their creed was a form of messianic Christian despotism combined with an intolerance of the Chinese cultural tradition. Even while the Qing emperor was still holding court in Beijing, the Taiping Heavenly Kingdom leaders were attempting to redistribute land and putting their ideas into practice, such as allowing women an unprecedented amount of freedom. They failed to extend their control to the north of the country, however, and eventually the Qing army, helped by Western arms, crushed them in 1864. During the campaign, Emperor Hongwu's palace was destroyed and his tomb looted. The Taiping Rebellion marked a turning point in the fortunes of the Qing dynasty, which never recovered from the blow dealt to it by such a forceful challenge to its authority.

Only two decades earlier, Nanjing had been the site of another tragedy—at least for the Chinese: the signing of the 1842 treaty with the English which was to end the first Opium War and lead to the opening up of China to trade with the West (on unequal terms). The Treaty of Nanking in 1842 foreshadowed later agreements which gave other Western powers a foothold in China, and heralded a new phase in China's relations with the outside world. It confirmed that the Qing government was totally incapable of defending the nation from superior Western navies and opium traders. The loss of sovereignty which resulted from granting concessions to foreigners was a source of profound humiliation to the Chinese.

Yet if the city has suffered in history, it has also seen days of splendour and fame as a centre of culture and Buddhist scholarship, particularly during the Tang dynasty. It was then that Nanjing was the home of the poets Li Bai (Li Po) and Bai Juyi (Po Chu-i), whose works are considered among the finest in Chinese literature.

CITY SIGHTS

The **Nanjing Museum** houses an excellent collection representing more than 30 centuries of Chinese history. Here you can see a jade burial suit, dating from the Han dynasty, which was believed to prevent physical decay. Small rectangles of jade were wired together to cover the body from head to foot, and a jade disc was then inserted into the corpse's mouth. Archaeologists discovered that the suit, alas, did not have the desired effect. The exhibits of the museum have been arranged chronologically, so visitors with little time can select the dynastic period in which they are most interested.

The **Museum of the Taiping Heavenly Kingdom** is fascinating for two reasons: its exhibits give a detailed picture of the rebel state set up by Hong Xiuquan, the 19th-century failed scholar who believed he could create the Kingdom of Heaven on earth, and it has a fine Ming dynasty garden which has survived the political vicissitudes of the city.

(Following pages) *The iconic Yangzi River Bridge, at Nanjing. It was the first bridge to properly link the two halves of the country split by the Yangzi. Completed in 1968, its double-tiered road-rail design continues to funnel much of the trade today, helping Nanjing to prosper.*

POLITICS IN COMMAND

O ne afternoon when we were making dazibao [big-character posters], Little Mihu came running into the classroom waving a magazine and shouting, "Big discovery, big discovery!" We clustered around. Little Mihu was holding the May issue of China Youth. He jabbed his finger at the back cover, a scene of young people carrying bundles of wheat in baskets slung on shoulder poles. Behind them stretched a golden ocean of wheat.

"Look at the red flag in the background," Little Mihu said excitedly. "It's fluttering toward the right. On the map, right is east and left is west. So the wind must be blowing from the west. Chairman Mao says the east wind should prevail over the west, but here the west is prevailing over the east!"

That was not all. Little Mihu turned the back cover sideways and traced his finger through the wheatfield, pointing out some light-colored streaks. "Here are four characters, do you see?" "Oh my!" somebody gasped. "Long live Kai-shek!" I saw it too, the veiled message in praise of Kuomintang leader Chiang Kai-shek.

The magazine passed from hand to hand. We were shocked that the enemies of socialism would be so bold as to issue a public challenge and amazed that they had figured out such a clever way to do it. Now we understood why the newspapers were warning us that counterrevolutionaries had wormed their way into the very heart of the Party's cultural apparatus. Nothing could be taken for granted anymore.

A few days later, Little Bawang pointed to Chairman Mao's portrait at the front of our classroom and exclaimed, "Look! Chairman Mao has only one ear!" Sure enough, the face was turned slightly to the right, showing only the left ear. A few students laughed. "What are you laughing about?" Little Bawang snarled. "This is a serious political problem. Every normal person has two ears, so why did this painter paint Chairman Mao with only one?" The class divided into two schools of thought. Yuling and I and a few others saw the missing ear as a question of artistic realism. But Little Bawang's view won over a majority. They began discussing whether to report the missing ear to the School Party Committee.

Literary Excerpt

The China Youth cover was the talk of Yizhong. Everyone was on the lookout for more incriminating evidence, and every day fresh dazibao reported the latest findings. One group of students claimed to have found a snake on the face of Lenin, whose portrait hung beside the portraits of Mao, Marx, and Stalin in the back of the school auditorium and several other meeting rooms. Others said the snake was no more than a shadow on one side of Lenin's nose. Another group found a sword hanging over Chairman Mao's head in a photograph that showed him standing on the rostrum in Beijing's Tiananmen Square. Others said the sword was a painted beam. There were a few more imaginative discoveries, but none was as convincing as that pernicious message on the back cover of China Youth.

The search spread. Nothing was immune from suspicion. Taking their cues from the newspapers, students found problems with short stories, novels, movies, and plays. The critiques that appeared on the walls each day became more and more intricate. The headline-style dazibao were joined by much longer xiaozibao, "small-character posters."

One poster criticized a literature textbook for spreading decadent bourgeois ideas because it included a poem about young people's minds turning to love in the spring. One chastised our geography teacher, Teacher Liu, for entrancing us with descriptions of the grasslands of Mongolia and the mountains of Xinjiang instead of inspiring us with Mao Zedong's revolutionary thought.

By now, layer upon layer of paper covered the school walls. The debate had expanded far beyond the bounds of the Three Family Village, although the Three Villagers' names still appeared here and there, usually covered with big red X's, the symbol used on court decrees to signify the death sentence.

Gao Yuan, *Born Red*

Gao Yuan was the son of a high-ranking official who was targeted by the Cultural Revolution. Gao himself got caught up in the Red Guard movement before entering military service. He then studied in Beijing, met an American girl, moved to the United States and penned *Born Red*.

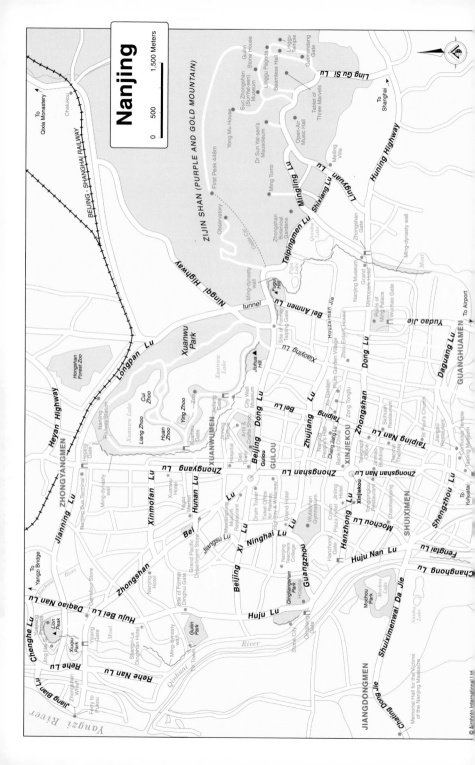

The old **city walls**, more extensive than anything that remains in Beijing today, are worth exploring—perhaps as part of an evening stroll. In the 17th century, these walls were the longest in the world and today, even in a state of decay, they are still a magnificent sight. The **Zhonghua Gate** and the **Heping Gate**, built with a mortar mixture of rice-gruel, paste and lime, are the only two to have survived from the Ming dynasty, and they vividly illustrate the insecure nature of those times—when the possibility of insurrection meant that hundreds of thousands of ordinary Chinese were made to undergo forced labour.

Within walking distance of each other, in the city centre, are the Ming **Bell Tower** and **Drum Tower**. The bell was used, as elsewhere, to sound the dawn, and the drum was beaten when the city gates were closed at dusk. Nanjing's two most well-known parks are **Xuanwu Lake Park** and **Mochou Lake Park**. In recent years, another scenic area has been developed around the **Confucius Temple** (Fuzi Miao), close to a stretch of the **Qinhuai River**. First built in the 11th century, the temple was destroyed in 1937 and reconstructed in 1986. It is flanked by shops and restaurants, and, together with the river, makes for a lively area to wander in.

Nanjing

Every morning at seven o'clock people gather in this small park in Nanjing to enjoy an hour of dancing before going to work. [Kevin Bishop]

Another of Nanjing's historical sites is the **Jiangnan Examination Hall**. The original examination hall, in which aspiring scholars of the region would gather in the hope of passing the civil service examination and winning an appointment to the imperial bureaucracy, has long since disappeared. During the Ming dynasty, it encompassed more than 20,000 individual cells in which the candidates would undergo their mental ordeal during nine days of examinations. These sometimes lasted one month. A new exhibition hall includes a reconstruction of some cells, and displays documents related to the history of imperial examinations, as well as inscribed tablets dating from the Ming, Qing and Republican periods.

MODERN NANJING

A great achievement of Nanjing is its bridge across the Yangzi River, which was built despite the withdrawl of the Russian engineers who designed it. The **Yangzi Bridge**, with its road and rail platforms, is six-and-a-half kilometres (four miles) long, and was completed in 1968. The bridge is a symbol of national pride and is important in Chinese communications. Before its construction, all north-south traffic through China had to make the crossing by ferry.

In the city centre, at 30 Meiyuan Xincun, travellers interested in Chinese communist history can visit **Zhou Enlai's house**. Here the late premier lived and worked when negotiating with the Kuomintang after the defeat of the Japanese.

Another popular place to visit, particularly for Chinese tourists, is the **People's Revolutionary Martyrs' Memorial**. It stands on the original site of the Rainbow Terrace, a place of Buddhist pilgrimage. It is said to have won its name after the eloquent preaching of a sixth-century monk so moved the Buddha that he sent down a shower of flowers which turned to pebbles. These pretty agate pebbles are collected, polished and sold as souvenirs. They are most beautiful when wet—whether with rain or submerged in water in a small bowl. Traditionally, the glistening pebbles are displayed along with New Year narcissi or goldfish.

OUTINGS FROM NANJING

East of the city are the **Purple and Gold Mountains**, which are home to some of the most famous sights of Nanjing. One of these is the **Observatory**, built on the summit of one of the peaks. It houses a fine collection of astronomical instruments, including a Ming copy of a Han dynasty earthquake detector. Also in the collection is a bronze armillary sphere, designed by the Yuan dynasty astronomer, Guo Shoujing, in 1275.

The most visited sight in the Purple and Gold Mountains is **Zhongshan Ling**, the mausoleum of Sun Zhongshan, better known in the West as Dr Sun Yat-sen. He is considered the father of the Chinese Republican Revolution. Dr Sun rose to prominence in the early years of this century as an activist in the anti-imperial movement. Prior to that, he lived in exile abroad (in 1896 he gained much publicity when he made a narrow escape after being kidnapped by Chinese secret service agents in London). In 1911, when news of the Qing overthrow reached him, Dr Sun returned to China and became the first president of the new republic. He did not have the support or personality to stop military leaders from taking power into their own hands, and he died a disappointed man in Beijing in 1925. You reach the mausoleum, which has a roof of brilliant, sky-blue tiles, after a spectacular climb up nearly 400 wide granite steps.

On the way to the mausoleum, visitors usually stop off at **Ming Xiaoling**, the tomb of the first emperor of the Ming dynasty. The tomb was looted during the Taiping Rebellion, but it is worth coming to see the pastoral site and its quiet Spirit Way, lined with stone warriors, scholars and beasts.

Also in the mountains is the **Linggu Monastery**, which is notable for its Ming **Beamless Hall**. This hall is made of bricks without any supporting pillars. It was constructed over a mound of earth which was subsequently scooped out on completion of the building, thereby leaving the hall standing in pillarless splendour.

The wooded **Qixia Mountain** lies 25 kilometres (16 miles) east of Nanjing, and is home to one of the oldest surviving monasteries in southern China. The present buildings of **Qixia Monastery** all date from this century, but there is a famous library with many ancient Buddhist scriptures. Within the monastic grounds there is an octagonal stone stupa, carved with images from the life of Buddha, which dates back to 601. A short walk from this stupa is a rock face carved with Buddha images. It is known as **Thousand Buddha Cliff** (Qianfo Yan, a name used at many sites throughout China), and has carvings dating from the early seventh century.

One hour by car, to the northeast of the city, there are stone carvings from the fourth and fifth centuries. This was a period of political chaos in China, when a series of short-lived dynasties ruled different regions of the country, and the carvings reflect this. They are scattered across the fields at 31 different sites, and all are remains of aristocratic and imperial tombs of the period. They are known collectively as the **Southern Dynasties' Stone Carvings** (Nanchao Shiku).

Nanjing

HISTORY AT REST

—By *Travis Klingberg*

Most visitors to Nanjing never stop at the Ming Imperial City. In fact, though many tour groups pass by on their way to other sites, most would never notice. The site is now a run-down park. Not a single building from Nanjing's glory days remains—all that is left is the name, Ming Gugong, and a few stone remnants.

Nanjing is not new, and it's not old. It's a city with a glorious past: the capital of dynasties, the centre of the world. It's also a city that has been sacked multiple times over, and there are places like the Imperial City where the scars still show.

A large gate and a sales window stand at the north end of the park, though no one bothers selling tickets. The park has no walls and visitors freely come and go from all sides, stopping at the teahouse, browsing cheap toys sold from towering bamboo racks, napping on the grass. Huskers sell lighters, laser pointers, albino rabbits in purple cages, and multicoloured kites of all sizes.

In the days when the founding Ming emperor Zhu Yuanzhang ruled China, the Imperial courtyards and temples were ringed by concentric walls—the Palace City Wall, the Imperial City Wall, the Capital City Wall, the Outer City Wall. Now, the few remaining fragments of the palace are bounded only by busy streets and rusted landscape fencing. Hand-tooled column footings from Ming-era buildings are scattered throughout the park, though no one seems to mind. They make good benches, and they don't really get in the way of the amusement rides, where children shoot at robot dinosaurs that bob and roar with tinny ferocity. The imperial axis—the kind that still anchors the entire city of Beijing—is now a mere sidewalk, marked off with numbers for street festival booths and crisscrossed by men struggling to get their kites aloft.

Meridian Gate, the main gate to the Imperial City, is the only part of the city that still stands above knee height. A plaque at the gate explains that the area had been razed in 1853 in "a war". At Zhu Yuanzhang's tomb, set on the green hillside overlooking the city, a similar historical plaque informs visitors that the tomb had been burned out in the same year, also in "a war". The destruction of an entire imperial city, along with the desecration of an emperor's tomb, is no small event, yet here was the ancient Ming Imperial City razed to the ground in an anonymous conflict. In a city such as Nanjing, ravaged so many times over the last 150 years, the omission of which war, by whom, is glaring.

In 1853, the Taiping Heavenly Kingdom, a band of peasants with revolutionary ambition, stormed Nanjing, destroying the Ming buildings. This was that "war". In the Communist era, the Taiping revolutionary spirit in itself was enough to make them People's Heroes, though the Taipings soon built their own imperial palace—this time a Heavenly Palace—that looked suspiciously similar to the Ming palace they had destroyed. Once the revolution was put down, the Taiping palace, too, was burned to the ground.

So goes Nanjing's history. In recent years, Nanjing has renovated or built minor sites of cultural interest, such as a museum to Zheng He, the early Ming dynasty ocean explorer. Yet to this day, most of Nanjing's big tourist sites are locations of significant political and military importance. The Imperial City is not even a minor tourist site, and is essentially forsaken. All that remains are column footings and the vague foundations of temples and reception halls. No one seems to mind.

The feudal glories of the Ming and the peasant revolutionaries of Taiping are equally treasured parts of China's official history, and Nanjing is the nexus of them both. Nanjing's glories have all been bittersweet: The Ming dynasty was founded here, but was moved to Beijing 53 years later. The Qing dynasty controlled the area for two centuries, but was routed by the Taipings and then was undermined by a group of secular reformers with visions of a modern China. (It's no subtle irony that Sun Yat-sen, the legendary father of modern China, is interred on the same hillside as feudal emperor Zhu Yuanzhang.) Warlords fought for power in Nanjing only 90 years ago, eventually yielding to the Kuomintang, who accelerated the development of a modern capital city. That development was stunted, however: The Japanese invaded in 1937 and terrorized the city. Then, little more than a decade later, China's civil war ended with the Communists in power and Beijing as the new national capital.

For most tourists, this tumultuous history dominates Nanjing. A bronze *ding*, a traditional three-legged ceremonial vessel, sits on the white stone steps leading to Zhongshan Ling, Sun Yat-sen's tomb. It was a gift to mark Sun's interment, bearing wishes befitting an emperor. The ding also bears two crater-like indentations from Japanese tank artillery: a giant tin can after target practice. Most people who notice the craters touch them tenderly, as if they were open wounds.

Special Topic

A message posted at the exit to the Nanjing Massacre Memorial reminds visitors to "Never Forget". Photographs document the atrocities committed by the Japanese army, and the excavated mass grave speaks on its own. The sufferings of countless individual Chinese have been subsumed by the totemic death count posted at the front gate: 300,000.

The Presidential Palace, Nanjing's most interesting historical site, still contains the garden retreat of Qing viceroys, Hong Xiuquan's bedroom, Sun Yat-sen's residence, and Chiang Kaishek's office. Visitors get their tickets punched at the same gate where the Qing, then the Nationalists, then the Japanese, then the Communists raised their respective flags, each proclaiming victory. By the time the Communists captured Nanjing in 1949 and announced—from Beijing—the founding of New China, Nanjing was exhausted.

Nanjing has since grown to be a thriving city with a quiet pride. Its residents have no arrogance about cultural or economic superiority, like their counterparts in Beijing or Shanghai, and most would say it's a good place to live. Many streets, including main traffic arteries and roundabouts, are lined by small businesses and plane trees, whose branches explode into a canopy of foliage in the warm months. There is a building boom, a consumer boom, a new subway, high-end coffee and ice cream. Nanjing's prime universities are nationally ranked, and the city is one of the three key military command centres that guard the coast—a prominent launching point for national political careers. The city in many ways has already outgrown its history, which now resides most comfortably in libraries and the tightly edited tourist experience.

Most Nanjing residents have visited Zhongshan Ling and Ming Xiao Ling, or at least know of them. If pressed, many can relate the city's past glory, home to the founders both of the Ming dynasty and modern China. However, it's more likely to find locals unconcerned about the glories and pains of the past, choosing instead to look to the future. For them, history's scars are the places you have to pay to get in to, and except during occasional flaring of political tensions, history seems something better left alone. Imperial City rest in peace.

Since 1997, Travis Klingberg has lived and worked in Sichuan, Beijing and Nanjing and has travelled much of China's heartland. He has worked as a writer, editor and guide.

BEIJING

Beijing lies just south of the rim of the Central Asian steppes and is separated from the Gobi Desert by a green chain of mountains, over which the Great Wall runs. The Great Wall was built and rebuilt by a succession of Chinese emperors to keep out the marauding hordes of nomads who from time to time swept into China—in much the same way as the wind from the Gobi still sweeps in seasonal sand storms which suffocate the city. The rocks beneath the city yield bitter water, which is barely drinkable, and only the presence of a few sweet springs made the growth of an imperial capital possible.

Modern Beijing lies in fact on the site of countless human settlements which date back half a million years. Visitors can see the site, outside the city at **Zhoukoudian**, where *Homo erectus Pekinensis*, better known as Peking Man, was discovered in 1929. The name Beijing—or Northern Capital—is by Chinese standards a modern term. It dates back to the 15th century, when the Ming emperor, Yongle, planned and built the city in its present form. One of the city's earlier names was Yanjing, a name given in the Liao dynasty (947–1125). The name refers to a nearby mountain, but is often mistaken to mean City of Swallows. Beijing does host a large summer community of swallows, which make their homes in the capacious eaves of the ancient wooden buildings. At twilight, **Qianmen**, the gate standing on the south side of Tiananmen Square, is circled by roosting swallows. This scene on a summer evening remains much the same as it must have been throughout the centuries, except that the gate now stands lonely and obsolete, no longer buttressed by the old city walls which were torn down on the orders of Mao.

Beijing first became a capital in the Jin dynasty (1115–1234), but it experienced its first phase of grandiose city planning in the Yuan dynasty under the rule of the Mongol emperor, Kublai Khan, who made the city his winter capital in the late 13th century. Kublai Khan's Beijing was known in Chinese as Dadu, but the Venetian explorer, Marco Polo, who may have visited the city at the time of Kublai Khan, knew it by the name of Khanbaliq. On his return to Europe, Marco Polo wrote a vivid account of his travels across Central Asia to China, which he called Cathay. However, his contemporaries did not believe his stories, and they nicknamed him *Il Milione*, saying his tales were thousands of lies. In fact, many of his descriptions of Cathay were inaccurate (there were some interesting omissions—including tea, bound feet and the Great Wall, for example), and many modern scholars are convinced he journeyed no further than the Near East: the rest is hearsay.

Beijing

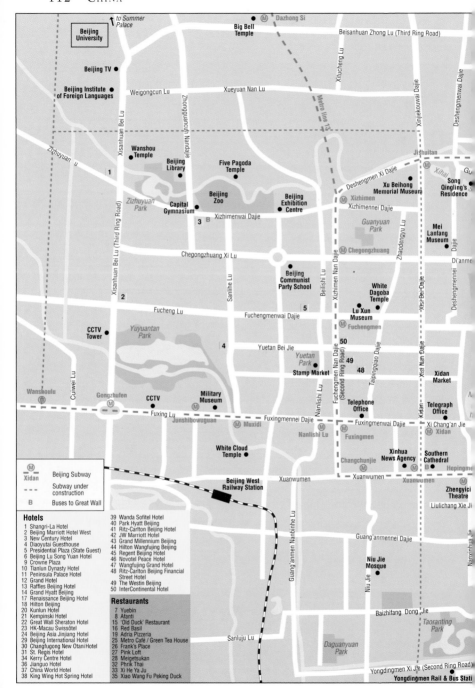

to Summer Palace

Beijing University

Dazhong Si

Big Bell Temple

Beisanhuan Zhong Lu (Third Ring Road)

Beijing TV

Beijing Institute of Foreign Languages

Weigongcun Lu

Xueyuan Nan Lu

Metro line 13

Xiluchuang Lu

Xinjiekouwai Dajie

Deshengmenwai Dajie

Zizhuyuan Lu

Zhongguancun Nandaihe

Xisanhuan Bei Lu

Jishuitan

Xihai

Gu

Wanshou Temple

Beijing Library

Five Pagoda Temple

Deshengmen Xi Dajie

Xu Beihong Memorial Museum

Song Qingling's Residence

1

Zizhuyuan Park

Capital Gymnasium

Beijing Zoo

Xizhimennei Dajie

Beijing Exhibition Centre

Xizhimen

Guanyuan Park

Zhaodengyu Lu

Xisi Bei Dajie

Mei Lanfang Museum

Dajie

Xisanhuan Bei Lu (Third Ring Road)

3 B

Xizhimenwai Dajie

Chegongzhuang Xi Lu

Saniihe Lu

Beishi Lu

Xizhimen Nan Dajie

Chegongzhuang

Di'anme

Deshengmennei

2

Fucheng Lu

Beijing Communist Party School

5

Fuchengmenwai Dajie

White Dagoba Temple

Lu Xun Museum

Fuchengmen

Xidan Market

CCTV Tower

Yuyuantan Park

4

Yuetan Bei Jie

Yuetan Park

Stamp Market

50

49

48

Fuchengmen Nan Dajie (Second Ring Road)

Taipingqiao Dajie

Xisi Nan Dajie

Cuiwei Lu

Wanshoulu

Gongzhufen

CCTV

Military Museum

Fuxing Lu

Junshibowuguan

Fuxingmennei Dajie

Muxidi

Fuxingmenwai Dajie

Nanlishi Lu

Nanlishi Lu

Telephone Office

Fuxingmen

Fuxingmenwai Dajie

Telegraph Office

Xi Chang'an Jie

Xidan

Xidan

White Cloud Temple

Xuanwumen

Xinhua News Agency

Changchunjie

Xuanwumen

Southern Cathedral

Hepingme

Beijing West Railway Station

Xuanwumen

Xuanwumen

Zhengyici Theatre

Liulichang Xie Ji

Guang'anmennei Dajie

Niu Jie Mosque

Niu Jie

Baizhifang Dong Jie

Taoranting Park

Guang'anmen Nanbinhe Lu

Sanluju Lu

Daguanyuan Park

Nanxinhua Jie

Yongdingmen Xi Jie (Second Ring Road)

Yongdingmen Rail & Bus Stati

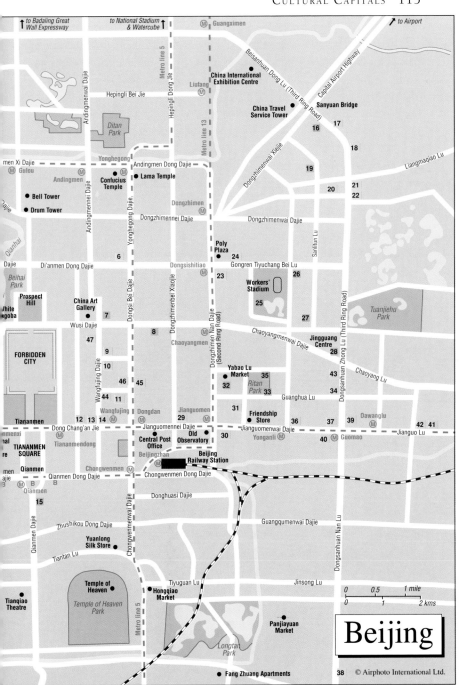

↑ to Badaling Great Wall Expressway
↑ to National Stadium & Watercube
↗ to Airport

Ⓜ Guangximen

Beisanhuan Dong Lu (Third Ring Road)

Capital Airport Highway

Andingmenwai Dajie

Hepingli Dong Jie

Metro line 5

Liufang

Ⓜ

Metro line 13

Hepingli Bei Jie

China International Exhibition Centre

Ditan Park

China Travel Service Tower

Sanyuan Bridge

16   17

men Xi Dajie

Yonghegong

Andingmen Dong Dajie

Dongzhimenwai Xiejie

Liangmaqiao Lu

Ⓜ Gulou

Andingmen Ⓜ

Confucius Temple

● Lama Temple

18

19

Andingmennei Dajie

Yonghegong Dajie

Dongzhimen

Ⓜ

20   21
22

● Bell Tower

● Drum Tower

Dongzhimennei Dajie

Dongzhimenwai Dajie

Sanlitun Lu

Qianhai

Dajie

6

Di'anmen Dong Dajie

Dongsi Bei Dajie

Dongsishitiao

Poly Plaza

24

Gongren Tiyuchang Bei Lu

26

Beihai Park

23

Workers' Stadium

Prospect Hill

China Art Gallery

7

Dongzhimenbei Xiaojie

25

27

Jhite agoba

Wusi Dajie

8

Chaoyangmen

Dongzhimen Nan Dajie (Second Ring Road)

Chaoyangmenwai Dajie

Jingguang Centre

28

Dongsanhuan Zhong Lu (Third Ring Road)

Tuanjiehu Park

47

FORBIDDEN CITY

9

Wangfujing Dajie

10

46

45

Yabao Lu Market

32

35

43

Chaoyang Lu

44

11

Ritan Park 33

34

Tiananmen

12   13   14

Wangfujing

Dongdan

Jianguomen

29

31

Guanghua Lu

Dawanglu

Ⓜ

42   41

Dong Chang'an Jie

Jianguomennei Dajie

Friendship Store

36

37

39

nal

al

re

TIANANMEN SQUARE

Tiananmendong

30

Jianguomenwai Dajie

Yonganli Ⓜ

40 Ⓜ Guomao

Jianguo Lu

Qianmen

Central Post Office

Old Observatory

Beijing Railway Station

men

ajie

Chongwenmen

Ⓜ

Beijingzhan

3 Ⓜ B

Qianmen Dong Dajie

Chongwenmen Dong Dajie

Dongsanhuan Nan Lu

Ⓜ Qianmen

15

Qianmen Dajie

Chongwenmenwai Dajie

Donghuasi Dajie

Guangqumenwai Dajie

Zhushikou Dong Jie

Yuanlong Silk Store

Tiantan Lu

Metro line 5

Tiyuguan Lu

Jinsong Lu

0   0.5   1 mile
0   1   2 kms

Temple of Heaven

Tianqiao Theatre

Temple of Heaven Park

Hongqiao Market

Beijing

Longtan Park

Panjiayuan Market

● Fang Zhuang Apartments

38   © Airphoto International Ltd.

Little of it remains in today's Beijing, except for the layout of **Beihai Park**, and remnants of Dadu's city wall between the northern legs of the third and fourth ring roads. However, the Beijing municipal government has begun reconstructing parts of the wall, using new materials, in an effort to show the wall's range and size. Liang Congjie, an environmental activist whose mother argued against tearing down the city wall in the 1950s as a government official, has called the new wall "a fake antique". The city of Beijing that visitors see today was the grand conception of Emperor Yongle, the Ming ruler who, having usurped the throne, moved the capital north from Nanjing. Most of the eminent historical sites in the city date either from the Ming or later Qing dynasties. The substantial modern transformation of the city has been executed by the present government, which on coming to power in 1949 decided to make Beijing its capital and to modernize the old city by demolishing the Ming city walls, destroying the commemorative arches (to widows and local dignitaries, among other honoured citizens), and replacing them with wide new roads and concrete housing blocks. The intimate network of *hutong*—or lanes—was partially redeveloped, thus taking away the distinct pattern of neighbourhoods which had given the city such human proportions. A few of the old hutong districts remain north and south of the Forbidden City, but the city centre is dominated by the imposing Stalinesque buildings put up around Tiananmen Square in 1959 to mark the 10th anniversary of the founding of the People's Republic, cleaned and revamped for the 1999 50th anniversary celebrations, and joined by increasing numbers of glossy office towers.

The Cultural Revolution (1966–76) also caused the destruction of many of Beijing's historic and religious treasures in the name of revolutionary purity. During the anti-intellectual purges of the Cultural Revolution, there were many cases of famous scholars being killed or committing suicide. Perhaps the most infamous was the death by drowning of the writer, Lao She. Of all the writers of the 20th century, it is Lao She who writes with the most authentic voice about Beijing, its people, neighbourhoods and lowlife, especially before 1949.

The leadership of the present Chinese government is trying to make good the ravages of the Cultural Revolution with restoration work and rebuilding. One problem is that the skilled craftsmen, whose forefathers built and maintained the imperial city for generations, are a dying breed, and today's craftsmen often lack the necessary skills and knowledge of materials to save buildings, frescoes and carvings. Some restored murals have crude colouring and lines worthy of chocolate-box design. Even so, there is still enough to see in the city, and beyond, to keep an enthusiastic sightseer busy for a long time. Also worth mention is Beijing's hosting of the 2008 Olympic Games, which gave its municipal authorities carte blanche to build a number of futuristic edifices—such as the **National Aquatics Center** (aka the Watercube), the **National Stadium** (the Bird's Nest) and the **Grand National Theatre** (the Egg)—that qualify as scenic attractions in their own right.

A cautionary note, however: Beijing's explosion of vehicular traffic from 170,000 in 1994 to three million in 2007 has resulted in a monumental gridlock problem—average rush hour traffic speed is now a mere 6kph—so unless you can conveniently use the new expanded subway system, be prepared for travel times between city sights to be frustratingly lengthy.

CITY SIGHTS

The **Forbidden City** (Imperial Palace, Gu Gong) was the home of emperors from its creation by Emperor Yongle in 1420 until Pu Yi, who reigned briefly as the last Qing emperor, left it in 1924. Since 1925 the palace has been the National Palace Museum, the largest and most important museum in China. Its exhibition halls and vaults hold some one million treasures and despite the removal of a substantial portion of the original collection to Taiwan in 1949, it remains one of the most important museums of Chinese artwork in the world.

The vast pageant of halls, white marble terraces and deep red walls is now used to display many exhibitions ranging from court costumes to the imperial collection of clocks and, in the dry autumn months, rare paintings. (Much of the imperial art collection was taken to Taiwan before 1949.) The entire complex of the Forbidden City, covering 74 hectares (183 acres), was designed to overawe the visitor while reinforcing the majesty of the Son of Heaven, as every Chinese emperor was known. The palace requires a visit of at least half a day, and it can be daunting in the heat of summer, the time at which the emperor and his court retreated to cooler lakeside palaces. The palace is at its most beautiful after a light winter snowfall. To see the golden roofs at their most brilliant at any time of year, try to get a view at dawn from an upper floor on the west wing of the **Grand Hotel** or its Palace View Bar, or from Coal Hill.

Another stunning sight is the **Temple of Heaven** (Tiantan). This is actually a wonderful sequence of temples and altars set in a park as part of Emperor Yongle's grand design. Heaven—or *tian*—was considered the source of harmony and spiritual authority by Chinese philosophers, and so it came to symbolize the source of imperial power. The Temple of Heaven was the site of imperial sacrifices at the winter solstice to keep order and harmony on earth. The architecture reflects that sense of order: the northern wall of the complex is curved in a half-circle to symbolize heaven, and the

Beijing

(Following pages) *Snow covers the Forbidden City as the sun rises over Beijing. The Imperial Palace has occupied this site since the late 13th century, but the present layout was established by the Yongle emperor of the Ming dynasty in the early 15th century.* [William Lindesay]

southern wall is built as a square to symbolize earth. Whereas most imperial buildings have yellow tiles (the imperial colour) on their roofs, the blue tiles here are said to 'reflect' the colour of the sky. The main buildings and altars are also built in tiers of three to create nine dimensions of surface. Nine is the mystical number in Chinese tradition, and it also symbolizes heaven. At other times of the year, the emperor made additional sacrifices at the **Altars of the Sun, Moon and Earth**. These sites have been transformed into public parks and can be found in the east, west and north of the city, respectively.

The original water park of Kublai Khan is now **Beihai Park**. Nothing remains here from the Yuan dynasty period except a vast, black jade bowl carved with sea monsters. Made for Kublai Khan in 1265, the bowl is displayed in the **Round City**, near the south entrance to the park. At the centre of Beihai Lake is a small hill on which stands a Tibetan-style **White Dagoba**, built in 1651 to honour the Dalai Lama's visit. The lake is actually only half of a larger one. The southern half lies hidden behind the high red walls of **Zhongnanhai**, once also part of the imperial park and now the residential complex of senior Communist Party leaders. No foreigner, unless he is a high-ranking dignitary, can visit the lakeside villas and steam-heated tennis courts used by China's privileged few. Ordinary Chinese and foreign tourists must take their pleasures on the north shores of the lake at Beihai, with boating in the summer and skating in the winter. Most of the buildings visited today date from the Qing dynasty. The park's **Fangshan Restaurant**, which specializes in the imperial cuisine of the Qing dynasty, is a popular place to host lunches and dinners.

Directly to the north of the Forbidden City across the street from the north gate in Jingshan Park lies **Coal Hill**, also known as Prospect Hill, though few refer to it as either anymore. Jingshan offers a fine view of the Imperial Palace to the south and Beihai Park to the west. The hill was constructed from the earth removed to dig the palace moat. It was called Coal Hill because the coal to heat the palace floors was stored in the hill. It played a sad part in Chinese history, since it was on its eastern slope that the last Ming emperor hung himself when his capital was overrun by rebel troops in 1644.

By the time the Jesuit fathers arrived in China in the 16th century, much of China's previous scientific knowledge had been lost, due to dynastic change and the resulting destruction and upheaval. In order to impress the Chinese emperors with the superiority of the Christian faith (a faith that had persecuted Galileo for his scientific discoveries), the Jesuit missionaries set about casting fine astronomical instruments and challenging the accuracy of the Chinese court astronomers' predictions. This was not a minor challenge, since the emperor—as Son of Heaven— was responsible for the accuracy of the calendar, and thus the harmony of the empire.

The Jesuits' astronomical instruments are on display at the **Imperial Observatory**, which is at the intersection of the Second Ring Road and Jianguomennei Da Jie. Ming and Qing pieces are also displayed on an open-air platform which was once a section of the city wall. Yet despite their great prestige at the Qing courts of Emperors Kangxi and Qianlong, and their work in the field of science, the Jesuits failed to achieve their objective of converting the imperial household.

Tiananmen Square is a vast 20th-century creation named after the Forbidden City's southernmost gate—the **Gate of Heavenly Peace**. In the centre stands the **Monument to the People's Heroes**, and behind that **Chairman Mao's Mausoleum** (open to the public in the mornings only), which was built within six months in 1977 by a volunteer work force of 10,000 Beijing residents (Chairman Mao died on 9 September 1976). Previously the square gave an uninterrupted view from the city gate of **Qianmen** to the outer walls of the Forbidden City. On the west side of the square sits the Stalinesque **Great Hall of the People**, where party and national congresses are held. On the eastern side stands the huge **National Museum of China**, which is currently closed for a major revamp and enlargement. The work is scheduled to continue until the end of 2009, but once finished the museum, with 192,000 square metres of floor space, will be the largest in the world and home to more than a million cultural relics.

The square has been a stage for significant events in China's modern history. Mao received millions of Red guards there in 1966 at the start of the Cultural Revolution, and 10 years later it witnessed mass protests calling for the arrest of the Gang of Four. In the spring of 1989 unrest in the square threatened chaos on a larger scale, something the authorities were not prepared to countenance and in early June the inevitable crackdown took place. Beijing authorities again briefly closed the square in 1999. It emerged, repaved in granite as well as areas of green grass apparently imported from the United States, in time for the 1999 National Day parade.

Beijing is rich in museums. The Forbidden City is a vast museum in itself, besides housing several separate collections such as clocks and watches, ceramics, paintings and so on. There are also museums devoted to China's revolutionary history, and to special interests such as aviation and archaeology. Two other places are worth a visit if time allows. The **National Library**, which has more than 13 million volumes including rare books and manuscripts, has recently been opened to the public. The **Beijing Art Museum** is located in the grounds of the Wanshou Temple, which for years had been occupied by the army, and displays an eclectic collection of Ming and Qing artefacts, as well as paintings from the Republican period.

Many of the city's old temples have been restored and opened to the public and are clearly shown on widely available English-language tourist maps.

Beijing

Jugglers exhibiting in the court of a Mandarin's Palace. [Wattis Fine Art]

The **White Dagoba Monastery** (Baita Si) can be found in the Taipingqiao district, west of Beihai Park. Built in the late 13th century under the supervision of a Nepalese architect and restored in 1999, it is a quiet place seldom visited by tourists. Its white dagoba (dome-shaped shrine) makes it easy to spot. To the northeast lies the **Lama Temple**, which is known in Chinese as Yonghe Gong—the Palace of Peace and Harmony—because it was originally the residence of a prince. When this prince ascended the throne as Emperor Yongzheng (reigned 1723–35), the complex of buildings was converted into a temple in accordance with custom. Under the next emperor, Qianlong, it became a centre of learning for the Yellow Hat sect of Tibetan Buddhism. It has a fine collection of Tibetan bronzes and paintings, but its most well-known treasure is a huge statue of Maitreya, the Future Buddha. More than 23 metres (75 feet) tall, this piece of sculpture is said to have been carved out of a single sandalwood tree.

Outings from Beijing

Legend has it that the Yongle emperor (reigned 1402–1424) picked the location for the **Ming Tombs** when out hunting to celebrate his birthday. While resting, local peasants came to wish him long life, so he renamed a nearby mountain Longevity Mountain and suggested to court geomancers that the valley be considered as a site for hosting the royal tombs. It satisfied the requirements of *fengshui*, literally 'wind-water' geomancy, a spiritual version of good vibes. It was sheltered from the evil-spirit bearing northern wind by mountains, while it possessed a wide-open aspect to the south, conducive to the approach of benevolent forces.

A grand view of the immense National Stadium, taken from the roof of the Watercube, with its futuristic plastic panelling. [Peter Danford]

Royal parties would travel for two days from the Imperial City to perform ancestor worshipping rites at the tombs. Now the site can be reached in less than one hour via the new Badaling Expressway.

The entrance to *Shisanling*, meaning 13 tombs, is announced by a towering marble *pailou*, or portico. At 33 metres (36 yards) in length and 10.5 metres (11.5 yards) in height, it is said to be the largest in China. However, it is unique because ornate carving normally produced in wood has been achieved remarkably in marble. It has five arches and was erected by the Jiajing emperor in 1540. Only the emperor would pass beneath the central arch whose tablet bears no characters, as it was unfitting for anyone to write anything about the Son of Heaven. The six supporting column bases have superb symbolic reliefs on their four faces: lions for strength, *makara* (water creatures) for fertility, and five-clawed dragons symbolizing the emperor. Statuettes of *qilin* lions, symbolizing good administration and peace, complete the arrangement.

A few hundred metres further on stands the Great Red Gate. Like all that follows, it was built as the approach to the Yongle emperor's tomb, **Changling**, but subsequently served the whole mausoleum. There used to be a pillar and gateway, *xiamamen*, or 'dismount (from horses) gate' here, but this has disappeared. Only the emperor's body was allowed to pass under the central arch. Next is the stele pavilion serving the whole mausoleum. It is flanked by four *hua biao*, marble columns, on which fabulous dragons are carved. Inside the pavilion, the stele is mounted on a huge *bi xi*, a tortoise-like creature, said to be a descendant of the dragon and able to bear enormous burdens. The tablet has inscriptions on both faces: that on the south face, 3,500 characters long, praises the Changling tomb. It was composed by Yongle's son and written by a famous calligrapher. The north face inscription has a 13-line poem by Qianlong (reigned 1736–1795)—one for each tomb—whose dynasty, the Qing, maintained the mausoleum.

CHINESE OPERA

P eking Opera has its origins in southern China, but was adopted by the Qing court in the 19th century and thus came to be known as *Jingju*, meaning 'capital opera'. It is best known for its percussive style of music and the use of wooden clappers (rather like oblong castanets), which are used to mark the time of the actors' movements. There are only four tempos which set the mood of the scene: the slow tempo is used for scenes of reflection or when the actor is thinking out loud; the medium tempo is used during narrative; a fast tempo is used for moods of gaiety or excitement; and a free tempo is used for interludes between the action. Actors either sing in a falsetto style or in natural voice. The warrior characters have special techniques for singing, pushing their voice through the lower front part of their cheeks in order to create a deep, gruff effect. Chinese audiences love to applaud a particularly fine solo, which requires great voice control and range.

Chinese opera is different from its Western counterpart in many ways, but no difference is as striking as the painted faces seen on the Chinese stage. Ancient Greek dramas were performed behind masks for dramatic effect, but the Chinese opera demands that many of its characters have their faces painted in elaborate patterns to denote personality. Audiences, through their familiarity with the art, can tell the good and bad characters apart—they know that red faces belong to heroes and white faces indicate treachery. In the past the illiterate and poor learnt their history and legends through opera performances. Not all painted faces are elaborate and multicoloured. Some require only a layer of rouge over the face with white contours around the eyes and thick black eyebrows (the eyes are emphasized by the simple method of sticking tape at the corners to pull the eyes upwards). As a rough guide, the young female and male 'good characters' have unpatterned, rouged faces, while the warriors have elaborate face markings. Clowns are easy to distinguish with their white blob of paint in the centre of their faces. Maidservants and page boys wear little make-up and usually have two little jaunty topknots of hair. The faces of the gods are painted a brilliant gold, and the animal spirits have faces painted to resemble the animal in question.

The stage will have very few props; instead they will be suggested by the actors miming an action to tell the audience what must be imagined. For example, you may see an actor 'row' across the stage by bending his body as if balancing on a boat and sculling from the stern with one oar. A character who is about to ride a horse flourishes his tasselled whip and makes a mounting movement. A man who is leaving a room takes an elaborate step while pulling at the hem of his robe (all traditional Chinese houses have raised steps in their doorways). Great emotion is expressed by the shaking of the hands in the sleeves of the tunic. Shy love is shown by the woman turning her head behind her hand. These and other tiny gestures by the actors give important information to the audience, gestures which can be read after only a little experience of Chinese opera.

The stories of traditional operas usually have complex plots full of twists and turns. Plot rather than character development is the way in which suspense is injected into the drama. This is because there is no character development as we know it in the West; the painted faces of the characters are given at the beginning of the play and there is no change of either character or make-up in the course of the action. Bad characters are vanquished, not transformed. It is understandable that the plays most popular with foreign visitors are the acrobatic martial operas, which need little explanation. Yet even the martial spectacles are more exciting for having their plots unravelled. A particular favourite is *San Cha Kou* or *Where Three Roads Meet*. This tale is of mistaken identity and includes a fight in the dark between two heroes and an innkeeper. The three actors mime a fight as if they were in pitch dark. It is so convincing you forget the actors can really see one another. Their eyes never meet, and at one point one of the actors moves his sword into the air as if trying to catch the moonlight on its blade. It is thrilling stuff, so much so that it inspired the English playwright Peter Shaffer to write *Black Comedy* after he saw a performance in the late 1950s.

Regional Chinese opera can be just as exciting and colourful as its metropolitan cousin. In Sichuan and Shaanxi operas you will often find the role of a comic dame sung by a man. In the *Yueju* style of opera of the Zhejiang region, all the parts are played by women and the music is softer, with more strings, wind instruments, and less percussion than northern opera. The classical *Kunqu* style, which originated in Kunshan, is still popular with older audiences in present-day China. There is a Kunqu troupe based in Beijing which performs quite regularly in the capital. They have one lively story in their repertoire concerning a wastrel husband who, as a young man, sold his wife. His punishment is to be taken into her service, on her secret instructions, and then to run errands while she pretends that she does not know who he is. He is filled with shame and heats her wine with trembling hands, dreading that she will recognize him. The story has a fine comic climax, in which the man is persuaded to marry an unknown bride, who turns out to be—yes—his wife, who has of course forgiven him. Chinese audiences delight in these tales of misfortune, forgiveness and reconciliation.

Special Topic

Beyond the tower beckons the avenue of statues comprising the **Spirit Way**. First come a pair of *wang zhu*, guiding posts, to show any wandering spirit the way back to its resting place. Twelve pairs of beasts follow, both mythical and real, providing a guard of honour for the spirits. Each beast appears first standing, then sitting, operating in a shift system to allow resting. The real animals, camels, horses and elephants, symbolize the vast geographical extent of the great Ming empire with camels indigenous to Central Asia, horses to the northern grasslands, and elephants to the subtropics of the southwest. The elephant, or *da xiang* in Chinese, is also highly auspicious as it is a homonym for 'great universe'. Mythical *qilin* and

In Peking Opera, a simple rouged face usually denotes a young, "good" character. [CGS]

xiezi represent the government's good administration and justice. Human figures begin with military officers to symbolize the empire's strength and security, while high civil officials, advisors to the emperor, make up the final four pairings. Each holds an elongated *hu*

tablet, used to make notes during audiences with the emperor. The symbolism combines to remind those entering the mausoleum of the magnificence of the

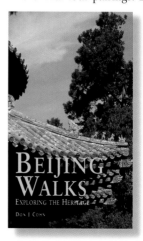

Ming empire and dynasty. The end of the Spirit Way is marked by a protective screen: evil spirits were thought only able to travel in straight lines, hence the stone curtain thwarted their attempts at violating the sanctity of the mausoleum. Screens also appear in individual tomb courtyards.

Odyssey's guides to Beijing provide far greater detail on how to fully appreciate this historic city.

Twelve sets of stone animals guard a section of the seven-kilometre-long 'Spirit Way' that forms the approach to the Ming Tombs, 50 kilometres northwest of Beijing. [William Lindesay]

Nearly six and a half kilometres (four miles) ahead stands the red-walled, golden-roofed surface architecture of Changling, beneath which the Yongle emperor's body and treasures are thought to lie undisturbed. All 13 tombs have similar plans: a circular mound enclosed by a tumulus wall under which subterranean chambers were dug. This tomb head, the sole realm of the spirit, was adjoined by rectangular courtyards which made up the approach. The arrangement symbolizes a round heaven above a square earth.

Changling's main attraction is its massive Hall of Heavenly Favours, where the spirit received its living descendents. The massive roof is supported by 60 wooden columns, each one a single trunk of *nanmu* from the southwest. Jesuit Matteo Ricci recorded seeing similar timbers being transported along the Grand Canal on his own journey to Beijing around 1595 and estimated that they must have taken three years to be transported from their native place.

Dingling, the tomb of the great Wanli emperor (reigned 1573–1620), is the only Ming tomb to have been excavated, from 1956–58. Its vaulted marble palace, deep underground, can be visited. It consists of six interconnected chambers, now bare except for original marble thrones and replica coffins. There are three of each: Wanli was buried with his empress Xiaoduan, and concubine Xiaojing.

Zhaoling, the tomb of the Longqing emperor (reigned 1567–1572), is being restored. However, those with more time would be well advised to visit some of the unrestored tombs. All have caretakers who readily permit those interested few to stroll around. By doing so, the construction of courtyard walls and stele-tower roofs can be better appreciated in tranquil, eerie surroundings which are now the haunt of birds nesting in thujas: evergreen trees planted around five centuries before to nourish the deceased in the tumuli beneath.

Further away from Beijing, and so less crowded with visitors, are the **Eastern Qing tombs** in Hebei Province. They are set in a peaceful farm landscape, backed with towering mountains. The carvings on their Spirit Avenues are notably different from their Ming counterparts—the officials in the Qing avenues have pigtails in the Manchu fashion and wear Buddhist rosaries (the Manchus were very interested in this religion). The two long-lived emperors, Kangxi and Qianlong, are interred here—as is the infamous Empress Dowager Cixi who, at the end of the 19th century, took control of the government and was responsible for obstructing the necessary reforms that might have averted the fall of the Qing dynasty.

A favourite haunt of the Empress Dowager was the wonderful series of lakeside halls and pavilions to the northwest of the city. This is poetically called in Chinese **Yiheyuan** (The Garden for the Cultivation of Harmony). We in the West know it as the **Summer Palace**. Here the Empress Dowager had a private opera stage built in the palace, as she did in the Forbidden City, so as to be able to enjoy whole days of theatrical entertainment. Following destruction by the Anglo-French forces in 1860, she refurbished the park using money earmarked for the modernization of the Chinese navy, and built the superstructure of the famous marble boat at the north shore of the garden's Kunming Lake. The lake is a popular place for boating in summer, and is glorious for ice-skating in winter, with its willow-fringed shore and marble bridges. Overlooking the lake and close to the marble boat is a fine restaurant, Tingliguan, which is popular for banquets.

At one time there was another Qing imperial retreat, **Yuanmingyuan** (Garden of Perfection and Brightness). Foreigners often refer to it as the Old Summer Palace. It lies close to the newer Yiheyuan and is a romantic ruin of marble columns, broken fountains and scattered terraces. First bestowed on one of his sons by Emperor Kangxi in 1709, Yuanmingyuan was enlarged and restored under Qianlong. The ruins found at the site today are all that is left of the Western Mansions, a complex of palaces, halls and pavilions designed in European style by Jesuits for Qianlong. Yuanmingyuan was looted and blown up by foreign troops in 1860. Part of an expeditionary force sent by European governments in retaliation for the incarceration and murder of envoys sent to obtain the emperor's signature to trade concessions forced on the Qing by the British.

A similar day's outing can be made to the **Fragrant Hills** (also known as the **Western Hills**), particularly in the autumn months when the folds of the small mountains are burnt gold and red with the dying leaves. This certainly provides a serene contrast to sightseeing in Beijing. If you plan ahead, you can visit the **Temple of the Sleeping Buddha** (Wofo Si) and the **Temple of the Azure Clouds** (Biyun Si), since they are en route to the hills. As its name suggests, the Temple of the Sleeping Buddha houses a recumbent statue. In lacquered bronze, it measures five metres (16 feet). The Temple of the Azure Clouds is a lovely place to visit in spring, when the peach and apricot trees are in blossom. The Fragrant Hills was an imperial park at the time of the nomad emperors of the Jin and Yuan dynasties. They made it their own game reserve. Sadly, there is little wildlife left, but a series of small temples set amidst the trees makes the park a quiet haven for peaceful walking, reading poetry and a breath of fresh air. Of particular interest in the park is the 16th-century garden of the Study of Self Knowledge, with its circular pool enclosed by a walkway. A recent addition to the park is a cable car which carries passengers to the top of the hills in 18 minutes.

Close to the east entrance of the park is the Fragrant Hills Hotel, designed by the celebrated Chinese-American architect I.M. Pei. It is a wonderfully simple design, inspired by classical Chinese architecture and interpreted in a modern way, but, under poor management since its opening, it has not fulfilled its potential of becoming one of the best hotels in China.

Chengde (formerly known to Europeans as Jehol) was another summer and hunting resort favoured by the Qing Court. Its expansive grounds, which included lakes, forests and a hunting park, were larger than both the Forbidden City and Yihe Yuan (the Summer Palace at Beijing) combined. It lies beyond the Great Wall and can be reached by train (5.5 hours) or vehicle (three to four hours) from Beijing. It was created by the cultured Emperor Kangxi, who planned a palace with lakes and parks in a sheltered river valley surrounded by mountains. Kangxi's grandson, Emperor Qianlong, doubled the number of landscaped beauty spots and had eight magnificent temples built, each of which was to reflect the different religious practices of the various domains of the Chinese empire. Only seven of these remain, since one was dismantled and removed by the Japanese early last century. One of the largest was inspired by the Dalai Lama's Potala Palace in Lhasa. Chengde fell from favour as a summer retreat in 1820, when Emperor Jiaqing was struck dead by lightning there.

Beijing

HIGH AND LOW

The rickshaw men in Peking form several groups. Those who are young and strong and springy of leg rent good-looking rickshaws and work all day. They take their rickshaws out when they feel like it and quit when they feel like it. They begin their day by going to wait at rickshaw stands or the residences of the wealthy. They specialize in waiting for a customer who wants a fast trip. They might get a dollar or two just like that if it's a good job. Having struck it rich they might take the rest of the day off. It doesn't matter to them—if they haven't made a deal on how much rent they'll have to pay to the rickshaw agency. The members of this band of brothers generally have two hopes: either to be hired full time, or to buy a rickshaw. In the latter case it doesn't make much difference if they work for a family full time or get their fares in the streets; the rickshaw is their own.

Compare the first group to all those who are older, or to all those who, due to their physical condition, are lacking in vigor when they run, or to all those who, because of their families, do not dare waste one day. Most of these men pull almost new rickshaws. Man and rickshaw look equally good so these men can maintain the proper dignity when the time comes to ask for the fare. The men in this group work either all day or on the late afternoon and evening shift. Those who work late, from four P.M. to dawn, do so because they have the stamina for it. They don't care if it is winter or summer. Of course it takes a lot more attentiveness and skill to work at night than in the daytime; naturally you earn somewhat more money.

It is not easy for those who are over forty and under twenty to find a place in these two groups. Their rickshaws are rickety and they dare not work the late shift. All they can do is start out very early, hoping they can earn the rickshaw rental and their expenses for one day between dawn and three or four in the afternoon. Their rickshaws are rickety and they run very slowly. They work long hours on the road and come out short on fares. They are the ones who haul goods at the melon market, fruit market, and vegetable market. They don't make much but there's no need to run fast either.

Very few of those under twenty—and some start work at eleven or twelve—become handsome rickshaw men when older. It is very difficult for them to grow up healthy and strong because of the deprivations they suffer as children. They may pull a rickshaw all their lives, but pulling a rickshaw never gets them anywhere. Some of those over forty have been pulling rickshaws for only eight or ten years. They begin to slow down as their muscles deteriorate. Eventually they realize that they'll take a tumble and die in the street sooner or later. Their methods, charging all that the traffic will bear and making short trips look like long ones, are quite enough to bring their past glory to mind and make them snort with contempt at the younger generation. But past glory can scarcely diminish the gloom of the future and for that reason they often sigh a little when they mop their brows. When compared to others among their contemporaries, however, they don't seem to have suffered much. They never expected to have anything to do with pulling rickshaws. But when faced with a choice between living and dying, they'd had to grab the shafts of a rickshaw. They were fired clerks or dismissed policemen, small-time merchants who had lost their capital, or workmen who had lost their jobs. When the time came when they had nothing left to sell or pawn, they gritted their teeth, held back their tears, and set out on this death-bound road. Their best years are already gone and now the poor food they eat becomes the blood and sweat that drips on the pavement. They have no strength, no experience, and no friends. Even among their coworkers they are alone.

Lao She, *Rickshaw* (1936), translated by Jean M James

Shu Qingchun (1899–1966), born in Beijing of Manchurian ethnicity, wrote under the pen-name Lao She. He had his first great literary success in 1936 with the publishing of *Luotuo Xiangzi (Camel Xiangzi)*. During World War II, he lead anti-Japanese writers in China. After the war, in 1949, he became the vice chairman of the union of writers. Unfortunately, the Cultural Revolution's cruelty towards intellectuals drove him to suicide. Some people considered him as a contender for the 1968 Nobel Prize.

CITIES TRADITIONAL AND MODERN
SHANGHAI

By Chinese standards, Shanghai is a very modern incarnation. Although its antecedents go back to the Warring States period (475–221 BCE), when it was just a small fishing village on a tidal creek near the mouth of the Yangzi River, it's gradual transformation into a flourishing trading city gathered enormous momentum in the 19th century when it became one of the treaty ports and thus was 'internationalized'. It has since become the world's seventh largest city, as well as the nation's biggest port and manufacturing base.

It was that very position near the mouth of the Yangzi, China's main trade artery, which made Shanghai so attractive to 19th-century merchants from Europe and America. Modern Shanghai owes its development, cityscape and pre-eminence to that strange conjunction of Western traders and regional Chinese entrepreneurs who flocked there to make their fortune in the late 19th and early 20th centuries.

Shanghai was one of the five ports opened to foreign commerce and residence by the Treaty of Nanking in 1842. Bound up with the idea of a treaty port was the principle of 'extraterritoriality', which gave foreign residents immunity from Chinese laws. As it was convenient for the self-governing foreign inhabitants to be grouped together in specific areas, settlements or 'concessions' were set aside for them. At one time Shanghai had British, French and American concessions, until the British and American communities merged and became the International Settlement.

The communist government was not well disposed towards Shanghai when it took over in 1949; it was suspicious of Shanghai's history of decadent prosperity, entrepreneurial spirit and political independence. At the same time, the new leadership was keen to cash in on the city's wealth and business infrastructure. Yet it starved the city of the funds needed for redevelopment and modernization, while much of the money the city generated was creamed off to develop the poorer inland regions. The Shanghainese have always resented this, especially as they are prone to consider themselves more quick-witted and capable than the northerners in Beijing.

In the new political climate where economics are increasingly in command, Shanghai now finds itself being asked to take a lead role in spearheading the development of the socialist market economy. Just as Chinese society needs innovative

Shanghai

(Left) *Nanjing Road is Shanghai's main shopping thoroughfare by day or night. [Peter Danford]*
(Following pages) *A 1935 portrait of The Bund. [John Warner Publications]*

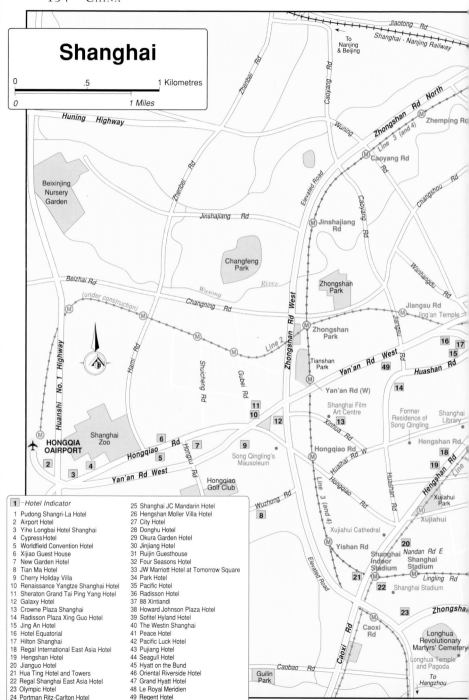

Shanghai

0	.5	1 Kilometres
0		1 Miles

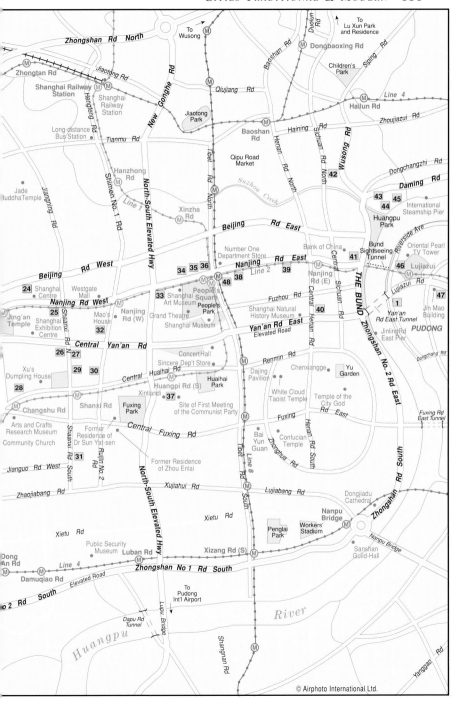

individuals to get wealthy and act as catalysts to inspire others on the road from rags to riches, the country needs entrepreneurial cities to do the same.

Shenzhen and other Special Economic Zones (SEZs) were established by Deng Xiaoping to do just that in the early 1980s. At that time Shanghai was overlooked by investors seeking footholds in China: it could not offer SEZ-type privileges. Deng equalized the ground rules after a tour of Shanghai in 1992, envisioning the development of 'Big Shanghai' with the construction of the Pudong New Area and Waigaoqiao Free Port. Moreover, the city's development augurs well by way of its *guanxi*, or connections.

Deng's immediate successor, Jiang Zemin, till recently the country's president and general secretary of the Communist Party, was born near and educated in Shanghai, where he rose to the position of city mayor. Former premier, pragmatist and economic wizard Zhu Rongji, is also an ex-mayor and was party chief of Shanghai.

Just as you don't go to New York to see colonial-style village America, so you don't go to Shanghai for a glimpse of China's imperial past. What the city does offer is a good view of treaty port identity, modern Chinese life, and perhaps a look at the nation's future—in the new industrial areas, and in the emergence of a new generation of young people who, in all but name, have left behind their revolutionary heritage and are getting on with the good things in life.

CITY SIGHTS: TRADITIONAL

Although Shanghai is a modern and industrial city, most Chinese and foreign visitors like to start their sightseeing with a trip to the old **Chinese city**, known as **Nanshi**. Here the streets are not built on an orderly grid system, as they are in the former International Settlement area, but run hugger-mugger in a mesh of lanes and alleyways. This is part of the charm of the place, but it is probably less picturesque for those who live here—the overcrowding means that homework, knitting, chess, preparing the dinner and even family quarrels often take place in the street.

It is also an area famed for its shopping. Unlike the large department stores of the famous **Nanjing Lu**, which sell anything from cameras to canned food, these small shops are speciality ones. Look out for shops with tea, fans, *bonsai* (miniature trees, known in Chinese as *penjing)* and singing birds. In the old city south of Nanjing Lu, you can add to your shopping list long cotton underwear for less than a few dollars, fans with Chinese opera characters, pot plants and patterned silks.

This quarter is popular with locals, too, thanks to its restaurants and the **Huxinting Teahouse**. This is set in the middle of a pond and is reached by a nine-turn, zigzag bridge. It has arched eaves and is painted red, making it a perfect setting for a leisurely cup of tea and traditional Chinese snacks.

On the other side of the pond is a slightly scruffier establishment, which serves delicious steamed dumplings known as Nanxiang dumplings. Made of minced pork, steamed in a thin pastry skin and dipped in vinegar and slices of ginger, they are so popular that the small restaurant can be identified simply by the sight of steam escaping from its windows and the crowds around its door.

A grander restaurant to visit nearby is the **Lubolang** (Walkway of the Jade Waves). This is famous for its steamed and baked Shanghai-style snacks, which include such lyrically named delights as Moth Eyebrow dumpling—a baked crescent of wafer-light pastry filled with shrimps and delicate vegetables. If you cannot get a seat in the restaurant—and it is always packed, especially near the windows which overlook the lake—you can buy snacks from the window downstairs to take away.

The **Yu Garden**, adjacent to the Lubolang restaurant, is a good place to walk off that lunch; it has marvellous vistas of pools, pavilions and rock gardens. The garden is attractive but it is often overcrowded with sightseers. It was laid out in the 16th century by a Ming official who made the garden to please his father. Only two

Shanghai

Shops on Sungkiang Road, circa 1900s, included a tobacconist, bookstore and noodle shop among others. [CGS]

hectares (five acres) in size, it recreates a wild landscape in miniature, with strange rocks, still pools, running water, meandering paths which offer changing vistas, and small pavilions in which to sit, dream or watch the moon. The garden also has an interesting history as the headquarters of the 'Society of Little Swords', an offshoot of the Taiping Rebellion in the mid-19th century. In fact, this association saved the garden from the destructions of the Cultural Revolution, since the 'Little Swords' were deemed to be early revolutionaries.

The city has some attractive temples, too. In the old quarter, there is the Taoist **Temple of the Town God**, very active and an architectural curiosity.

In the northwest of the city stands the **Temple of the Jade Buddha** (Yufo Si), named after its two exquisite milk-white jade Buddhas, which were brought from Burma in the 19th century. One of the Buddhas is seated, and the other is recumbent, the latter position symbolizing the Buddha's attainment of enlightenment. It is an active temple. The monks are used to visitors, who may, if they wish, attend the religious services here.

At the western end of Nanjing Lu is the **Jing'an Temple**, dating back to the last century, when it was popularly known to foreign residents as the Bubbling Well Temple. It has a colourful history, and was once presided over by an abbot who was famous for his rich wife, seven concubines and White Russian bodyguard.

To the southwest of the city, near a small park, stands the **Longhua Temple**, with its seven-storey pagoda. The temple was founded in the third century, although the pagoda in its present form dates from the tenth century and the other buildings are all from the Qing dynasty. In a bid to attract tourists, the tradition of holding a temple fair here in spring—the season of peach blossoms which can be seen in the adjoining Longhua Park—has been revived.

CITY SIGHTS: MODERN

Modern Shanghai was largely a product of European colonialism and much of the architecture, whether civic or suburban, still reflects that heritage. The **Bund** and Xujiahui Cathedral are part of the Western legacy. The Bund is probably the most famous thoroughfare in China. It's official name is Zhongshan Dong Yi Lu, though the Shanghainese call it Waitan. It should be noted that the local government is now substituting *Road* for *Lu* as part of their efforts to encourage the use of English.

The Bund stretches along a section of the Huangpu River, and is bounded on the other side by spectacular colonial buildings. In the 1930s, those buildings housed

The Shanghai Grand Theatre, opened in September 1999, and designed by French architects. Its huge steel roof is equal in weight to the steelwork of the Eiffel Tower. [CGS]

the offices of foreign trading firms and banks, so the Bund was then Shanghai's equivalent to Wall Street. Much of the 1930s skyline remains, including the old Hongkong and Shanghai Bank building, with its broad facade, portico and dome now home to the Pudong Development Bank after being vacated as the city's Communist Party headquarters in 1996.

The most striking skyline is now opposite the Bund in the rapidly developing Pudong, where the 88-storey Jin Mao building, housing the Grand Hyatt hotel in its higher storeys, is topped only by the Oriental Pearl TV Tower.

The port, the largest in China, is worth visiting just to gain an idea of the amount of traffic which flows through it. Shanghai's wharves stretch for 56 kilometres (35 miles) along the shores of the Huangpu River and, unlike the northern ports which ship more than they receive, the bulk of Shanghai's port traffic is incoming. Short rides on the Huangpu, as far as the mouth of the Wusong River (also known as Suzhou Creek), are offered from the Beijing Dong Lu wharf on the Bund.

The **Municipal Children's Palace** is as interesting for its setting as for its child prodigies. The palace is housed in the pre-1949 residence of the wealthy stockbroking family of Kadoorie. The Kadoories left Shanghai for Hong Kong, where today they are of considerable influence in the region's business community. Their former mansion is now a centre for children of exceptional abilities, who can pursue their studies or activities with special training facilities. Visitors can see athletic or musical performances given by the children.

For those who can't resist pandas, even if they are in captivity, **The Shanghai Zoo** in the western suburbs is of interest. There are also golden-haired monkeys, which once lived wild in the Yangzi gorges, and rare Yangzi River alligators.

Chinese revolutionary history was made in Shanghai with the founding of the Chinese Communist Party in 1921. The house where the founding members gathered, and the **site of the First National Congress of the Chinese Communist Party**, can be visited at 76 Xingye Lu, just north of Fuxing Park. Former Chinese Communist Party General Secretary Jiang Zemin chose a residence in this area as his retirement residence after he officially stepped down from all his government positions in 2003. In the Hongkou district north of the city, you can also find the residence of the writer Lu Xun (1881–1936). He was a pioneer of modern Chinese language and literature. A museum of his life and work can be found in the nearby **Hongkou Park**, where his tomb is placed at the bottom of a bronze statue of the writer.

Shanghai Museum, which is located on the refurbished People's Square, was reopened in October 1996 to much fanfare. Formerly housed in an antiquated bank building, the stunning new facility, designed to resemble a Shang ritual bronze, houses an impressive and comprehensive collection of Chinese *objets d'art*. Among the permanent collections are one of the finest bronze exhibitions in the world, Buddhist sculpture, Chinese painting and calligraphy, ceramics, Ming and Qing furniture, jade, antique coins and a fine collection of national minority costumes.

SHANGHAI NIGHTLIFE

I f you prefer to eat, drink and listen to music, rather than sitting up in the evening with a book and a cup of jasmine tea, then Shanghai is the city for you. It has innumerable restaurants featuring cuisines of nearly all of China's culinary regions. The international hotels now offer anything from saunas and discos to English-style pubs, and the old hotels of the 1930s have their own attractions—such as art deco interiors, shabby but grand dining rooms, billiard tables and bars. Most famous is the **Peace Hotel** on the Bund, which featured a legendary jazz band until 2007, when the hotel closed for a complete—and much needed—refurbishment. It will reopen in 2010 as the Fairmont Peace Hotel, and will undoubtedly be a must-visit Shanghai hotspot once again.

There are a growing number of trendy restaurants appearing on the scene in Shanghai. Probably the most popular of these is **M on the Bund,** the creation of successful Hong Kong restaurant and club impresario, Michelle Garnaut. The restaurant and drinks bar is situated on the top floor of a former bank building on the Bund. Its dazzling views across to Pudong and down the Bund are complemented by a jazzy décor and menu of fusion foods. However, the hottest number along Shanghai's famous riverfront now has to be Bund 18.

On most tour group itineraries is the **Shanghai Acrobatic Theatre.** It is certainly worth obtaining tickets for its virtuoso performances of juggling, tumbling and plate-spinning. The local opera performed in the Shanghai region is known as *Yueju.* A more melodic relative of the Peking Opera school, it has less percussion and more choruses than the northern style.

XINTIANDI

istoric architecture plays a major role in Shanghai's most stylish eating and entertainment area at Xintiandi, 'New Heaven on Earth,' which opened in 2001. The Luwan district government wanted to rejuvenate the area for the 50th anniversary of communist rule. Though an historic part of the former French Concession, this in itself was insufficient to safeguard the area from being razed to make way for new development. However, its hosting the building where the communist party was founded in 1921 gained it some security.

This Hong Kong initiated development is Shanghai's answer to London's Covent Garden. A whole block of archetypal 'shikumen' houses, dating from the early 20th century, have been fabulously refurbished and recreated to perfection. Such shikumen, or stone frame door, houses—a cross between the British terraced house and the Chinese courtyard dwelling—are fast disappearing across the city, only to be replaced by faceless high-rise apartment blocks. Here they are preserved in an environment where East meets West, and where the past and present collide.

A neighbouring modern block contains shops, a cinema and a chic boutique hotel. The area is fringed by the impressive Taipingqiao Park, where Shanghai's largest downtown man-made lake mirrors this marriage of old and new.

Shanghai

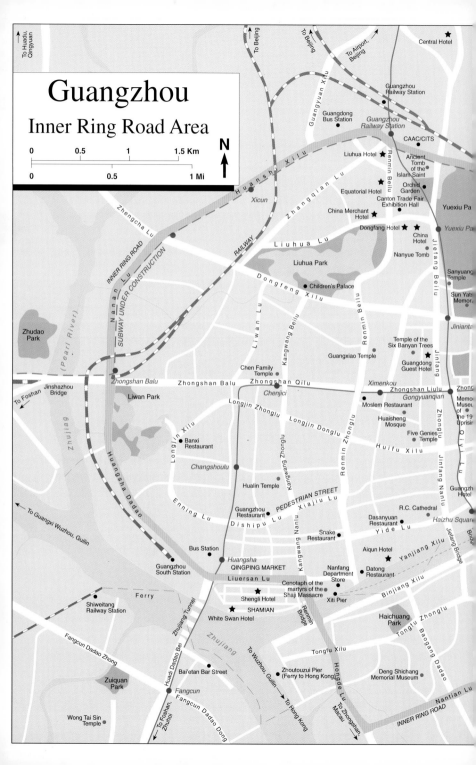

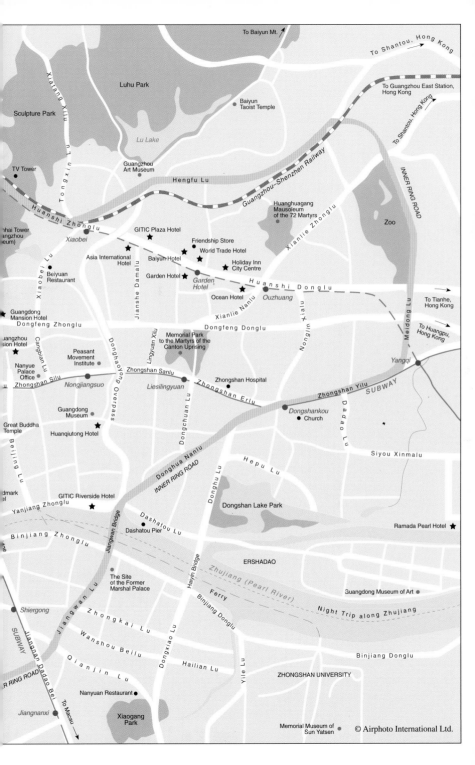

To Baiyun Mt.

To Shantou, Hong Kong

To Guangzhou East Station, Hong Kong

To Shantou, Hong Kong

INNER RING ROAD

Luhu Park

Baiyun Taoist Temple

Sculpture Park

Lu Lake

TV Tower

Guangzhou Art Museum

Hengfu Lu

Guangzhou–Shenzhen Railway

Huanghuagang Mausoleum of the 72 Martyrs

Zoo

Xianlie Zhonglu

Huanshi Zhonglu

hai Tower angzhou eum)

Xiaobei

GITIC Plaza Hotel

Friendship Store

World Trade Hotel

Xiaobei Lu

Asia International Hotel

Baiyun Hotel

Holiday Inn City Centre

Jianshe Damalu

Beiyuan Restaurant

Garden Hotel

Garden Hotel

Huanshi Donglu

To Tianhe, Hong Kong

Ocean Hotel

Ouzhuang

Xianlie Nanlu

Meihua Lu

Guangdong Mansion Hotel

Dongfeng Zhonglu

Cangbian Lu

Xianlie Nanlu

Dongfeng Donglu

To Huangpu, Hong Kong

uangzhou sion Hotel

Lingyuan Xilu

Memorial Park to the Martyrs of the Canton Uprising

Nonglin Xilu

Yangqi

Nanyue Palace Office

Peasant Movement Institute

Donghaoyong Overpass

Zhongshan Sanlu

Zhongshan Hospital

Zhongshan Yilu

SUBWAY

Zhongshan Silu

Nongjiangsuo

Liesilingyuan

Dongchuan Lu

Zhongshan Erlu

Dadao Lu

Guangdong Museum

Dongshankou Church

Great Buddha Temple

Huanqiutong Hotel

Beijing Lu

Siyou Xinmalu

Donghua Nanlu

INNER RING ROAD

Hepu Lu

Donghu Lu

dmark el

GITIC Riverside Hotel

Dongshan Lake Park

Yanjiang Zhonglu

Dashatou Lu

Ramada Pearl Hotel

Binjiang Zhonglu

Jiangwan Bridge

Dashatou Pier

Haiyin Bridge

ERSHADAO

Zhujiang (Pearl River)

Guangdong Museum of Art

The Site of the Former Marshal Palace

Ferry

Night Trip along Zhujiang

Shiergong

Jiangwan Lu

Zhongkai Lu

Dongxiao Lu

Binjiang Donglu

Binjiang Donglu

SUBWAY

Wanshou Beilu

Hailian Lu

Yile Lu

ZHONGSHAN UNIVERSITY

R RING ROAD

Dadao Bei

Qianjin Lu

Jiangnanxi

To Macau

Nanyuan Restaurant

Xiaogang Park

Memorial Museum of Sun Yatsen

© Airphoto International Ltd.

GUANGZHOU

Guangzhou (Canton) is the capital of Guangdong Province, one of China's richest and—in the river plains—most fertile regions. With a subtropical climate, an extensive coastline and a mesh of tributaries of the Pearl River, which forms a rich alluvial delta, Guangdong Province produces an abundance of seafood. Indeed, the amount of fish, meat, vegetables and fruit available throughout the year makes the offerings of a northern Chinese table look poor by comparison. The Cantonese gourmet will eat an astonishing diversity of foodstuffs, some of which will never feature on a northern menu, such as pangolin, dog, snake, monkey, cat or even bear's paw. Such adventurous tastes both impress and appall Chinese from other regions.

The Cantonese have always been considered a distinct group in the Chinese world. All regions of China have their different dialects, but few are so difficult to master as Cantonese, with its imploding consonants and a more complex tone system than that used in the northern dialect of Mandarin or *Putonghua*. Separated from the Yangzi area by an east-west mountain chain and far from the early centres of Chinese civilization in the Yellow River basin, Cantonese culture has been relatively isolated, allowing the province to develop its own identity as well as its own distinctive dialect.

The sea has been part of the same process, endowing the people of Guangdong with their outward-looking and venturesome spirit. The long coastline facing out into the South China Sea, towards the islands of Southeast Asia and the shipping routes to India and the Middle East, means that Guangdong Province has always had better links with the outside world than other parts of China. It certainly has a history of being a conduit for new ideas and religions. Arab traders made their way up the Pearl River to the city of Guangzhou as early as the seventh century, leaving behind small communities of Muslims, with their mosques and imams. What they took away from China was more enduring than the porcelains and silks in their vessels. The Arabs absorbed Chinese ideas and inventions, most of which were ultimately to have a profound impact on the West. The Christian Crusades against the Arabs in the 12th century brought Europe into contact with such inventions as gunpowder, the magnetic compass, the stern-post rudder and papermaking, all of which had originated in China, unknown to the Europeans who learnt these new sciences from the Arabs.

In economically lean times, the sea has also offered an escape: the waves of emigration of the Cantonese over a long period have resulted in the establishment of Chinatowns in many Southeast Asian, North American and European cities.

In the 15th century, the Portuguese traders and Jesuit missionaries who arrived in Guangzhou—guided by compasses which had been invented long before in China—found a wealthy, cosmopolitan city which already had centuries of experience in trading with foreigners. Indeed the Portuguese were shocked that they were viewed as just one more contingent of barbarians who were after Chinese silks and porcelains. British ships came in the 17th century and were followed by Protestant missionaries. For a time, these European merchants and missionaries behaved in accordance with Chinese law and customs. The law required all foreign trade to be confined to Guangzhou. But as trade expanded, Western traders began to find this restriction increasingly irksome and started pressing for freer conditions of commerce than were allowed by imperial regulations. Their moment came when they possessed the arms and warships to offer a military challenge to the Chinese. By this time, the British had also established an extensive mercantile empire in India. This was the setting for the arrival of Guangzhou on the stage of international history.

In 1839 the British opened fire on Guangzhou after the British Parliament had voted to go to war in order to sustain its lucrative opium trade with China. This trade in Indian-grown opium had developed as an easy means of exchange for Chinese silks and teas. It was, however, considered pernicious by many Chinese government officials, who persuaded the Qing court to put a stop to the trade in 1839. The British responded by adopting Palmerston's 'gunboat diplomacy'. The subsequent Opium War brought a humiliating defeat for the Qing troops whose weapons and tactics were too outdated to deal with the superior firepower and the highly manoeuvrable ships of the British navy. The Treaty of Nanking, which concluded the war in 1842, opened four other Chinese ports to foreign trade and thus broke Guangzhou's monopoly. By the early 20th century, Shanghai had eclipsed Guangzhou as China's major port.

Nonetheless, the late 19th century was a period of prosperity for Guangzhou. It remained a city of great intellectual and political ferment. By the 1890s, an anti-Qing movement was gathering momentum in Guangdong Province, fuelled by the Qing government's inability to curb the activities of foreign traders and missionaries—activities much resented by the Chinese. This resentment erupted in 1900 in the form of the Boxer Rebellion, which swept over North China and left hundreds of foreigners and Chinese converts to christianity dead. The turmoil temporarily masked the activities of anti-imperial revolutionaries in the south. Under the leadership of Cantonese Dr Sun Yat-sen, they were busily forming cells and soliciting overseas

Plant seller, Canton 1799. [Wattis Fine Art]

*Traditional arts are still very much alive and hopefully will remain so,
in spite of the general fascination with the new.*

Chiuchiao-style embroidery shop in Shantau, eastern Guangdong Province.

Chinese support for their planned revolution. In fact, it was in Guangzhou itself that the October 1911 Revolution, which overthrew the Qing dynasty, was foreshadowed. In April of that year, an uprising led by anti-Qing activists was defeated by imperial troops at the Battle of Canton. Over 100 young revolutionaries died in the fighting. When the October Revolution came, the city quite peacefully went over to the Republican side, and there was little bloodshed.

Guangzhou was badly damaged and suffered a large loss of civilian life during the Japanese occupation of the 1940s. There was much resistance to the occupation, and many communist-led cells organized sabotage operations in the area. Yet it was only after the 1949 Revolution, when the Communist Party came to power, that political struggle became an everyday reality in Guangzhou. In the 1950s, the anti-landlord movement led to mass executions of peasants who were rich enough to have rented out land or to have employed workers. And in common with other major cities, Guangzhou experienced severe disruption during the Cultural Revolution (1966–76).

Much urban renewal has been accomplished since then, although the city still gives an impression of sprawling untidiness. Still, the shabby, impoverished atmosphere of the 1970s has been converted into bustle and brashness by the unprecedented prosperity that has come with the economic reforms of the last decade. Guangzhou's great advantage has been its proximity to the former British territory of Hong Kong, which provided the city with an invaluable link to the developed West. With the territory's return to Chinese sovereignty, it remains to be seen whether the link with the new Special Administrative Region of China will remain largely unique to Guangdong Province, or exert a wider, weaker influence.

Almost the entire Chinese population of Hong Kong either migrated from Guangdong Province or is descended from natives of the province. A familiar sight in the early 1970s was Hong Kong people thronging the railway station on the eves of holidays or festivals, scrambling to get to Guangzhou and beyond to visit their relatives. Nowadays the traffic between Hong Kong and the port of Guangzhou is more hectic than ever.

Hong Kong businessmen and manufacturers have relocated entire factories to Guangzhou and its surrounding towns. Many of these factories are in Guangdong's three Special Economic Zones, **Shenzhen**, **Zhuhai** and **Shantou**, which were opened to attract foreign trade and investment, and which offer lower labour costs than in the more developed Asian countries.

CITY SIGHTS: TRADITIONAL

The oldest and least visited temple in Guangzhou is **Guangxiao Temple**. For those with an interest in Zen (Chan in Chinese) Buddhism, the Guangxiao Temple is of great historical significance. It was here in the Tang dynasty that the Sixth Patriarch of Zen Buddhism, Hui Neng, was initiated into the monkhood. Hui Neng taught that enlightenment can be attained in a flash of illumination, and does not necessarily have to be earned through systematic discipline and study. That doctrine is the core of Zen Buddhism. The temple is also of architectural interest. Despite frequent repairs and rebuilding over the centuries, the Great Hall retains its Song dynasty dimensions. In the temple compound you can find an early Song iron pagoda, which was originally built for another temple and moved to its present site in 1235. At the entrance to the temple is a small antique shop.

More popular on tourist itineraries, however, is the **Temple of the Six Banyan Trees** (Liurong Si), with its nine-storey pagoda, the Huata. Founded in the fifth century, some time after the Guangxiao Temple, it is also associated with the Sixth Patriarch. Its present name dates from the Song dynasty, when the poet and calligrapher, Su Dongpo, came south to Guangzhou and, impressed by the trees of the temple, wrote two characters meaning 'Six Banyans' as an inscription. The two characters are engraved on stone in the poet's calligraphy, and this tablet (or stele) can still be seen near the temple entrance. Here is also a Song bronze statue of the Sixth Patriarch, as well as several fine Qing brass Buddhas.

An interesting example of an ancestral temple, few of which have survived in modern China, is the **Chen Clan Temple** (Chen Jia Ci). Built in the 1890s, it is a splendid example of traditional southern architecture of the late Qing period. Chen (Chan in Cantonese) is a very common surname in the province; members of the Chan family from 72 counties in Guangdong founded this temple to give a proper setting for ancestor worship and Confucian studies. In the moral order expounded by Confucius, education, loyalty and filial duty were all stressed. The spirit tablets of the ancestors are no longer in the central hall at the back, and in fact the clan temple now serves as the Guangdong Provincial Folk Arts Museum, which displays examples of carving on a variety of materials, such as walnut shells, ivory and wood. Carving is the most striking feature of the temple halls: the surfaces of its window frames, doors and pillars are all elaborately decorated with carving and sculpture. Even the eaves and roof ridges are floridly ornamented with clay figurines.

The arrival of the Arabs in the seventh century also brought a new religious centre to the city. The **Huaisheng Mosque** is one of China's earliest mosques, and is believed to have once stood at the edge of the Pearl River. The river has shifted its course, and the mosque now lies in the city centre, just south of Zhongshan Lu on Guangta Lu. It has a fine, plain, stone minaret, known as the Guangta, indicating the early date of the mosque's foundation—most late mosques having small pavilions in place of the minaret. Visitors can climb the minaret for a view of the city.

CITY SIGHTS: MODERN

hilst the new airport may be the most spectacular modern building in the vicinity, in order to gain an impression of how European traders once lived, it is worth visiting **Shamian Island**, a one-kilometre (two-thirds of a mile)-long sandbar in the Pearl River. The Chinese authorities gave the land to Europeans in the 19th century, to be their residential base, along with extraterritorial rights. Once on the island, the Europeans were no longer subject to Chinese law or supervision. Shamian was made an elegant enclave with large mansions, churches, a yacht club and tennis courts. Now the area has been tastefully restored making it an interesting place for a leisurely walk. An excellent five-star hotel, the **White Swan**, with a glass atrium lobby, waterfalls, trees and swimming pool, has been built here and makes a convenient place to relax and enjoy a cool drink.

On the Pearl River, freighters wait to unload.

Guanxiao Temple, founded at the end of the 4th century, is one of the oldest structures in Canton. It was a regular destination for monks from India who came to China to lecture, spread Buddhism and supervise scriptural translations.

These days traders from all over the world come annually to the spring or autumn **Chinese Export Commodities Fair** (Canton Fair) sponsored by China's foreign trade corporations. The Fair, established in 1957, used to provide the only opportunity for business exchanges between China and the capitalist West. Today, each session of the fair is still attended by some 30,000 business people even though more direct exchanges at factory and provincial levels are now the norm.

For locals, just as much bargaining and trading goes on daily at the **Qingping Free Market**, where over 2,000 stalls sell all sorts of farm produce from fish, meat and fruit to goldfish and Chinese herbal medicine.

Just west of Haizhu Square on Wende Lu lies the **Roman Catholic Cathedral**, open to worshippers again after serving for many years as a warehouse. It was built in granite by a French architect and was consecrated in 1863.

The **Mausoleum of the 72 Martyrs** is a memorial to the young revolutionaries who lost their lives in the Battle of Canton. Donations for the memorial, which was built in 1918, came from patriotic overseas Chinese as far away as Canada and Chile. The mausoleum is constructed in a bizarre blend of styles, with a miniature Statue of Liberty, an Egyptian-style obelisk, and two traditional Chinese guardian lions!

The founding father of the Chinese Republic is commemorated in the **Sun Yat-sen Memorial Hall**, with its brilliant blue tiles. Inside there is a 4,700-seat auditorium used for concerts, operas and other shows.

The city's earliest contribution to communist revolutionary history is remembered in the **Peasant Movement Institute**, which was once the headquarters of such activists as Mao Zedong, who set up a school to educate young cadres. The Institute is housed in a Ming dynasty Confucian temple, and is therefore both historically and architecturally interesting.

Another incident in communist revolutionary history was the so-called Canton Uprising of 1927. The uprising, led by the Chinese Communist Party, resulted in the establishment of a soviet government, the Canton commune. This took place just before the Kuomintang army pushed northwards to unify the country. The Kuomintang, or Nationalist Party, was founded shortly after the 1911 Revolution. It ruled China, often in name only, until 1949, after which it established on Taiwan what it once claimed to be the legitimate government of China. In the early 1920s, the Kuomintang had formed an uneasy alliance with the communists, who then proceeded to infiltrate Kuomintang ranks. The situation was highly unstable, as the radicals and conservatives within the party continued to compete for control of policy. In 1927 the alliance collapsed and Chiang Kai-shek, leader of the Kuomintang, moved quickly to suppress the radicals and communists. In reaction, the Chinese Communist Party in Guangzhou revolted and took over the city with much bloodshed and destruction. However, the Canton commune was just as bloodily crushed, with about 5,000 suspected communist activists or supporters put to death. This event is remembered in the **Memorial Park to the Martyrs of the Canton Uprising**, where local people now go boating or strolling. A fine chrysanthemum fair is held here every autumn.

Botanists and amateur gardeners will also enjoy the **South China Botanical Garden**, the finest of its kind in China. Founded in 1958, it is administered by the Chinese Academy of Sciences and is set in 300 hectares (750 acres)—large enough to find a quiet spot, even in hectic Guangzhou.

Finally, the **Municipal Museum** is worth visiting for three main reasons. It is housed in a Ming dynasty watchtower, the Zhenhai Tower, built by a general in 1380; it gives a fine view over the city and it has an interesting collection of historical documents. Even better is the **Nanyue Museum** and **Royal Mausoleum**, with burial treasures from the tomb of a king who ruled here in 200 BCE.

OUTINGS FROM GUANGZHOU

Many adventurous travellers explore the countryside of Guangdong Province by bus. This is quite easy to do, since there are now good bus services to the towns and villages. Those with less time to explore by themselves can join a tour to one of the farming centres outside Guangzhou, such as **Dali**. Dali town, formerly a People's Commune encompassing 19 villages, is surrounded by paddy fields, vegetable plots and orchards. Another standard tour from Guangzhou is to **Foshan**, 28 kilometres (17 miles) southwest of the city. Foshan has a famous ceramics industry, and is also well known for its folk arts such as paper-cutting, lantern-making and carving. The town has retained many fine old temples which, like most Cantonese temples, are brightly decorated with roof figures, colourful murals and carved doors. The **Foshan Ancestral Temple**, dedicated to a Taoist deity, was first built in the 11th century.

An excursion can also be made to **Conghua Hot Springs**, 80 kilometres (50 miles) to the north of the city. If you wish to stay, there are hotels and guest villas on the spot. A bath in the mineral water from the 12 hot springs in the area, which varies in temperature between 30°C (86°F) and 70°C (158°F), is meant to help those suffering from such ailments as arthritis, hypertension and digestive disorders. The resort is set in a pleasant green landscape along the Liuxi River.

Overseas Chinese are sometimes interested in visiting the **former residence of Sun Yat-sen**. The father of the Republic was born in Cuiheng Village, in Zhongshan, in 1866.

Across the Pearl River delta from Cuiheng is **Shenzhen**, the first Special Economic Zone to be established in China. These zones are interesting if you have a desire to see what economic progress is taking place in China today, but Shenzhen has also tried to attract tourists by offering other amenities. Its most successful venture is the '**Splendid China**' exhibition. Splendid China is a heritage park in which all the most renowned monuments and scenic sights in China are reproduced in miniature. You will see a Temple of Heaven, for example, reduced to a tenth of its real size, or the cliffs of the Three Gorges of the Yangzi River rising just two metres above a shallow stream. The exhibits have been made with great attention to detail and authenticity, and laid out in pleasant grounds studded with kiosks selling light refreshments and souvenirs. Unfortunately, much of the historical information provided is wildly inaccurate, and favours a view of history sympathetic to the Han majority at the expense of China's minority peoples.

Next to this park is the **China Folk Culture Village**, where you will find superb, full-sized reproductions of buildings from all over China, with an emphasis on the minority areas. People from these areas work here, giving folk dance performances.

Should you wish to visit Shenzhen, it should be noted that it is closer to Hong Kong than Guangzhou, and therefore easier to access it from Hong Kong.

Guangzhou

Shenzhen's metropolitan sprawl disappears into the distance from the Lo Wu border crossing—ironically, the green belt at the bottom and left is Hong Kong territory. [Kasyan Bartlett]

Tianjin docks continue a 19th century international trade tradition. [James Montgomery]

TIANJIN

ianjin (Tientsin), a leading commercial centre on the River Hai in northern China for many decades, has grown into one of the country's powerhouse industrial and manufacturing cities. It is one of China's four municipalities, important urban areas under direct control of the central government (the other three are Beijing, Chongqing and Shanghai), and yet despite its significance to China's overall economy, it is not a major destination for foreign travellers unless they are in China on business. A short train or bus ride from the capital, the city with its large artificial harbour, is the port for Beijing. In recent years it has come to be considered by foreign businessmen as more go-ahead than Shanghai (the other major Chinese port) in its efforts to attract overseas capital.

A European trading community was established here in the 19th century. The Western powers which had been pressing for trading privileges saw Tianjin's importance as the gateway to North China and were eager to gain a foothold in the city. They were able to achieve this at the conclusion of the second Opium War in 1858, when the Treaty of Tientsin was signed authorizing the establishment of French and British concessions in the city. From the end of the 19th to the beginning of the 20th centuries, more concessions were given to Japan, Germany, Russia, Austro-Hungary, Italy and Belgium. As a result of these settlements, Tianjin inherited a mixture of architectural styles as well as improved shipping facilities.

The catastrophic Tangshan earthquake of 1976 forced Tianjin to substantially redevelop its urban infrastructure. Nevertheless, some buildings, such as those around Heping Lu and Jiefang Lu on the Hai River's west bank, remain from treaty port days.

Visitors to Tianjin usually go to one of the city's famous **carpet factories**. Woven by hand from painted patterns placed on the weaver's loom, the carpets are made in a variety of patterns and sizes, the most popular are classic designs with traditional motifs. The weaver interprets the pattern and colour matches the wool. Once woven, the carpets are hand-trimmed with electric scissors to create an embossed effect.

Two handicrafts from the Tianjin region—kites and New Year posters—are famous throughout China. The kites are made in fabric or paper, and are stretched over thin bamboo frames. Designs can range from a basket of peonies to a goldfish. The New Year poster workshops in Hexi district produce brightly decorated pictures, which the Chinese like to paste up in their homes during the lunar New Year. The posters traditionally feature fat babies, the god of longevity, maidens plucking lotuses (lotus seeds being symbols of fertility), and door gods.

Tianjin

Tianjin's traditional arts and crafts can be purchased on the **Ancient Culture Street** along the River Hai close to the city centre. The street incorporates the renovated 14th-century temple to the local goddess of fishermen, which contains a folk museum. While exploring Ancient Culture Street, try the famous Tianjin steamed dumplings called *goubuli baozi*. The name means, disconcertingly, 'dogs won't touch them'. Yet despite their name, they are delicious. These *baozi* are also sold in **Food Street**, a complex of 110 restaurants and snack shops in the south of the city.

Businessmen whose itineraries demand extended stays in Tianjin would be advised to make a trip to **Shanhaiguan** where the Great Wall meets the Bohai Sea in a pleasant coastal town. Other such day trips can be made to the lakeland region of **Baiyangdian** to the south, in Hebei Province. Here, tourists take water tours of the lakeside villages, which thrive on fishing, ducks and reed weaving. To the north of the city, within the municipal boundary, is the **Temple of Singular Happiness** (Dule Si), in Jixian district. This Buddhist temple was founded in the seventh century and is famous for the 11-headed Guanyin (Goddess of Mercy) statue. The eastern gate of the temple is the earliest of its kind extant in China.

A sketch of the first railway train at Shanghai, June 1876, artist unknown.
[Hongkong and Shanghai Bank Group Archives]

THE INVISIBLE HAND

O ld T'ung-pao felt his being reassert itself. His years had indeed not been lived in vain! It would be a plentiful year. He walked among the tall stalks and caressed them. There would be a four-picul harvest! Sometimes when his fingers felt of the heavy, drooping ears, he half-imagined there might even be five piculs out of every mow [mu; unit of land]. Every ear was so full! He began to calculate the future. No exaggeration to count on four and a half piculs. Surely not. That meant he would be able to reap forty piculs altogether. Six and four-tenths piculs went to the tax collector. He would still have over thirty piculs. Figuring conservatively at ten dollars a picul, that meant three hundred dollars! That would pay off the best part of his debts. He couldn't imagine a price of less than ten dollars a picul! He and all his neighbors would be relieved of their burdens by one good harvest. Heaven surely had good eyes!

But while Old T'ung-pao contemplated his grain and his rosy dreams, the rice merchants in town, like Heaven, had eyes in their heads, and their eyes were only for their own profit. Before the rice was even cut, the price began to fall. During the reaping—the villagers were cutting down the fruits of months of toil, and piling their grain in neat stacks—the price in town fell to six dollars a picul. While they were grinding out the grain, the price fell further to four dollars. Finally, when they packed their coarse, plentiful rice into market, they could barely sell it at three! The rice merchants looked coldly at their outraged faces.

"That's today's price," they said coldly. "It'll be lower still tomorrow."

Debt collectors were busy in the village pursuing their debts. Would they take rice for the debts? Well, yes. The coarse rice at two-ninety. White rice at three-sixty.

Old T'ung-pao stood confused and silent amid the ruins of all his rosy calculations.

Mao Dun, 'Autumn Harvest', 1932

Shen Dehong, (1896–1981) a journalist, communist ideologue and cultural critic, took the pen-name Mao Dun, meaning "Contradiction". Born in Zhejiang Province, he went on to study at the Peking University, but did not graduate. Although a naturalistic writer himself, his tastes were broader, such as his admiration for Leo Tolstoy. He acted as Mao Zedong's secretary and culture minister until 1964, survived the Cultural Revolution and proceeded to write his memoirs, which were unfinished when he passed away.

CITIES IN A LANDSCAPE

While the following four cities (Wuxi, Suzhou, Hangzhou and Guilin) were historically renowned for the beauty of the natural features within which they are set, and although tourism inevitably focuses on their historical and geographical virtues (as does this book), it is important to note that modern China is reforging all these cities and their environs to a sometimes startling degree.

Wuxi, Suzhou and Hangzhou are all incredibly prosperous cities, part of the Yangzi Delta Region that has become a centre for electronics and software development as well as light industry. Modernization has been rampant, and consequently visitors may be nonplussed on arrival by the sight of high-tech buildings, international brand-name shops and Western-style shopping malls.

However, as the following pages show, despite the surge towards tomorrow's world, much of the past is still protected by local governments wise to the need to preserve their rich heritage.

WUXI

Three thousand years ago, two fugitive princes from the north settled in an area close to present-day Wuxi. They and their descendants set up a new state and called their capital 'Mei'. In around 200 BCE, the town was renamed 'Youxi'—which means 'with tin'—when reserves of the metal were discovered nearby. Later, when the deposits ran out, the city's name was changed to Wuxi or 'without tin'.

Since the seventh century Wuxi has benefited from the fact that the Grand Canal runs through its centre. The Grand Canal was built by the Sui emperor Yangdi to link the north and south of his realm, and to transport grain from the fertile Yangzi valley to the arid north. Visitors can stand on any of the city's many bridges and watch boats pass by, just as they have done for over a thousand years. Yet despite the city's strategic position on the canal, Wuxi did not prosper—as did neighbouring Yangzhou—until the early part of this century. It was then that Wuxi burgeoned as a centre of silk-reeling and weaving (although silk production had long been a major industry of Jiangsu Province, in which Wuxi is located).

The great attraction of Wuxi is Taihu, a lake about seven kilometres (four miles) outside the city. Its expanse of shining water set between soft hills mirrors the sky in all its moods, and fishermen trawl its waters for the fish which play such an important part in the cooking of Wuxi. Along the shores are orchards growing the best of sweet oranges, peaches and Chinese plums. The shallow edges of the lake are harvested for their freshwater shrimps, lotus roots, seeds and water chestnuts. The lotus seeds are ground into a sweet paste for buns or simmered in a sugary soup; the water chestnuts are used in savoury dishes to create a crisp, light contrast to the meat. And beyond the orchards are the mulberry fields, supplying the leaves which go to feed the countless silkworm larvae whose cocoons will be spun into silk thread for the factories of Jiangsu Province.

CITY SIGHTS

The **Plum Garden** (Mei Yuan) is a particularly popular place in spring, when thousands of plum trees are in blossom. The best time to eat the plums themselves is in late summer. Another sylvan pleasure is the **Li Garden**, which is modern by neighbouring Suzhou standards. Yet it is well worth seeing, since it contains all the elements of a classical Chinese garden in an idyllic setting.

Chinese visitors to Wuxi invariably come away with one or two *ni ren*, or clay dolls, made at the **Huishan Clay Figurine Workshop**. The tradition of making clay figures dates back to the Ming dynasty. At the workshop, which may be visited, you will find brightly painted figures in traditional round shapes of dozing monks, fat babies and smiling children holding fish, coins or lotus flowers (the symbols of plenty, prosperity and fertility). In recent years, new shapes have been introduced which reveal the influence of Western cartoons. Look out for a Chinese 'Snow White and the Seven Dwarfs', as well as some very blonde nymphs.

Much of Wuxi's surrounding arable land is patterned with groves of mulberry bushes, so it is hardly surprising to learn that there is a thriving silk industry here. Visitors are often taken to the **Number One Silk Reeling Mill** or the **Number One Silk Weaving Factory**. The **Zhonghua Embroidery Factory** is also open to visitors. (During the Cultural Revolution, the traditionally lyrical names of shops and businesses were considered a 'feudal' relic and all factories were renamed by their size, be it Number One or Two, or by some patriotic label such as Red Flag or East is Red. Sadly, these names have stuck.)

OUTINGS FROM WUXI

Lake Taihu has 90 islands in all. The visitor can enjoy them and their related sights either by taking one of the shallow-draught ferry boats or by cruising across the lake in a grander dragon boat (in fact, a gaily decorated barge). **Turtle Head Island** is the most popular destination for pleasure craft on the lake. Here visitors can walk through bamboo groves and paths lined with flowering shrubs, or climb to get a view of the entire lake from **Deer Peak Hill**. Chinese holiday-makers like to savour the peace of the island by finding a quiet spot on the rocky foreshore to read, chat and enjoy a family picnic. The lake is equally popular with government officials from neighbouring cities, who can come for a rest at one or other of the many sanatoriums and government holiday villas built along the shore.

From Wuxi, a trip on the **Grand Canal** can be arranged through various travel agents or online. This can be either a short three-and-a-half-hour excursion which incorporates a meal on board the boat, or a tour of several days covering 220 kilometres (136 miles) and including visits to Changzhou, Zhenjiang and Yangzhou. Similar tours are offered at all the Jiangsu towns on the Grand Canal.

When first constructed the canal linked the northern city of Luoyang, which the Sui emperor Yangdi chose as his capital, with the southern town of Yangzhou in Jiangsu Province. Later it was extended as far as Beijing in the north and Hangzhou (in Zhejiang Province) in the south. The canal's construction was completed in an astonishing six years, bringing great suffering to the conscript labourers who excavated the canal and lined it with vast slabs of stone. During the six years, bridges were also constructed across the canal and its embankment was paved to make roads. The canal was of economic, political and military importance, ensuring the emperor a constant supply of rice and other products from the river-washed farmlands of the Yangzi basin to the arid lands of the north. It was also important for the speedy despatch of troops to the south. However, the vast public works scheme undertaken by Emperor Yangdi undermined the popularity and finances of the dynasty. The result was that in 618, only one year after Yangdi died, the country was swept by a rebellion bringing the Tang dynasty to power. Today, the canal is no longer a strategic artery, but it does function as a commercial route. Barges ply between canal cities, carrying agricultural produce and bulk goods too expensive to transport by the overworked rail system.

Finally, a day trip to the neighbouring city of **Yixing** is highly recommended, both for its teapots and its tea. The simplest way is by car, as Yixing is only 60 kilometres (36 miles) from Wuxi, on the opposite side of Lake Tai. Yixing is the home of the famous **Purple Sand Pottery Factory**, where you can see traditional clay teapots being made. The dark, reddish-brown and blue teapots are unglazed, their fame resting on a sophisticated simplicity of form. Older versions of Yixing ware can be seen in the **Pottery Museum**. Modern craftsmen can turn out teapots shaped as pumpkins with a dragon's head on the lid—when the tea is poured the dragon's tongue protrudes! Other designs include small squirrels running across branches, or a handle shaped as a simple twist of bamboo. In fact, the range and variety of Yixing teapots is astounding and can satisfy any aesthetic taste.

SUZHOU

uzhou is notable for its intimacy of scale as a city and its tradition as a centre for refined garden design. If Hangzhou can be described as a city set within a landscape , Suzhou is a series of landscapes set within a city. (The beauty of both cities was extolled in the well-known saying, 'In heaven there is paradise, on earth Suzhou and Hangzhou'.)

A casual stroll around Suzhou will not immediately reveal the gardens; they are hidden behind high walls. The gardens were the creations of scholar-artists, who made their own private, landscaped retreats from the cares of the outside world. They are not simply areas for tending and planting, but are also artistic conceits designed in harmony with rocks, pools, plants, decorative windows, pebble mosaics, walkways and carefully devised vistas. In addition, they are laid out as settings in which to entertain as well as retire, to observe the changing moods of the seasons as well as the light and shade of the passing day.

Suzhou's fame dates back to the Tang dynasty, when its beauty and affluence were praised in poetry. Yet its origins can be traced to a very much earlier period. It is believed that a settlement was first built on the present city site during the sixth century BCE, when the marshlands of the region were reclaimed. From these earliest times, Suzhou was known for its canals, which crisscrossed the low-lying land. The canals had steep humpbacked bridges, under which sailed the river craft which carried the city's traffic. Marco Polo, who may have visited the city in the 13th century, claims the city canals had 6,000 stone bridges. Most of those canals have disappeared with the need to reclaim more and more land for building, so that only 168 of the original thousands of stone bridges are left standing. Nevertheless, Suzhou remains an attractive and graceful city, with its low-eaved, whitewashed houses and tree-shaded streets. In the old city quarters, there is even a flavour of traditional village life, now that the economic reforms of the last decade have allowed families to set up their own street stalls, selling anything from dumplings to handmade inkstones.

According to Chinese tradition, Suzhou women are among the fairest of their sisters, and their local dialect is so charming that even a quarrel is attractive to overhear. Suzhou women are also famed for their skill at needlework.

CITY SIGHTS

The great period of garden-making in Suzhou was during the Ming dynasty (1368–1644), when it was recorded that the city contained over 250 gardens. Today, it is known that over 100 still remain, but only a handful of the more famous ones have been renovated and opened to the public.

Suzhou

One of the smallest and yet most remarkable is known as the **Garden of the Master of the Fishing Nets** (Wangshi Yuan). A garden was first built here in the Song dynasty, but its present form and name date from the late 18th century, when the scholar, Song Zongyuan, bought the property. A walk through the garden with its bridges and carefully devised views is particularly rewarding. Some visitors may recognize the Hall for Eternal Spring, which has been recreated in the Metropolitan Museum of Art in New York.

The larger and more open garden known as the **Garden of the Humble Administrator** (Zhuozheng Yuan) is part park and part a restored Ming garden. In the park section, visitors can stroll by the small pond and enjoy hot snacks served at a nearby stall. The classical Ming garden has a pool patterned with islands and bridges, one island of which—the Xiangzhou—is said to suggest a moored boat. In the small enclosed Loquat Garden are a series of decorative pebble pictures.

The oldest extant garden in the city is reputed to be the **Pavilion of the Blue Waves** (Canglang Ting), dating back to the Song dynasty. The garden was re-landscaped in the Ming dynasty and then destroyed in the Taiping Rebellion of the mid-19th century. It was restored in 1873. The garden has an imposing artificial hill and an open vista to an adjacent, willow-fringed canal.

Another seductively named garden is the **Lingering Garden** (Liu Yuan). With stylized landscapes in an ornamental setting, this large 16th-century garden is famous for its classical round doorways known as moon gates. These and other geometrically-shaped doorways provide natural frames for viewing the plants, pools and rocks beyond. The garden pool is framed by vast rock formations, which create the impression of mountains.

For the connoisseur of rocks, the **Forest of Lions Garden** (Shizi Lin) is a favourite. It was laid out in the Yuan dynasty (1279–1368) under the supervision of the painter Ni Zan, and is thus one of Suzhou's most admired gardens. The garden was also the childhood home of the Chinese American architect, I.M. Pei. It has a fine collection of rocks, one of which is so large and eroded that it has small caverns and grottoes through which you can actually walk. Oddly shaped rocks were an indispensable feature of Chinese gardens; they were regarded as aesthetic objects and the most ornamental and coveted ones were those dredged from the bottom of Taihu Lake near Wuxi.

A 1980 scene typical of old Suzhou, one of the most famous cities on the ancient Grand Canal. Sadly, the sailing vessels are rarely if ever used these days; however, strenuous efforts are being made to preserve what's left, and to regenerate as much of China's canal systems as is feasible.

The **Garden of Harmony** (Yi Yuan) is a Qing-dynasty garden which has been modelled on earlier Ming ones. It too has a number of rocks dredged from Taihu Lake, which have been arranged as a mountain frame for the pond. It is interesting to note that this, like other classical Chinese gardens, does not have the dynamic, fluid quality of the Japanese garden. In the Chinese version there is a pleasure in the composed harmony of elements and the appreciation of devised contrasts.

East of the city is the quieter **Plough Garden** (Ou Yuan), which is recommended if you want to escape the crowds. This is an important consideration, since in the warmer months the crowds in Suzhou's gardens almost obscure the view. The best idea is to visit the gardens just as they open in the morning or—if you want to take special photographs—go to your guide and see if you can arrange a visit before opening time.

As far as temples are concerned, staying in Suzhou would be incomplete without a visit to the **Cold Mountain Monastery**. This monastery has been immortalized in a Tang-dynasty poem by Zhang Ji, copies of which are painted on fans or carved on inkstones and sold as Suzhou souvenirs. The temple was founded in the fifth century and is adjacent to a small, attractive canal, spanned by a high-arched bridge which is featured in the name of the poem, 'Midnight at Maple Bridge':

The moon sets, a crow calls in the frosty air,

Under dark maples and fishermen's lamps, I toss in troubled sleep.

Cold Mountain Monastery stands outside the city walls,

And the chimes of its midnight bell are wafted to my boat.

The monastery's bell has disappeared and the Ming replacement was taken to Japan and lost. The present bell, cast in 1906, was given by a Japanese Buddhist delegation. Cold Mountain Monastery is also famous for its association with the Tang-dynasty Buddhist monk-poet Han Shan, who stayed here at one time.

Opposite the Lingering Garden, you will find the **West Garden Temple**, designed by the scholar, Xu Shitai, in the Ming dynasty. The main curiosity is a pond where a reputedly 300-year-old turtle lives.

Of the many stone bridges remaining in Suzhou, the most famous lies in the southeast of the city and is known as the **Precious Belt Bridge**. It is over 1,000 years old, built in 816, and it has 53 arches. In its present form, it is a 19th-century restoration of the original. The bridge is so named because an early governor of the city is said to have sold a precious belt in order to raise funds to build it.

The **North Temple Pagoda**, easy to find because of its height, is a prominent landmark of Suzhou. It was built in 1582 and has been restored so that visitors can safely climb up to get a good view of the city. In the central district of the city stand the **Twin Pagodas**, which were built in the Song dynasty. They are all that remain of an earlier Tang temple.

The **Folk Custom Museum** and the **Drama and Opera Museum** are fascinating places to visit for those interested in Chinese culture. The city's old Confucius Temple now houses a **Museum of Stelae** (stelae are inscribed stone tablets). The most interesting of these is a Song-dynasty constellation chart and a Yuan city map, which shows Suzhou as it was in the early 13th century. The new **Suzhou Museum** was designed by world-famous Chinese architect I.M. Pei; it is a wonderful fusion of modernistic architectural style and traditional themes, and houses over 3,000 cultural relics, most notably excavated artefacts, Ming and Qing paintings and calligraphy, and ancient craftwork. The museum is located on Dongbei Street next to **Zhong Wang Fu**, the most complete historic complex of the 19th-century Taiping Heavenly Kingdom.

In common with several other towns in Jiangsu Province, Suzhou has long been an important centre of silk production; the industry had certainly become highly organized by the 16th century. It is not surprising that the art of embroidery developed too. The **Research Institute for Embroidery**, set up in 1957, is well worth a visit. It has its own museum showing the development of embroidery stitches and motifs, and there is a shop. Some of the most outstanding examples of embroidery show perfect stitching on both sides of the silk, and the reversed image is made to stunning effect.

Suzhou also has a tradition of making intricately carved sandalwood fans, which can be bought at the **Sandalwood Fan Factory**. The fans keep their fragrance for years, and traditionally were dowry gifts.

OUTINGS FROM SUZHOU

To the northwest of the city is **Tiger Hill**. It is a wonderful sight, with its leaning pagoda, waterfalls, spring, rocks and landscaped paths. The hill was built in the Zhou dynasty (1027–256 BCE) as a burial mound for a local ruler, the King of Wu. Legend has it that a tiger guards the tomb—hence its name.

For another half-day outing, the **Dongshan** area, 40 kilometres (25 miles) southwest of Suzhou on Taihu Lake, and **Changshu**, about the same distance to the north, both offer a glimpse of rural life.

Suzhou

HANGZHOU

lthough Hangzhou was once an imperial capital in the Southern Song dynasty (1127–1279), the city is better known as a pleasure resort. Specifically, it is best known for its **West Lake**, which has been celebrated over the centuries in both song and verse. Marco Polo, who may have visited Hangzhou in the 13th century, wrote lyrically of the pleasures of the lake and concluded, 'indeed a voyage on this lake offers more refreshment and delectation than any other experience on earth'.

Without West Lake, Hangzhou would have been just another prosperous city thriving on its position as the southern terminus of the Grand Canal, and on its two agricultural industries of tea and silk. But with West Lake, Hangzhou has gained a status not far short of paradise. If Suzhou's loveliness as a city of gardens is almost entirely man-made, Hangzhou has little need of artifice to enhance its natural beauty. The city skirts the shore of a wide, shallow lake rimmed by green and gentle hills, on the slopes of which are grown the famous Longjing tea of the region and mulberry leaves for the silkworm larvae.

The modern city is, alas, less prepossessing. It was virtually destroyed during the Taiping Rebellion in the mid-19th century, and underwent extensive modernization and industrialization after 1949. Walking around Hangzhou today gives the visitor little idea of the glories of its time as the capital of the Southern Song, a period famous for great cultural achievements. Little remains, too, of its later imperial heritage. It is only when contemplating the lake that one understands why, in the Yuan, Ming and Qing dynasties, Hangzhou was an imperial resort, and why the two famous long-lived Qing emperors, Kangxi and Qianlong, each made six visits to the city.

Hangzhou has a rich literary heritage. The city and West Lake have been the setting of numerous folk-tales and scholars' stories. In one tale recorded by a Ming collector of folk legends, Feng Menglong, a white snake maiden, aided by her blue fish maidservant, falls in love with an ordinary mortal during a rainstorm on West Lake. The story ends tragically when the white snake and blue fish are captured by a Buddhist monk, made to revert to their original animal forms, and then imprisoned under a pagoda. The pagoda is said to have been the Thunder Peak Pagoda, which once overlooked the lake from its southern shores but tumbled down in 1924.

This is not the only such tale. In an earlier story, told by a Tang scholar, the Qiantang estuary to the south of West Lake—which once joined it as part of the same tidal basin—was reputed to be the home of a hot-tempered dragon. It is no wonder

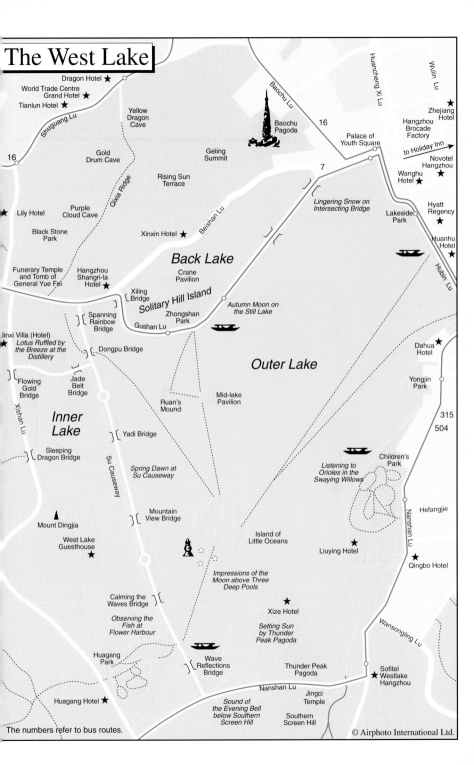

The West Lake

Dragon Hotel ★
World Trade Centre
Grand Hotel ★
Tianlun Hotel ★

Shuguang Lu

Yellow
Dragon
Cave

Baochu Lu

Baochu
Pagoda

16

Huancheng Xi Lu

Wulin Lu

Zhejiang ★
Hotel

Hangzhou
Brocade
Factory

Palace of
Youth Square

to Holiday Inn

16

Gold
Drum Cave

Geling
Summit

7

Novotel
Hangzhou ★

Wanghu
Hotel ★

Qixia Ridge

Rising Sun
Terrace

Lingering Snow on
Intersecting Bridge

Hyatt
Regency

★ Lily Hotel

Purple
Cloud Cave

Black Stone
Park

Xinxin Hotel ★

Beishan Lu

Lakeside
Park

Huanhu
Hotel

Hubin Lu

Back Lake

Funerary Temple
and Tomb of
General Yue Fei

Hangzhou
Shangri-la
Hotel ★

Crane
Pavilion

Xiling
Bridge

Solitary Hill Island

Autumn Moon on
the Still Lake

Spanning
Rainbow
Bridge

Zhongshan
Park

Gushan Lu

Jinxi Villa (Hotel)
★ Lotus Ruffled by
the Breeze at the
Distillery

Dongpu Bridge

Outer Lake

Dahua ★
Hotel

Yongjin
Park

Flowing
Gold
Bridge

Jade
Belt
Bridge

Ruan's
Mound

Mid-lake
Pavilion

Xishan Lu

Inner
Lake

Yadi Bridge

315
504

Su Causeway

Sleeping
Dragon Bridge

Spring Dawn at
Su Causeway

Listening to
Orioles in the
Swaying Willows

Children's
Park

Hefangjie

Mount Dingjia

Mountain
View Bridge

Nanshan Lu

West Lake
Guesthouse ★

Island of
Little Oceans

Liuying Hotel ★

Qingbo Hotel ★

Impressions of the
Moon above Three
Deep Pools

Calming the
Waves Bridge

Xize Hotel ★

Observing the
Fish at
Flower Harbour

Setting Sun
by Thunder
Peak Pagoda

Wansongling Lu

Huagang
Park

Wave
Reflections
Bridge

Thunder Peak
Pagoda

Sofitel
★ Westlake
Hangzhou

Huagang Hotel ★

Nanshan Lu

Jingci
Temple

Sound of
the Evening Bell
below Southern
Screen Hill

Southern
Screen Hill

The numbers refer to bus routes.

© Airphoto International Ltd.

then that the estuary is famous for its tidal bore, which can reach six metres (20 feet) in height. Such a phenomenon would be easy to associate with mischievous dragons who are known to make their homes in lakes, rivers and clouds.

West Lake's two most renowned literary associations are with the Tang poet, Bai Juyi (Po Chu-yi), and the Song poet, Su Dongpo. They both served as governors of the city, and both were responsible for major earthwork projects designed to safeguard West Lake from flooding. The lake has two major causeways named after the poet-governors who commissioned their building. The causeways now have attractive lakeside walkways, planted with willows and flowering trees.

CITY SIGHTS

Many scenic places in China traditionally have a number of famous vistas, and the West Lake is no different. Some time in the Song dynasty, ten 'prospects' were selected for the lake, but their original locations are not known. The sites now designated as the Ten Prospects were marked in the Qing dynasty. Fanciful names given to the views were carved on stone tablets and placed at the sites. Today, with the help of a map and a guide, the visitor can still see 'Spring Dawn at Su Causeway', 'Observing the Fish at Flower Harbour', 'Listening to the Orioles in the Swaying Willows', 'Lotus Ruffled by the Breeze at the Distillery', 'Setting Sun by Thunder Peak Pagoda' (the pagoda has gone), 'Autumn Moon on the Still Lake', 'Impressions of the Moon above Three Deep Pools', 'Lingering Snow on Intersecting Bridge', the 'Sound of the Evening Bell below Southern Screen Hill' (the bell has disappeared, as has the Jingci Monastery in which it hung), and a little way from the lake, 'Twin Peaks Piercing the Clouds'.

The best way to start a visit to the lake is to take a boat from the northern shore to the central **Island of Little Oceans** (from where can be seen 'Impressions of the Moon above Three Deep Pools'). The island is man-made and has been cleverly contrived to enclose four small lakes, which creates the effect of lakes within a lake. Here a small pavilion serves refreshments, including the famous West Lake lotus root simmered into a sweet broth. Three stone lanterns jutting out of the water close to the island are sometimes lit with candles at night to create the impression of three moons reflected in the water.

The **Su Causeway**, named after the poet Su Dongpo, is an excellent place to stroll and enjoy a view of the lake. Small bridges intersect the causeway, and thus it is sometimes known as Six Bridge Dyke. The causeway is particularly beautiful in spring when the willow, peach, camphor and horse-chestnut trees are in bud and blossom. At the northern end of the Su Causeway is a prospect—'Lotus Ruffled by the Breeze at the Distillery'. It is here that visitors come in summer to see the deep pink lotus blossoms.

Solitary Hill Island, the largest of the lake's islands and easily found near the Hangzhou Shangri-La Hotel, is linked to the shore by Xiling Bridge as well as the famous **Bai Causeway**, named after the poet Bai Juyi. On the island is the **Xiling Seal Engraving Society** where visitors can order a seal carved with their name in Chinese. The **Zhejiang Museum** and its adjacent botanical garden on the island are also worth exploring. Another of the Ten Prospects can be seen from the southeast corner of the island—'Autumn Moon on the Still Lake'. It was here that Emperor Qianlong of the Qing dynasty had a pavilion built so as to be able to enjoy the prospect. On the north shore of the lake stands the **Tomb and Temple of Yue Fei**, a popular place to visit for Chinese tourists because of Yue Fei's reputation as a patriot. Yue Fei, a general who served the Southern Song dynasty, led several successful campaigns against the Jin nomads, who had conquered North China and driven the Song emperor southwards to a new capital in exile at Hangzhou. General Yue Fei incurred the jealousy and distrust of the prime minister, Qin Hui, who had the general murdered in 1141. When Yue Fei's reputation was restored, his remains were interred in Hangzhou and the temple was established.

Also on the north shore of the lake is the slender **Baochu Pagoda**, which was first built in the tenth century. The present structure dates from 1933. A small adjacent teahouse offers an attractive view over to the south of the lake, where the remains of the seven-storey brick **Thunder Peak Pagoda**, which fell down in 1924, are now dwarfed by the attractive **Leifeng Pagoda**, which stands out regally on a hillock and offers superb views over the lake and surrounding city from its upper levels.

Overlooking the nearby Qiantang estuary is the impressive 13-storey, dark red, wood-and-brick structure of the **Pagoda of the Six Harmonies** (Liuhe Ta). It was first built in 970 on the site of an earlier pagoda which served as a lighthouse. The pagoda's name refers to the six codes of Buddhism—to strive for the harmony of body, speech and thought, and to renounce physical pleasures, personal opinions and wealth. Visitors can ponder on these codes as they climb the pagoda for a view over the river.

There are other reflective spots in Hangzhou. Of its several parks, the best for gardening enthusiasts is the **Botanical Garden** on the western outskirts of the city. It has a fine medicinal herb section and is in a peaceful rural setting. North of the Hangzhou Shangri-La Hotel are three caves, which are open to visitors: Purple Cloud Cave, Gold Drum Cave and Yellow Dragon Cave. They are crowded on rainy days, when sightseeing below ground becomes an attractive option.

Hangzhou

Not far from the Botanical Garden is the tea-growing area that takes its name from the 'Twin Peaks Piercing the Clouds' prospect. Another tea plantation is found on the road past the Pagoda of the Six Harmonies, at Meijiawu. Both cultivate Hangzhou's famous Dragon Well (Longjing) tea. To learn about Hangzhou's other important industry, it is worth arranging a visit to the **Silk Printing and Dyeing Complex** or the **Du Jinsheng Silk Weaving Factory**.

OUTINGS FROM HANGZHOU

If your plans allow an extended stay in Zhejiang Province, there are several short or day outings to be made from Hangzhou. To the west lies the **Lingyin Temple**, notable because of its woodland setting next to the **Peak that Flew There** (Feilai Feng). According to legend, the peak, actually a limestone outcrop, was once part of a holy mountain in India before it spontaneously flew to Hangzhou. The Peak that Flew There is famous for its Yuan-dynasty Buddhist carvings, but earlier carvings in the rock-face date back to the tenth century. The open-air teahouse next to it is an excellent place to sit and drink a cup of pale green Longjing tea and look at the Buddhist carvings. The temple buildings have been destroyed several times since its founding in the fourth century; the present ones are restorations from the 1950s. Close to the temple is the Taoguang Hermitage, offering walks through bamboo groves and, at the top of the path, a fine view over the city.

Longer outings from Hangzhou offer a chance to see the neighbouring towns of **Shaoxing** and **Ningbo**. Neither of the towns features on the standard tourist circuit, but both of them are interesting. Shaoxing is only a 70-kilometre (43-mile) ride away from Hangzhou, to the southeast. It is a canal town, surrounded by many lakes, and has old and attractive buildings and temples. Besides fishing, Shaoxing people also live by the town's traditional industry of making rice wine—visitors can ask to go to a tasting at the Shaoxing Winery. Another famous site in Shaoxing is the old home of Lu Xun, the 20th-century writer, and a museum dedicated to him. Ningbo is further—the train from Hangzhou takes three and a half hours. Being a coastal port, Ningbo's fortunes have long been tied to trade and shipping. It was one of the five Treaty Ports established in 1842, and it is one of the 14 coastal cities opened by the Chinese government to foreign investment in 1984. Apart from its seafaring traditions, Ningbo also has a reputation for producing tough mercantile inhabitants who are particularly hardheaded in business. Its most famous son was, however, the Kuomintang leader, Generalissimo Chiang Kai-shek. From Ningbo, there is a steamship service to **Putuoshan** (*see* page 281), an island off the Zhejiang coast, which has one of China's nine sacred mountains.

Lingyin Si (Temple) was founded in the 4th century, and its beautifully reconstructed halls are still filled with pilgrims, making it a rewarding day trip from Hangzhou. [Jeremy Tredinnick]

GUILIN

uilin is one of China's best-known cities on account of its beautiful landscape of limestone mountains, likened in a Tang poem to jade hairpins. The city has been popular with sightseers for over 1,000 years, and many famous poets and painters have lived and worked here, celebrating its river and mountain scenery.

Once the capital of Guangxi Province (the capital was moved south to Nanning in 1914), Guilin has always been a prosperous commercial centre, profiting from its proximity to the Ling Canal which links the two major river networks of the Pearl and the Yangzi. This canal was built in the second century BCE, during the reign of Qin Shi Huangdi, the first emperor of China, who used it to link the middle regions of his empire around the Yangzi with the far south. But central government control of Guangxi was only intermittent, and the province remained a frontier region of the Chinese empire until the time of the Tang dynasty (618–907). Many Guangxi people are not ethnic Chinese. Around 35 per cent of the population are Zhuang, the most populous minority group in China. However, the land they occupy covers over 60 per cent of the province, and thus the province has been designated a Zhuang Minority Autonomous Region.

Guilin lies along the west bank of the Li River, and was once a walled city. However, widespread destruction during the Japanese occupation in the Second World War, along with a recent modernization and industrialization programme, have left the city drab and undistinguished amidst its mountains. In the 1980s tourists began coming here in increasing numbers, both Chinese sightseers who had been made prosperous by the economic reforms, and foreign visitors encouraged by the expansion of hotels and air services. The city was inundated with tourists, with the result that prices rose higher and higher. So why come to Guilin at all? The answer is simple—its landscape of abrupt mountains amidst verdant river plains still has the ability to refresh and enchant the senses.

CITY SIGHTS

The city sights of Guilin are of nature's rather than man's making. However, the small mountains which punctuate the river plain have been embellished with delicate pavilions, winding paths and carvings. It is great fun to climb one of these mountains and gaze out over the city and the **Li River**, where fishermen pole their bamboo rafts through the lazy current while their cormorants dive for fish.

In the city centre, the best-known peak is **Solitary Beauty Peak** (Duxiu Feng), which was once part of a 14th-century palace of the Emperor Hongwu's nephew, Zhou Shouqian. The calligraphy on the peak's rock-face dates from the Tang and Ming dynasties.

Close to Solitary Beauty Peak is **Fubo Hill**, named after a famous general of the Han dynasty. Halfway up the hill is a cave where the Goddess of Mercy, Guanyin, was worshipped. Fubo Hill has many fine stone inscriptions and carvings; those outside the Cave of Guanyin are attributed to the Qing painter, Li Pingshou.

Another interesting hill, this time with four peaks, is the **Hill of Piled Silk** (Diecai Shan). It offers sweeping views over the Li River and the city to the south. It also has many fine stone carvings, some again from the hand of Li Pingshou. The hill has several Buddhist altars, which were built between the tenth and the 13th centuries.

The small group of peaks which make up **West Hill** (Xi Shan) was once famous for its Buddhist statuary. They are all but gone after Red Guards smashed them in the 1960s. However, when the more popular hills in the centre of town are crowded, this is a good place to wander in quietly and enjoy a view over the countryside.

South of the city centre are two hills which cannot be climbed but are interesting for their resemblance to animals—**Camel Hill** and **Elephant Trunk Hill**. The latter juts out into the Li River at its junction with Peach Blossom River, and at dusk looks extraordinarily like a larger-than-life elephant drinking from the river. Camel Hill is found on the eastern bank of the Li River, past Seven Star Park. The park, so called because of its peaks arranged as the stars of the Big Dipper, contains the attractive covered Flower Bridge. It is in the environs of the park that you find the **Seven Star Hill** and **Cave**. Underground caves are often found in limestone areas, since the rock easily erodes in water, forming vast caverns below ground level. The Seven Star Cave contains dripping stalagmites and stalactite pinnacles, all illuminated with coloured lights. Other caves worth visiting are Reed Flute Cave, White Dragon Cave (beneath South Creek Hill), and Returned Pearl Cave (beneath Fubo Hill).

OUTINGS FROM GUILIN

The **Li River** boat trip is undoubtedly the highlight of most people's visits to Guilin. It is not too hard to understand why, for even the most well-travelled visitor finds the quiet, pastoral landscapes along the river enchanting. Setting out downstream just beyond the city (return journeys upstream are also available), the boat passes a landscape of manicured fields shaded by leafy bamboo groves and punctuated with

Guilin

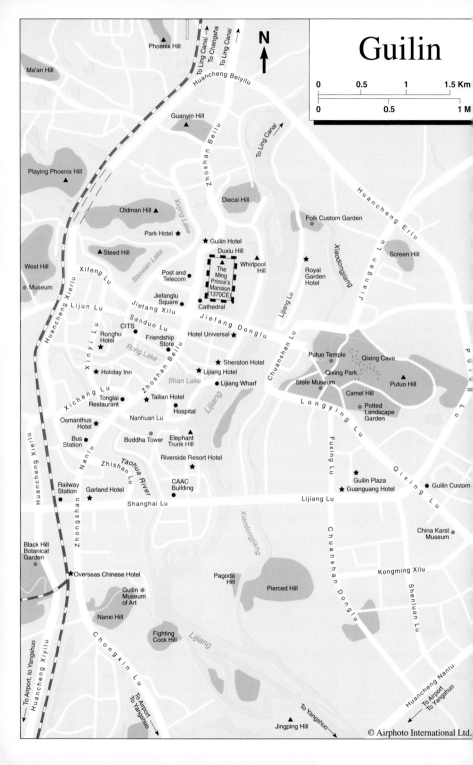

Guilin

Phoenix Hill

Ma'an Hill

Playing Phoenix Hill

To Ling Canal
To Changsha
To Ling Canal
Huancheng Beiyilu

Guanyin Hill

N

0   0.5   1   1.5 Km
0   0.5   1 M

Zhoshan Beilu

To Ling Canal

Huancheng Erlu

Diecai Hill

Oldman Hill

Xiang Lake

Folk Custom Garden

Park Hotel

★ Guilin Hotel
Duxiu Hill

Xiaodongjiang

Screen Hill

Steed Hill

Whirlpool Hill

★ Royal Garden Hotel

West Hill

Xifeng Lu

Baoxian Lake

Post and Telecom

The Ming Prince's Mansion (1370CE)

Museum

Huancheng Xierlu

Lijun Lu

Jiefanglu Square
Jietang Xilu

Jiefanglu Xilu

Sanduo Lu

Cathedral

Jiefang Donglu

Lijiang Lu

Chuanshan Lu

CITS

Xinyi Lu

Ronghu Hotel

Friendship Store

Hotel Universal ★

Putuo Temple

Qixing Cave

Zhoshan Beilu

Rong Lake

★ Sheraton Hotel

Qixing Park

★ Holiday Inn

Shan Lake

Lijiang Hotel

● Lijiang Wharf

Stele Museum

Camel Hill

Putuo Hill

Xicheng Lu

Tonglai Restaurant

Tailian Hotel

Lijiang

Longying Lu

Potted Landscape Garden

Nanhuan Lu

● Hospital

Osmanthus Hotel

Nanlu

Bus Station

Buddha Tower

Elephant Trunk Hill

Fuxing Lu

Qixing Lu

Zhishan Lu

Riverside Resort Hotel

Taohua River

Railway Station

Garland Hotel

CAAC Building

Shanghai Lu

Lijiang Lu

★ Guilin Plaza
★ Guanguang Hotel

● Guilin Custom

Zhongshan

Xiaodongjiang

Black Hill Botanical Garden

Chuanshan Donglu

China Karst Museum

★ Overseas Chinese Hotel

Pagoda Hill

Pierced Hill

Kongming Xilu

Shenluan Lu

Guilin Museum of Art

Nanxi Hill

Fighting Cock Hill

Lijiang

Chongxin Lu

To Airport, to Yangshuo
Huancheng Xiyilu

To Airport
To Yangshuo

To Yangshuo

Huancheng Nanlu
To Airport
To Yangshuo

Jingping Hill

© Airphoto International Ltd.

(Top) *A classic scene within classical scenery, Yangshuo, 1980;* (bottom) *An inspirational view from Half Moon Hill, a popular climbing spot near Yangshuo.* *[Jeremy Tredinnick]*

steep, bizarrely-shaped hills. The hills have fanciful names, which are in the Chinese tradition of making a picture when looking at landscapes—Crown Rock, Conch Hill, Jade Lotus Peak and Snow Lion Peak are examples. These karst limestone formations evolved millions of years ago, when the area was under the sea. The process of erosion of the rock over a long period created the strange shapes we see today. On the river you will see fishermen with the trained cormorants who catch fish for them.

The boat ride downstream usually stops at the village of **Yangdi**, but the karst scenery can be seen all the way to Yangshuo (83 kilometres from Guilin). However, dropping water levels on the Li make navigating stretches of the river increasingly problematic, so only certain sections may be possible depending on the time of year. **Yangshuo** is an enchanting market town that has unfortunately been increasingly overrun by tourism in recent years. Inundated by streams of visitors daily, Yangshuo has adapted to cater to both the Western backpacker scene and the Chinese tourist market and even has its own website (*www.yangers.com*). Nevertheless, the town's smaller, more village-style atmosphere (coach tours excluding) and setting among beautiful and inspiring surroundings make it a hotspot for all forms of tourism. A great way to experience its scenery is to rent a bicycle and explore the surrounding villages and countryside at your own pace, biking through cultivated farmland that stretches out idyllically to the base of impressive peaks. Indeed, Yangshuo has become something of an adventure sport centre, with rock climbing, mountain biking, caving and river kayaking all popular among outdoor enthusiasts.

You can visit the **Ling Canal** (Ling Qu) by going to the small county town of **Xing'an**. Over 2,000 years old, the canal symbolizes the extent of the military power of China's first dynasty, the Qin, which had its capital at Xi'an, over 1,000 kilometres (620 miles) to the north. The canal joins the two major river systems of the Pearl— which flows into the sea south of Guangzhou—and the Yangzi, which joins the ocean just north of Shanghai. The joining of these two river systems was of great strategic and economic importance. By means of the inland water route, the government could transfer grain from the rice-growing areas to feed the less well-endowed north, while at the same time it could despatch troops to the south to quell the rebellions of the traditionally troublesome minority peoples.

To the north of Guilin lies an imposing range of rugged mountains that are home to a number of different minority people including Zhuang, Yao and Dong. They are upland rice farmers living in small clan villages that overlook verdant tiers of terracing that rise over 300 metres in places. A day trip from Guilin to **Longsheng** (one of the townships in the mountain region) is recommended both for the magnificent scenery and the chance to explore some minority villages.

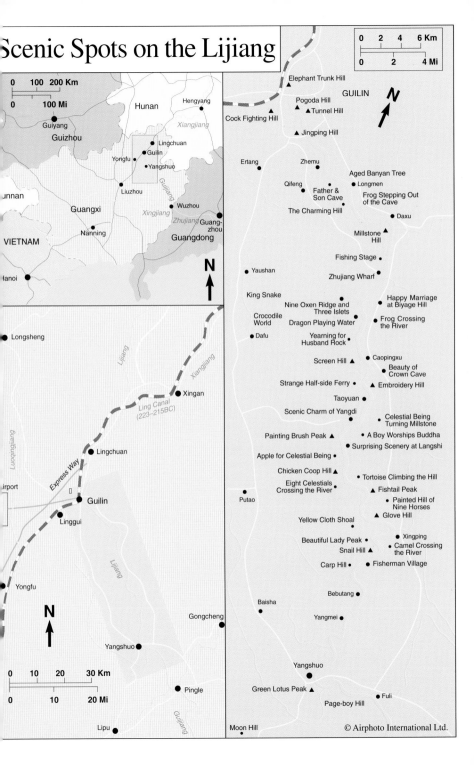

Scenic Spots on the Lijiang

0 100 200 Km

0 100 Mi

Guizhou
Guiyang
Hunan
Hengyang

unnan
Guangxi
Yongfu
Lingchuan
Guilin
Yangshuo
Liuzhou
Xiangjiang
Wuzhou
Zhujiang
Guang-zhou
Guangdong

VIETNAM
Nanning
Hanoi

Longsheng

Lijiang
Xiangjiang
Xingan
Ling Canal
(223–215BC)

Lingchuan

Express Way

Guilin
irport

Linggui

Lijiang

Yongfu

Gongcheng

N

0 10 20 30 Km

0 10 20 Mi

Yangshuo

Pingle

Guijiang

Lipu

0 2 4 6 Km

0 2 4 Mi

Elephant Trunk Hill
Pogoda Hill
Tunnel Hill
GUILIN
Cock Fighting Hill
N
Jingping Hill

Ertang
Zhemu
Aged Banyan Tree
Qifeng
Father & Son Cave
Longmen
Frog Stepping Out of the Cave
The Charming Hill
Daxu
Millstone Hill

Fishing Stage
Yaushan
Zhujiang Wharf

King Snake
Nine Oxen Ridge and Three Islets
Happy Marriage at Biyage Hill
Crocodile World
Dragon Playing Water
Frog Crossing the River
Dafu
Yearning for Husband Rock

Screen Hill
Caopingxu
Beauty of Crown Cave
Strange Half-side Ferry
Embroidery Hill
Taoyuan
Scenic Charm of Yangdi
Celestial Being Turning Millstone
Painting Brush Peak
A Boy Worships Buddha
Surprising Scenery at Langshi
Apple for Celestial Being
Chicken Coop Hill
Tortoise Climbing the Hill
Eight Celestials Crossing the River
Fishtail Peak
Putao
Painted Hill of Nine Horses
Yellow Cloth Shoal
Glove Hill
Beautiful Lady Peak
Xingping
Snail Hill
Camel Crossing the River
Carp Hill
Fisherman Village

Bebutang
Baisha
Yangmei

Yangshuo
Green Lotus Peak
Fuli
Page-boy Hill
Moon Hill
© Airphoto International Ltd.

KING OF THE PEDANTS

When I was twelve, I got a job as a waiter in the Prosperity for All over on the edge of town. The boss said I was too young and stupid-looking to wait on the long-gown crowd in the side room, but he could use me to help out behind the bar. Now the short-jacket crowd was easy to deal with, but even so there were quite a few of them who would run off at the mouth and stir up trouble there was no call for, just because they couldn't keep things straight in their own heads when they ordered.

So I'd ladle the yellow wine out from the big earthenware crock and into a pot, and they'd watch like hawks to make sure I didn't slip any water in. They never felt at ease until they'd seen the pot safely placed in the hot water. Under supervision like that, cutting the wine wasn't easy. And so it wasn't long before the boss decided I wasn't cut out for that job either. Luckily the person who'd gotten me the job had a lot of prestige, so the boss couldn't just up and fire me even if he'd wanted to. And so he made me into a specialist. From then on I would tend to nothing but the boring business of warming the wine.

From one end of the day to the other I'd be, standing behind the bar. Though I performed my assigned task to the best of my ability, it was downright monotonous. And what with the stern face of the boss and the unfriendliness of the customers, I was never able to loosen up. The only time I could relax a bit, and even have a laugh or two, was when Kong Yiji came around. And that's why I still remember him even now.

Kong Yiji was the only customer in a long gown who drank his wine standing up. A big tall fellow with a scraggly grey beard, he had a face that was pale and wrinkled. And every so often, sandwiched in between those wrinkles, you'd see a scar or two. Kong wore a long gown just like the gentry, but it was so raggedy and dirty you'd swear it hadn't been patched or washed in at least ten years. When he talked, he always larded whatever he had to say with lo, forsooth, verily, nay and came out with a whole string of such phrases, things that you could half make out, and half couldn't. Because his family name was Kong, people nicknamed him Yiji. They got the idea from the first six words of a copybook that was used in teaching children how to write characters: ABOVE—GREAT—MAN—KONG— YI—JI, a string of words whose meaning you could half make out, and half couldn't.

Literary Excerpt

One day he came to the wineshop and all the regulars, as usual, started to eyeball him and laugh. Somebody yelled, "Hey there, Kong Yiji, you've put a few new scars on that old face of yours!"

Without responding, Kong looked straight toward the bar and said: "Warm two bowls of wine and let me have a saucer of fennel beans." He set out nine coppers all in a row.

Someone else kept the fun going by shouting, "You must have been caught stealin' again!"

Kong Yiji opened his eyes wide in indignation and replied, "How dare you, without a shred of evidence, besmirch a man's good name and even—"

"What good name? Wasn't it the day before yesterday I saw you trussed up and beaten with my own eyes?"

Kong's face flushed red and the veins stood out on his temples as he began to defend himself. "The purloining of volumes, good sir, cannot be counted as theft. The purloining of volumes is, after all, something that falls well within the purview of the scholarly life. How can it be considered mere theft?" Tacked onto that was a whole string of words that were difficult to understand, things like The gentleman doth stand firm in his poverty, and verily this and forsooth that. Everyone roared with laughter. The space within the shop and the space surrounding the shop swelled with joy.

Lu Xun, *Kong Yiji* (1919), translated by William A Lyell

Lu Xun, or Lu Hsün, (1881–1936) is called the father of modern Chinese literature. His first story *A Madman's Diary* is considered to be the first story written in Modern Chinese. Lu Xun chose to write the way people talk. Lu Xun (a pen name, his real name was Zhou Shuren) wrote stories, poetry, essays, literary criticism and literary history. His stories were published in literary journals of the time and were then collected and published as books. He has three volumes of short stories.

EXPEDITIONS
INNER MONGOLIA

The grasslands of China's Inner Mongolia Autonomous Region are relatively little visited by tourist groups. This is a shame, since the region offers some of the most tranquil, undeveloped landscapes in the whole country. With a northwesterly wind blowing off the Siberian steppes, winters are harsh in the region but summers are warm and glorious. From May to September, herds of cattle, sheep, goats and camels roam the grasslands, and Mongolian herders follow their animals, using as a home the decorated felt tents which we know as *yurts*, but which the Mongolians themselves call *ger*.

The Mongolian people are the descendants of the armies of Genghiz Khan, who conquered the entire land mass of Central Asia, from the Caspian Sea to the present borders of North China, in the early 13th century, and who—under Kublai Khan—

A Mongolian woman, in traditional costume for a local festival, helms a ship of the desert.

The Five Pagoda Temple in Hohhot. [Brianna Laugher, licensed by Creative Commons Attribution ShareAlike, http://creativecommons.org/licenses/by-sa/2.5]

went on to conquer the whole of China and to found the Yuan dynasty. Their original homeland was the northeast corner of what is now Mongolia, the highland country sandwiched between Russia in the north and the People's Republic of China in the south. Known as Outer Mongolia, this vast area was at one time controlled by the Qing empire until, in the early part of the 20th century, it gained independence with Soviet help. The territory remaining within the People's Republic of China—Inner Mongolia—has since been administered as an Autonomous Region. The Mongolian people are thus divided by an international boundary between Mongolia and Inner Mongolia within the People's Republic of China.

During the reign of Kublai Khan, Tibetan Lamaism had gained favour among the Mongol aristocracy, and the Mongols remain followers of this form of Buddhism to this day. The influence of this religion can be seen in their arts and temple architecture.

Latent Mongolian nationalism has made the Chinese government acutely sensitive about their northern border, shared with Russia. In the 1960s, during the Cultural Revolution, the use of the Mongolian language, dress and customs was prohibited. Today, the teaching of Mongolian in schools and universities has been reintroduced, but the Mongolians of China believe their culture is doomed because Chinese is now the language of education—and thus of privilege. They fear the destiny of the Manchus, whose language ultimately became a relic of their nomadic past. Migration of Han Chinese into the territory has diluted the proportion of ethnic Mongolians in the population, who now account for only 17 per cent compared with some 80 per cent of Chinese.

Most foreign travellers come to Inner Mongolia to visit the high-altitude grasslands and experience the nomadic lifestyle. However, the model yurts laid on for foreign guests are usually situated in pastoral areas which provide permanent winter dwellings for the herders and their families. These are a welcome innovation for the Mongolian nomads, although they do not reflect the hardships of a traditional nomadic lifestyle. On the other hand, this lifestyle has undergone radical changes anyway, as a result of increasing cultivation of forage crops.

There are three such places open to tourists outside Hohhot, the capital of Inner Mongolia. **Xilamulunsumu** can be reached as part of a day trip from Hohhot. Visitors can stay here in yurts specially set aside as a 'motel', complete with washing facilities. The more distant communities of **Huitengxile** and **Baiyinhushao** require an overnight stop. All offer traditional Mongolian hospitality: a yurt, butter, tea and mutton ribs. You may also be offered fermented mare's milk and even a Mongolian-style singalong. The Mongolians are enthusiastic singers and, when there are no Chinese around, they enjoy singing of those 13th-century battles when they conquered the Chinese.

Visit a yurt 'motel' and dress up in Mongolian costumes to pose for photographs alongside tasselled camels. You may prefer, however, to strike out across the grasslands on horseback or by jeep. The rolling hills and limitless expanse of undulating meadows may seem monotonous at first glance, but travel quietly and you will be pleasantly surprised. You can catch glimpses of wildfowl bathing in the shallow pools lying in small hollows. Wild irises grow amidst the grass, and skylarks rise from the pastures, singing into the clear blue heavens. Lone herdsmen watch their flocks grazing, occasionally moving them on with a flick of their lasso whip. Sometimes, by the verge of a track, you will see a white arrow pointing seemingly to nowhere. These are used by aircraft pilots to help them find their bearings.

HOHHOT

The present capital of Inner Mongolia was founded in the 16th century by a group of nomads known as the Tumet. The city grew and prospered under the Qing dynasty, and with the founding of the People's Republic of China in 1949, it was renamed Hohhot—meaning 'Blue City' in Mongolian.

The city has a liveliness imparted by the outgoing nature of its Mongolian inhabitants. City-dwelling Mongolians are hard to distinguish from the Chinese because they wear the same clothes. But the Mongolian is more gregarious and spirited in his outlook on life than his Chinese cousin.

The history of the region is well documented in the **Museum of Inner Mongolia**. The museum cannot be missed, since a white statue of a prancing horse rises from its roof. During the Cultural Revolution, Chinese officials turned the statue so that it faced Beijing. Now the statue once again faces north towards the grasslands.

Popular on tour itineraries is a visit to the **Tomb of Wang Zhaojun**. Wang Zhaojun was a Han dynasty princess who, in the first century, was married off to a barbarian chieftain to seal an alliance. Chinese are taught to consider her marriage an act of self-sacrifice—a potent reminder of how the Chinese have traditionally viewed their nomadic neighbours. No-one knows whether the tomb is really hers.

The Mongolians adopted the Tibetan Buddhist faith in the Yuan dynasty, and Inner Mongolia had many fine lamaseries before the Cultural Revolution. Some of those damaged monasteries are now being restored. Of particular interest in the city is the **Dazhao Monastery**, founded in the 16th century. Nearby, the **Xilitu Monastery** is the home of a Living Buddha (*huo fo*), a Chinese term for an incarnate lama who forms part of a lineage of spiritual masters. The present incarnation of the Living Buddha is sometimes introduced to foreign journalists.

For many, the most attractive sight of Hohhot is the **Five Pagoda Temple** (Wuta Si). In fact, it is not really a temple but rather a stupa with five small stupas on its roof, which was once part of a long-destroyed monastery. Inside stands what is said to be China's oldest star map (actually in Mongolian), carved in stone. A wealth of finely worked carvings cover the exterior of both the main stupa and the five roof stupas.

Inner Mongolia has a large community of Chinese Muslims (known as 'Hui'). Their **Great Mosque** (Qingzhen Si) of Hohhot is open to visitors. It was built in the 17th century and, like all late mosques built in China, it has no minaret. In imperial times there was an order for minarets to be replaced by pavilions, in which were placed inscriptions reminding the Muslims of their loyalty to the emperor.

NO WAY OUT

During the long summer Turfan [Turpan] is undoubtedly one of the hottest places on the face of the earth, and the thermometer registers around 130°Fahrenheit in the shade, but it is not hot all the year round and in winter the temperature falls to zero Fahrenheit. The heat is accounted for by its geographical location, which is in a depression watered by no river of any size, and lying below sea-level. Between May and August the inhabitants retire underground, for the mud or brick houses, even though they have deep verandahs and spacious airy rooms, are intolerable by day. In each courtyard there is an opening which leads by a flight of steps to a deep dug-out or underground apartment. Here are comfortable rooms and a kang spread with cool-surfaced reed matting and grass-woven pillows which help the people to endure the breathless stagnation of the midday hours; they eat and sleep underground and only emerge at sunset., and all necessary business is done then, but people avoid the living and sleeping rooms of their houses because they are infested with vermin. There are large and virulent scorpions which creep under sleeping-mats, drop on to the unconscious sleeper from the beams or hide themselves in his shoes. One jumping spider with long legs and a hairy body as large as a pigeon's egg leaps on its prey and makes a crunching noise with its jaws. Turfan cochroaches are over two inches in length, with long feelers and red eyes which make them a repulsive sight. All these creatures know how to conceal themselves in sleeping-bags and rolls of clothing, so that man is handicapped in dealing with them. Apart from these virulent monsters, the inns provide every variety of smaller vermin such as lice, bugs and fleas, and each is of an order well able to withstand all the patent nostrums guaranteed to destroy them. On account of these pests the people of Turfan sleep on wooden beds in the courtyards, but the constant watering of the ground results in swarms of mosquitoes, which torment the sleeper almost beyond endurance.

Mildred Cable, *The Gobi Desert*

Alice Mildred Cable (1878–1952), a British missionary, arrived in China in 1902. Originally assigned to Huozhou, Shanxi, she befriended Evangeline and Francesca French; the three travelled as itinerant missionaries bringing Christianity to the farthest reaches of the Gobi desert and Xinjiang.

In the eastern suburbs of Hohhot stands a rare piece of architectural history. The **Wanbuhuayanjing Pagoda** dates from the tenth century and has survived with little change, despite a series of renovations over the centuries. The pagoda is a beautiful brick and wood structure in seven storeys.

BAOTOU

Baotou, Inner Mongolia's only major industrial centre, is very much the creation of the town planners of the 1950s. It is the site of major iron, steel and coal industries. Located to the west of Hohhot and connected to it by railway, the city offers very little for the sightseer, but beyond the city are several interesting destinations.

A two-hour bus ride into the Daqing Mountains takes you to the **Wudang Monastery**. (A more expensive, and rather more comfortable, option is to hire a jeep for the day.) This Tibetan-style monastery, belonging to the Yellow Hat sect, remains an important spiritual centre for Mongolian Buddhists today. In the main halls are richly coloured murals dating from the late-18th century. The largest monastery in the region, it encompasses accommodation for monks and continues a tradition of Buddhist festivals and ceremonies, sending monks out to pray for rain when the grasslands are dry.

South of Baotou is a possible tomb-site of **Genghiz Khan**. Since he is father of the Mongolian people, this spot has become a focal point for Mongolian festivities. In spring every year, a *suduling*, very similar to the Highland Games in Scotland, is held near the tomb. Young Mongolian men gather to test their prowess in the skills of wrestling, spear-throwing and riding.

From Baotou, visits to a part of the **Ordos Desert** can be arranged. The tours take visitors to a place known as **Noisy Sands Bay** (Xiangshawan), where the sands have such a high silica content that they literally rumble when you slide across them.

THE SILK ROAD

Beyond the western fringes of China stretch the gravel and sand deserts and barren mountain ranges of Central Asia. This vast expanse of barely inhabitable land was once home to nomadic tribes and small pockets of settlers, who farmed the land wherever oasis springs watered the earth. Depending on their own military strength and organization, these tribes were sometimes able to pose a considerable threat to the border regions of the Chinese empire. In the second century BCE, the Han emperor, Wu Di—as a defensive measure against further incursions by some of the nomads—sent large expeditionary forces into Central Asia to find allies among other tribes to help him in his border campaigns. It was through such diplomatic activity and contacts that Chinese influence was extended westwards. The power of the Han dynasty brought an era of stability to those Central Asian lands—and from this balance of forces arose the opportunity for establishing that great trade route known as the Silk Road. In fact, the route from the settled lands of China to the **Karakoram Mountains**, which separate the modern borders of China's Xinjiang Uyghur Autonomous Region, Kashmir and Pakistan, was well known to a few intrepid traders of even earlier times. The Chinese love of jade, much of which comes from the Kunlun range, made the hard journey across the deserts and mountains worth the effort for the high premiums paid in the palaces of China. By the time of the Han dynasty, it was Chinese silk—prized in the noble homes of the Near East and the Roman Empire—that gave the major impetus to the development of the routes which we now call the Silk Road. The road was in fact a chain of caravan trails, reaching north across the Gobi Desert, west across the Taklamakan, then as far south as present-day India and Iran, before leading to Antioch on the eastern shores of the Mediterranean. China controlled these trade routes to the west, while drawing in great wealth.

Along with trade came travellers—and with them, ideas. The Silk Road may have seen the exchange of small but precious gems, porcelain, furs and silk, but in the long term the greater exchange was of science, religion and art. In the Han dynasty, the Silk Road brought Buddhism to China, and by the Tang dynasty, Islam, Nestorian Christianity and Zoroastrianism were to find roots in Chinese soil. The two latter faiths never flourished beyond the Tang dynasty, but Islam was to grow to be a major force in Chinese culture, particularly in the areas spanned by the Silk Road. It remains the dominant religion in Xinjiang.

The modern traveller, journeying through regions which were once part of the Silk Road, will find it easy to conjure up images of those early wandering imams and monks, bringing their faith to Central Asia's oasis towns. Large communities of Muslims continue to flourish, and vast Buddhist cave shrines mark the passage out from China to the beginning of the Taklamakan Desert. But it should not be forgotten that it was along this route that the Chinese inventions of the compass, gunpowder and paper were carried westwards—inventions which were eventually to unleash the forces which would bring about the demise of the Silk Road. Advances in navigation first made by the Arabs, and later by the Iberian nations of Spain and Portugal, were to lead to a flourishing maritime trade with China. And it was this opening of the sea routes that in turn brought ruin to the oasis kingdoms and cities built on the wealth of the caravanserai.

Today, a journey along the entire length of the Silk Road is more feasible than at any other time since the 1930s. Within China, between Xi'an and Kashgar, scores of cities, towns and counties directly on the Silk Road have opened up to foreign travel. Crossings between China and Kazakhstan and Kyrgyzstan are now possible, and beyond, travel into Uzbekistan is possible. Land crossings between Turkmenistan and Iran are now also feasible with valid visas, making an unbroken overland odyssey from Turkey available to the intrepid.

FROM XI'AN TO LANZHOU

Xi'an (*see also* page 84), formerly Chang'an, marked the traditional starting point of the Silk Road in the journey to the west. Modern Xi'an, now a provincial capital, does not have the imperial trappings of its grand past but still holds remainders of its former glory. The **Shaanxi Provincial Museum** has many treasures of Silk Road days—Tang figurines depicting hook-nosed merchants from Western Asia, stelae with Nestorian Christian inscriptions, and coins from as far afield as Greece.

In tracing the Silk Road, many modern travellers choose to fly or take the direct train from Xi'an to Lanzhou, the capital of Gansu Province and the best place to begin an organized tour of the Silk Road. However, for the visitor with time to spare, a series of train and bus trips between the two cities is recommended because of the wealth of archaeological sites which can be visited en route. The journey yields as many side-trips as the traveller can afford—to the small towns along the route to Lanzhou, and to the southern grasslands of Gansu where Tibetan and Mongolian communities of herders live interspersed with the Hui (Chinese Muslim) people.

[Above] *Uyghur worshippers leave Kashgar's Idkah Mosque in southwest Xinjiang.* (Right) *Tashkurgan's stone fort, romantically situated in China's High Pamirs. [Jeremy Tredinnick x2]*

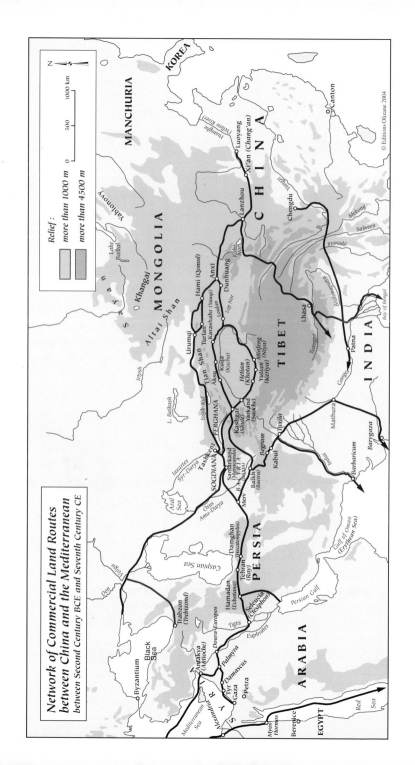

Network of Commercial Land Routes
between China and the Mediterranean
between Second Century BCE and Seventh Century CE

Relief :
more than 1000 m
more than 4500 m

© Editions Olizane 2004

Xianyang is the site of the capital of the Qin dynasty which unified China in 221 BCE. The Afang palace of the first emperor has been excavated, but little now remains. We are left only with the descriptions of its grandeur recorded in the *Shi Ji*, a history compiled in the Han dynasty. It is said that the megalomaniac Qin emperor had replicas of the palaces of his defeated rivals built within his own palace, and brought artefacts from the conquered states to be used in his own household. Indeed, in the excavations at Xianyang, coins from the distant southern state of Chu were uncovered.

West of Xi'an lies **Baoji**, the home of the early Zhou dynasty culture. For those interested in the extraordinary bronzes of this era, the **Baoji Bronze Culture Museum** should be visited.

A once important city for Silk Road traders, Baoji is now a major rail junction. The city, set on the banks of the River Wei, has a quiet and prosperous air. Its most striking sight is the Ming dynasty **Jintai Monastery**, built high on a hill overlooking the city and the surrounding mountains. In the monastery is a stele carved in the calligraphy of the famous scholar-general Cao Cao, a prominent military leader during the Three Kingdoms period. This general was the ruler of the state of Wei from 220 to 265, and is famous for his poetry as well as his calligraphy. The inscription in the Jintai Monastery is in the 'melon-skin' style (and barely legible even to the Chinese).

Tianshui is the first town you reach after crossing the border between Shaanxi and Gansu provinces. Famous for its carved lacquerware, Tianshui was the birthplace of Li Guang, the famous 'Flying General' of the Western Han dynasty. He was sent by his emperor to fight the Huns (Xiongnu) of Central Asia, and helped bring peace and prosperity to the region. His tomb, where only his possessions could be buried after his death in battle, can still be visited.

Just beyond the city of Tianshui is the major Buddhist cave complex of **Maijishan**. The name, which means 'Wheat Rick Mountain', refers to the shape of the small mountain, which rises in a blunt-ended cone of soft yellow stone. Maijishan is one of the five most important Buddhist cave centres, the others being Yungang in Datong, Longmen at Luoyang, the great Mogao caves at Dunhuang (also situated in Gansu), and Dazu in Sichuan (*see* also pages 94, 196, 225). Many of the caves are almost inaccessible, but the outer face of the mountain is carved with magnificent Buddha images. The interior of the caves is decorated with frescoes and clay statues.

A few miles to the north of Maijishan rises **Xianren Cliff** (Immortal Cliff). Many of the carvings here date back to the fifth century. Within the caves there is an eclectic mix of statues: Buddhist and Taoist figures as well as Confucian sages stand side by side.

Northwest of Tianshui, on the northern bank of the River Wei, stands a whole complex of caves and temples. These caves, situated in Wushan County, are little visited and floods sometimes cut off access. On one cliff face, known as **Lashao Temple**, are carved the three figures of the Sakyamuni Buddha and his two disciples. The Buddha is sitting serenely in the lotus position and his two disciples stand on either side, holding lotus blossoms. These carvings were originally painted and some of the colours still remain. Beneath the Buddha's feet is a series of bas-reliefs featuring strange animals, some of which bear a close resemblance to the carved lions seen in Persian sculpture.

Sprawling along the banks of the Yellow River, **Lanzhou**, the capital of Gansu Province, is an industrial centre for the northwest. The city's main attractions are the treasures in the **Gansu Provincial Museum**. It is in this museum that the visitor can find the famous cast-bronze flying horse which was sent on a cultural tour of major world capitals in the 1970s. The horse, a magnificent representation of the new breed of horses that had been brought along the Silk Road from Ferghana (Uzbekistan) to the Han court of China, dates from the second century. The Ferghana horses' superior speed and stamina made them extremely valuable. The bronze sculpture vividly portrays the speed of the Ferghana steed, with its flared nostrils, windswept mane and tail, and one of its hooves poised on the back of a flying swallow. Fine examples of Neolithic pottery, known as Yangshao ware, are also in the museum, along with Zhou ritual bronzes and a reconstruction of a Han tomb.

EXPEDITIONS FROM LANZHOU

Binglingsi is an important Buddhist cave complex dating from the fifth century and added to for the next 1,500 years. It lies upstream on the Yellow River from Liujiaxia Dam, which is 70 kilometres (43 miles) southwest of Lanzhou. Between spring and autumn, when the water level of the river is high enough, you can get to it by taking a two-hour boat ride from the dam. The hundreds of caves with their statues and wall paintings depict the life and works of Buddha and his disciples. Some of the carvings show Indian influences. When the dam was built, the lower-level caves were submerged, although the best statuary was saved and moved to higher sites.

(Preceding pages) *Dunhuang's Mogao Caves complex, the greatest repository of Buddhist cave art in China; and the nearby Mingsha sand dunes—China is fighting a constant battle against the encroachment of the desert on to farmland in its northwest region, where the continual movement of sand has swallowed several ancient cities, such as Loulan and Niya, which once thrived on the Silk Road. [Wong How Man]*

Labrang Monastery is one of the most important Tibetan Yellow Hat Sect monasteries in China. Situated southwest of Binglingsi, in the small town of Xiahe, it is the focal point of the local Tibetan community. Labrang was founded in 1709 under the patronage of the Qing Emperor Kangxi. It became an important centre of worship and religious instruction due to the continued benefaction of the Qing emperors, who were much attracted to the Buddhist faith. Labrang is also the home of numerous incarnate lamas. The sprawling complex now houses 1,000 monks, but previously it had more than 4,000. Originally, too, it owned most of the surrounding farmland, but the communist regime confiscated the land and destroyed part of the monastery. Since the lamasery is an important spiritual site, it maintains the traditional calendar of Buddhist festivals. It is likely that visitors will see part of the religious life of the lamasery and, if lucky, may even see one of the great debates held publicly by the lamas. At New Year, the lamas perform demon mask dances to usher in good fortune for the coming year.

Xiahe itself offers a glimpse into a semi-nomadic Tibetan community which lives by farming and herding. Many of the small traders in the town are Muslim, though they sell the paraphernalia associated with Tibetan lamaism such as prayer wheels and sutras.

On the road to Labrang lies the small town of **Linxia**, the capital of the Hui Autonomous Prefecture. The Hui people are Chinese Muslims, whose ancestors adopted the faith during the Tang dynasty when Arab and Central Asian merchants travelled to, or even settled in, China. As a reminder of the region's Arab connections, the tomb of an Arab missionary stands on the summit of a local hill. In Chinese, the imam was known as Han Zeling, but his Arab name is believed to have been Hamuzeli. The Dongxiang minority people also live in this area. They too are Muslims, like the Hui, but their bright blue eyes and aquiline noses betray more Western antecedents. Linxia is a lively town with a muted Han Chinese presence. Numerous teahouses, restaurants and small shops line the narrow streets. Here you can try sanxiangcha (three-flavoured tea), a delicious blend of green tea, rock sugar and 'dragon eyes' (the fruit known most widely as 'longan'), or browse among the carpets, prayer mats, knives and Tibetan jewellery offered for sale. From the top of Wanshouguan, a Taoist temple built in the Ming dynasty and recently restored, there is a sweeping view of the town's 20-odd mosques.

From Lanzhou to Urumqi

After leaving Lanzhou, the inhospitable nature of the old Silk Road and surrounding landscape becomes increasingly evident. To the south lie the barren slopes of the Qilian range; to the north, the Gobi Desert stretches beyond the western limits of the

Great Wall. The winds in this region are fierce. Crops are grown in the crevices of flat stones laid out across the fields to keep the earth from blowing away. Except where streams and springs give life to patches of vegetation, the land is bone-dry. With a little imagination, the modern traveller can readily understand the difficulties faced by the Silk Road merchants who travelled by foot with a camel caravan. Today, train and bus make the journey far easier.

After the railway leaves Lanzhou, it turns northwestwards towards **Wuwei**, a city in the Gansu or Hexi Corridor. It was at Wuwei that the famed Flying Horse of Gansu was discovered. Continuing westwards, the track reaches **Jiayuguan**, the pass which marks the western limit of the Ming Great Wall (*see* special section on the Great Wall page 299). Many people break their train journey here to see the Ming fortress, built to guard the strategic pass between the Qilian Mountains to the south and the Black Mountains to the north. It is also here that some of the earliest segments of the Great Wall can be seen. Much of the wall, which has crumbled to an undulating earth mound, dates back to the Han dynasty and bears no resemblance to the Ming sections north of Beijing.

In a barren area on the outer limits of the Gobi, 20 kilometres (12.4 miles) northeast of Jiayuguan, are 1,400 tombs dating back to between the Wei and Jin Dynasties (220–420). Two of the tombs, excavated in 1972, are open to the public and have been curiously named the Wei-Jin Art Gallery. Positioned deep in the earth at the bottom of a steep set of stone steps, this is the largest subterranean "art gallery" in the world, containing colourful murals depicting routine life in those days.

From Jiayuguan, the journey to **Dunhuang** is usually by bus or train—a new rail link now runs right through to Dunhuang from the main line at Liuyuan. However, visitors on a tighter schedule fly in, as Dunhuang does have an airport.

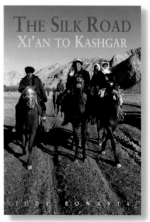

The Buddhist caves located at **Mogao**, which is served by minibuses from Dunhuang, are found in hills 25 kilometres (16 miles) away. There are approximately 2,100 carvings. Although the caves were first worked in the fourth century, no carvings from that era have survived intact. The earliest caves that can be seen date from the fifth century. Monks and craftsmen lived and worked in Dunhuang for more than four centuries, and the caves reflect the changes of style during that period.

A mural from the Mogao Grottoes, Dunhuang.

Besides carvings, the murals of Dunhuang are one of the Silk Road's most impressive landmarks. There are over 45,000 square metres of mural painting. The early wall paintings, dating from the Northern Wei dynasty, take their theme from the Jataka stories of Buddha's life. The execution is dynamic, with swirling clouds and apsaras (Buddhist angels) trailing floating ribbons. This was to give way later, during the Sui dynasty, to paintings which show a greater stillness of composition. These paintings include fewer illustrations from the Jataka tales and more serene iconographic Buddha and Bodhisattva figures.

In the early 1900s, a succession of orientalists came and carried away thousands of the paintings and documents stored in the caves, among whom were Sir Aurel Stein (whose collection can be seen in the British Museum in London and the National Museum in New Delhi) Paul Pelliot (his finds are in Paris' Musée Guimet and Bibliothèque Nationale) and Albert von Le Coq (Museum für Indische Kunst, Berlin).

The caves lie behind and below the huge **Mingsha Sand Dunes**, for many an equally attractive site (visitors can climb them, slide down them on snowboards, even paraglide over them), and close to the caves is a small, sickle-shaped lake, the **Crescent Moon Pool**, mysteriously set amidst the encroaching dunes.

Northwest of Dunhuang, the railway crosses into the **Xinjiang Uyghur Autonomous Region**, an extensive territory sharing international boundaries with India, Pakistan, Afghanistan, Tajikistan, Kyrgyzstan, Kazakhstan, Russia and Mongolia. The oasis town of **Turpan** (pronounced *Tulufan* in Chinese), on the railway line to Urumqi, is an extraordinary contrast to the barren gravel desert on all sides. Where the line of fields and trees ends, the desert begins with a brutal abruptness. An important way-station on the northern section of the Silk Road, the Turpan oasis was a centre of Buddhism in the early centuries AD. The Uyghurs migrated to and took over the Turfan region in the ninth century and were primarily Buddhist (with some Nestorian

Christians and followers of Manichaeanism) but converted in the 13th and 14th centuries under pressure from the Islamic invasions that came from southern Xinjiang.

Turpan, lying in a depression well below sea level, has extremes of temperature which can swing from a high of 43°C (109°F) in summer to a low of -32°C (-26°F) in winter. The water for the Turpan oasis comes from a system of underground channels called *karez* which bring the snow melt from the nearby Tianshan range. This system distributes water from the base of the mountains along channels that slope less than the geographical depression, thus ensuring that the water flows closer to the ground by the time it reaches the town. Some historians believe this ancient system (as old as 2,000 years) may have been introduced to the Turpan region from Persia where similar irrigation systems are in use. In the fields surrounding Turpan are grown sweet grapes and the famous Hami melon. Some of the grape harvest is dried in the open in the town (Turpan's seedless white raisins are exported). Besides raisins, the brightly coloured fabrics worn by Uyghur women and Muslim caps are also found in the main market of the town. Small restaurants on either side of the market serve mutton kebabs and rice pilaf, as well as pastries and noodles.

One of the city's most famous sights is the **Emin Minaret** at the Suleiman Mosque, founded in the late 18th century. This circular minaret, built in the Afghan style of unglazed mudbricks arranged in bold geometric patterns, is much photographed.

Beyond the city rise the **Flaming Mountains**, whose deep-red rocks absorb the sun's heat and create furnace-like temperatures. Travellers walking in the mountains have found the soles of their shoes melting in the heat. Set amidst these mountains is the Buddhist cave centre of **Bezeklik**. The complex is also known, like many others on the Silk Road, as Thousand Buddha Caves. Carved between the fifth and 14th centuries, they have been very badly damaged, but some fine Tang frescoes have survived.

Turpan is close to the ruins of two ancient cities which were abandoned when trade along the Silk Road fell into decline at the end of the Yuan dynasty. **Gaochang** (Karakhoja) was a first-century walled city of which very little now remains save for massive crumbling walls and foundations. The cemetery of Gaochang, known as **Astana**, has had some of its tombs excavated, one of which—from the Tang dynasty—contains fine murals. The smaller abandoned city of **Jiaohe** (Yarkhoto) has an incredible setting on the top of a cliff, an island at the confluence of two rivers.

Urumqi, capital of the Xinjiang Uyghur Autonomous Region, is an important transportation hub for modern travellers. Xinjiang has 11 airports, the highest number for any region in China, and so travellers can choose to reach the more remote destinations by air in preference to road journeys, which can be dusty, hot and tiring, not to mention time-consuming. A railway line skirts the north of the Taklamakan Desert to Kashgar (known as Kashi in Chinese), which is the westernmost city within China's borders. Kashgar is the starting point for the journey along the Karakoram Highway to Pakistan. Two separate passes, the Torugart and Irkeshtam, lead to the Kyrgyz Republic.

The city of Urumqi is modern and, by and large, lacking in attractive architecture. In recent years it has jumped on the skyscraper bandwagon, but it has also smartened up its public parks and rejuvenated its Erdaoqiao Market bazaar area. Though Urumqi may have a uniformity common to most major Chinese cities, its inhabitants are widely dissimilar. The majority of the people in Xinjiang are Uyghurs and Kazakhs. Both are Muslims, but they are also well known for being heavy drinkers, and evenings out can be raucous affairs. Within the city all ethnic groups wear similar clothing, but you will still see many Uyghur men wearing the *dopa* skull cap. A visit to the new **Xinjiang Uyghur Autonomous Region Museum** is essential; it has an important collection featuring the region's early history and material on the ethnic minorities, including extraordinary mummified corpses from Xinjiang's ancient desert graves.

EXPEDITIONS FROM URUMQI

The most popular, and perhaps the most overrated of expeditions, is to the Tien Shan (Heavenly Mountains) and Tianchi (Heaven Lake). The journey up into the cool alpine meadows of the Tien Shan is a welcome relief after the heat of the desert, but the trip is crowded on weekends and holidays, so be warned. Cruises on the lake, which lies some 1,900 metres (6,300 feet) above sea level, are available.

The day trip to **Nan Shan** (Southern Mountains) is a more attractive alternative, since fewer people make the journey. The Kazakh people graze their flocks of sheep on the summer pasture here from May through mid September. During summertime the rich pastureland is dotted with the felt yurts favoured by the Kazakh. They enjoy equestrian sports and are often quite happy to put on a display of local polo. Tour group visitors are usually invited into the local yurt for a meal of home-baked bread, cheese and mutton kebabs.

The Urumqi-Almaty railway is an unusual but interesting way to enter Central Asia from China—the journey takes 40 hours. Travellers with valid Kazakh visas can buy tickets in Urumqi.

Riders show off their steeds at Kashgar's Livestock Market. [Kevin Bishop]

A golden eagle perches on the arm of a Kyrgyz horseman. [Wong How Man]

Rising in the Tien Shan, the Yili River gives its name to the Yili Kazakh Autonomous Prefecture, with its capital at Yining. An interesting side-trip can be made from Urumqi to **Yining** (Gulja), not so much for any Silk Road associations but because it has flourished in recent years as a result of increased trade across the Chinese-Kazakh border. The city was opened to foreign visitors only in 1990, and is accessible by either bus or plane from Urumqi. Yining is 60 kilometres (35 miles) from the international border, and still retains a frisson of Russian feel to it, even though Chinese development has seen most of the Russian architecture disappear. Kazakh herders live mainly on the grasslands surrounding the city and higher up the valley in the picturesque Narat Grasslands. As one would expect in a pastoral community, yoghurt and cheese are widely available. The Kazakhs like a hard goats' cheese called *kurut*, which is available in the markets; and yoghurt as well as a home-brewed beer made from honey and wheat are sold from ubiquitous refrigerators around the city.

FROM URUMQI TO KASHGAR

long the northern fringe of the Taklamakan on the new railway line lies **Kucha**, formerly an important trading post along the Silk Road. The old city, centred on the main mosque and bazaar, retains much of the flavour of medieval Central Asia. Small teashops serve a spicy soup of dumplings made with mutton, turnips and red peppers. The Friday market is a huge melee with donkey carts, horses and thousands of Uyghurs all involved in the selling of saddles, melons, silk, rugs, embroidered caps and other wares. Some 65 kilometres (40 miles) northwest of Kuqa, the **Kizil Thousand Buddha Caves** are located in an attractive setting on the bank of River Muzat. First hewn in the fourth century, the caves were abandoned with the spread of Islam in the 14th century. Of the 236 caves, only 75 have remained intact. The statuary has all disappeared, but strange murals depicting man-beasts, double-headed birds and Buddhist immortals remain. The chief interest here are a number of wall paintings which show a strong Indo-Hellenic influence.

Kashgar (Kashi) has a long history stretching back over 2,000 years. Situated at the foot of the Pamir Mountains, the city stands at the point where traffic along the great trade routes crossed over the high passes into what is today's Pakistan, Tajikistan and the Kyrgyz Republic and beyond. For much of the Han and Tang dynasties Kashgar was under Chinese control, but the indigenous people of the region are believed to be Indo-European in origin, now mixed with Mongol and Turkic blood. At the end of the 19th and beginning of the 20th century—during the struggle between Britain and Russia for control of Central Asia which was later referred to as the 'Great Game'—Kashgar with its foreign consulates was a listening post in the intrigues and intelligence-gathering activities of the two powers.

Despite its earlier role as a meeting point for Buddhist monks and craftsmen, the city is now thoroughly Islamic in character, although now framed by inevitable Chinese modernization. It is smaller than Urumqi and the city centre is easy to explore on foot or bicycle. Because of Kashgar's trade with Central Asia, its bazaars are full of goods from the Indian subcontinent. There is a choice of hats of every description: fur-trimmed, embroidered and plain. Silks are on sale, as are semiprecious stones and the beautiful hand-woven rugs of the region. The Sunday Bazaar is particularly exciting—colourful, lively, and seen as an occasion for all who go there; six kilometres southeast of the city the Sunday Livestock Market is the place to watch Tajik and Kyrgyz horsemen showing off their riding skills.

THE ROADS TO PAKISTAN AND KYRGYZSTAN

The Karakoram Highway route from Kashgar to the Pakistani border over the **Khunjerab Pass** is one of the most spectacular road trips in the world, crossing frozen high-altitude plateaus and cutting through the precipitous Karakoram Mountains.

As the road heads south, travellers pass through the small town of **Gez**, which has a large community of Kyrgyz people. The Kyrgyz are nomadic herders, whose women have a liking for elaborately embroidered head cloths, heavy silver jewellery, and waistcoats decorated with buttons. From Gez, the road ascends steeply and passes the two great peaks of Mount Kongur and Mount Muztagata. Around **Tashkurgan**, in the midst of the Pamir Mountains, live the colourful Tajik people. The Tajiks are pastoralists descended from Persian stock, and still wear richly hued traditional clothing, the women using buttons, tassels and silver discs to decorate their plaits.

From Tashkurgan, it is two hours by road to the Pakistan border. In earlier days, the route was extremely hazardous and entire camel caravans could be frozen to death on the passes when a snowstorm swept in. Luckily, the modern traveller on the Silk Road is better insulated against such dangers, and there's a scheduled bus service from May to November and private transport at other times—but even today it is still a journey requiring planning and involving no little sense of true adventure.

Two passes connect Kashgar with **Kyrgyzstan**, and these have become a popular land route into and out of Xinjiang. The **Torugart Pass** is the most northerly and quickest way to Naryn and Bishkek, but must be arranged through a tour agency. The **Irkeshtam Pass** leads to the town of Osh, and a weekly public bus is available. Talk of a border crossing into **Tajikistan** opening for tourists at the **Kulma Pass** near Tashkurgan keeps intrepid travellers excited, but at time of press the talk had still come to nothing.

The Silk Road

TIBET

There are many mountains in the world, but few have contained such a uniquely spiritual civilization as the Himalayas of Tibet. Tibetan history began to be recorded in the seventh century, when Buddhism took root in the country. Buddhism blended with the ancient indigenous animistic beliefs of Bon and became the core of Tibetan culture. In time the people of these mountains created a society in which monasteries acted as the centres of learning, of medicine, and ultimately of economic and political power. Thus a group of warrior tribes was transformed into a theocratic state.

Yet the peaceful doctrines of Buddhism did not always prevent the Tibetans from warring with each other, or with their neighbours. Due to the high altitude and scarce soils, farming was limited to a few river valleys, where only barley could be grown successfully. Tibet therefore could not develop a social system of settled farming communities in the manner of its Chinese neighbours to the east. The young men of Tibet could only herd, trade or join a monastery. Up until the middle of this century, the term 'monk' covered the widest possible range of character and activity. Some monks were cooks, others were the craftsmen of the brotherhood, and a chosen few were educated to become lamas—those who, in turn, transmitted Buddhist teachings and the traditions of Tibet's culture and medical knowledge to others.

The great unifier of Tibet, King Songsten Gampo, patronized the establishment of Buddhism in the seventh century, along with the development of a Tibetan script in which the scriptures themselves could be written. He also made tactical marriages to two Buddhist princesses, one Nepalese and one Chinese. The king's descendants ruled Tibet until the middle of the ninth century, when the monarchy came into conflict with the monasteries. After the last king was assassinated by a monk, rival monasteries created power bases, and the country was divided into regional spheres of influence. Tibet's earliest monasteries were controlled by rival sects, the most powerful of which were the Red Hats. In the 14th century, a scholar named Tsong Khapa founded the Yellow Hat Sect, which subsequently eclipsed the older Red Hat Sect and proved to be a force for reunification.

From the Yellow Hat Sect evolved a lineage of reincarnating master monks known as Dalai Lamas, a title meaning 'Ocean of Wisdom'. In the 17th century, during the tenure of the Fifth Dalai Lama, his ascendancy over all other lamas was established, and he was proclaimed to be the reincarnation of Chenrezi, the Bodhisattva of Compassion (the Tibetan version of India's Avalokitesvara, and China's Guanyin).

A Tibetan woman's colourful clothing is matched by the turqoise beauty of Lake Yamdrok-Yamtso to the southwest of Lhasa. [Jeremy Tredinnick]

The Fifth Dalai Lama ruled from Lhasa but brought Shigatse, the second city of Tibet, under his control by enhancing the power of that city's Yellow Hat monastery, Tashilhunpo. Tashilhunpo's abbot had been the Dalai Lama's tutor and, in honour of his wisdom, the Dalai Lama had him named the Panchen Lama, meaning 'Great Scholar'. The Panchen Lama was then proclaimed to be a reincarnation of the Amitabha Buddha, thus making his status in Shigatse unchallengeable.

In the following centuries, Tibet's theocratic government came to exercise ecclesiastical influence at the Qing court. The Qing rulers, who were Buddhists, often invited high-ranking Tibetan lamas to Beijing to teach and advise their court. However, by the late 19th century, the British in India and the Russians had become alert to the possibility of using Tibet as a pawn in their power game for control of Central Asia. This scheming in turn reminded the Qing rulers of the importance of Tibet in Chinese political concerns. In 1904, the British sent the Younghusband Expedition into Tibet to force a treaty of trade and friendship on the Tibetans. In 1910, it was China's turn to invade Tibet, seeking political concessions. The 13th Dalai Lama fled to Darjeeling and requested British aid to oust the Chinese. But it was the newly unified Chinese communist government which finally gained control of the country, sending in its own army to 'liberate' Tibet in 1950.

The traditional way of life continued until an abortive uprising in 1959. After this the 14th Dalai Lama fled with 80,000 followers over the Himalayas into India, leaving Tibet essentially under Chinese military-backed control. Over the following years several thousand monasteries were destroyed and monks, nuns and lamas were forced by their Chinese protectors to embark on productive jobs. New roads and airfields were constructed making Tibet more easily accessible from China. The 14th Dalai Lama has remained in exile, declining to return if he is allowed only to settle in Beijing.

In the 1980s the Chinese introduced a policy of limited economic autonomy and religious freedom and a programme of restoration for the monasteries was launched. At the same time more and more Han Chinese were migrating, with the result that Lhasa and Shigatse are now predominantly Chinese. Settlers are encouraged with guaranteed jobs and housing, special loans and wages higher than they would be able to earn elsewhere in the country.

The Chinese have set a high value on Tibet's strategic importance. The borders of Greater Tibet have been redrawn with whole Tibetan regions absorbed into the surrounding provinces of Qinghai, Gansu, Sichuan and Yunnan. Yet despite Chinese rule and migrations of both Han Chinese and Hui Muslims into their communities, the Tibetans retain their sense of cultural identity, though this is being continually eroded.

Tibet

It is hardly surprising that in the bleak but majestic landscapes of Tibet's highlands, the world of the spirit seems more real than the world of men. The silent landscapes of snow and ice, mountains, lakes and meadows have an unearthly beauty, inspiring veneration not only in the Tibetans for whom this beauty is a part of their everyday life, but in all those who experience it.

LHASA

Because of Lhasa's altitude, 3,500 metres (12,000 feet) above sea level, most visitors need to take it easy the first few days in order to become acclimatized to the thin air. The best way to do this is to start your itinerary with a few short outings, taking rests in between. Strolls around the city and out along the banks of the **Lhasa River** are an excellent and not too taxing introduction to life in Tibet.

Chinese influence is apparent in the sharp contrast between the old Tibetan part of Lhasa and the newer section of the city constructed since the 1960s. Clustering round the Jokhang Temple, the old district contains a web of narrow lanes and houses of rough-hewn stone, brightened with whitewashed walls and painted woodwork. The new section of the city is drabber, and is dominated by wide boulevards with housing and office blocks set well back from the road behind high compound walls.

Many Tibetans still dress in their traditional costumes—mainly because the clothes are so well adapted to the rigours of the climate. A garment common to both men and women is the *chuba*, a thick belted coat made from sheepskin. In winter the men wear felt or fur hats. The women wear their hair in braids or tucked under coloured scarves, and—on special occasions—elaborate headdresses. Their long dresses are usually black, brown or blue in colour, but the working pinafores of woven stripes (only worn by the married women of Central Tibet) are brightly coloured.

The two great sights of Lhasa are the Jokhang Temple and the Potala Palace. The **Jokhang Temple** is the home of the most precious Buddha image the country possesses—the Sakyamuni Buddha, brought from China by the Tang dynasty princess Wen Cheng, who was married to the great King Songsten Gampo. In the main hall of the temple is a set of murals showing the arrival of Princess Wen Cheng in Tibet. The Jokhang is the most important site of pilgrimage in Tibet, and worshippers throng its halls and shrines. It is customary for them to circumambulate, in a clockwise direction, round the Holy of Holies, which contains the gilded and bejewelled statue of Sakyamuni. The roof of the Jokhang can also be visited.

Built on a hill overlooking the city, the **Potala Palace** is Tibet's best-known landmark. Once the spiritual and temporal palace of the Dalai Lama, it is now a

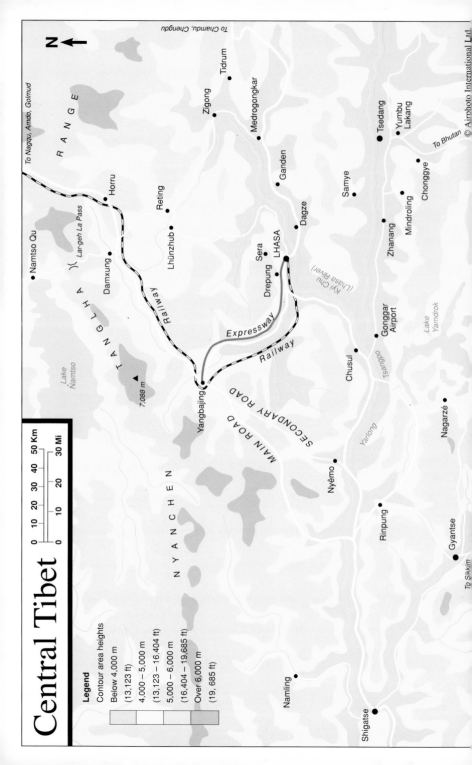

Central Tibet

© Airphoto International Ltd.

Legend

Contour area heights

Below 4,000 m
(13,123 ft)

4,000 – 5,000 m
(13,123 – 16,404 ft)

5,000 – 6,000 m
(16,404 – 19,685 ft)

Over 6,000 m
(19, 685 ft)

Scale: 0 10 20 30 40 50 Km / 0 10 20 30 Mi

N

To Nagqu, Amdo, Golmud

To Chamdu, Chengdu

To Bhutan

To Sikkim

TANGLHA RANGE

NYANCHEN

Namtso Qu

Lake Namtso

Lar-geh La Pass

Damxung

Horru

Reting

Lhünzhub

7,088 m

Railway

Yangbajing

Expressway

Sera
Drepung
LHASA

Dagze

Ganden

Zigong

Tidrum

Medrogongkar

Samye

Kyi Chu (Lhasa River)

Railway

MAIN ROAD

SECONDARY ROAD

Chusul

Gonggar Airport

Zhanang

Mindroling

Chonggye

Tsedang

Yumbu Lakang

Lake Yamdrok

Tsangpo

Yarlong

Nagarzé

Nyêmo

Rinpung

Gyantse

Namling

Shigatse

museum with shrines and chapels maintained by monks. The Potala has two sections, known as the White and Red Palaces. The White Palace, built in 1653, rises in terraces to the central Red Palace, built in 1693, which is crowned with an ornate gilded copper roof. Inside the Potala, most of which is off-limits to visitors, there are open chapels and galleries which have fascinating wall paintings. The apartments of the 13th and 14th Dalai Lamas are open to visitors. The innermost room of the 14th Dalai Lama's apartment is left exactly as it was on the day of his flight to India in 1959. Visitors may also see the tomb of the 13th Dalai Lama, which consists of a huge stupa.

A walk around the old section of Lhasa is full of discoveries: small temples being restored and lovingly decorated, street stalls selling anything from snacks to daggers, prayer flags fluttering above walls, and glimpses into the courtyards of Tibetan homes. At the heart of this section is the **Barkhor pilgrim path**, the street encircling the Jokhang Temple. As pilgrims are constantly walking around it in a clockwise direction (this is true of all Buddhist sites in Tibet), it is wise to follow suit in order not to offend or collide with them. On the Barkhor, devout pilgrims often make the circuit in a series of full-length body prostrations.

Southeast of the Barkhor Pilgrim Path is the **Muslim Quarter** of Lhasa, which has a mosque and *halal* restaurants. The **Tibetan Hospital of Traditional Medicine** (Mentsikhang) makes a fascinating visit for those interested in herbal remedies and their history. Traditional medicine was once taught in the monasteries, the most famous of which was the old medical college on the summit of Chokpori Hill in Lhasa. It was reduced to rubble by the Chinese army in 1959, and a huge television antenna was erected on the site. Religious pilgrims still circumambulate the hill, which has many beautiful carvings, paintings and holy sites around its slopes.

Tibetan carpets, with their Buddhist motifs, are extremely attractive, and one can watch them being made at the **Lhasa Carpet Factory**. Tibetan performing arts are being revived, and the **School of Tibetan Performing Arts**, founded in 1980 as a gesture of Chinese tolerance, allows foreign visitors to attend music and opera rehearsals.

After years of closure, small city temples are now functioning. The **Ramoche Temple** in the north of the city, and the cave temple of **Palalubu** at the foot of Chokpori, are open to foreign visitors. Less frequently visited are the monasteries of **Chomoling**, **Muru Ningba**, **Tengyeling** and **Ani Gonpa**. The last is Lhasa's only nunnery and worth a visit.

Travellers exploring the city should make time for an outing to **Gumolingka Island** in the Lhasa River—a favourite summer picnic place for Tibetans. Tibetans are generally friendly and welcoming and, in their love of open-air picnics, can show zealous hospitality. Foreign travellers have been known to reel back to their hotels in a stupor after generous (and unrefusable) refills of local liquor.

You can also visit the old summer palace of the Dalai Lama, the **Norbulingka** (Jewel Park). The palace lies just southwest of the the Lhasa Hotel (formerly the Holiday Inn) in the west of the city. It was built by the Seventh Dalai Lama as a summer retreat and has fine palaces, gardens, ponds and pavilions. Within a five-minute walk of the Lhasa Hotel is the Tibet Museum which houses a remarkably rich collection of Tibetan artefacts. Despite its emphasis on the historic relationship between China and Tibet, the museum's well laid-out series of galleries introduce different aspects of Tibetan culture. These include some rarely seen before texts on Tibetan medicine, Chinese and Tibetan documents from the Yuan, Ming and Qing periods and a number of exquisite Buddha images.

Set against the bare hillside of Mount Gephel Utse, on the western outskirts of Lhasa, the **Drepung Monastery** was once the largest and the wealthiest in Tibet. A Yellow Hat foundation, the monastery was served by senior monks who were instrumental in the training of Dalai Lamas and who specialized in esoteric psychic practices. It was also the home of the Nechung, the State Oracle who, in trance, advised the Dalai Lama on important decisions. Drepung was divided into four Tantric Colleges, each of which had its own special field of learning. In the chanting hall of the **Loseling College**, there is a model doll of the State Oracle in the regalia worn for prophecy. The chanting hall of the **Ngapa College** is also worth a visit—on its red doors are beautiful gold drawings depicting the history of the Dalai and Panchen Lamas. If there is chanting going on, visitors are usually still allowed to stay as long as they walk round the edge clockwise and refrain from making any noise.

On the northern outskirts of Lhasa lies **Sera Monastery**, a Yellow Hat Sect monastery which was once rival to the Drepung. Set against Tatipu Hill, Sera had three Tantric Colleges which were famous for their Bon tradition of occult teaching. Monks have returned to Sera and can be seen at prayer in their deep red robes and distinctive yellow hats which sweep upwards like a curved shell over their forehead. Worth looking for is the image of the horse-headed god in the **Sera Je College** chanting hall. The treasure of the monastery is the gilded Chenrezi image, the Bodhisattva of Compassion, of whom all Dalai Lamas are said to be incarnations. The Chenrezi image is in the **Tsokchen College** chanting hall. Be sure to visit Sera Monastery in the afternoons to catch the daily ritual of "debating monks". Sera is considered to be the most intellectually rigorous of the great monasteries and part of a monk's training is debating. Each afternoon the debating courtyard is a sea of maroon robes as monks pair off and engage in heated discussions relating to esoteric teachings.

The **Droma Lhakang Temple** lies 27 kilometres (17 miles) south of Lhasa. It is dedicated to the Indian Tantric master, Atisha, who came to Tibet in the 11th century. Atisha settled in Tibet to teach, and he was instrumental in the revival of Buddhism after two centuries of fighting and destruction which followed the overthrow of the royal family in the ninth century. The temple has many images of the Tibetan goddess, Tara, who was the guardian deity of Atisha. Tara is said to have been a princess who, when challenged by monks saying that a woman could never achieve enlightenment, set out to prove them wrong. When Tara did achieve enlightenment, she was deified. It is easy to identify her image, since it is usually depicted in white or green.

A family makes a spiritual outing to the Potala Palace.

To the east of Lhasa, 70 kilometres (45 miles) distant, is the Yellow Hat Sect monastery, **Ganden**. Once Tibet's third largest religious community after Drepung and Sera, it was destroyed by the Chinese army in 1959 but was later rebuilt and is now in active use.

GYANTSE

The traveller in Tibet often visits Gyantse on the way to Shigatse. Gyantse gives the impression today of being a small and inconsequential city, but that was not always so. Commanding the junction of two main caravan routes, one to India and the other to Nepal, the fortified city was of strategic and military importance and of great wealth. Until the early part of this century, Gyantse was Tibet's third city and a important gathering-point for nomads, who would come to sell their wool for export.

The wealth of the city was manifested in the foundation of **Palkhor Monastery**, built in the 14th century. The monastery has been badly damaged, but on no account should it be passed by. Its Nepalese-style stupa with painted eyes is of great interest. Known as the **Kumbum**, meaning 'Place of a Thousand Images', the stupa has a gilded tower topped by a parasol wrought in filigreed metal. The monastery itself has a vast wall, on which large *tangkas*—Buddhist paintings on silk—are hung in the open air during the summer months.

Gyantse's 14th-century fortress, or *dzong*, was damaged by British artillery in 1904, during the Younghusband Expedition. The fortress was further damaged by Chinese troops in the 1960s, but still retains rare and magnificent murals painted in the Nepalese Newari style. Whereas both Lhasa and Shigatse have undergone extensive modernization, Gyantse remains refreshingly traditional; a rather dusty Tibetan town that invites exploration by the visitor.

SHIGATSE

Shigatse is set in the valley of the country's major river, the **Yarlong Tsangpo**. This river is better known by its Indian name, the Brahmaputra, for it flows from the western mountains of Tibet down through India to the Bay of Bengal. Near Shigatse, the broad Yarlong Tsangpo waters farm fields around the city.

The journey to Shigatse from Lhasa is usually made by a direct route along the Yarlong Tsangpo River, where the road is cut dramatically from cliffs alongside the rushing waters. An alternative southern route, filled with grand vistas, passes Yamdrok Yamtso Lake and Gyantse. Finally, a long, difficult northern route, rarely travelled, traverses the breathtaking grasslands and bleak terrain of the high plateau. Many travellers visit Shigatse by one route and return to Lhasa by another.

Shigatse once rivalled Lhasa for the political and spiritual control of Tibet. It was a centre of monastic learning, and had its own noble families, who used their wealth to found monasteries and thus create power bases. The city was dominated by the Red Hat Sect until the time of the Fifth Dalai Lama who, with the backing of a Mongolian warlord, managed to subdue rival sects and unite the country under the leadership of the Yellow Hat Sect. The Panchen Lama, abbot of **Tashilhunpo Monastery**, reinforced the rule of the Dalai Lama from Lhasa.

Perhaps because the Panchen Lama at the time—the tenth—became the 'guest' of the Chinese in Beijing in the 1960s, Tashilhunpo was spared the worst of the excesses of the Cultural Revolution. It has now emerged once more as an active centre of worship and teaching. A Yellow Hat order, Tashilhunpo was founded in the 15th century, but it came to pre-eminence in the 17th century with the naming of its abbot as the first Panchen Lama. The sixth Panchen Lama is considered to be the greatest.

Tashilhunpo is a beautiful monastery, for it rises in stately terraces to a central gilded roof with decorated eaves and finials. Its distinctive rose-coloured walls are inset with dark wooden windows that are brightened with whitewashed borders. The monastery still practises the art of making *mandalas* (abstract meditation pictures) of coloured sands. Its courtyard has a high *thangka* wall, on which the huge coloured pictures are unfurled in the sun during festivals.

Visitors can view the **Panchen Lama's Palace**, which remains uninhabited. In the palace is a temple containing the tomb of the fourth Panchen Lama; it has a stupa wrought in gold and precious stones. On the upper level of the temple hang embroidered *thangkas* made for the monastery in Hangzhou in the 1920s. Of special interest are: the Panchen Lama's throne displayed in the main chanting hall; the sutra hall where the Buddhist canon (scripture) is kept; the 20th-century statues of the Maitreya Buddha made in gold, copper and brass; and the roof with its chapels.

Travellers can join worshippers on a walk back to Shigatse from the monastery on a pilgrim path (again, the walk has to be done in this direction, since the route is clockwise).

Twenty-two kilometres (14 miles) south of the city is **Shalu Monastery**, a Red Hat Sect monastery founded in the 11th century. The original buildings were demolished by an earthquake, and the present structure dates from the 14th century, when it was rebuilt in Mongolian style. Its most famous abbot was Butön, who was a clever administrator and a brilliant historian of Buddhism. The monastery was celebrated for its occult training, and still preserves outstanding murals, especially huge, floor-to-ceiling *mandalas*.

Tibet

FROM SHIGATSE TO NEPAL

From Shigatse, there is a route to Nepal which is highly recommended for adventure travel. Despite the lack of comfort on the journey, this route is popular because of the breathtaking contrasts of scenery visible from the road. The traveller passes through upland river meadows and dun-coloured deserts, crosses passes offering spectacular vistas of the Himalayan peaks, and drops down into the warmer forest glades of Tibet's border with Nepal. The trip also offers a chance to see more off-the-beaten-track monasteries and villages. There are places for food and lodgings on the way.

A new bus service between Lhasa and Kathmandu started up in the spring of 2005, but not without some teething pains in the first few months. The direct service is scheduled to make a round trip once per week, departing Kathmandu on Tuesdays and Fridays. However, travellers going from Kathmandu to Lhasa using this service should try to sort out their visas one week or more in advance.

A one-month visa for Nepal can be obtained in one working day from the Nepalese consulate in Lhasa. The consulate is also able to give up-to-date information on the condition of the road to Nepal. Now that tours are conducted on this route, independent travellers are advised to organize their transport well in advance since it may not be easy to find at short notice. It is possible to hire a jeep with driver from Shigatse to the border. Two days after setting out from Shigatse the traveller can expect to reach Zhangmu, where the border crossing may be made. Once over the border, a variety of onward transportation to Kathmandu will be waiting for the traveller. Depending on the state of the roads, the final lap of the journey to Kathmandu can be done in about eight hours. From late June to September, the rainy season, the roads can be treacherous and certainly time-consuming to travel on. Travelling from Lhasa to Nepal is said to be less strenuous than vice versa, since the rapid change in altitude on the ascent to Lhasa can cause great fatigue and dizziness. Those already acclimatized to Lhasa's altitude will find the descent more comfortable.

West of Shigatse stand the almost unearthly walls of **Sakya Monastery**. Its name means 'tawny soil', and its massive windowless walls rise from the earth like an enormous abstract painting of grey and maroon, with a single white-and-yellow stripe breaking the colour change. It was once the leading Red Hat Sect monastery of the region and enjoyed Mongolian patronage during the Yuan dynasty, when one of its abbots went to the court of Kublai Khan to convert the emperor. Kublai Khan made the monastery the centre of power in Tibet during his reign. The monastery has suffered damage, but sections of the 13th-century building can still be seen.

Tashilhunpo Monastery, Shigatse.

On the road to Nepal, a detour can take the traveller to the base camp of Mount Everest, at a tiny monastery site called Rongbuk. If you decide to trek here, you must do so only after careful preparation, with enough food for ten days and adequate sleeping and cooking equipment.

North of **Nyalam**, on the road to Nepal, is a cave where the eccentric Buddhist saint and poet, Milarepa, spent much of his life. He is famous for his severe asceticism, acts of compassion and wild songs of poetry. The cave is close to a monastery dedicated to Milarepa, which was destroyed in the Cultural Revolution, but now restored by craftsmen and artists brought in from Nepal to help.

The last Tibetan town before crossing the border is **Zhangmu**, built steeply on the hillsides.

WHEN TO VISIT TIBET

The high altitude and general dry atmosphere create some exacting conditions for visitors—some of the highest UV rates in the world and frequently windy conditions which can chap the skin. Travellers also should think seriously before travelling in the colder months. By late February and early March it starts to get warm during the day, and the Tibetan spring can be quite lovely. The summer is the most popular tourist season, when visitors often have a chance to observe Tibetan festivals and celebrations—of either a religious or sporting kind. Keep an ear to the ground for news of Tibetan horse races, wrestling matches and drinking sessions, which take place throughout the warmer months. Rain falls intermittently through June to September in southern Tibet. The Tibetan lunar New Year falls in January or February. Although it is cold then, it does provide a wonderful opportunity to enjoy a week of archery contests, religious dances and other ceremonies. The last day of the old year sees a dance by lamas in masks; this is when evil influences are driven out to usher in an auspicious New Year.

Winter is actually a good time to visit Lhasa as the city becomes a centre for pilgrimage for Tibetan nomads from across the expanse of "Greater Tibet" (including Amdo Tibetans from Qinghai and Gansu provinces and the Khampa of Sichuan and Yunnan provinces). The temples are full to overflowing with magnificently dressed men and women who flock to Lhasa to fulfil a lifelong wish that is held dear by Tibetans everywhere.

THE LAND OF THE BLUE POPPY

ext day we ascended the valley which is dominated by the highest peak in this part of the range, a ponderous blunt-headed buttress of dark rock, where snow lies in the gullies all the year round, though the glaciers have long since disappeared.

At first we followed the flower-girt stream which now wandered with divided waters over a flat sandy channel, starred with red and white saxifrage, and anon rushed noisily between bush-clad gravel banks where tall yellow poppies nodded to us as we passed. Presently, leaving the stream and ploughing knee-deep through Rhododendron we began to climb more steeply over very uneven hummocky country, interrupted here and there by grassy alps, where numbers of yaks were browsing. The black tents of the herdsmen were visible at the foot of the slope just across the stream…

…Presently shrubs grew more scattered and finally died out. Masses of pale-grey rock lay in disordered heaps. Small level pockets of sand occurred here and there along the stream, and before us the stony ground rose steeply in every direction, barren and forbidding. We were again in the land of the blue poppy.

Of this magnificent plant (Meconopsis speciosa) I will give some details. One specimen I noted was 20 inches high, crowned with 29 flowers and 14 ripening capsules above, with 5 buds below—48 flowers in all. Indeed the plant seemed to go on throughout the summer unfurling flower after flower out of nowhere—like a Japanese pith blossom thrown into water—for the stem is hollow and the root shallow. Another 8 bore fruits, 15 flowers and 5 buds. But for a certain perkiness of the stiff prickly stem, which refuses any gracefulness of arrangement to the crossed raceme, and the absence of foliage amongst the blooms, these great azure-blue flowers, massed with gold in the centre, would be the most beautiful I have seen. The Cambridge blue poppy is, moreover, unique amongst the dozen species of poppy-wort known to me from this region, in being sweetly scented. On one scree I counted no less than 40 of these magnificent plants within a space of a few square yards.

Frank Kingdon-Ward, *Himalayan Enchantment, An Anthology*, 1990

(Left) *Rongbuk Monastery, watched over by Chomolungma, Goddess Mother of the World, aka Mount Everest.* (Top) *The multi-tiered Kumbum stupa in Gyantse.* (Above) *Pilgrims walk and prostrate their way around the Jokhang Temple in Lhasa.* [Jeremy Tredinnick x3]

SICHUAN

The vast inland province of Sichuan in southwest China is shaped like a deep dish, with a lowland river plain wedged within a serrated rim of towering mountains. To the west the foothills of the Himalayas jut skywards in snowy chains, and to the north the deep-brown folds of the Longmen range separate Sichuan from the neighbouring province of Shaanxi. To the east, the turbulent Yangzi and its tributaries flow between the deep cuts of mountain ranges which sweep from north to south.

Sichuan, which means 'four rivers', is named after the four tributaries of the Yangzi: the Jialing, Minjiang, Tuojiang and Wujiang. The rivers run in deep gorges through sparsely inhabited upland regions, before they reach the rich soils of the alluvial plains at the centre of the province.

The fertile river plains of Sichuan are the granary of China, producing enough rice and wheat to export surpluses to other parts of the country. With 11 frost-free months, fertile soil and an abundance of rainfall, double cropping and three rice harvests a year are possible. The villages of the lowland regions of Sichuan are prosperous and attractive, tucked into bamboo thickets amidst glittering fields of wet paddies and neat terraces of vegetable fields and orchards. The agrarian reforms implemented throughout China in the past few decades were pioneered here by Premier Zhao Ziyang in the late 1970s. At that time he was head of the provincial party committee in Sichuan. He was so successful in restoring Sichuan's agricultural economy that the Sichuanese coined a rhyme: *Yao chi fan, zhao Ziyang*. Translated, it means, 'If you want to eat, find Ziyang', thus making a pun on *zhao*, which means 'find', as well as sounding the same as his surname.

The most remote mountainous regions of Sichuan are populated by minority peoples. In the far west of the province, for example, there are large communities of Tibetans, and in the south, the Yi congregate around Liangshan. Perhaps these are the most attractive regions for the foreign visitor to explore. But there are more accessible and equally attractive destinations in Sichuan, such as the Buddhist caves of Dazu, the holy mountain of Emeishan, and the ethereally beautiful highland reserves of Jiuzhaigou and Huanglong. Of the province's major cities, visitors are most likely to visit Chengdu, the capital, and Chongqing, which in fact became independent from Sichuan when it was created a municipality in March 1997, before steaming east down the Yangzi.

For details of the Yangzi port cities, including Chongqing, *see* page 252. For the Buddhist mountain of Emeishan in western Sichuan, *see* page 341.

Sichuan

CHENGDU

Chengdu may be a large, modern city, but its ways are more those of the countryside than the town. Life is taken at an easy pace, teahouses are always full, and market stalls overflow with an abundance of farm produce brought in from the surrounding villages. The city centre is softened by trees shading the pavements and wide boulevards. The old city hugs the Jin River in a tangled pattern of lanes overhung by two-storey frame houses painted a dusky red. Chengdu rose to prominence in the Three Kingdoms period (220–265) as the capital of the state of Shu (even today, Sichuan is referred to by the name of Shu). Chengdu is the provincial capital, however Chongqing is, within the region, the greater industrial centre.

The city was once among the most splendid in China, with its own grand city walls (pulled down in 1949) and Vice-Regal Palace, destroyed in the 1960s. Today enormous changes to Chengdu's downtown overwhelm the remains of its past history, and with these new developments much of its former charm.

In the rural western suburbs of Chengdu stands **Du Fu's Thatched Cottage**. Du Fu (712–770) was a Tang poet who lived in Chengdu for a brief but productive period during which he wrote more than 200 poems. During the later Song Dynasty, a thatched cottage shrine was built in memory of the original cottage, which he described in the poem 'My thatched cottage is wrecked by the autumn wind'. The present buildings date from 1500 and 1811, when major restorations were undertaken. In the front hall are two wooden screens, one of which has a biography of the poet carved out in Chinese characters. In the shrine itself stand clay figurines of Du Fu, which date from the Ming and Qing dynasties. The garden walks around the shrine are lovely, and many different types of bamboo have been planted to shade the paths. There is a lively teahouse in the grounds.

Set in the southern suburbs of the city are a series of halls called the **Zhuge Liang Memorial Halls**. They commemorate the great military strategist Zhuge Liang, who was adviser to the King of Shu in the Warring States period (475–221 BCE). The halls were first built in the fourth century, but the present buildings date from 1672. On display are three bronze drums, believed to have been used by the armies of Shu under Zhuge Liang.

Wenshu Yuan, also known as the Manjusri Temple, is located south of the railway station. The temple is dedicated to the God of Wisdom or, by his Sanskrit name, Manjusri. On the way to the entrance, you will walk down a narrow lane flanked by stalls selling all that is necessary for worshipping in the temple—'hell money' for burnt offerings, candles, firecrackers and so on. Wenshu Yuan is the headquarters of the Chan (Zen) Buddhist sect in Sichuan.

(Top) *The mountain scenery near Jiuzhaigou and Huanglong is verdant and impressive.*

(Left) *An algae-coloured lake in the Jiuzhaigou region of northern Sichuan.* [Jeremy Tredinnick x2]

(Right) *A type of junk known as a* laohuaqiu *passes the great Buddha at Leshan. A photograph taken in the mid-1980s.* [Bill Hurst]

A symbolic offering of multicoloured arrows on the slopes above Langmusi, a Tibetan monastery on the Sichuan-Gansu border. [Jeremy Tredinnick]

Finally, the **Precious Light Monastery** (Baoguang Si) is worth a visit. It was founded in the Han dynasty and houses a fine collection of Buddhist treasures as well as modern paintings. Its 1,000-year-old Sheli Pagoda is a beautiful structure which is Chengdu's own version of a leaning tower—its top eight storeys tilt slightly to one side. A craft market held outside the monastery walls is popular with both local and foreign visitors.

OUTINGS FROM CHENGDU

One of the world's first irrigation systems can be found outside Chengdu. This vast hydraulic system at **Du River Dyke** (Du Jiang Yan), was created in the third century BCE by Li Bing, a minister in the ancient state of Shu. Its scale and sophistication are a tribute to the scientific genius of ancient China. The network of dykes and canals not only controlled flood levels on the Minjiang, a major river in Sichuan, but also created an irrigation system vital to the agricultural development of the region. Close to the dyke are several old temples, one of which— the **Two Princes Temple**—is dedicated to Li Bing and his son.

One of the most splendid sights Sichuan has to offer is the great statue of the Maitreya Buddha carved on a river cliff at **Leshan**. The statue overlooks the confluence of the Min, Qingyi and Dadu rivers to the south of Chengdu. Carved in the eighth century, the seated Buddha is 71 metres (220 feet) high, and is the largest Buddha image carved in China. It has a gentle and serene face, which is now overhung with trees growing in the gardens at the cliff top. It is also out of proportion and slightly grotesque. The best way to see the statue is to take a boat along the river. On either side of the statue stand carved warriors who, though they are imposing, are dwarfed by the size of the Buddha.

Opened to tourists in 1982, the **Buddhist Caves of Dazu**, to the southeast of Chengdu, are reason enough to visit Sichuan. The caves are scattered over 40 different locations and contain more than 50,000 carvings dating from the Tang and Song dynasties. Because the carvings are in Sichuan, an area historically isolated from the strongholds of power either in the north or around the lower Yangzi valley, they have escaped much of the destruction suffered by Buddhist centres elsewhere. The two most visited cave complexes are **Beishan** and **Baodingshan**. However, adventurous visitors can easily reach the more remote cave centres with the help of local guides.

The sculptures of Beishan date from the late Tang dynasty and are best seen at a the site known as Fowan, a crescent-shaped cliff within walking distance of Dazu town. Look for the carvings of grottoes number 136 (known as the 'Wheel of the Universe') and number 245, which illustrates the 'Western Paradise' and consists of

Seated statue of Guanyin with 1,000 arms, Baodingshan, Dazu Buddhist Grottos. [Sydney Wong]

more than 500 figures. The sculptures of Baodingshan date from the Southern Song Dynasty and are found at 13 different locations. The monk, Zhao Zhifeng, made the master plan for these Buddhist carvings, and a miniature of that master plan survives to this day. The rock sculptures are concentrated at Dafowan, where you will find a series of narratives based on the Buddhist scriptures. But what is special about them is the inclusion of everyday scenes of rural life.

The highway from Chengdu to the border with Shaanxi Province is known as the 'Ancient Road to Shu', famous in Chinese history as one fraught with danger and obstacles. Today, the traveller can make the journey by hiring a jeep or by local bus. The only link between the remote region of Sichuan and the northern provinces of China, the route—with its high mountain passes—was of great strategic importance, especially in times of war. Many of the stories associated with this route relate to the Three Kingdoms period, when the state of Shu was at war with its northern rival, the Wei. On the way north there are five famous passes—Seven Bends (Qipan), Skyward (Chaotian), Flying Immortals (Feixian), Heavenly Might (Tianxiong) and Sword Gate (Jianmen).

The small town of **Jian'ge** is remarkable for its ancient wooden buildings, which have survived from the Ming dynasty. North of Jian'ge is **Guangyuan**, the last city before Sichuan ends and Shaanxi begins. The city is notable for being the birthplace of Wu Zetian (625–705), the only woman sovereign in Chinese history.

Northern Sichuan encompasses areas of great natural beauty. Two of these are the nature reserves of **Jiuzhaigou** and **Huanglong**. Getting to them is much easier today than in years past, as there is now an airport—a mere 40-minute flight from Chengdu—within an hour or two's bus ride from both sites, while a long linking ring road of well-maintained tarmac allows for smooth transit on good coaches (8–10 hours' travel in each direction). A good argument for going by road is the mountainous area you pass through, which offers some of the most stunning landscapes in China. Jiuzhaigou, a valley more than 2,000 metres (6,500 feet) above sea level, is named after the nine Tibetan settlements in the area. It is studded with crystalline lakes, rimmed by snowcapped mountains and splashed by waterfalls. Huanglong is also a highland valley, but here the terrain has been marked by the steady depositing of calcium carbonate over aeons of time, so that strange-looking limestone formations crop up here and there, washed by icy snowmelt and broken by shallow pools of mineral-laden water. The cool highlands are the natural haunt of the giant panda, but the number of these shy creatures has been much depleted, and they are rarely seen in the wild nowadays.

THE ROAD TO TIBET

Public Security Bureau regulations concerning the openness of the the road to foreigners notwithstanding, the overland route to Tibet passes through hostile terrain making it a most difficult journey. The route west of Chengdu has been gradually opened to foreign tourist travel and it is now possible to travel overland from Chengdu west to Kangding, Batang, Litang, Derong and south into Yunnan province to Deqin and Zhongdian. Travel to Lhasa through eastern Tibet is possible but special application must be made. Road conditions are variable at best and accommodation is rustic but the magnificent landscapes and traditional lifestyle of the Khampa Tibetans make this a memorable journey.

On the first day's travel west escaping from the masses and humidity of the Sichuan Basin, buses reach **Ya'an**. The country to the west is wild and steeped with the history of the Red Army's passage through the region in summer, 1935 on their Long March. Nationalist leader Chiang Kai-shek came to Ya'an thinking he was finally going to wipe out Mao's Red Army. At the very least he expected to prevent them crossing the torrent of the Dadu River at the town of Luding, an action which might have forced them to perish in remote western parts. The two leaders were just 80 kilometres apart. Between them was Erlang Shan, a 3,437-metre (11,275-foot) pass (the road across it has now been rebuilt by the People's Liberation Army).

Miraculously, Mao's forces captured 'the Fixed Bridge of Lu', named after the engineer who built it in 1701 for the Kangxi Emperor. Nationalists defending **Luding Bridge** had removed its wooden planks, leaving only bare chains, but miraculous heroism won the day. Mao's forces escaped through northern Sichuan, evading the Nationalists completely by crossing high mountains and an uninhabited grassland plateau, before making their way towards northern Shaanxi to establish a new revolutionary base area.

Kangding, in the the Ganzi Tibetan Autonomous Prefecture, is the next town west of Luding; it has remained Tibetan in character, despite recent influxes of Chinese settlers. Kangding is famous for being a historic trading town that marked the border between the Chinese and Tibetan worlds.

At **Xinduqiao**, the highway divides into two sections. The northern part goes through Ganzi, Maniganggo and the Chola Mountains, to Dege and Qamdo. The southern section goes via Batang. Both roads offer views from the high passes over the folded mountain mass of the Qinghai-Tibetan plateau. Dege, on the northern run, is well worth a visit, since it has a traditional Buddhist printing press, where sutras are printed by hand from wood blocks. Also on the northern route is Qamdo, the largest town in eastern Tibet. The men of Qamdo have a reputation for being fierce warriors and hunters, who in earlier times made their living from banditry.

MINORITIES

Fourteen different minority groups live in Sichuan: the Tibetans, Yi, Miao, Qiang, Hui, Tujia, Bouyei, Naxi, Bai, Zhuang, Dai, Mongolian, Manchu and Lisu. Their communities are predominantly in the remote mountainous regions of the north, west and southwest of Sichuan, although several of these minorities can be found in other Chinese provinces as well. Many of their districts are being opened up by local authorities in order to attract foreign travellers and bring greater prosperity to the minorities. Of special interest are the Qiang people, who live in **Maowen County**, north of Chengdu. The Qiang are known for their small castle-like dwellings, which were built on hilltops. The castles are no longer inhabited, but they were made with such fine craftsmanship that they are still standing after several hundred years. Their women are skilled at needlework. To this day, they retain their distinctive dress of brilliant-coloured robes and cloth turbans decorated with tassels.

Yunnan

China's minority nationalities are known for their annual festivals held in southwest China. [Opposite, Wong How Man. This page: top left, bottom right by China Photo Library; top right by CGS; bottom left by Tom Nebbia]

YUNNAN

Yunnan Province, in China's far southwest, is of special interest to many travellers because of its large and diverse population of minority peoples. Twenty-two different ethnic minorities live in this province which borders Burma, Laos, Vietnam and Tibet. Many of these peoples have lifestyles, religious customs and costumes more in common with their Tibetan and Southeast Asian neighbours than with the Han Chinese.

The presence of these peoples endows Yunnan with a different atmosphere to China's northern provinces. Until quite late in its history, the region was not directly under Chinese control. Its earliest inhabitants were the Dian people, the same name that is given to Kunming's lake, and they were known to have lived around Kunming in the first millennium BCE. Wonderful bronze implements from their culture have been found in excavations outside the city (these are now on display in the Yunnan Provincial Museum in Kunming itself). During the Tang Dynasty, the Nanzhao Kingdom held sway over Yunnan, later to be replaced by the Dali in the 12th century.

In the next century, the Mongol conquerors of China brought Yunnan under the aegis of their Yuan Dynasty. As a means of controlling their new territory, the Mongols brought in Muslims to settle in the area and act as their political agents. Yunnan's Muslim population has grown and thrives to this day. Yet even as late as the Ming and Qing dynasties, the imperial court saw Yunnan as a distant and unattractive outpost, using it in much the same way as the British used Australia in the late 18th and 19th centuries—as a place for dumping unwanted persons.

Yunnan is also the original home of many of the plants and trees which were introduced to the West from China. Camellias, rhododendrons and tea, to name but three, all trace their origins to the high plateau in China's southwest which is Yunnan. The plateau rises steeply towards the northwest and the Himalayan mountain chains, while the lower-lying regions are in the south, on the borders of Burma, Laos and Vietnam. Its average elevation is about 2,000 metres (6,000 feet).

The plateau's high altitude and the tropical location of the province give it a mild climate throughout the year—ideal for travellers, even in winter months. The province has long been known as the Land of Eternal Spring. Three great rivers flow south through Yunnan from its northern border with Tibet: the Salween, Mekong and Yangzi. The Salween and Mekong continue on into Burma and Laos, but the Yangzi turns in an enormous loop to flow north into neighbouring Sichuan Province.

There are four great adventure destinations in Yunnan: Dali, Lijiang, Zhongdian and Xishuangbanna. Though they have become very popular with China travellers, they are still largely unspoilt. All the regions are renowned for their natural beauty of setting, historic sites and, of course, their minority peoples. Dali, Lijiang and Zhongdian lie to the northwest of Kunming, the provincial capital, in the high plateau region of Yunnan. Xishuangbanna is in the south of the province, where the tropical jungles and riverside villages make the region a natural geographical and cultural extension of Southeast Asia.

The popularity of these destinations should neither deter the independent traveller from including them on an itinerary, nor detract from the exploration of other, less well-documented regions. Yunnan, perhaps more than any other region except Tibet, appeals to the traveller for whom the journey itself is the adventure.

KUNMING

As is the case in Chengdu, and indeed in the majority of China's larger cities and towns, most of old Kunming has been raized to the ground and replaced with often ugly office towers and high-rise dwellings. Even the legendary lake at Kunming, Dianchi, once described as like a blue-glazed dish edged with a painted trim of green, is increasingly hedged in by intensively cultivated market gardens. However the lake still has considerable charm and Yunnan's gentle climate combine to make Kunming—the capital of the province—appealing even in the winter months when much of the rest of China is too cold to attract many visitors. But it is the variety of peoples in the region which usually draws travellers to Yunnan, and for many travellers, Kunming is simply a staging post for journeys to the towns and villages of these peoples, rather than a destination in itself. But even if time does not allow a journey far beyond Kunming, there are many opportunities to learn about the minorities and to see their handicrafts in the museums and shops of the city.

CITY SIGHTS

A good starting place for a visit to Kunming is the recently revamped **Yunnan Provincial Museum**, which provides an excellent introduction to the region's ancient cultures. It is here that you will also see the fine bronzes of the Dian Kingdom, which dates back to 1200 BCE. These bronzes deserve careful scrutiny, as they show detailed scenes of daily life. The animal bronzes are especially noteworthy. Also well worth a visit is the **Museum of Minority Nationalities**, located south of the city near the north shore of Dian Lake. This excellent museum displays extensive collections

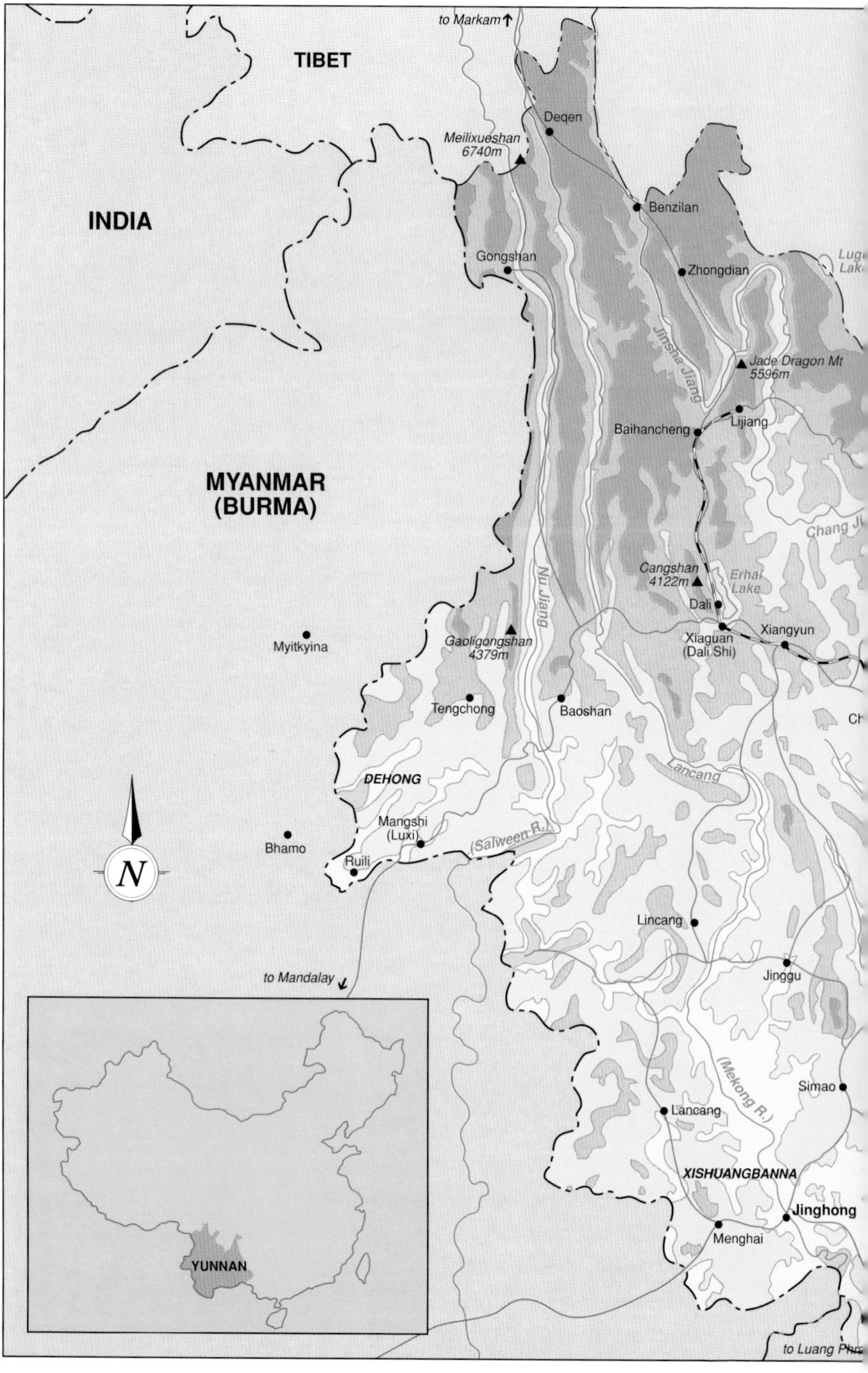
to Markam
TIBET
INDIA
MYANMAR
(BURMA)
Deqen
Meilixueshan
6740m
Benzilan
Gongshan
Zhongdian
Jinsha Jiang
Jade Dragon Mt
5596m
Lijiang
Baihancheng
Cangshan
4122m
Erhai
Lake
Dali
Xiaguan
(Dali Shi)
Xiangyun
Nu Jiang
Myitkyina
Gaoligongshan
4379m
Tengchong
Baoshan
Lancang
DEHONG
Mangshi
(Luxi)
(Salween R.)
Bhamo
Ruili
N
Lincang
Jinggu
to Mandalay
(Mekong R.)
Simao
Lancang
XISHUANGBANNA
Jinghong
Menghai
YUNNAN

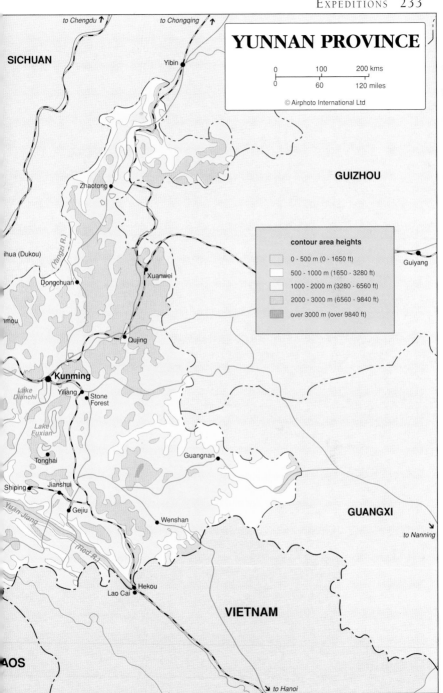

Yunnan

detailing all of the province's 22 ethnic groups and their wildly varying lifestyles. You will note that the Dai women, whose villages lie close to the borders of Laos and Burma, wear the sarong that is seen all over Southeast Asia.

Close to the zoo in the north of the city is the Buddhist **Yuantong Temple** and its adjacent park. The park is famed for its flowering shrubs and trees: cherry in spring, rhododendrons in summer, chrysanthemums in autumn and camellia or magnolia in winter. The temple itself dates back a thousand years or so, and has been attractively restored.

Just south of Jinbi Lu are two ancient pagodas dating from the ninth century—**East** and **West Temple Pagodas**. The oldest surviving structures in Kunming, they are historically and architecturally invaluable. The East pagoda can be visited on Shulin Jie and is notable for its multiple eaves and sublime shape. On its summit stand four 'golden roosters' (copper, actually). The West pagoda can be reached along a broad pedestrianized street created in classical style, and passing an impressive and accurate recreation of the massive Ming Dynasty main fortified city gate.

Yunnan's large Muslim community dates back to the Yuan Dynasty. Five mosques are open in Kunming, and can be visited if proper attire is worn and cameras are used with discretion. The largest mosque is on Shuncheng Jie, in an Islamic neighbourhood which is also worth exploring for its small shops and *halal* (Muslim) restaurants.

OUTINGS FROM KUNMING

In a woodland setting about 12 kilometres (seven and a half miles) northwest of Kunming lies the **Bamboo Temple**. A legend tells of the temple's foundation in the Tang, when two princes chased a rhinoceros to a spot where monks appeared holding staves of bamboo, which then miraculously turned into groves of bamboo. The temple is noted for its 500 *luohans*—finely crafted, idiosyncratic statues of holy men, created in the late 19th century.

In the northeast of the city about 11 kilometres (seven miles) away, the **Copper Temple**, or Golden Temple (Jindian), can be reached after a dramatic climb through pine woods. The attractive temple with its wrought-copper roof stands on a marble terrace and is dedicated to the Taoist deity, Zishi.

Most travellers to Kunming will want to take one of the numerous ferries which traverse **Dianchi** at various points. The western shores of the lake rise steeply towards **Western Hill**, a range of four mountains famous for its temples and magnificent views. The **Huating Temple**, Kunming's largest Buddhist monastery, has an imposing garden with an ornamental lake, the enclosing decorative wall of which connects several stupas. Higher up the mountain is the **Taihua Temple**, which also has a garden setting of great charm. The back of the temple has a hall dedicated to the Guanyin, Goddess of Mercy. In her Indian incarnation, she was depicted as a male. However, the Chinese have endowed her with the grace and compassion of a Buddhist Virgin Mary. Beyond the Huating Temple rises the **Sanqing Temple**, a Taoist shrine. There is little left of the original interiors, but a rest at the temple teahouse is recommended before a walk to **Dragon Gate**, where the view of the lake below is unsurpassed. A chair lift goes to the top of the mountain.

Daguan Park, on the north shore of the lake, contains a pavilion which houses a cultural treasure in the form of a poem inscribed on its facade. Written by a Qing dynasty scholar, it extols the beauty of the scenery of Kunming. The park itself is attractive, with a landscape of lakes and willow-edged causeways.

On the eastern and southern shores of the Lake Dianchi, fields and villages stretch down to the water. A bus or taxi journey to some of the smaller villages and towns will show rural life just beyond the city. A visit to the small town of **Jinning** is recommended for its museum honouring the birthplace of Zheng He, the great Ming dynasty eunuch admiral. His expeditions beginning in 1405 took him as far as Arabia and Africa, well in advance of the journeys of the Portuguese and Spanish explorers. These expeditions did not result in China establishing a trading empire, however. The museum shows the extent of his seven great voyages, which he achieved with the aid of the Chinese-invented compass.

Seventeen kilometres (10 miles) northwest of the city lies the **Kunming Botanical Garden**. The mountains and valleys of Yunnan harbour over half of China's indigenous trees and flowers. Many flowering shrubs, such as the rhododendron and camellia, which people from the West now see as a natural part of their own landscape, were first collected in Yunnan by European plant-hunters. Close to the garden is the colourful Taoist temple known as **Black Dragon Pool**. As with many dragon legends, the dragons of this story were destructive, only being mastered by a Taoist scholar who banished nine of them and tamed the tenth. This one is said to live in the pool.

The most popular day trip from Kunming is the **Stone Forest**, 126 kilometres (79 miles) southeast of the city. This can be reached by coach tours or, for the more adventurous, by train to **Yiliang** and from there by bus. The Stone Forest is a strange place, with limestone pinnacles and rocks standing like petrified trees. The outcrops are not a fossil forest but the result of water erosion—just like the mountains of Guilin, except on a smaller scale. The area is the home of the Sani people, who delight in offering their handicrafts to visitors and often give song and dance performances in the local hotel.

Yunnan

Karst limestone pillars of the Stone Forest.

DALI

est of Kunming, elevation 1,900 metres (6,100 feet), 400 kilometres (250 miles) along the old Burma Road, stand the **Cang Shan** (Azure Mountains), whose slopes rise in soft furrows above the lakeside plain of Dali. The richness of the plain's black soils, the marble deposits buried in the mountains, the waters of **Erhai Lake** (Ear Lake) teeming with fish, and the ribbons of small streams which water the fields, all help to make Dali a prosperous region.

Dali is the name of the region and of the region's principal town. It was once the capital of the Nanzhao Kingdom, when Yunnan was ruled by its own tribal people. At the height of its power in the eighth and ninth centuries, the Nanzhao Kingdom sent armies to conquer parts of present-day Burma and Laos, and periodically fought with Tibet and Tang China. In the tenth century, the kingdom was renamed Dali, but it was only brought under Chinese rule in the Yuan dynasty.

The predominant ethnic group in Dali is the Bai, whose young women adorn themselves in bright red tunics, multicoloured aprons and intricate hats with tassels, braided ribbons and woven fabric.

There are regular sleeper buses from Kunming to Dali, and the airport near Xiaguan handles numerous daily flights to and from Kunming. A long-anticipated railway connection between Kunming and Xiaguan has opened to passengers. The new **Kunming/Dali Express Highway** has cut the overland trip to approximately 4.5 hours, so numerous ways exist to reach western Yunnan.

Xiaguan has a lakeside park with a botanical garden famous for its camellias, azaleas and magnolia. Also in Xiaguan is a **Tea Factory**, where Yunnanese tea is processed into 'bricks' for export to Tibet and the rest of the world. Worth seeing in the city are several mosques and the impressive Dali Prefectural Museum.

The more attractive stone-built town of Dali itself, with its whitewashed walls and grey tiled roofs, invites exploration. In the north of the city stand the **Three Pagodas** (San Ta), the largest of which is striking in its unadorned simplicity of form. These pagodas, once part of a great temple complex, are among the finest in China. Close to the Three Pagodas is the **Marble Factory**, where the stone is cut and polished to reveal natural patterns resembling clouds and mountains. Supplies come from the Azure Mountains and have been quarried for 1,200 years. This famous local industry is invoked every time the Chinese word for marble is used—*dalishi* (Dali stone). Each Monday morning, a vast and colourful country market draws farmers and artisans from all around to the town of Shaping at the north end of Erhai Lake. This happy, rustic gathering amazes visitors with the range and peculiarity of its country products.

The perfect way to enjoy the local sights is by boat on Erhai Lake. CITS arranges boat trips or, with a little bargaining, you can hire boats on the waterfront. The western shore of the lake is flat, with cultivated fields, and the rocky eastern shore is interesting for its small, dry-stone-walled villages, with their moored fleets of boats. The lake's islands are worth exploring: **Golden Shuttle Island** for its Buddhist temple and pavilion, and **Xiaoputuo Island** for its picturesque temple dedicated to the Goddess of Mercy, Guanyin.

Outings from Dali

To the northeast of Dali rises **Chicken Foot Mountain** (Jizushan), so named because of its striated ridges which resemble a chicken's foot. Formerly this mountain drew Buddhist and Taoist pilgrims from far and wide, and its slopes were studded with temples and monasteries. Sadly, all the most important religious sites were very badly damaged during the Cultural Revolution, and little remains of Jizushan's former glories. However, a seventh-century pagoda has survived, as have small sections of the old walnut forests which once supplied timber to the people of the plain.

For those with time to spare, a visit from Dali to the renowned Buddhist caves of **Stone Treasure Mountain** (Shibao Shan) is highly recommended. The caves are in a remote area north of Dali, 130 kilometres (81 miles) away, but they reward the traveller with carvings dating back to the Nanzhao Kingdom. Of special interest are caves depicting life under the Nanzhao, and the excellent stone sculptures of Buddhist deities and teachers.

After viewing the grotto, take the steep descent to Shaxi Village, heading down the winding stone steps beside the parking lot. The village, the last remaining way station along the ancient Tea and Horse Caravan Trail, stands out starkly in the distance, a patchwork of traditional rooftops in the middle of the lush Shaxi Valley. The trail, which once stretched some 3,500 kilometers from Xishuangbanna in Yunnan to Tibet, dates back to the Tang dynasty, but for the most part came to an end with liberation in 1949. As the name suggests, the trail was once used to transport brick tea from Yunnan and Sichuan to Tibet, where these products were exchanged for the small but sturdy Tibet-bred horses. It fell into disuse when modern transportation routes connected southwest China with Tibet.

The first stop is the Shaxi Marketplace, the last remaining market along the old trail. The World Monument Fund has put the market square on its list of the 100 most endangered sites in the world. The ancient influence of the different peoples who passed through here can still be seen today in the mixed styles of architecture and the

confluence of religious traditions. The square retains much of its original architecture, including an old opera stage, merchant guesthouse and temple, making it an excellent example of how commerce, religion and entertainment all merged in this village centre. The Swiss Federal Institute in Zurich is collaborating with the local government to preserve the old marketplace, the historic village around it, and the idyllic Shaxi valley.

The Xingjiao Temple, of the Bai esoteric sect of Buddhism, was built in 1415 during the Ming Dynasty, and is being renovated. A mural on the wall of the main hall of the temple, titled Sakyamuni descends to hell, is rare because it depicts Sakyamuni as a female. This may be due to the traditional respect the Bai people have for women. The valuable frescoes, which are being restored by European experts, date back to 1417.

The inn on the square, where muleteers stayed, is still there. They slept on top of large wooden boxes, their possessions safe inside. The windows of the wooden structure, which are placed just above the beds, had bars so the muleteers could keep an eye on their horses at night. Plans call for the inn to be revived as a tourist hotel. The former agricultural bank will be converted into a teahouse where local musicians will perform. The old opera stage will become a museum introducing local gods. The town also has beautiful traditional architecture, the mud-brick East Gate, wide enough for just two horses to pass through side-by-side, and a beautiful old arched stone bridge.

The early iron suspension bridge called **Rainbow Bridge** (Jihongqiao) may also be visited. The Chinese people were the first in the world to build iron suspension bridges. This one is a reconstruction dating from 1475, but a similar bridge is known to have existed at this site for a thousand years or so. Inscriptions carved on nearby cliffs attest to the role played by the Rainbow Bridge in linking the area with India, Burma and Siam.

LIJIANG

P art of the delight in going to Lijiang lies in the journey itself. Formerly, one had no choice but to go by road from Dali, a magnificent 196-kilometre (122-mile) journey through narrow fertile valleys, mountains and forest glades of rhododendrons and azaleas, all culminating in an unforgettable view of the **Jade Dragon Snow Range** above Lijiang. Today, however, the rail line has been extended from Dali to Lijiang, and a small airport between Heqing and Lijiang handles flights from Kunming; the short trip affords a spectacular hour in the air.

Moso woman in the village of Ninglang northeast of Lijiang.
The Moso, a sub-group of the Naxi, still adhere to a matrilineal society. [Wong How Man]

Lijiang is the home of the Naxi people, who speak a language of the Tibeto-Burman group, and dress in black or deep blue. Other smaller minority groups live around Lijiang, including the Lisu, Pumi and Nuosu Yi. The Pumi are more brightly clad than the Naxi people, and the Lisu can only be seen by visiting the more remote districts close to the Nujiang (the Chinese name for the Salween River).

The Naxi were traditionally a matriarchal tribe, whose property was passed through the youngest female child; the men were in charge of gardening, music-making and child-rearing. In the present more liberal climate in China, the traditional Naxi orchestras are being revived. The Naxi are also notable for their shamanist traditions. Shamans (spirit mediums) were common in ancient China, and they still survive amongst the remote Siberian tribes, in Korea, and in Tibetan communities. The shamans, or *dongbas*, of the Naxi were responsible for transmitting the learning of the tribe into their own pictographic script—now being translated into Chinese in a concerted attempt to preserve the Naxi heritage.

Lijiang, elevation 2,400 metres (7,800 feet), falls into clear parts: old and new (though the "old" part is in fact virtually all new too, since a 1996 earthquake levelled most of the original buildings). The old town is infinitely more interesting, with its pebbled paths, potted mountain plants and small restaurants serving *baba*—deep-fried wheat cake, offered with a variety of fillings. It is now a "UNESCO World Heritage Site" (the entire old town has been rebuilt and even enlarged but using strictly authentic traditional methods and materials). The park known as **Black Dragon Pool** is the principal attraction of the town, with its **Moon Embracing Pavilion** (a modern reconstruction, since the Ming pavilion was burnt down in 1950 by a drunken cadre and his mistress in a fit of suicidal romanticism—or vandalism). An adjacent building is used to house the **Dongba Cultural Research Institute**, and another, the **Dragon God Temple**, is a setting for flower and art shows. The **Five Phoenix Hall**, a piece of whimsical architectural bravura, was once part of the now defunct Fuguo Temple. The hall is one of two buildings from the temple which were transferred intact to the Black Dragon Pool park in recent years.

Fuguo was one of the Five Famous Temples of Lijiang, the remaining four of which dot the hillsides that surround the Lijiang Plain. These temples were founded

The Moon-Embracing Pavilion at Black Dragon Pool in Lijiang, with Jade Dragon Snow Mountain (Yulongxueshan) in the background. [Jeremy Tredinnick]

under the patronage of Mu Tian Wang, the 17th-century Naxi king. He was a religious man, instrumental in the growth of the Red Hat Sect of Buddhism in his domain. The **Jade Summit Temple** (Yufeng Si) is famous for its setting in a pine forest, and for a camellia tree which in late February or early March flowers in such profusion that locals claim it has 20,000 blossoms. A trip to the **Temple of Universal Benefaction** (Puji Si) includes a pleasant walk up a mountain trail. In the temple, Tibetan thangkas have survived destruction, as have a few Buddha images. A few miles south of the town, the **Peak of Culture Temple** (Wenfeng Si) was famous in its time as a meditation centre. Above the temple is a hole in the earth, near a sacred spring where monks would stay for over three years to engage in intense meditation. The fourth temple to survive, the **Zhiyun Si**, in the nearby town of Lashiba, is now a school.

OUTINGS FROM LIJIANG

The mighty Yangzi River sweeps through the northern part of Yunnan, and can be seen at the dramatic **Tiger Leaping Gorge** (Hutiao Xia) as it roars through a deep canyon that rises nearly two miles to the snowy summits above. According to legend, a hunted tiger was able to make its escape from one side of the narrow gorge to the other in one single bound. At the point where the Yangzi makes its great turn northwards lies Shigu (Stone Drum) village, so named because of a memorial stone drum commemorating a victory by Chinese and Naxi troops over a Tibetan force in 1548. **Shigu** is known in modern Chinese history as a crossing-point of the Red Army on its Long March. During the winter of 1934–1935 the Red Army troops reached Shigu, where the local citizens helped ferry them across the river to escape the Nationalist troops in pursuit.

The village of **Nguluko** (Yuhu) is typical of the smaller Naxi villages in its setting. In the 1920s it was the home of the Austro-American explorer and botanist, Joseph Rock, who pioneered research on Yunnan's flora and Naxi ethnology. Joseph Rock's summer house is now open to visitors. It includes a small exhibition of Rock memorabilia and some period photographs. The ancient town of **Baoshan**, to the north of Lijiang, is a rare sight because it is one of China's few remaining walled towns.

Baisha, once the capital of the Naxi kingdom, is now a sleepy farm village at the foot of the Yulongxueshan. The collection of 15th century Baisha murals is housed in an original 15th century Ming structure. They incorporate the pragmatic nature of the Naxi—Tantric Buddhist deities; Mahayanna Bodhisattvas, Daoist immortals and Naxi shaman coexist in an etheral netherworld that reflects the Naxi's sense of tolerance for different beliefs.

ZHONGDIAN

Zhongdian is the name of both a huge county and the town that is its seat. It forms one of three counties that make up Yunnan's Diqing Tibetan Autonomous Prefecture; Tibetans call their home Gyelthang, not Zhongdian, an introduced Chinese name. The area has now been officially named *Shangri-La*.

The region has a great range in elevations, from Meilixueshan (Mount Kawakarpo) at 6,740 metres (22,110 feet) which borders Tibet, to 1,480 metres (4,850 feet) deep in the gorges of the Yangzi, Salween and Mekong rivers. Plant hunters and geographers in the first half of this century prized Zhongdian for its natural riches, and it is largely for the forested mountains and high plateau grandeur that visitors come today.

Direct flights to Kunming, Chongqing, Guangzhou and other domestic destinations have brought large numbers of tourists to the area from China's urban areas and it must be admitted that Zhongdian town has a tacky feel to it now. However, once you leave the town itself the surrounding country is gorgeous and the long, thrilling overland trip to Lijiang is worth the sacrifice of time and comfort; rarely in the world does one see such beautiful scenery. Fine domestic architecture, fields of colour and rarified air give the journey between Lijiang and Zhongdian a magical quality.

The town itself, at 3,160 metres (10,400 feet), has an old section entirely in local Tibetan style. Sights in and around Zhongdian include a park, with a view over the entire town, a wooden bowl factory, and the large Yellow Hat Sect monastery of **Songzhanling**, founded in the 17th century. A few kilometres north of town lies **Napa Hai**, a huge lake that forms part of a nature preserve. Twenty-five kilometres east of Zhongdian is the serene alpine lake of **Bita Hai**.

The best known natural wonder in the region is **Baishuitai** (White Water Terrace), which lies some two hours by car south from the town. At the head of a steep valley are a series of stepped terraces, white and encrusted, each with a small pool of clear, shallow water. Such terraces can be found in Turkey and New Zealand, but the ones here are particularly beautiful because of the dramatic setting. The flow of water and the extent of the terraces is greatest in March, when thousands of pilgrims and tourists come to picnic and drink the water. It is believed to have curative powers and to help women conceive.

XISHUANGBANNA

Located in the south of Yunnan Province, and bordering Burma and Laos, is the Xishuangbanna Dai Autonomous Prefecture. The Dai people are one of Yunnan's

Yunnan

*An idylic hamlet, Meirendao, on the banks of the Jinsha Jiang has succumbed
to prolific dam construction—and its population relocated by the government
to evade the swollen waters. [Wong How Man]*

largest minority groups. About a third of the total population live in Xishuangbanna along with 12 other minority groups and a few Han Chinese.

Scarcely anything is known about the early history of the Dai. Their language and culture suggest that the Dai share a common ancestry with the Thais. What *is* recorded is that in the second century BCE Dai chieftains sent tributary missions to the Han emperors. Between the eighth and 12th centuries Xishuangbanna was incorporated into the Nanzhao and Dali kingdoms. From the 14th to the 19th century a policy of pacification was practised by the Chinese imperial administration to keep control of the border areas. But it did not deter first the French—with their base in Indochina—and then the British from encroaching into this southwestern outpost. The incursions were short-lived, however. During the first half of the 20th century, Yunnan, in common with many other areas in China that were far from the seat of government, was controlled by a warlord. The area was taken over by the communists in 1950 and—except for the tragic decade of the Cultural Revolution, when minority peoples were treated atrociously—Xishuangbanna has enjoyed relative autonomy in local administration.

Most Buddhists in China are followers of the Mahayana sect (or Tantric in Tibet) but the Dai are followers of Theravada (as are the Burmese and Laotian people.) Their temples and stupas closely resemble such architecture found in Southeast Asia.

The sheer cliffs of Tiger Leaping Gorge, through which the Yangzi thunders. [Jeremy Tredinnick]

Similar to Thailand's Songkran celebration, the Dais famously hold a water splashing festival. For three days in the middle of April, the Dai go around splashing each other—and any passerby—with water. It is symbolic of a legendary triumph of the forces of good over a destructive demon and an occasion for the washing away of sins. During the festival a shortage of transportation and lodgings makes visiting difficult.

Xishuangbanna's tropical monsoon climate is similar to that of northern Laos and Myanmar (Burma). The rainy season extends from June through late September. The administrative capital, Jinghong's airport receives numerous flights from Kunming as well as links to Dali, Lijiang, Beijing, Shanghai and other Mainland cities. There are also international connections to Thailand.

Jinghong is an attractive city of 95,000. Its wide streets are lined with oil and coconut palms and its colourful central market overflows with tropical fruits. Tourism fuels the local economy, abundant hotels serve Chinese tour groups escaping the grey winters of northern China. The **Tropical Crops Research Institute** in the city's western district is popular. Beyond Jinghong, close to the Mekong River, are many interesting Dai villages. Their stilt houses, common throughout Southeast Asia, address the problem of river flooding. Dai house roofs are similar to double-eaved Malay and Thai roofs, offering maximum ventilation and protection from heavy tropical rains. Markets brim with Dai, Hani and Jinuo women in colourful embroidered clothing sell jewellery and handicrafts.

An early morning one-hour boat ride down the Mekong takes you to **Menghan**, a small Dai village with a few dusty roads and an excellent market. The village stands on **Olive Plain** (Ganlanba), covered with large plantations of rubber and fruit.

At the town of **Menghai**, west of Jinghong, tea growing and processing is the main industry. The tea grown is the famous Pu Er variety. At nearby **Mengzhe**, also an area of tea plantations, is the **Manlei Great Buddha Pagoda.**

Another fine expedition is to follow the road from Jinghong to the Burmese border. **Damenglong**, 70 kilometres (43 miles) southwest of Jinghong, is just eight kilometres (under five miles) from Burma. Burmese traders cross the border on Japanese motorbikes and tractors to bring Burmese cosmetics, jade and farm produce to exchange for China-made household goods and motor parts. Close to Damenglong is the **White Pagoda**, a 13th-century structure with eight small stupas surrounding a taller, central spire. Devout Buddhists leave offerings of money, flowers, fruit and embroidered cloth at the 'footprints of the Buddha' in the shrine inside the base of the pagoda. Amongst nearby paddy fields and hills is lush vegetation with beautiful hikes, right up to the Burmese border.

CHINESE PAINTING

C hinese painting has a long and eminent history, being considered the ultimate accomplishment of the Chinese scholar. There are, however, two traditions of Chinese painting—the scholar and the professional/artisan. Both these traditions have overlapped and influenced each other, but in general the scholar tradition has retained the greatest prestige.

The development of the scholar tradition becomes clear with the advent of the Tang Dynasty, even though few of the surviving Tang paintings are original. They are mainly copies made in later centuries. Indeed, copying was considered an important part of the practical study of painting, and there is a long tradition in Chinese painting—as in the other arts—of learning from past masters.

By the Song Dynasty—considered by many to be the apogee of Chinese landscape painting—there was an established tradition of painting styles and repertoires as well as a rich vocabulary of symbols and emblems used as an inner language in the paintings. The main categories of subject matter evolved into four classes—landscape, people and objects, birds and flowers, grass and insects. Of the four, the most esteemed was that of landscape. In the Northern Song Dynasty, masters such as Li Cheng, Fan Kuan, Guo Xi and Xu Daoning created magical, monumental landscapes and mists in which, if humans had a place at all, it was a minor one.

It is in these classic landscapes that the fundamental difference between Western and Chinese painting can be identified: perspective. After Giotto's work in 13th-century Italy, Western painting developed with a single fixed perspective. However, Chinese painters, although they were aware of perspective, rejected the device of a single disappearing point, creating instead landscapes in which the viewer *becomes* the traveller within the painting. The problems which such a technique creates are solved by the inventive use of space and by giving the picture shifting layers of perspective. Expanses of mist and water convey subtle shifts of vision. As you view a hanging scroll, your eye moves upwards to the summit of the mountains in a series of scene-changes. With a horizontal scroll—traditionally viewed an arm's length at a time—the same effect is achieved from right to left.

The second major difference between Western and Chinese art lies in the medium itself. Most Western masterpieces are worked in oil. Chinese paintings are worked in black ink on silk or absorbent paper, sometimes using mineral colours—and those sparingly. The two traditional colours of Chinese painting are blue and green. Since the artist chose to capture the spirit or essence of his

Special Topic

subject, rather than recreate it in loving detail, the use of black ink in a variety of tones and strokes has always been much more evocative than definitive in intention. Using brush and ink leaves no room for error. Once the brush is on the paper, it must be moved with strength and fluency if the painting is not to be rendered lifeless. Unlike the artist in oils, the Chinese painter has no chance to change or paint over his initial strokes. The importance of the brushstroke meant, in turn, that the development of the Chinese artist was intimately linked to that of the calligrapher. The scholar painter aimed to achieve an easy, inspired fluency of style which was unerring. To some extent, this explains why the noted poet and calligrapher of the Song Dynasty, Su Dongpo, saw the arts of poetry, painting and calligraphy as indivisible. In Chinese art, part of the beauty of the painting lies in the poem which the artist selects to write at the side of his work, as well as the style in which he decides to write it. Manuals on brushwork were compiled so that young artists could admire and copy the past masters, learning, for example, how they painted trees in winter or spring and precisely which brushstrokes they used.

Nature was the major preoccupation of the Chinese scholar artist. He made choices of subject in harmony with his own mood and the season of the year. Indeed, he believed that nothing could be painted without an understanding of the essential character of nature. Thus, landscape painting for him was less a celebration of the individuality of a particular place than an evocation of the spirit of *all* landscapes, captured in one particular scene at one particular season.

In his treatment of birds, animals and flowers, the Chinese painter also had little in common with his Western counterparts. The *nature morte* (still-life) of European painting would have been distasteful to him. The Chinese tradition is to show animals and flowers alive in their natural setting. Much attention is paid to detail here, and the artist is expected to depict how the plant or tree changes with the seasons, how an animal or bird moves and stands. This does not mean that Chinese renderings of flora and fauna are realistic. Rather, they are 'true' to the nature of the subject.

This also applies to the inner vocabulary of the Chinese painting. These emblems and symbols are an important part of the artist's intent. The four favourite subjects of the scholar painter are bamboo, plum, chrysanthemum and orchid, all of which reflect the qualities which the scholar strives to achieve in his own conduct. The bamboo bends but is not broken. The plum blossoms in winter, rising above adverse conditions, as does the chrysanthemum, while the orchid represents fragrance and elegance of form. The scholars of the Ming and Qing dynasties turned these four subjects into a veritable fashion.

Landscape, ink and colour on paper, Li Huashen. [Hanart T Z Gallery]

THE YANGZI RIVER

T he Yangzi River (Changjiang, or Long River, to the Chinese, the Yangtze to traditionalists) offers travellers many kinds of expeditions. Although steamers no longer ply upriver from Shanghai (improvements in road and rail links have made this an uneconomical alternative), there are a variety of modern and luxurious cruise ships that explore the stretch of river between Wuhan and Chongqing, including the spectacular Three Gorges. But for those keen to see the remote upper reaches of the Yangzi—impossible to navigate due to its turbulent course through mountain meadows and narrow gorges—overland expeditions to northern Yunnan, Tibet, and even as far as the river's source in Qinghai, are possible.

The Yangzi is a great waterway, although navigation on it was fraught with difficulty until the latter half of the 20th century. Since 1949 the government has been attempting to keep the waters in check with various substantive hydraulic schemes. The latest of these is the massive **Three Gorges Dam** (Sanxia Ba), about 40 kilometres (25 miles) upriver from Yichang. Rising water levels in the gorges have made necessary the relocation of over one million people and scores of historical sites. The waters will rise a further 40 metres (131 feet) between 2007 and 2009 to a final height of 175 metres (574 feet) above sea level, and the Daning River will then disappear. Yet the 'taming' of the Yangzi has not taken away the sense of adventure.

Few travellers can fail to be impressed by the dawn voyage through the towering walls of the Three Gorges. But the river also has its less spectacular, but still memorable moments and sights: the evening flight homeward of geese across the bows of the ship, a glimpse of a riverside pagoda, the passing of small craft with their lamps lit at night, or the thick flow of the river as it pushes past the shoreside fields of young rice.

With a little imagination, the history of the river can be brought to life, too—the epic battles of the Three Kingdoms, Kublai Khan crossing the river with his navy on his way to conquer the Song empire of the south, and more recently, the tea clippers of the 19th century which raced from Hankou (now part of Wuhan) to London and New York with the first of the season's tea.

THE RIVER JOURNEY

Yangzi travellers can choose the slower upstream journey, embarking at Wuhan or Yichang, or the downstream trip embarking at Chongqing. The legendary journey through the Gorges can be made in style on a variety of comfortable, international-standard cruise ships. The cruises usually involve daily shore visits or excursions on small boats to explore tributary streams.

The Yangzi River

Chongqing is the usual embarkation point for the journey downstream. The new municipality, established in 1997, is the main industrial centre of southwest China. It served as the country's capital during the Sino-Japanese War, when the city's notorious foggy weather saved it from Japanese bombers. Chongqing's history dates to the fourth century BCE, then known as Yuzhou. Its modern name Chongqing means 'Double Celebration', adopted by a Song dynasty prince-cum-emperor from Yuzhou.

Built at the confluence of the Yangzi and Jialing rivers, it was a settlement of strategic importance, serving as the capital of the ancient state of Ba during the fourth century BCE. Little is known about the men of Ba, except that they buried their dead in wooden coffins which were then placed on cliff ledges or in caves high above the river.

Set on a promontory on the north bank of the Yangzi, the city has outgrown its original site and spilled over to the adjacent banks of both the Yangzi and Jialing. Cable cars and bridges connect the newer districts of Chongqing with the older cliffside city centre. Most visitors are taken to **Eling Park** at dusk to view the city's attractive, steep lamplit streets sweeping down to the dark waters below. First thing in the morning, visit the **Chaotianmen** docks to see the harbour and all the river craft as passengers disembark from their upstream cruises. Previously everyone negotiated long flights of slippery, slimy steps up to the city. Thousands of porters known as the *bang bang jun* (help army), with their bamboo poles and ropes, would carry luggage and cargo up the staircases. Although the rise in water level behind the Three Gorges Dam has reduced the flight of steps to a minimum, the *bang bang jun* are still there to assist passengers with their luggage when they board or disembark cruise ships.

The following riverside towns are in the same order as they appear going downstream from Chongqing. While historical background is given, bear in mind that most of these towns will be partially or completely submerged by the new dam. Entire new towns constructed nearby lie above the final water level.

Fuling was the site of the royal tombs of the state of Ba (fourth to second centuries BCE). The most important archaeological treasure in Fuling is a set of carvings consisting of 14 fish and stone inscriptions giving information on ancient hydrology and cosmology, the oldest of which was carved in the Tang dynasty (618–907). Known as the White Crane Ridge, the carvings have been preserved *in situ* in a specially constructed, 250-metre (820-feet) long, underwater museum.

The nearby town of **Fengdu** was traditionally known by its nickname of 'Ghost City' and it has a temple dedicated to the King of the Underworld. This strange association dates back to the Han dynasty, when two scholar-recluses who lived in the town were believed to have achieved immortality. The combination of their names results in the title 'King of the Underworld'. It is most apt, as Fengdu township was torn down before the rising waters of the Yangzi could smother it. The temple, however, is above the waterline and is protected.

The name of **Shibaozhai** means 'Precious Stone Fortress'; the precious stone in question is a 220-metre-high (720-foot) rock on the north bank that, from afar, is said to resemble a stone seal. (Seals in traditional China were carved at the base and used as a form of official signature.) In 1662, during the Qing dynasty, a temple was built on top of the rock. Originally the temple could only be visited by climbing up an iron chain, but in the late 19th century a nine-storey wooden pagoda was built next to the rock so that the ascent could be made by staircase. An extra three storeys were added in the 20th century, and now the 12-storey red pagoda rises alongside the rock to the base of the temple. The rising waters of the river now surround the pagoda, which has been preserved on an island behind a dam of its own.

Wanxian (now called Wanzhou) is an ancient river port and once had a thriving junk-building industry; the boats were constructed from cypress wood found in the nearby hills. The city's market is well known for delicious, locally grown citrus fruits and a wide selection of bamboo and rattan handicrafts. On the outskirts of the town is **Taibai Rock**, where the Tang dynasty poet Li Bai (Li Po) is said to have stayed. The rock face around the memorial pavilion to the poet is covered with stone inscriptions.

South across the river, the town of **Yunyang** is famous in stories from the Three Kingdoms period (220–265). It is said that General Zhang Fei of the Kingdom of Shu (which covered most of present-day Sichuan) was assassinated in Yunyang. In his honour, the **Zhang Fei Temple** was built and contains stone carvings from the fifth and sixth centuries. The temple has been relocated above the projected water level about three kilometres (less than two miles) upstream, opposite the new town.

Fengjie, guarding the western entrance of the Three Gorges, is also associated with the Three Kingdoms period. It was here that Liu Bei, the King of Shu, died in despair after his armies were routed by the forces of Wu. The famous general of the state of Shu, Zhuge Liang, trained his troops in military strategy in the fields around Fengjie.

Baidicheng—or White Emperor City—can be reached by ferry from Fengjie. It offers splendid views into the mouth of the Qutang Gorge, and has a temple which was originally dedicated to the mythical White Emperor. In the Ming dynasty the temple was re-dedicated to General Zhuge Liang. One of its halls contains a 'Forest of Stelae', a collection of tablets which includes several rare stone carvings. The Bamboo Leaf Poem Tablet, on which the characters of a poem are engraved in the form of three bamboo branches, is one of only three of its kind in China.

The Zhailouge Pavilion as it was circa 1979—it has been saved from the rising water level of the dammed Yangzi by a protective coffer dam. [Tom Nebbia]

THE THREE GORGES

The Three Gorges of the Yangzi extend for 200 kilometres (125 miles) of the river's course, and span the boundary of Chongqing Municipality and Hubei Province. The first gorge on the downstream voyage is the Qutang. It is the shortest gorge, but visually the most dramatic. The second, the Wu (Sorceress) Gorge, is flanked by enchanting scenery of forest-clad slopes rising into strangely formed mountain peaks. The final gorge, the Xiling, is the longest of the three.

Before the construction of the Three Gorges Dam, the gorges pushed the river into a funnel of furious water, which in places had a velocity of 80,000 cubic metres (105,000 cubic yards) a second. At some points, the river was squeezed to a width of less than 100 metres (330 feet), and the water flow could reach 25 kilometres (15 miles) an hour. Following the completion of the dam the water level has already risen approximately 65 metres to135 metres (443 feet) above sea level. Between 2007 and 2009 the waters are due to rise a further 40 metres (131 feet). The Three Gorges remain, but with altered geography, making both the river's flow slower and water in its gorges deeper and wider. Doubtless, ships' captains welcome the easier and safer navigation.

The most spectacular of the gorges, the **Qutang Gorge**, was known to foreigners in the 19th century as 'The Windbox'. The name seems inappropriate on a fine day with a light mist hanging between towering cliffs, which themselves soar in deep shadow to over 1,200 metres (4,000 feet) either side of the river. Yet in a storm, with a high water level, the gorge was impossible to navigate, and many lost their lives while travelling through the Qutang. Look out for the Meng Liang stairway, a series of holes on the rock face which stops halfway up the river cliff. High on the slopes of the rock face were found some of the 2,000-year-old coffins from the state of Ba. It is a picture of the entrance to Qutang Gorge that appeared on the reverse of the old five yuan banknote (still to be found in circulation), and now decorates the latest ten yuan notes.

The twelve peaks of **Wu Gorge** all have poetic names. They include Fir Tree Cone Peak, the Gathered Immortals Peak, and the Assembled Cranes Peak. As the Chinese have a great love of weaving legends around strange natural phenomena, these gorges and mountains are therefore among their best-loved landscapes. The most renowned peak in this sense is **Goddess Peak** (Shennu Feng), which is said to resemble the figure of a maiden kneeling in front of a pillar. Legend has it that the young goddess was the daughter of the Queen Mother of the West, who fell in love with this lonely spot and made her home here.

Installation of one of the Three Gorges Dam's Francis-type turbines is an amazing feat in itself.
[China Yangtze Three Gorges Project Development Corporation]

At the end of Wu Gorge the town of **Badong** has been rebuilt three kilometres (less than two miles) upstream, as its predecessor was submerged by the rising waters. Opposite this, connected by a new suspension bridge, is the north-bank town of **Guandukou**, which sits at the mouth of the **Shennong Stream**. Since the completion of the dam, the increased water level has meant that this tributary has become navigable further up its course.

Passengers on some cruise ships now disembark here and transfer to a smaller vessel for a journey up the Shennong Stream, through tranquil scenery of verdant river cliffs and terraced fields, to **Bamboo Gorge**. Here they board small, traditional wooden boats known as *wan dou jiao*, or peapod boats, due to their shape. Teams of trackers—local Tujia tribesmen—skillfully paddle the boats upriver through the narrow, steep-sided gorge. On reaching shallower sections, they jump into the water and haul the boats over the rapids with traditional bamboo ropes, accompanied by the chants used for centuries by trackers on the Yangzi. In the quieter reaches of the gorges, golden-haired monkeys still roam in chattering bands. The region is famous for rare medicinal herbs.

Xiling Gorge, the next on the river, runs for 75 kilometres (45 miles) through slopes planted with orange groves. The gorge is divided into seven smaller gorges, the most famous of which are the Gorge of the Sword and the Book on the Art of War, the Gorge of the Ox's Liver and Horse's Lung, the Gorge of the Yellow Ox, and the Gorge of Shadow Play. The shoals and rapids within Xiling were the most treacherous of all obstacles in the Three Gorges. Until the 1950s, boats were hauled over them by trackers, whose backbreaking job would guarantee them an exceedingly short lifespan. A folk song about one of the most dangerous shoals has the following words: 'May the gods protect us as we sail through the Blue Shoal. If the Dragon King gets angry, then both men and boats are finished!' The Blue Shoal, like other river obstacles, was dynamited in the 1950s to make the Yangzi safer for navigation.

Approximately the mid-point of the Xiling Gorge, at Sandouping, is where the giant **Three Gorges Dam** is positioned. Vessels to and from Yichang and Wuhan must pass through five massive step locks. There are two sets of locks, one for upstream and one for downstream traffic. Cruise passengers are now able to visit the dam site, where there is a viewing platform and visitor centre.

Yichang marks the end of the upper reaches of the Yangzi and the beginning of the broader, middle reaches of the river. The city was an important river port, where goods were unloaded from the larger ships used further downstream, or from the smaller ships which travelled upstream through the gorges. West of the city is the

Three Travellers Cave, named after three Tang dynasty poets who first met there. It is famous for its Tang and Song inscriptions of poetry. The hill above the cave is an excellent place to go to enjoy a view of the eastern entrance of the Xiling Gorge. Yichang also marks the site of the legendary Yiling Battle between the states of Shu and Wu in the third century. The Wu army was smaller and weaker, but it used fire to destroy the camps of the Shu army. The King of Shu, Liu Bei, was bitterly disappointed after this battle and died soon afterwards in Fengjie. Further downstream on the north bank is the town of **Shashi**, with its riverside **Pagoda of Longevity**, built in the reign of Emperor Qianlong in the Qing dynasty.

Dongting Lake, below Shashi, was once China's largest freshwater lake. However, silting and land reclamation have reduced its size, and now it ranks second. Legends about Dongting abound. One Tang dynasty story has the lake as the home of the King of the Dragons. The lake was part of the intricate waterway system which allowed goods from the very south—as far as Guangzhou—to be brought by way of the Xiang River (a tributary), through the lake, to towns along the Yangzi. The lake was the scene of extensive flooding in the summer of 2002, with record rains bringing the inland body to the edge of inundating the neighbouring city of Yueyang.

THE LOWER RIVER

The triple city of **Wuhan**, which spans the confluence of the rivers Han and Yangzi, is for many travellers the end or the beginning of their river cruise. Wuhan has always been the Yangzi's main inland river port, since it marked the furthest point to which seagoing vessels could sail. In the 19th century, the city became a Treaty Port and grew rich on the tea trade which was centred on **Hankou** (one of the three connected cities).

Hankou, still the commercial centre of Wuhan, was declared a treaty port in 1861 as a result of concessions forced on China following the Opium War. Five Foreign Concessions (British, Russian, French, German and Japanese) were established shoulder-to-shoulder astride the north bank of the Yangzi River. The foreign concessions were all closed down by 1927, but many fine examples of turn-of-the-century European architecture still grace the bund area along Yanjiang Dadao and the streets north of the bund. The Wuhan City Government began to renovate many of these buildings in 2000.

The bund area was also renovated and reopened as a pleasant Riverside Promenade, which at 9.8 kilometres is eight times longer than that of Shanghai's Bund. On the other side of Yanjiang Dadao are a number of Western buildings dating back to the early 1900s. Highlights include the former German Consulate (1918), the Banque De L'Indo-chine (1917), the American Consulate (1905), the home of Song Qingling

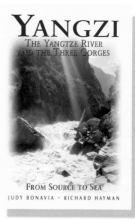

(1896), Hong Kong and Shanghai Bank (1917) and the National City Bank of New York (1921).

Head west along Yanjiang Dadao until you reach the Customs House, a Renaissance building erected in 1921. Turn right here on to Jianghan Street, better known now as the Pedestrian Walking Mall, or Buxing Jie in Chinese. The road was laid out in 1900 and marked the boundary between Chinese-inhabited Hankou and the concessions; it became a 1.2 kilometre pedestrian mall in 2000. Here, wonderful European architecture is juxtaposed by newer Western façades: McDonald's, KFC and Pizza Hut, as well as a few international and local brand-name shops.

In Hanyang, there are two famous sights—the Lute Pavilion and the Buddhist Guiyuan Monastery. The Lute Pavilion comprises a series of terraces and pavilions set amidst attractive gardens. It lives up to its musical name, since it is now a popular place with elderly music lovers who gather here for open-air performances. The Guiyuan Monastery was founded in the Qing dynasty and became an important centre for Chan (Zen) Buddhist scholarship. It has a collection of 500 carved and gilded *luohans* (Buddhist disciples), which are considered works of great craftsmanship. Inside the monastery is a vegetarian restaurant.

Wuchang, which sprawls along the opposite bank of the Yangzi River, is linked to an important event in Chinese revolutionary history. It was here that the military uprising started, which was ultimately to topple the Qing dynasty and bring about the founding of the Republic of China. Visitors can see the **Headquarters of the 1911 Revolution**, which is known locally as the Red House. A statue of Dr. Sun Yat-sen stands outside the building. Another place of special interest in Wuchang is the **Hubei Provincial Museum**, which houses artefacts excavated

(Right) *The Three Gorges Dam sluices can discharge 102,500 cubic metres (3,620,000 cubic feet) per second at their maximum capacity (excluding discharge through the generating units). Each of the dam's 23 deep outlets measures seven metres wide by nine metres high (23 feet by 29.5 feet). The 22 main outlets (pictured) each have an eight-metre (26.25 feet) clear width. The discharge section, located in the central section of the dam and at the centre of the river, links two hydropower stations. [Huang Zhengping]*

from the Warring States period tomb of the Marquis of Zeng. An impressive collection of 65 bronze chime bells forms only part of the tomb's treasures.

The Yellow Crane Tower is neither the original tower, nor is it the original site, but it remains a symbol of Wuhan. Chinese poets ascended the steps throughout history to praise the surrounding scenery. First built in 223, Yellow Crane Tower was originally located a short distance from here, on the bank of the Yangzi River. The complex has been rebuilt many times, most recently in 1986.

To rub elbows with the locals, take in the show at the base of the Changjiang Bridge, northwest of the Yellow Crane Tower. Every afternoon at 2pm, elderly opera buffs in costume and heavy makeup stage Chu opera, a Hubei province original, on a makeshift park stage. Another attraction is the neighbourhood grannies, who do a traditional drum dance. Hawkers peddle traditional medicine, fortunetellers shake their bamboo joss sticks, mahjong and card sharks hustle and curbside masseuses pound people's backs. There are even a few street dentists, bent over open-mouthed patients in folding chairs.

East Lake is a great place to escape city life. Six times larger than Hangzhou's West Lake, East Lake covers a total water area of 33 square kilometres, making it the largest urban lake in China. The lake has numerous pavilions, museums, botanical gardens and an aviary surrounding it. There are also places to sun bathe, swim and fish.

Zhongshan Warship, originally located at Baishazhou, was originally built for the Qing government by the Japanese in 1910. It was later destroyed in a Japanese bombing attack in 1938. In 1997, workers successfully salvaged the Zhongshan from the Yangzi River. The ship has been refurbished and is now a museum.

Hubei's excellent cuisine is reason enough to visit Wuhan. As a crossroads for nine provinces, Hubei has been influenced by other regions of China and its menu is varied and interesting. The food is excellent and cheap, even in the most expensive-looking restaurants. Popular local dishes include: steamed Wuchang fish, or bream, sparerib and lotus-root soup, hot-dry noodles, and doupi—pancakes stuffed with pork, other meat, and either mushrooms or shrimp.

The Wuhanese take breakfast so seriously that they have even coined their own name for this daily rite, *guozao*. The best place to sample a local breakfast is Hubu Lane, tucked away in a corner of Wuchang. Hubu Lane has more than 100 small eateries lining both sides of the street turning out breakfast favourites from around China. The most popular dish in the alley is *reganmian*, or hot dry noodles. A variety of seasonings can be added to the noodles: sesame oil, finely chopped garlic, diced radish, vinegar, white pepper, mustard tuber, ginger, scallion and chili—but the sine qua non is sesame paste.

WATER, WATER, EVERYWHERE, NOR ANY DROP TO DRINK . . . —By Olivia Walker

China's rapid economic development has had a stark impact on its rivers and lakes, resulting in an environmental problem that the country must face for the foreseeable future. In China many lakes are so polluted that they turn a Day-glo colour: lakes such as the Dianchi, Tai and Chao have experienced toxic algae blooms so bad that the government has had to find alternative drinking water for millions. This situation is becoming progressively worse as industrialization continues; the waste dumped into Dianchi almost doubled from 58 million cubic metres in 1999 to 97 million in 2004. With China's available water resources per capita being just a quarter of the world average, and more than 300 million of the rural population lacking access to safe drinking water, this is an environmental and humanitarian crisis of worrying proportions.

On a scale of A to E, with A indicating top water quality, and E categorized as water 'not to be touched by any part of the human body', 26 per cent of China's seven major water systems achieved a grade E, as did nine of its largest lakes. In Lake Dianchi for example, until its first wastewater plant was built in 1990, 90 per cent of Kunming's wastewater was pumped untreated into the lake. The lake water is now undrinkable despite several billion US dollars spent trying to clean it up, and it is believed that over 55 per cent of the lake's fish population has been killed off by disease.

One solution has seen towns and cities use underground aquifers for water, but this has actually added to the problem, with water tables falling as much as three metres in some northern cities

Special Topic

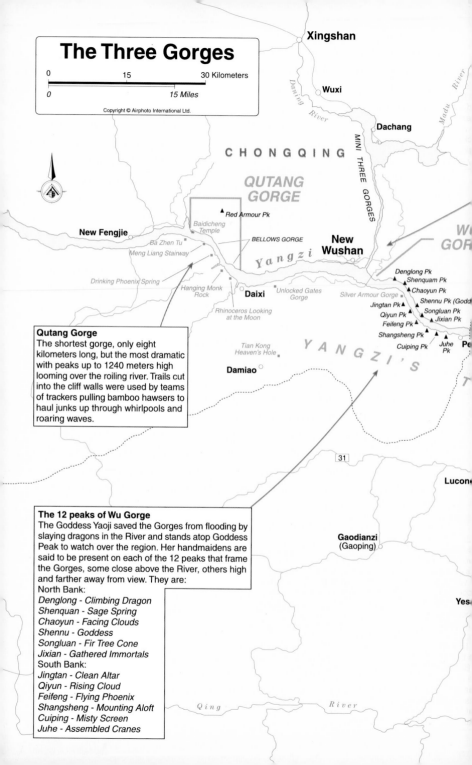

The Three Gorges

0 15 30 Kilometers
0 15 Miles

Copyright © Airphoto International Ltd.

Xingshan

Wuxi

Dachang

CHONGQING

QUTANG GORGE

MINI THREE GORGES

Daning River
Madu River

Red Armour Pk
Baidicheng Temple
BELLOWS GORGE
New Fengjie
Ba Zhen Tu
Meng Liang Stairway
Drinking Phoenix Spring
Hanging Monk Rock
Daixi
Unlocked Gates Gorge
Rhinoceros Looking at the Moon
Yangzi

New Wushan

Silver Armour Gorge
Denglong Pk
Shenquam Pk
Chaoyun Pk
Shennu Pk (Godd
Jingtan Pk
Songluan Pk
Qiyun Pk
Jixian Pk
Feifeng Pk
Shangsheng Pk
Cuiping Pk
Juhe Pk

W
GOR

Pe

Tian Kong Heaven's Hole
Damiao

YANGZI'S

31

Lucon

Gaodianzi (Gaoping)

Yes

Qing River

Qutang Gorge
The shortest gorge, only eight kilometers long, but the most dramatic with peaks up to 1240 meters high looming over the roiling river. Trails cut into the cliff walls were used by teams of trackers pulling bamboo hawsers to haul junks up through whirlpools and roaring waves.

The 12 peaks of Wu Gorge
The Goddess Yaoji saved the Gorges from flooding by slaying dragons in the River and stands atop Goddess Peak to watch over the region. Her handmaidens are said to be present on each of the 12 peaks that frame the Gorges, some close above the River, others high and farther away from view. They are:
North Bank:
Denglong - Climbing Dragon
Shenquan - Sage Spring
Chaoyun - Facing Clouds
Shennu - Goddess
Songluan - Fir Tree Cone
Jixian - Gathered Immortals
South Bank:
Jingtan - Clean Altar
Qiyun - Rising Cloud
Feifeng - Flying Phoenix
Shangsheng - Mounting Aloft
Cuiping - Misty Screen
Juhe - Assembled Cranes

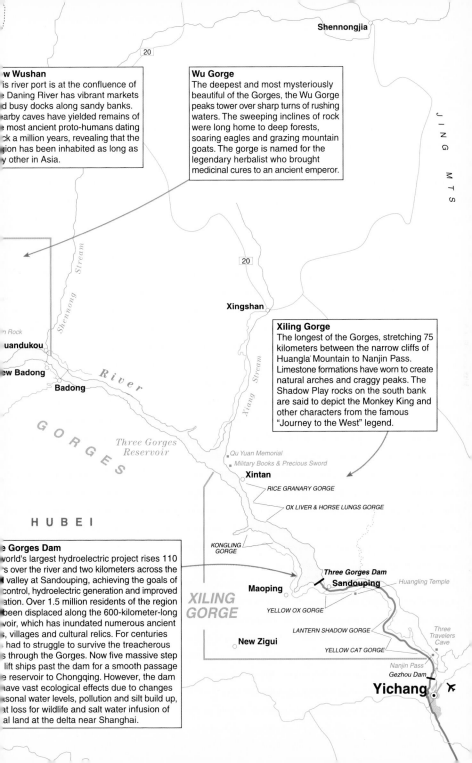

Shennongjia

20

w Wushan
is river port is at the confluence of
e Daning River has vibrant markets
d busy docks along sandy banks.
arby caves have yielded remains of
e most ancient proto-humans dating
ck a million years, revealing that the
jion has been inhabited as long as
y other in Asia.

Wu Gorge
The deepest and most mysteriously
beautiful of the Gorges, the Wu Gorge
peaks tower over sharp turns of rushing
waters. The sweeping inclines of rock
were long home to deep forests,
soaring eagles and grazing mountain
goats. The gorge is named for the
legendary herbalist who brought
medicinal cures to an ancient emperor.

J I N G   M T S

20

Xingshan

Xiling Gorge
The longest of the Gorges, stretching 75
kilometers between the narrow cliffs of
Huangla Mountain to Nanjin Pass.
Limestone formations have worn to create
natural arches and craggy peaks. The
Shadow Play rocks on the south bank
are said to depict the Monkey King and
other characters from the famous
"Journey to the West" legend.

Shennong Stream

n Rock

uandukou

ew Badong

Badong

R i v e r

Xiang Stream

Qu Yuan Memorial
Military Books & Precious Sword
Xintan

RICE GRANARY GORGE

OX LIVER & HORSE LUNGS GORGE

G O R G E S

Three Gorges Reservoir

KONGLING GORGE

H U B E I

e Gorges Dam
world's largest hydroelectric project rises 110
s over the river and two kilometers across the
l valley at Sandouping, achieving the goals of
control, hydroelectric generation and improved
ation. Over 1.5 million residents of the region
been displaced along the 600-kilometer-long
voir, which has inundated numerous ancient
, villages and cultural relics. For centuries
had to struggle to survive the treacherous
s through the Gorges. Now five massive step
lift ships past the dam for a smooth passage
e reservoir to Chongqing. However, the dam
have vast ecological effects due to changes
sonal water levels, pollution and silt build up,
at loss for wildlife and salt water infusion of
al land at the delta near Shanghai.

Three Gorges Dam
Sandouping

Huangling Temple

Maoping

XILING
GORGE

YELLOW OX GORGE

LANTERN SHADOW GORGE

Three Travelers Cave

New Zigui

YELLOW CAT GORGE

Nanjin Pass
Gezhou Dam

Yichang

including Beijing. Some experts believe that towns in Hebei have used aquifers to such an extent that they will soon be sitting on 'hollow ground'. The World Bank has estimated China's annual economic loss due to water shortages from pollution at US$20 billion, although the full environmental impact is still being evaluated.

Pollution is thought to have significantly reduced rainfall in hilly areas of China, in some cases by up to 50 per cent. Emissions from factories, power plants, cars and agricultural burning all pump polluting particles into the atmosphere, which act as an inhibitor to the formation of rain droplets. In the past few decades China's rapid industrialization has produced vast amounts of particle pollution known as the 'Asian haze'.

Fisheries have incurred an estimated loss of around US$530 million through disease, infection and poison to their stock. Human health has similarly been affected and research is ongoing into the link between high levels of water pollution and rising cancer rates. This issue received intensive publicity when 'cancer villages' appeared on polluted stretches of the Huai River and Tai Lake in Jiangsu Province. A survey in 2003 by the Chinese Health Ministry found that over 480,000 people die of liver, stomach, intestine and bladder cancer in rural areas each year.

The Chinese government is, however, well aware of its water crisis and the huge effect it will have on future development. With this in mind, water issues are supposedly at the top of the political agenda and the National People's Congress has overhauled the country's 23-year-old water pollution law, the first major revision in a decade. Of course, overcoming China's pollution problems will incur phenomenal cost—though in all probability far less in the long term than the economic losses caused by the negative effects of pollution.

A realistic and lasting overhaul will need to address the lax emission standards for industry, the flouting of pre-existing laws by businesses and the overall failure to build new water treatment facilities. The truth is that the problem will persist until a more effective monitoring and punishment system is put in place—the system as it stands is too fragmented, with different agencies in charge of interlinked aspects of water treatment, resulting in a lack of responsibility and obligation. To achieve long-term environmental, economic *and* humanitarian gain a single institution and more legislative tools are needed.

China's Herculean task is to reconcile its economic development with its environment as soon as possible, as the two cannot be mutually exclusive. Some argue that the industrialization taking place in China may be harming the environment and public health but still does 'more good than harm for the country's overall development'. Yet to be economically stable in the long term China cannot ignore its water crisis or its many other environmental issues. Returning China's water resources to a healthy state is a huge responsibility—unless urgent action is taken the flood of serious issues will swell and inundate the country, with predictably disastrous results. Perhaps the best way for the powers-that-be to envisage the situation is as a huge opportunity: to build a better environmental infrastructure, increase public awareness and develop a conscientious conservation ethic that will save and enhance China's otherwise almost unlimited potential.

Needless to say, travellers to China will in the main be happily unaware of its water issues—hotel water supplies are of international standard, as are virtually all urban service industry facilities. Only in remote rural areas should care be taken.

Special Topic

In the evening try dinner at one of the outdoor restaurants on Jiqing Street. Diners pack the area each night to be entertained by the some 300 licensed performers who work the street, roaming from table to table, restaurant to restaurant, in search of an audience. The extravaganza comprises guitarists, banjo players, opera performers, accordianists, erhu players, comedians, rock singers, artists, shoeshine kids and flower girls. The average tableside show costs 10 RMB per song.

Leaving Hubei Province, the next port of call is **Jiujiang**. Once an important river port for the tea trade, Jiujiang now thrives on its cotton industry. The city lies just west of **Poyang Lake**, one of China's best-known nature reserves, a wintering ground for rare white- and red-crested cranes, as well as storks and wildfowl. Jiujiang is the stopping-off point for visits to the mountain resort of **Lushan**. Lushan is attractive in spring, when the azaleas are in flower, but it receives a heavy swell of visitors in the summer months, when the mountains offer a cool retreat from the baking temperatures of the Yangzi plain. Close to Jiujiang is **Stone Bell Hill**, which overlooks the spot where Poyang Lake meets the Yangzi. The hill is chiefly of interest for its unsolved mystery—nobody can quite give an explanation for a strange bell-like sound that can be heard on the hill, though some people believe it is caused by flowing water. In the Song dynasty, the poet Su Dongpo was so intrigued by the hill that he came here three times.

Xiaogushan, below the mouth of the Poyang, is a small riverine island which, through silting, has now become part of the north bank of the river. Legend tells of a maiden, Xiaogu Niang Niang, who when eloping with her lover on a flying umbrella, dropped her slipper into the river. The slipper miraculously turned into an island. The girl and her lover fell from the sky and became mountains divided by the river. There is a temple on the island dedicated to Xiaogu Niang Niang, which is visited by infertile women who come in the hope of bearing a child. Downstream, again on the north bank, is the octagonal Ming-dynasty **Zhenfeng Pagoda** of Anqing. By now the Yangzi is in Anhui Province. Anhui's two great scenic sites are the mountains of Huangshan and Jiuhuashan. The town of **Wuhu** is situated at the confluence of the Qingyi and Yangzi rivers. As this was a danger spot for navigation, a pagoda was built to act as a lighthouse. It was named **Zhongjiang** ('Mid-River') **Pagoda**, and does indeed mark the mid-point of the lower Yangzi, from the mouth of Poyang Lake to the estuary above Shanghai. For **Nanjing**, *see* page 98.

Zhenjiang was a city of great strategic importance in the Three Kingdoms period and it served as the capital of the state of Wu. It is here that the Grand Canal intersects the Yangzi, thus making Zhenjiang an important trading centre. The hills around the

The Twenty-four Bridge on Yangzhou's Slender West Lake. [Gisling/Wikimedia Commons, licensed under the GFDL]

city were the source of inspiration for many painters of the Southern Song school. In the middle of the river at Zhenjiang rises **Jiao Hill**, where the Song dynasty painter Mi Fei, and the poet Lu You, had stone inscriptions carved in their own calligraphy.

The nearby **Jin Shan** was once a riverine island, but silting has joined it to the southern bank of the river. The monastery of Jin Shan is still an important place of Buddhist pilgrimage. To the northeast of the city lies **Beigu Hill**, considered to be the most beautiful of Zhenjiang's hills. It appears in many of the stories in the *Romance of the Three Kingdoms* (*see* Recommended Reading, page 389).

To the north of the Yangzi, on the Grand Canal itself, lies the city of **Yangzhou**, once one of the wealthiest of Chinese cities. During the Tang dynasty, its merchants thrived on the salt trade (which was an imperial monopoly) and gave their patronage to the many artists who flocked here. Today Yangzhou has retained its traditional charms. One of the most delightful ways to pass your time here is to stroll through the lanes which thread between the city's canals. The buildings around the **Slender West Lake** are some of the finest, with their simple whitewashed walls and contrasting dark-grey tiled roofs, which sweep up into flying eaves. A large community of Arab traders resided in the city in the Yuan dynasty, and the city mosque, the **Xianhe Si**, dates from the 13th century. Puhaddin, who was a 16th-generation descendant of the Prohet Mohammed, came to China in the mid-13th century and was buried in Yangzhou. In the **Museum** there is a good collection of the works of the Eight Eccentric Painters of Yangzhou, who lived in the 18th century. Unlike most scholar-painters of the time, who regarded painting as a purely academic pursuit, these painters were so unconventional as to make their living from the sale of their works to the wealthy merchants of Yangzhou. For **Shanghai**, *see* page 131.

THE GOOD LIFE

Far away in the East, under sunshine such as you never saw (for even such light as you have you stain and infect with sooty smoke), on the shore of a broad river stands the house where I was born. It is one among thousands; but every one stands in its own garden, simply painted in white or gray, modest, cheerful, and clean. For many miles along the valley, one after the other, they lift their blue- or red-tiled roofs out of a sea of green; while here and there glitters out over a clump of trees the gold enamel of some tall pagoda. The river, crossed by frequent bridges and crowded with barges and junks, bears on its clear stream the traffic of thriving village-markets. For prosperous peasants people all the district, owning and tilling the fields their fathers owned and tilled before them. The soil on which they work, they may say, they and their ancestors have made. For see! Almost to the summit what once were barren hills are waving green with cotton and rice, sugar, oranges, and tea. Water drawn from the river-bed girdles the slopes with silver; and falling from channel to channel in a thousand bright cascades, splashing in cisterns, chuckling in pipes, soaking and oozing in the soil, distributes freely to all alike fertility, verdure, and life. Hour after hour you may traverse, by tortuous paths, over tiny bridges, the works of the generations who have passed, the labors of their children of today; till you reach the point where man succumbs and Nature has her way, covering the highest crags with a mantle of azure and gold and rose, gardenia, clematis, azalea, growing luxuriantly wild. How often here have I sat for hours in a silence so intense that, as one of our poets has said, "you may hear the shadows of the trees rustling on the ground"; a silence broken only now and again from far below by voices of laborers calling across the water-courses, or, at evening or dawn, by the sound of gongs summoning to worship from the temples in the valley. Such silence! Such sounds! Such perfume! Such color! The senses respond to their objects; they grow exquisite to a degree you cannot well conceive in your northern climate; and beauty pressing in from without moulds the spirit and mind insensibly to harmony with herself. If in

China we have manners, if we have art, if we have morals, the reason, to those who can see, is not far to seek. Nature has taught us; and so far, we are only more fortunate than you. But, also, we have had the grace to learn her lesson; and that, we think, we may ascribe to our intelligence. For, consider, here in this lovely valley live thousands of souls without any law save that of custom, without any rule save that of their own hearths. Industrious they are, as you hardly know industry in Europe; but it is the industry of free men working for their kith and kin, on the lands they received from their fathers, to transmit, enriched by their labors, to their sons. They have no other ambition; they do not care to amass wealth; and if in each generation some must needs go out into the world, it is with the hope, not commonly frustrated, to return to the place of their birth and spend their declining years among the scenes and faces that were dear to their youth. Among such a people there is no room for fierce, indecent rivalries. None is master, none servant; but equality, concrete and real, regulates and sustains their intercourse. Healthy toil, sufficient leisure, frank hospitality, a content born of habit and undisturbed by chimerical ambitions, a sense of beauty fostered by the loveliest Nature in the world, and finding expression in gracious and dignified manners where it is not embodied in exquisite works of art—such are the characteristics of the people among whom I was born. Does my memory flatter me? Do I idealize the scenes of my youth? It may be so. But this I know: that some such life as I have described, reared on the basis of labor on the soil, of equality and justice, does exist and flourish throughout the length and breadth of China.

Anonymous, *Letters from a Chinese Official;*
Being an Eastern View of Western Civilization, 1903

Literary Excerpt

FUJIAN

The coastal province of Fujian in southeast China is one of the areas least explored by foreign visitors. Yet the province offers some of the best sightseeing, historic sites and local cuisine found anywhere in China, with the bonus of a warm, subtropical climate which makes winter visits an attractive option. The four main cities of Fujian are the capital Fuzhou, Xiamen (Amoy), Quanzhou and Zhangzhou. In the west and north of the province lie the scenic Wuyi Mountains (*see* page 356).

Fujian has a long indented coastline backed by steep and rugged mountains where much of the soil is too poor for rice farming. The Fujianese have traditionally earned their living from the sea, and by growing fruit, vegetables and tea. Poverty and the beckoning seaboard had encouraged emigration since the end of the Song dynasty. In the 19th and early 20th centuries, the existing land tenure system forced many more poorer peasants to emigrate, and now the overseas Fujianese community is second only to that of the Cantonese. Most overseas Chinese from Fujian settled in Southeast Asia, with a large proportion in the Philippines. Taiwan, lying only 160 kilometres (100 miles) across from Fujian, has also had its share of Fujianese emigrants in the last three centuries. So many people on either side of the Taiwan Straits share common ancestors and speak the same dialect that the renewal of ties which has come with China's more liberal economic climate is hardly surprising. In spite of the tensions which exist across the Straits between Taiwan and mainland China, business continues to cement the relationship. Taiwan remains the single largest source of foreign investment in Fujian.

Fujian has a long history of trade with the outside world. In 1842—by the Treaty of Nanking—Fuzhou and Xiamen (then known as Amoy) were two of five Treaty Ports opened to foreign commerce and residence. The city of Quanzhou had a large foreign population during the Tang and Yuan dynasties, including many Arabs. Their descendants, and their converts' descendants, still live in distinct Muslim communities throughout the province. Many of Fujian's mountain people are not Han Chinese. One of the most distinctive minority communities is the She people. Young people from the She villages often work in the cities to save enough money to get married. The girls wear headdresses of bright scarves over a frame shaped like a coathanger without the hook.

There are some wonderful off-the-beaten-track places to visit in Fujian, if you are willing to take local buses and wander at will. If you are visiting in the warmer months, the coast has some lovely golden sand beaches. Local cooking places emphasis on what is readily available—fresh vegetables and seafood—and is delicious.

Fujian

With the influx of overseas Chinese tourists, who come back to visit their ancestral villages, new hotels have proliferated and transportation is much improved.

FUZHOU

The provincial capital, Fuzhou, has a glorious setting on the banks of the Min River, against a backdrop of mountains. It has grown up around three hills—Yushan, Gushan and Wushan—which are areas of scenic interest with numerous pavilions, temples and museums. The city is famous for its lacquerware and puppet troupe, but other reasons to visit the city are its excellent seafood restaurants, various craft factories, and excursions to the numerous old temples around the city.

Yushan lies in a striking location at the mouth of the Min River and, although small, it has three temples, several pavilions and the city's landmarks, the famous **White and Black Pagodas**. These pagodas were first built in the 10th century and each has seven storeys. You will also find the **Fuzhou Antique Shop** on Yushan.

West of Yushan lies the small hill of **Wushan**. The hill was originally a place of Taoist retreat. It has many small pavilions sited to offer views over the countryside and river estuary. There are several stone carvings on the hillside, the most remarkable of which is an image of Buddha on the southeastern slope. Close to Fuzhou University, the **Xichan Temple** is a lively city temple, which has been restored by donations from overseas Chinese.

Visitors will not want to leave Fuzhou without one momento of its famous 'Three Handicraft Treasures of Fuzhou'—Stone carving, lacquerware and cork sculpting—available at the craft factories or on Wusi Lu near the Overseas Chinese Hotel.

QUANZHOU

South of Fuzhou, on the banks of the Jin River, lies the ancient port city of Quanzhou. Its quiet, prosperous air belies its distinction as China's first port in the Song and Yuan dynasties. Though its harbour silted up in the Ming dynasty and is now of minor importance, it remains the commercial centre for the surrounding farmlands.

As a reminder of Quanzhou's maritime links, the Muslim community flourishes. From the Tang to the Yuan dynasties, Arab merchants traded and settled in Quanzhou, what they called 'Zaytun'—the Great Emporium. A short walk from the Overseas Chinese Hotel is the **Grand Mosque**. Built in the first years of the 11th century, it is still an active worship centre. Just east of the city is the burial site of two Tang dynasty era Muslim missionaries, **Lingshan** (Ling Hill).

(Following page) *Women of Hui'an County in Fujian Province. [Wang Gangfeng]*

Fujian

In the old quarter, to the northwest of the city, the **Kaiyuan Temple** is one of the most famous in the region. Founded in the Tang dynasty, it has some fine examples of Buddhist architecture and statuary dating from the Song dynasty. To the east is the **Ancient Boat Exhibition**, the remains of a Song dynasty seagoing ship excavated downstream of the city and now housed in this hall. A dramatic new museum, with towers shaped like junk sails, has opened with exhibits related to the era when Quanzhou was a big port on the so called 'Maritime Silk Road'.

ZHANGZHOU

Like Quanzhou, Zhangzhou was also a large port city, until its tidal creek silted up and it was eclipsed by the nearby port of Xiamen. Zhangzhou now serves as a market for the farmers of the rich, fertile plain of the Jiulong River. The area is famous for its tropical fruits, such as pineapples, bananas, lychees and *longyans* (Dragon's Eyes), as well as for the popular Chinese New Year flower, the narcissus, which is grown for special effect in water. The city is also renowned for its art galleries, craft factories and local opera troupes, which often give open-air performances.

XIAMEN

On the southern coast of Fujian, the thriving commercial city and port of Xiamen is one of the success stories of China's economic reform programme. The city is China's third Special Economic Zone, and it has a thriving electronics industry as well as a port with good facilities for seagoing vessels.

Its beautiful setting, on an island linked to the mainland by a narrow causeway, led to a ban on heavy industry in the city, giving it a relatively pollution-free atmosphere. Its rocky shores face several offshore islands on the eastern side, one of which—**Gulangyu**—is the city's own resort, with old villas and car-free lanes.

East of Xiamen's city centre and against the slopes of Wulao Mountain are the rising terraces and courtyards of Buddhist **Nanputuo Monastery**. It runs a vegetarian restaurant in a side courtyard and has one of China's few Buddhist schools. Not far away is the **Overseas Chinese Museum**, built by Fujian's favourite son, Tan Kah Kee, who made a fortune in Singapore and returned to his birthplace to give generously of his time and money. The museum tells the story of the Chinese diaspora.

The lovely island of Gulangyu has golden sand beaches for swimming in warmer months, narrow lanes full of hawker stalls, and the Lotus Flower Monastery, known locally as the **Sunlight Monastery**. It stands on the high point of the island called **Sunlight Rock**, which, climbed at dawn, gives an excellent view of the sunrise over the sea. The island has four churches, and every Christmas Eve a carol service is held there.

FOREIGN DEVIL

I always objected to halt at a city, but arriving at that of Liang-shan Hsien late on the afternoon of the third day from Wan, it was necessary to change the chai-jen [sedan-chair bearers] and get my passport copied. An imposing city it is, on a height, approached by a steep flight of stairs with a sharp turn under a deep picturesque gateway in a fine wall, about which are many picturesque and fantastic buildings. The gateway is almost a tunnel, and admits into a street fully a mile and a half long, and not more than ten feet wide, with shops, inns, brokers, temples with highly decorated fronts, and Government buildings "of sorts" along its whole length.

I had scarcely time to take it in when men began to pour into the roadway from every quarter, hooting, and some ran ahead—always a bad sign. I proposed to walk, but the chairmen said it was not safe. The open chair, however, was equally an abomination. The crowd became dense and noisy; there was much hooting and yelling. I recognised many cries of Yang kwei-tze! (foreign devil) and "Child-eater!" swelling into a roar; the narrow street became almost impassable; my chair was struck repeatedly with sticks; mud and unsavoury missiles were thrown with excellent aim; a well-dressed man, bolder or more cowardly than the rest, hit me a smart whack across my chest, which left a weal; others from behind hit me across the shoulders; the howling was infernal: it was an angry Chinese mob. There was nothing for it but to sit up stolidly, and not to appear hurt, frightened, or annoyed, though I was all three.

Unluckily the bearers were shoved to one side, and stumbling over some wicker oil casks (empty, however), knocked them over, when there was a scrimmage, in which they were nearly knocked down. One runner dived into an inn doorway, which the innkeeper closed in a fury, saying he would not admit a foreigner; but he shut the door on the chair, and I got out on the inside, the bearers and porters squeezing in after me, one chair-pole being broken in the crush. I was hurried to the top of a large inn yard and shoved into a room, or rather a dark shed. The innkeeper tried, I was told, to shut and bar the street-door, but it was burst open, and the whole of the planking torn down. The mob surged in 1500 or 2000 strong, led by some literati, as I could see through the chinks.

There was then a riot in earnest; the men had armed themselves with pieces of the doorway, and were hammering at the door and wooden front of my room, surging against the door to break it down, howling and yelling. Yang-kwei-tze! had been abandoned as too mild, and the yells, as I learned afterwards, were such as "Beat her!" "Kill her!" "Burn her!" The last they tried to carry into effect. My den had a second wooden wall to another street, and the mob on that side succeeded in breaking a splinter out, through which they inserted some lighted matches, which fell on some straw and lighted it. It was damp, and I easily trod it out, and dragged a board over the hole. The place was all but pitch-dark, and was full of casks, boards, and chunks of wood. The door was secured by strong wooden bars.

They brought joists up wherewith to break in the door, and at every rush— and the rushes were made with a fiendish yell—I expected it to give way. At last the upper bar yielded, and the upper part of the door caved in a little. They doubled their efforts, and the door in another minute would have fallen in, when the joists were thrown down, and in the midst of a sudden silence there was the rush, like a swirl of autumn leaves, of many feet, and in a few minutes the yard was clear, and soldiers, who remained for the night, took up positions there. One of my men, after the riot had lasted for an hour, had run to the yamen with the news that the people were "murdering a foreigner," and the mandarin sent soldiers with orders for the tumult to cease, which he might have sent two hours before, as it can hardly be supposed that he did not know of it.

The innkeeper, on seeing my special passport, was uneasy and apologetic, but his inn was crowded, he had no better room to give me, and I was too tired and shaken to seek another. The host's wife came in to see me, and speaking apologetically of the riot, she said, "If a foreign woman went to your country, you'd kill her, wouldn't you?"

Isabella Bird, *The Yangtze Valley and Beyond*, 1899

Isabella Lucy (Bird) Bishop (1831–1904) was
the first woman member of the Royal Geographical Society.
She travelled extensively and wrote numerous books.
She also founded several hospitals in both China and Korea.

SACRED MOUNTAINS

ountain climbing was a traditional pastime in ancient China. Emperors went to mountains to make sacrifices to heaven and the deities. Scholars went to draw inspiration for poetry and painting. Mystics went to become Buddhist monks or Taoist hermits. Ordinary people went to pray and worship. Thus mountain climbing in China was more than a sport. It was a popular religious and cultural activity. This partly explains why Chinese mountains are so well laid out with walking trails, stone markers, hermitages, monasteries, guesthouses and tea pavilions. Several sacred mountains have been selected as World Heritage Sites.

The Chinese have divided their mountains between Taoist and Buddhist peaks. Taoists were philosophers with an interest in alchemy, herbal medicine and the general world of nature. They regarded the pursuit of immortality and oneness with the cosmos as a way of life. The common people, however, also established and worshipped a pantheon of Taoist deities. The Buddhists believed that the path to enlightenment lay in good works, a knowledge of the Buddhist scriptures, and in meditation far from the everyday world. Both Taoists and Buddhists therefore saw mountains as a natural refuge. In early times, the religious affiliation of a mountain was not so clearly defined—Buddhist and Taoist communities often shared the same mountain. Today, however, the divisions are clear. The four Buddhist mountains are Emeishan in Sichuan (*see* WHS page 341), Wutaishan in Shanxi, Putuoshan off the coast of Zhejiang, and Jiuhuashan in Anhui Province. The five Taoist mountains are Taishan in Shandong Province (*see* WHS page 323), Huashan in Shaanxi, Northern Hengshan in Shanxi, Southern Hengshan in Hunan and Songshan in Henan. Huangshan in Anhui Province belongs to neither category, and is not a holy mountain though it is a World Heritage site (*see* WHS page 326).

The Southern and Northern Heng mountains and Mount Song have not been included here, since they are not easily accessible to foreign travellers (though many would say this is a very good reason to visit them). All of the sacred mountains described here are popular with foreign visitors; in fact, some of them have become so popular, especially with overseas Chinese and Hong Kong visitors, that they have been officially designated as 'Tourist Zones' (Jiuhuashan and Putuoshan, for example). Few travellers would plan to scale all the peaks of China's mountains, but a trip to at least one of them could be included as part of a regional tour. Some of the more enterprising international travel companies now include mountain trips as part of their itinerary.

*A state-of-the-art, Austrian-built, gondola lift whisks sight-seers 1,610 metres
to the top of Huashan's north peak in just five minutes. [Paul Mooney]*

HUASHAN

uashan, with its fearsome five peaks, rises over 2,400 metres (8,000 feet) above the plains of Shaanxi Province, to the east of Xi'an. The mountain was once off-limits to foreigners, but even after opening it was only for the fittest, bravest travellers. The mountain paths were carved out of bare rock in many places and lead past dizzying precipices. However, a new cable car and improved mountain paths now make Huashan accessible to most visitors.

Like Taishan to the east, Huashan is a Taoist mountain and a site of imperial sacrifices. History records that the founders of the Shang and Zhou dynasties made sacrifices on this mountain, which dominated a strategic pass at a great bend of the Yellow River. Its peaks are dotted with small Taoist shrines and large temples, some of which are used as guesthouses. The most spectacular view can be had from the **West Peak Monastery**, which sits astride a narrow ridge of bald granite, topped with wind-sculpted pine trees.

WUTAISHAN

To the northeast of the city of Taiyuan, in Shanxi Province, soars the five-peaked mass of Wutaishan. The mountain is sacred to Buddhists. It represents Manjusri, the Bodhisattva of Transcendent Wisdom, known in Chinese as Wenshu. Being close to the grasslands of Inner Mongolia, Wutaishan was a frequently visited place of pilgrimage for Mongolians who had adopted the Tibetan version of the faith.

In the centre of the small town of Taihuai the temples and monasteries seem also to jostle for space as much as the crowds do. Those in the surrounding countryside are quieter, but easily reached by bus or on foot, and those on the surrounding five peaks either on small group tours or by chartered jeep or minibus from the town. Although much has undergone heavy-handed restoration, there's still some rare Tang architecture in the area—tucked away between Taihuai and the county town of Wutaixian are the two oldest surviving halls in China. Nights are cool even in mid-summer, so dress appropriately.

PUTUOSHAN

Putuoshan rises out of the sea off the coast of Zhejiang Province. This rocky island, seven kilometres (four miles) long by five kilometres (three miles) wide, is a remarkable sanctuary of peace and beauty, which has been a Buddhist site of pilgrimage since the Tang dynasty. In the early 13th century, it was dedicated to Guanyin, the Goddess of Mercy, by an imperial decree.

Now designated a 'Tourist Zone', Putuoshan is reached by boat from Ningbo or via the larger island of Dinghai. Like other religious establishments, Putuoshan's monasteries were closed during the Cultural Revolution, and the thousands of monks and nuns who lived there were forced to return to their towns and villages. Some of the original Buddhist inhabitants have now returned, and in the last few years the island has again become an active centre of Buddhist worship.

The three great monasteries of Putuoshan are the **Puji Si**, **Huiji Si** and **Fayu Si**. The Puji Si buildings date from the Qing dynasty, but the tiles of the roof of the monastery's Great Hall come from the Ming palaces of Nanjing, destroyed by the Manchu troops when they conquered China in 1644. Located on Buddha's Peak, the Huiji Si is a Ming foundation which can be reached by bus or up a flight of 1,000 stone steps—a challenge for the very devout who ascend it by prostrating themselves at every third step. The Fayu Si, a later foundation than Puji Si, has an attractive setting, rising in terraces amidst tree-clad slopes.

JIUHUASHAN

The Buddhist peaks of Jiuhuashan lie south of the Yangzi River in Anhui Province. Jiuhuashan is dedicated to the Bodhisattva Dizang. Its 90 peaks rise as high as 900 metres (3,000 feet) against the backdrop of a wooded plain. The trails make comfortable walking, except for those to the summit, and just under 100 monasteries have survived to this day. The most prominent of these, the **Dizang Si**, is dedicated to Dizang. This Bodhisattva is believed to be able to open the gates of hell to release the suffering souls, so the monastery was by tradition a point of pilgrimage for bereaved relatives. Some of the mountain temples were founded as early as the fourth century, but most of the buildings that have survived to this day date from the Qing period.

HONG KONG SPECIAL ADMINISTRATIVE REGION

S o long regarded as a gateway to China, especially since China opened its doors to tourism in the late 1970s, Hong Kong remains a good place to begin a China tour, being served by almost every top airline in the world at discount rates. Moreover, purpose-built rail links make it possible to board a train in Kowloon directly to Guangzhou, Beijing or Shanghai. Hong Kong is a fascinating blend of the Orient and Occident, scenic wonder, economic miracle and shopping paradise.

The main centres of population in Hong Kong are Hong Kong Island itself and Kowloon. The Island and the tip of Kowloon peninsula were ceded to Britain 'in perpetuity' by the so-called 'Unequal Treaties' which concluded the two Opium Wars between Britain and China in the 19th century. Thereafter, Hong Kong flourished as the base for British opium trading. In 1898, Britain leased more of Kowloon and the

Hong Kong

(Opposite page) *Central district, a financial hub, as seen from above Tsim Sha Tsui.* (Left) *The Big Buddha on Lantau Island is one of Hong Kong's major tourist attractions, especially now that a cable car from the MTR rail line at Tung Chung can whisk visitors up to it in some style.* [Jeremy Tredinnick]

New Territories from China for a period of 99 years. That lease expired in 1997, hence the historic agreement to return Hong Kong to Chinese sovereignty spelt out in the Sino-British Joint Declaration made in 1984.

By its bizarre, overnight change of ownership on 30 June–1 July, 1997—one day the concern of British Cabinet ministers in London's Downing Street, the next that of the Chinese Communist Party's Politburo in Beijing's Zhongnanhai—Hong Kong's traditional attraction as a destination for travellers has been enhanced by its appointment with history decided upon in 1984 between the late Chinese leader Deng Xiaoping and the then British Prime Minister, Margaret Thatcher.

Hong Kong, now part of the big country again albeit a special one bearing the name of Special Administrative Region (SAR), continues to function mostly autonomously. According to the SAR's Basic Law, Hong Kong will be able to maintain its capitalist economy for 50 years, accommodated ideologically in Beijing by Deng Xiaoping's 'one country, two systems' concept.

The lease of 1898 gave Hong Kong a large number of offshore islands as well as the New Territories. It is these islands, and the remoter areas of the New Territories, which offer a glimpse into Hong Kong's older rural world, soon to be gone forever. The farmers of the New Territories and the outlying islands are mainly Hakka people; the women are easy to identify, since they wear a traditional headdress of a woven rattan hat with a black cloth fringe. In the New Territories, you can still see the traditional walled villages of the Hakka (fortified against their Cantonese neighbours, with whom they rarely inter-married in the past). One of these villages, Sam Tung Uk in Tsuen Wan, is now preserved as a museum in the middle of a highrise estate.

Hong Kong's rural life is dying as farmers get older and their better educated offspring take up work in the city. After all, Hong Kong is the fourth largest financial centre and one of the biggest ports in the world. Business dominates Hong Kong. If you walk down a busy street in Central, the financial district on Hong Kong Island, you will see people consulting their wireless PDAs, likely getting an update on the stock market's movements. The value of trading on the Hong Kong Exchange may fall far short of Wall Street's, but it is still an important market for international dealers because of its regional position and its slot in the international time zones.

Business has made Hong Kong prosperous—and it shows. The biggest Paris and Italian fashion houses have several branches in Hong Kong; new buildings such as the 88-storey/420 metre IFC2 in Central and elsewhere are being designed by world-famous architects. The Bank of China headquarters was designed by I. M. Pei, the Chinese-American architect who was also responsible for a controversial building at the Louvre in Paris. Norman Foster's Hong Kong Bank building has been written up in all the architectural magazines. The Hong Kong Convention and Exhibition Centre in Wanchai and the airport at Chek Lap Kok are further examples of Hong Kong's building marvels. Hong Kong's image in the world has changed radically since the 1960s, when it was known for its sweatshops and jeans factories. Although it is still a large exporter of garments, Hong Kong now manufactures for top designers. Gone are the days when the label 'Made in Hong Kong' meant something cheap and shoddy. 'Made in Hong Kong' now has prestige and style, as one can quickly see just by milling around Central—the business district—during the working week. Its citizens, ever fashion-conscious, not only dress elegantly but are also particularly susceptible to the acquisition of status symbols. While Mercedes are ubiquitous, Hong Kong has the greatest concentration of Rolls Royces per square kilometre in the world.

CITY SIGHTS

The visitor to Hong Kong has a dazzling variety of choice over ways to spend time profitably in the Special Administrative Region. Many people enjoy the shopping, of course, and the wonderful restaurants and nightlife. But there are are other ways to spend your days—which could mean anything from a ferry ride to one of the outlying islands, a day out at the marine centre of **Ocean Park**, or a visit to one of the old temples or markets of Kowloon. Listed here is a small selection of possible sights and pleasures. The rest is up to the individual visitor.

The Peak, also known as Victoria Peak, is the mountain-top residential district of the rich and powerful. It is also a marvellous place to look out over the city, the harbour and the islands. If you are fit, and the weather is not too hot, you can walk to the top.

There are two shady, quiet paths—one starts from Magazine Gap Road, the other from Conduit Road. The most popular and comfortable way to the top is the eight-minute journey by the **Peak Tram**, which has its terminus just off Garden Road. Once at the top, you can walk up to the summit or take the circular trail which starts just to the right of the exit of the Peak Tram terminus. The **Peak Tower** (which looks like a cross between a lost spaceship and an antique Chinese vessel) has a coffee shop which offers good food with stunning window views. Over the road from the terminus, the **Peak Café** offers an airy setting for a meal or just a cup of tea.

Usually overlooked by foreign visitors but much loved by local residents, the **Botanical Gardens** can be found up the hill from Central, behind the former **Government House**. In the morning, old people gather to swap gossip and do their calisthenic exercises. The gardens are pleasant, but the small zoo is the main

attraction with its leopards, orangutans and wonderful landscaped aviaries full of rockpools, waterfalls and exotic foliage. The zoo is famous for its pioneer work in captive breeding of such endangered species as the Philippines Palawan Peacock and the Chinese Crane.

On the other side of Garden Road is **Hong Kong Park**, with a huge walk-in aviary, conservatory and Flagstaff House, a colonial relic from 1846, which was restored to house the **Museum of Tea Ware.**

For ordinary Hong Kong people, a ride on the **Star Ferry** is the cheapest way to cross the harbour. For visitors, the Star Ferry is also the best way to enjoy a view of the whole harbour from the water. The fleet of ten green-and-white Star Ferries all have 'star' in their names—Celestial Star, Morning Star, Solar Star, for example.

Between Central district and Western district there are two parallel roads, Queen's Road and Des Voeux Road, bisected by a series of small lanes. It is fun to explore the lanes while they last—some of them have disappeared in recent years in the wake of urban development. However, much has been preserved in the cleverly-restored **Western Market**. Some of the Cloth (Wing On) Alley merchants have stalls here, along with arts and crafts stores and restaurants.

OUTINGS FROM HONG KONG

The largest 'outlying' island is **Lantau**, off the west coast of Hong Kong Island itself. Despite the development of Hong Kong's state-of-the-art new airport on one side and Disneyland near its eastern tip, the island remains a haven of peace and quiet. The most well-known sight on Lantau is the **Po Lin Monastery**, with its giant seated Buddha—an impressive sight despite the commercialism surrounding it. A short walk away is the relatively new Ngong Ping theme village, and the upper terminus of the **Ngong Ping 360** cable car, which descends over steep hillside wilderness and across a bay to Tung Chung new town, only five minutes' drive from Chek Lap Kok Airport and connected to Kowloon and Hong Kong Island by the MTR underground rail system. The cable car had a problematic first few years, but it is a popular draw for mainland tourists, and is a scenic way to reach the Buddha. Man-made attractions aside, the island is worth visiting for its grand landscapes of cloud-tipped mountains, pastoral valleys and cove beaches. The walking trails are well marked and take you through some lovely scenery.

To the south of Hong Kong Island, **Lamma Island** is smaller than Lantau and has no cars. Sadly, one side of it is disfigured by the three enormous chimney stacks of

(Preceding pages) *Hong Kong Island's Central District is a forest of skyscrapers crowding the harbour. The Star Ferry piers have now been moved to reclaimed land alongside the piers for transport to the Outlying Islands. [Kasyan Bartlett]*

a coal-fired power station. It has a flourishing community of young people and is also visited on balmy evenings and at weekends by fleets of pleasure boats for its excellent waterfront seafood restaurants.

To the southwest of Hong Kong Island, **Cheung Chau** is famous for its Bun Festival, held every year in May. The festival features stilt-walkers, traditional costume parades and mountains of sticky buns (which, until the practice was discontinued as too dangerous, young men used to climb for a prize pinned to the top). Cheung Chau is now badly overbuilt and is a dormitory for Hong Kong commuters. Yet there are some pleasant pubs and bars, as well as a windsurfing school on the island.

Off the east coast of the New Territories lie the two lovely islands of **Ping Chau** and **Tap Mun**. Ping Chau, which lies close to China and is shaped like a grassy aircraft, can only be visited at weekends by public ferry. The absence of inhabited villages has made it a natural wildlife sanctuary, bright with butterflies, dragonflies and shy birds. The nearby island of Tap Mun is also small, but it has thriving villages, restaurants and a famous Tin Hau Temple popular with local seagoing fishermen (Tin Hau being a Taoist goddess worshipped in southern China and believed to protect fisherfolk). Tap Mun can be reached every day by ferry. Ferries to both islands depart from University, a stop on the Kowloon-Canton Railway.

In the eastern New Territories, the **Sai Kung** peninsula is the most beautiful and unspoilt area. This is because much of the land was designated as a Country Park in the 1970s. Visitors can explore the hills and seashore on walking trails, or pick up one of the small ferries which run between the villages. The beaches are clean and uncrowded, and the walks offer glorious views over **Mirs Bay** and the China coast. Further north, the town of **Fan Ling** is where the Royal Hong Kong Golf Club is sited.

SHOPPING AND ENTERTAINMENT

Central has all the most expensive brand-name shops. Prices may or may not be lower than New York or London, depending of course on currency fluctuations. Their best customers in recent years have been Asians, particularly Japanese and Taiwanese. Better value is offered at the factory outlet shops themselves, which sell goods made for export at knock-down prices. Lists of these factory outlets can be found in a shopping guide widely on sale in Hong Kong bookshops.

(Following pages) *In the shadow of Lantau Peak, Po Lin Monastery boasts the world's largest outdoor bronze Buddha, an impressive 34 metres (60 feet) high. A new 5.7-kilometre-long (3.5 miles) gondola ride, Ngong Ping 360, takes sightseers on a scenic journey from Tung Chung, near Chek Lap Kok International Airport, to a terminal at the Ngong Ping theme village, seen here at lower right. [Kasyan Bartlett]*

If you like shopping combined with some local colour, then try to visit some street markets by night. There are many throughout the Island and Kowloon, but the most popular with foreign visitors is **Temple Street Night Market** in Kowloon, near the Jordan Mass Transit or MTR (underground/subway) station. Here you can buy hand-painted T-shirts as well as taste a casserole of garlic snails. Another market is located around **Sai Yeung Choi Street**, near the Mongkok MTR station.

As far as eating is concerned, the choice is so diverse that it is best to contact the Hong Kong Tourism Board (www.discoverhongkong.com) for a comprehensive listing. If you have just come out of China and are longing for Western food, then Hong Kong has some of the best Western restaurants in the world. While the Continental restaurants in the top hotels, such as the Peninsula and the Mandarin, are always reliable, there is a host of independent French and Italian restaurants, not to mention fast-food outlets, in the gleaming shopping malls and areas such as Central, Tsim Sha Tsui and Causeway Bay.

Some of the most interesting local restaurants are the traditional teahouses, where the old-fashioned flavour of Chinese breakfast and lunch— *dim sum* (small steamed and fried snacks)—can be savoured. The best-known traditional teahouses are the Luk Yu in Stanley Street, on the Island, and the bird teahouse—where old men go with their pet caged birds—called Wan Loy, on Shanghai Street in Mongkok, Kowloon. It is almost impossible to find seats at these places, though, and one would do better to try a larger restaurant, possibly in an office-cum-shopping complex, which offers less 'atmosphere' but at least a reservation service.

Hong Kong is famous for its late, late nightlife. In Causeway Bay, the shops don't close until around 11pm every night. Popular in the Central district are **Lan Kwai Fong** and SoHo (*South of Hollywood Road*) where bars and discos can go on until 4am. Most hotels have good bars and nightclubs, some with live music. Many karaoke bars are scattered in the bright lights districts of Tsim Sha Tsui and Wanchai. The local hostess bars range from the cheap and cheerful to the very, very expensive. These should be visited with some caution and a prior look at prices.

Ocean Park on Hong Kong Island has many rides, but emphasizes nature and wildlife as opposed to the cartoons and movies celebrated at Hong Kong Disneyland. Ocean Park was the first to successfully breed dolphins in captivity, has interesting animals such as the Asian Small-clawed Otter and boasts a large aquarium. After nearly 30 years of serving Hong Kong, a substantial revamp of the park is under way, including a new rollercoaster, subzero "Ice Palace" and 7.6 million litre (15.9 million gallons) aquarium with underwater restaurant.

PARADISE LOST? —By Calum MacLeod

The other WTO (World Tourism Organisation) forecasts that by 2020 China will leapfrog France as the world's favourite destination, attracting 130 million international arrivals a year. The China National Tourism Administration is even more bullish, predicting 150 million by 2010. Combined with booming domestic tourism, how does this onslaught affect the tourist sites and their residents?

YOU SHOULD NEVER GO BACK, to disturb good memories with the shock of the new. Especially in China. "When I first came through that gate, it was an exhilarating experience, like finding a forgotten piece of old China," remembered James Kynge, a Financial Times correspondent, of the moment he entered the walled banking town of Pingyao in central Shanxi province. "But it has changed so quickly. Now people seem to have lost some of their warmth, everyone is out to make a buck, and some are engaging in all sorts of tricks, like the guy who just tried to charge me 85 *yuan* to get in, when there isn't even an entrance ticket!"

It is a familiar, selfish lament the world over. We can't help ourselves. The fleeting traveller holds moments frozen in time, but a return visit exposes the romance of the past to the harsh light of economic progress. And what progress there has been! Even previously 'off-the-beaten-track' destinations like Pingyao are on the frontline of a tourist invasion sweeping across China. Forget foreign encroachment, this is civil war. With more disposable income in their pockets, and more leisure time to dispose of it, armies of domestic tourists are laying siege to their nation's sights. This article offers some views from the trenches over the last four years of engagement, as China became the largest tourism market in the world—officials estimate that even with the negative impact of the SARS epidemic, domestic tourists notched up 870 million "person times" last year, down just 0.9 percent on the 2002 record.

To translate big numbers into real life, follow the march of commercialisation down the small lanes of Pingyao, one of China's last surviving walled cities. But watch out for the golf carts, packed with

Chinese tourists notching up the sights, and make way for the rickshaw pullers too, fighting for space and custom from the crowds window-shopping stalls crammed with identical kitsch. Western visitors can bemoan the loss of innocence—from the comfort of courtyard hotels, Internet cafes and foot massage parlours. What do locals make of their town's makeover? "The tourists have brought many good things to us," hotel owner Li Pingsheng recently told the BBC's Louisa Lim. "Many young people were unemployed, but now they're tour guides, or they run restaurants or hostels. Tourism gave us a livelihood, it gave us hope."

It will also serve eviction orders, if local authorities succeed with plans to relocate up to two-thirds of the 40,000 residents still within the city walls. For the people of Pingyao are victims of their hometown's success. With some six million visitors per year, tourism is now the town's lifeblood, but to keep its main arteries clear, in the hope of longevity, and more room for golf carts, the official diagnosis calls for removing the very people who make Pingyao a fascinating, living organism, and a picturesque slice of 'real' China, not just a museum of quaint roofs and tourist tat.

Over in Shangri-La, the exodus is well underway. For 60 years, nobody in southwest China's Yunnan province realised they were sitting on a goldmine of Western fantasy. Novelist James Hilton was sitting in Woodford Green, northeast London, when he coined the term Shangri-La for his Eastern Utopia of snow-capped peaks, teashops and Tibetan lamas serving up ethnic harmony and eternal happiness. 'Lost Horizon' (1933) was a bestseller, and the Frank Capra film proved a welcome wartime diversion, but Shangri-La's greatest trick has been selling its myth to Chinese tourists who have neither read the novel nor watched the movie.

Maverick music man Xuan Ke, a conductor in Lijiang and former political prisoner, placed 'Lost Horizon' in northwest Yunnan a decade ago, although Hilton never set foot in China, and the tourist industry has cashed in ever since. Over four million people a year now swamp the old backpacker trails on 'Shangri-La Tours' from Kunming to Dali, Lijiang and Zhongdian, or rather Shangri-La, as Zhongdian has changed its name. Officially. Hilton's fictional escape to paradise now boasts a real-life home;

arrive at Shangri-La airport in Diqing prefecture, before choosing a hotel, restaurant or karaoke bar of the same name.

Back in 1988, I remember retreating each night from Lijiang's atmospheric old town—the modern but dull new town offered the only guesthouses. Today, every house within the old town appears to house a hotel, restaurant, shop or gallery, many of them run by Han Chinese who have displaced the native Naxi. "This is a dangerous time," admitted Zhang Ahui, owner of the Sun Moon Café, whose rental payments enabled her Naxi landlord to upgrade to the new town. "We make money from tourism, but there is always a contradiction between development and preservation. More Chinese like me come to run businesses here, and the purity and customs of the Naxi are changing. If we develop too quickly, within a few years tourists will go elsewhere."

UNESCO, the organisation that bestowed the coveted 'World Heritage' status on Lijiang, Pingyao and 27 other sites in China, echoed such concerns in its 2001 report criticising tourism management in Lijiang and elsewhere. Environmentalists have decried the carving up of Jade Dragon Snow Mountain, Lijiang's signature backdrop, with cable cars, ski resorts and Asia's highest golf course. Yet Xuan Ke, the man who put the region on the map, is adamant that the benefits outweigh the risks. "I think we must continue to open up," he told this visitor to his theatre of octogenarian musicians, the town's premier nightspot. "I believe tourism does not destroy traditions, but helps to preserve them."

Similar arguments buttress the 87 other sites that China hopes will earn the 'World Heritage' badge of honour, and licence to print *renminbi*, as Beijing turns tourism into a major economic pillar. It is the longest such wishlist in the world, and would stretch much further but for the political storms of the last century. The challenge this century is not anti-feudal campaigns but rising living standards. City planners have to act quickly to stop local residents modernising in styles that break down tradition or the neighbourhood, though the city fathers themselves are often the culprits.

Different answers to the development debate are on display, and well worth your time, in the tourist testbed of Jiangnan, the area south of the Yangtse River in Jiangsu and Zhejiang provinces. Here half a dozen

Special Topic

shuixiang, or 'watertowns', compete for visitors on daytrips or long weekends from Suzhou or Shanghai. In Luzhi, an entrance ticket of 46 *yuan* buys you access to quintessential China: meandering canal walks, humpbacked bridges, fishermen and cormorants, old men and chess games, woodfronted shops selling pickled vegetables, noodles and pumpkin cakes. "We want to preserve the old character of Luzhi," an attendant told me in Baosheng temple, "so we are following the preservation plan of Tongji University in Shanghai. We know the river water is not clean, so from 2004 all houses in the old town have had to treat their wastewater, although this doesn't affect the factories outside the old town."

Plenty of work remains to be done, but the progress to date is in large part due to campaigning Professor Ruan Yishan and his team at Tongji. "The speed of urbanization took everyone by surprise," Ruan told writer Jasper Becker. "We managed to save a few [historic cities], but the destruction was so fast... At the beginning, people would not accept my views, but now they are ready to follow my preservation schemes and retain the original buildings." Ruan's first watertown project was Zhouzhuang near Suzhou, now overrun with 2.5 million visitors a year. In both Zhouzhuang and Wuzhen, a significant proportion of the original residents were resettled in new areas, while restoration work in Luzhi and Tongli has focussed on retaining the feel of living, working places.

Life remains very real for the farmers of Zhangbi, an ancient fort back in Shanxi province, where village chief Yang Chengrui envies the problems faced by his neighbours two hours' drive away in old Pingyao. "Do you want to invest?" Yang asked. "We want to develop tourism, new hotels and restaurants." "But they must be outside the fort walls and in character," interrupted local historian Zheng Guanggen, a retired fitter now wrestling with the contradictions of tourism. Zheng personally delivered Zhangbi's development plan to the Ministry of Construction in Beijing, and enthuses over the fort's dragon-style layout and multi-layered tunnel. In one temple painting, a filial son lies on his parents' bed for two hours before they retire, so that the mosquitoes will sate themselves on him and allow them a good night's rest. Zheng doubts that the youth of today is capable of such self-sacrifice or foresight. "The young people have no interest in our history or buildings," he complained. "They just worry about the rain and the harvest. They don't realise they could make their lives better through tourism."

In another of China's hidden gems, another man has seen the same light of tourist promise. Deep in southern Jiangxi province, village chief Dong Shaosheng is banking on tourism to preserve Liukeng, or 'River Pit', perhaps the most traditional village in China. While progress in the rest of the country brings a building boom of concrete, white tiles and blue glass, Liukeng's poverty and isolation have left intact a maze of narrow cobbled lanes between 'horse-head' stone walls concealing mansions from more prosperous times.

"By ourselves, we are unable to preserve these old houses," agreed village elder Dong Zhaorong. "We need visitors' money to help us." If they come, not only picturesque scenery and architecture await, but traditions and beliefs that survived Communist persecution. A funeral procession wound past Dong's house, the relatives clad in white, the Chinese colour of mourning, their heads swathed in sackcloth. A happier village tour takes place each Chinese New Year, amid torch parades and mask dancing, when a bust of the chief village god is carried to every household in Liukeng, dispensing good fortune for the year ahead.

Currently, few of the 5,000 residents derive revenue from the growing trickle of visitors, but the village chief encourages them to establish restaurants, guesthouses, and handicraft shops. For now the people of Liukeng live by more traditional means. After dawn, farmers lead their water buffalo out of the old village gates for a day in the rice fields. Down the lane in the herbalist shop, the white-coated proprietor delves for medicinal roots from a chest blackened with age. But pausing between cuts on a set of wooden chairs, a young carpenter asked, "What kind of souvenirs would foreign tourists like?"

[*China Review magazine, Autumn 2004, Issue 29, pp.24–26*]
Calum MacLeod is the Editor of *China Review* magazine
and Director of the Great Britain-China Centre.

Special Topic

MACAU

The former Portuguese-colony-now-SAR, Macau, or Macao as it is alternatively spelled, is a small enclave of islands most well known for its gambling casinos. Even Vegas's Big Players, such as hotel-casino magnate Steve Wynn, are attracted to the action, and the ostentatious success of the phenomenal Venetian Macao casino-resort has simply upped the stakes for entertainment and service-industry investors—where it will end is anybody's guess.

Today, in many ways Macau is unrecognisable from its relative obscurity and slightly quaint image of only a decade ago. With casino money funding its ambitions, Macau's leaders have spent heavily to create tourist attractions such as the sky-piercing, 338-metre **Macau Tower**, and the 120,000-square-metre **Fisherman's Wharf** themed entertainment park, located near the Macau Ferry Terminal and

(Top) *São Paulo's façade is the definitive icon of Macau and its historic centre. [Macau Government Tourist Office].* (Above) *The main building of the astonishing Venetian Macao is the largest building in Asia, and second largest in the world after Boeing's Washington-based aircraft plant. [Courtesy of the Venetian Macao-Resort-Hotel]*

boasting twin 40-metre-high 'volcanoes' with labyrinthine interiors, a Roman amphitheatre performance venue, as well as a host of gaming venues, restaurants and shopping areas. On top of the 170-metre summit of Coloane Island stands the world's tallest statue of the goddess **A-Ma** (also known as Tin Hau), and a new **A-Ma Cultural Village** based around a colourful temple complex is five minutes' walk downhill.

But despite the building bonanza of the last few years—most notably the sea reclamation between Coloane and Taipa islands that has resulted in the **Cotai Strip** ('Co' for Coloane, 'tai' for Taipa), home to the mind-bogglingly over-the-top **Venetian Macao-Resort-Hotel** complex, which is worth visiting as a tourist attraction in its own right—there is still much of old Macau to be found in its original city centre. The enclave's unique blend of Portuguese-Chinese flavours extends not only to its food, such as *bacalhao* (a fish dish) and Macanese egg-tarts, but also to its architecture—a legacy from the early 1500s when the first Portuguese traders arrived. Macau's historical treasures have been recognized by UNESCO (*see* page 371), and a wander through the back streets around **Senado Square** and southwest

uphill towards **Penha Church** still gives glimpses of unchanged Macanese life. Other attractive historical sites include the hilltop **Guia Fortress**, the atmospheric **A-Ma Temple** on the southern tip of the Macau peninsula, and old **Coloane Village**, a peaceful retreat that seems a world apart from the gambling utopia only a few kilometres away. An hour's ferry from Hong Kong, a border-bridge skip from Guangdong Province's Zhuhai, Macau is increasing its integration with the rest of China while offering gambling on a huge scale, but still managing to offer a fascinating if fragile glimpse of a unique cultural heritage.

Coloane's impressive A-Ma statue.
[Jeremy Tredinnick]

THE GREAT WALL

—William Lindesay

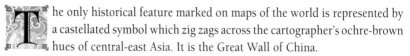 he only historical feature marked on maps of the world is represented by a castellated symbol which zig zags across the cartographer's ochre-brown hues of central-east Asia. It is the Great Wall of China.

Daunted by neither landscape nor distance on its tortuous journey from desert to sea, this superlative-defying defence system, the longest, oldest, most time-consuming, labour-intensive and material-demanding construction project in mankind's history, is far more than a landmark: it is part of the geography of North China, the world, and beyond.

Snaking along mountain ridges, the Great Wall dominates the landscape from miles around. From the air, where horizons are wider, the Wall still sits astride the horizons, reaching from where the sun rises to where it sets. And from the heavens, courtesy of satellite photography, we know the Great Wall is as prominent a geographical feature as the hand of nature at its most powerful in carving out the mighty valleys of the Yangzi and Yellow rivers.

ORIGINS

In history there have been three sub-continental scale Great Walls, built during Qin (221–206 BCE), Han (206 BCE–CE 220) and Ming (1368–1644) times. Intervening dynasties—including the Northern Wei (386–534), Northern Qi (550–577) and the conquest dynasties of the Liao (916–1125) and Jin (1115–1234)—also built walls and dug trenches for defensive purposes, but not on such a grand scale. However, by definition, having been constructed at the northern edges of the empires on imperial orders, they too were Great Walls of China.

No major threats to the security of Chinese empires ever came from the south, but in the north a variety of peoples—Xiongnu, Quitans, Jurchens, Mongols and Manchus—ethnically different to Han Chinese, inhabited the steppes and desert fringes. The Han settled in the fertile central plains, cultivated crops and built settlements, often walled, while the northerners were nomads and hunters who habitually invaded Han territory on horseback.

EVOLUTION

igh walls, running for long distances across open country and manned by guards, had been used as a means of preventing mass invasions since the Warring States period (475–221 BCE). They were made from rammed earth. Wall-building continued to play an important role in national defence strategies, with increasing sophistication. Rocks, bricks and mortar were used; construction scales grew ever greater; routing through the mountains was more ambitious to accentuate defensive capacity; and patrolling garrisons were provided with arsenals of ingenious weaponry for close and remote combat.

Wall-building innovation reached its acme during the Ming dynasty. Ironically, Manchu horsemen were allowed to pass through one of the Wall's most fortified passes, at **Shanhaiguan** on the Yellow Sea coast, by a renegade general (*see* picture on page 310). The invaders established the Qing dynasty (1644–1911) and wall-building was abandoned: future enemies would come not from the north, but from across the globe by sea to China's coast.

The Ming's brilliant construction therefore, designed to be insurmountable to the most determined and well-armed invader, was never truly tested.

THE MING DYNASTY DEFENCE

Remains of the Ming Great Wall stretch from Jiayuguan, along the Hexi corridor of Gansu Province, across the Ningxia Hui Autonomous Region and Shaanxi, along the Shanxi-Inner Mongolia provincial boundary, north of Beijing and through Hebei to Shanhaiguan on the coast. In the early 17th century, in response to the growing threat of Manchu invasion, this mainline structure was extended by the addition of the so-called Liaodong sidewall, stretching from Shanhaiguan, northeast to the Yalu Jiang, a river which today marks the border between China and North Korea.

The Beijing region boasts the most magnificent remaining sections since the Hongwu emperor (reigned 1368–1398) ordered the routing of the Great Wall through the Yanshan mountains. According to recent satellite surveys, the Beijing Municipality has 673 kilometres of Great Wall within its boundaries. Most of it was reinforced during the Yongle (reigned 1402–1424) and Wanli (reigned 1573–1620) periods.

Having suffered under barbarian rule for more than three centuries, the Hongwu emperor, who re-established native Han rule, decided that the building of a Great Wall was the basic means of border defence necessary to ensure that the Chinese empire would never again be conquered by the northerners. At the time, the Ming

The Great Wall

had their capital in Nanjing, which was in the centre of the fertile Yangzi region and well-supplied with grain, but distant from the volatile northern border where, as history had proved time and time again, dynastic stability was most at stake.

To guarantee good military control and loyalty in the north, the Hongwu emperor adopted a policy of *pan wang*, or princes guarding the border, by assigning some of his 27 sons to northern fiefdoms.

When the Yongle emperor took power in 1403, he decided to move the capital from Nanjing to Beijing. He had spent his youth in the Beijing region after his father's establishment of the dynasty in 1368, and was later given the title Prince of Yan and military control of a fiefdom. Very much a professional soldier with strong allegiance in the north, he was a veteran at thwarting Mongol threats and realized that keeping the hordes at bay would secure him a long reign, and the empire's stability.

To do that, he had the Great Wall reinforced on a massive scale and built lines of beacon towers to facilitate the conveyance of signals to the new capital. Meanwhile, Beijing was built into a bastion just south of this stupendous defence. The Imperial City had a moat and high defensive walls, and within it was constructed the Imperial Palace, also behind a moat and palace walls. All building materials were shipped along the Sui-built Grand Canal, whose renovation and improvement by the Yuan allowed the new capital to be kept well-supplied with grain from the south.

Most of the Wall north of Beijing follows mountain ridges and scales peaks: here the ramparts are virtually impossible for an invader to breach, let alone access on horseback. There were however, a few valleys through the mountains which had been used as passes since ancient times. These became strategic passes (most heavily-fortified sections) on the Great Wall: thicker, high ramparts were built at these points, and watchtowers were closer together. Double walls created loops in which invaders could be trapped and annihilated. Larger garrisons of men were stationed at passes.

To the invader, the system of ramparts must have appeared impregnable, masterminded by militarily brilliant strategists and architects. The Ming Wall should be regarded as being as technically advanced and militarily advantageous in its day as systems of spy satellites, radar and the nuclear deterrent are today.

In terms of its communicative role, the Great Wall was the medieval equivalent of the optical fibre of today. Guards in beacon towers would spread information concerning Mongol threats by smoke signal, cannon fire or drum beats, depending on weather conditions. The message could be carried along the Wall, then south to the emperor in the Imperial Palace.

(Left) *An invader's view of the formidable defences of the Great Wall. [William Lindesay]*

Within a matter of hours the emperor and his ministers could be made aware of threats and swiftly decide on counter-attacking measures. Had the capital remained in Nanjing, information might have taken several days to reach its destination.

The Great Wall's system of defence and communication was also supplemented by military expeditions into the heart of Mongolian territory to destroy encampments and burn grasslands. The Yongle emperor personally led many of them: Beijing served as the ideal platform from which to launch campaigns. Thus the Great Wall in many ways was the last line of defence and by no means the border of the empire.

Built to withstand attack from Mongol hordes and never seriously breached, Beijing's Ming Great Wall stands as a permanent monument to glorify the ingenuity of architects and military strategists, and a memorial to mourn the countless millions who were conscripted and died during its construction.

VISITING THE WALL

adaling, Juyongguan, Mutianyu, Jinshanling and Simatai have, to greater and lesser degrees, been reconstructed and 'opened' to tourism. It is necessary to purchase tickets to access the Wall at these places. Some sites now have cable cars to spare less able visitors heart- and leg-strain on the steep climbs. Those who enjoy hiking, and who have the neccessary time, can arrange to visit designated derelict sections beyond the reconstructed sections

There is simply too much Great Wall around Beijing to reconstruct, and that means several hundred kilometres of it exists in a wild, authentic state—remote, overgrown and crumbling but recent legislation to protect the fabric has placed tough restrictions on scaling many sections.

Badaling was the first section of Wall renovated for tourism. Just 65 kilometres north of Beijing, and accessible via the newly-built Badaling Expressway toll road, it is about one and a half hours' drive from the city. This most crowded section is beginning to show signs of tourism overuse as more than 10,000 people a day converge on the site during the high season and on holiday weekends. The strategic pass is quite magnificent, with the lower sections of the ramparts being composed of huge, pink granite blocks which are topped with kiln-baked bricks bound with mortar. Beacon towers are located within an arrow's flight of each other, and looking east and west the ramparts thrust and dip in and out of sight. From April to October the Wall is floodlit in the evenings.

The **China Great Wall Museum**, with nine exhibition rooms, is located at Badaling. Many weapons and Wall-related relics discovered in the vicinity are exhibited: a battle scene is recreated with models; and Wall-building techniques and battles are explained and chronicled with charts and drawings. Photographs of famous visitors, including 276 foreign heads of state from 143 countries, are also on show. Open 8am–4pm daily. Telephone 6921-1890 or 6921-1228. Another attraction adjacent to the museum, especially recommended for younger visitors, is the Great Wall Circular Vision Theater where a dramatized 15-minute film about the Wall's history and legends is projected onto an Omnimax circular screen.

Badaling is accessible by five tourist line public buses. Tour buses leave from just east of Qianmen opposite McDonald's; Beijing Railway Station west forecourt; and from opposite Beijing Zoo. From 6am–10am daily, April to November; 6.30am–10am, December to March. Buses travel directly from the city to Badaling then the Ming Tombs. Travel time is more than 90 minutes. Return services start from 1.30pm and end at 5.30pm in summer, earlier in winter. There are regular departures on scheduled air-conditioned services from Deshengmen all day. Most hotels offer minibus tours to the Wall and prices may range from 60–200 Rmb. Taxis can be hired for between 300 Rmb and 500 Rmb depending on how long the driver is required to wait, and vehicle type. There are also local trains from Beijing Station (not the new West Station) and Beijing North Station (also known as Xizhimen). Buy your ticket up to four days in advance (easiest at Beijing Station's ticket office for foreigners at the far left-hand corner of the concourse). These require an early start, but are useful in winter if the roads are snowbound.

Juyongguan can be seen by all en route to Badaling. Entering the valley heading north from Nankou, the sharp-eyed will detect linearities which describe a massive loop on the distant mountainside. Juyongguan was a second, 'insurance' line of defence, and reconstruction since 1990 has replicated the bastion's elaborate defence system of ramparts, gates and towers. A total of Rmb150 million (US$18 million), a record sum for relics reconstruction in China, has been invested in this site. Very little of the building material is original: most was removed by locals in search of readily-available building materials during the Qing and Republican periods. However, the view from the Wall's highest point on the western ridge is magnificent, affording one clear appreciation of the strategic nature of this pass which links the northern steppes with the plain of the south.

The Great Wall

The main reason to stop at Juyongguan lies at the foot of the Wall, between the old and new roads. Yuntai, the **Cloud Terrace**, once formed the base for three successively-built Yuan dynasty (1279–1368) pagodas. The remaining hexagonal 'language' archway has Buddhist reliefs of the Four Heavenly Kings in white marble on its northern and southern faces, while the interior of the structure has scripts in six languages which reflect both the extent of the Mongol empire and the many nationalities of Buddhism's adherents. The scripts are Nepalese Sanskrit, Tibetan, Phagspa Mongolian, Uyghur, Xi Xia and Han Chinese.

Mutianyu, 80 kilometres (50 miles) north of Beijing in Huairou County, is the second most visited section. Less crowded, visitors can climb up 1,000 steps or take the cable car to reach the Wall, and use a slide to descend.

Magnificent panoramas lie in wait, especially in fall. The thickly wooded slopes around Mutianyu provide a palate of autumnal tints to contrast with the whitish blocks of the Wall. For the energetic, a walk to the west is recommended. After one kilometre derelict ramparts are reached. A further 30–40 minutes' walk will take hikers to a prominent loop called the Oxhorn. The highest beacon tower for miles around still stands a few hundred metres further west. It rewards the adventurous with a bird's eye view westward across the precipitous Jiankou section which is extremely difficult to negotiate due to its crumbling condition, bushy overgrowth and near-vertical inclines (*see* picture on next pages).

Mutianyu is accessible by public bus tourist line number 6, departing from outside the Southern Cathedral (northeast corner of the Xuanwumen intersection, accessible from the subway station of the same name—*see* Beijing map on page 112–113.) There are frequent departures daily between 6am and 10pm from April to November, and only on Saturdays and Sundays, 7am to 9am, in other months. Buses also visit Hongluo (Red Conch) Temple and Yanqi Lake after leaving Mutianyu.

A dawn panorama over the jagged Jiankou section, west of Mutianyu, that spectacularly illustrates the enormous feat of engineering achieved by its Ming dynasty builders. [William Lindesay]

Travel time is about two hours. Return buses leave Mutianyu between 1pm and 5pm. Minibus tours also depart from various hotels, while taxis can be hired for 300–600 Rmb. Public buses leave Dongzhimen Bus Station, close to the subway of the same name, for Huairou, starting from 6am and every 15 minutes thereafter. From Huairou it is a short bus trip to Mutianyu. If necessary, accommodation can be found in Huairou, and a Ming dynasty style barracks has been constructed as lodgings on the Mutianyu Wall itself, about a kilometre west of the cable-car station.

Jinshanling and **Simatai**, adjacent sections of the Great Wall to the east of Gubeikou, are located 120 kilometres (75 miles) northeast of the capital on the boundary between Beijing Municipality and Hebei Province. These sections are regarded by most as Wall par excellence for their heights, solitude and plethora of watchtowers which dot the ramparts like fins on a mighty dragon. Formal access points for both sections are about five kilometres (three miles) apart as the crow flies, or 25 kilometres (15 miles) by road.

At Jinshanling (*see* picture on page 302), the Wall zig-zags up inclines and straddles between peaks like a suspension bridge of stone. Every turn in the defence and peak is marked with a tower. A particularly striking feature here are barrier walls, best described as mini battlements on the Wall pavement itself. They were built as a precaution against invaders mounting the Wall. Defenders could combat invaders while seeking protection from missiles behind the mini-battlements. In clear weather Miyun Lake, Beijing's main reservoir, can be seen.

A few kilometres eastward (about three hours' walk) at Simatai, is the most hair-raising challenge on the Great Wall near Beijing. Soon the reconstructed section is left behind as one climbs eastward and upward towards the perilous Simatai ridge.

The highest watchtower, dubbed the 'Tower for Viewing Beijing' for the vista available to its conquerors, can be reached only by negotiating an extremely narrow section of Wall. Sharp drops loom on both sides of this one-metre-wide path. Beyond is the Stairway to Heaven of barrier walls—a challenge whether you suffer vertigo or not. Those who lose their nerve halfway across are best advised to crawl on all fours.

Public bus tourist line number 12 from Xuanwumen, outside the Southern Cathedral, provides a service to Simatai. Departures, approximately every 30 minutes, are limited to weekends and state holidays. Travel time is three hours plus, and buses stop briefly at Bailongtan Pool on the way back.

Jinshanling and Simatai are east of Gubeikou which is on the Beijing—Chengde railway line. There are departures from Beijing Station which take three to four-and-a-half hours to reach Gubeikou.

An alternative is the minibus, from the east forecourt of Beijing Station. Frequent departures leave throughout the day from about 5am. The public bus from Dongzhimen is a slow alternative at 7.30am and 8.30am; or minibuses run the same route for about double the fare. All these modes of transport to Gubeikou would necessitate short onward travelling to Jinshanling and Simatai. Motorcabs are available. Alternatively, take the bus from Dongzhimen to Miyun, then a minibus directly to Simatai.

Purists who want to visit a non-tourist section would be advised to head for **Huanghuacheng**, 60 kilometres north of Beijing. Heavily reinforced during the reign of Wanli, these derelict, mighty ramparts cross a small valley in which a reservoir has been built. A special feature of the Wall and towers here are rocks of various provenance: pink granite, white dolerite and grey gabbro. This is a fine location to start a high-level hike, either east or west from the road. To the west, the first tower still contains a memorial plaque, dating from 1580, recording the good deeds of the garrison stationed there for the defence of the capital. To the east, the Wall climbs steeply towards the peak of the highest mountain around.

This section can only be reached by public bus from Dongzhimen, changing at Huairou for Huanghuacheng. Taxis cost between 300 and 500 Rmb, but although the route is actually very easy to follow, it is hard to find a Beijing taxi driver who knows the way. Take the road north from the Asian Games Village towards Lishui Qiao, then keep going north through Xiazhuang, following signposts for Sihai.

William Lindesay, OBE, travelled alone and on foot for a distance of 2,470 kilometres along the route of the Ming Great Wall between Jiayuguan and Shanhaiguan in 1987. He recounted his journey in Alone on the Great Wall *(Hodder, UK 1989; Fulcrum USA 1991;). Remaining in China since his adventure to research the Wall, he became concerned about the physical and spiritual destruction of the Great Wall cultural landscape and established the conservation group International Friends of the Great Wall (http://www.friendsofgreatwall.org) in 2001. Lindesay now works with the Beijing Bureau for Cultural Relics, UNESCO Beijing Office and the US-based World Monuments Fund to preserve the authenticity of the Great Wall.*

His latest book is Images of Asia: The Great Wall *(Oxford Univ. Press, Hong Kong, 2003). He is currently compiling a record of his personal discoveries and realizations conceived after having spent more than 1,000 days on and around the Wall under the title* Great Wall: An Exploration.

For travellers with the time to appreciate what Lindesay describes as "the story of the Wall as I have discovered it" (http://www.wildwall.com), the researcher offers Great Wall culture weekends and Wild Wall weekends based at either of his farmhouses, both located within 2.5 hours' drive from Beijing. Trips include Lindesay's personal guidance and storytelling, accommodation in renovated yet traditional farmhouses, all meals and return transportation from Beijing, with hotel or airport pickups. For details visit www.wildwall.com or fax (86) 10 6175 1982.

(Following left page) The Great Wall at Shanhaiguan snakes down the mountains and across the coastal plain to the sea. Despite having built the strongest Great Wall in history, the Ming dynasty's defences were breached here on this coastal plain by Manchu horsemen in 1644, who went on to establish the Qing dynasty. [William Lindesay]; (following right page) Exploring the Great Wall is both a cerebral and physical experience. [Anthony Cassidy]

The Great Wall

WORLD HERITAGE SITES

From natural wonders that predate the Paleolithic period to the more recent man-made triumphs of the Ming and Qing dynasties, China has many gifts to offer the world. The collective World Heritage Convention (WHC) sites within the country's borders are considered to provide a gateway of understanding between the Chinese and other peoples. These sites give us insight into the great diversity of influences that have helped form Chinese society.

Great strides are being made in protecting China's cultural and natural heritage, which is reflected in the growing number of sites the United Nations Educational, Scientific and Cultural Organisation (UNESCO) includes in its World Heritage List. There are now 35 sites within the country's borders that are considered to be treasures of the world at large. Since the historic centre of Macao (now spelt Macau), a unique blend of Portuguese and Chinese stylings, was inscribed on 15 July 2005, four new sites have been added: the **Sichuan Giant Panda Sanctuaries** and the Shang dynasty archaeological site of **Yin Xu** in 2006, and in 2007 the fortress homes of **Kaiping Diaolou and Villages** in Guangdong Province, and the vast **South China Karst** of Yunnan, Guizhou and Guangxi.

The criterion for choosing such sites is based upon guidelines originally set by UNESCO in 1972, when the organization ratified a Convention Concerning the Protection of the World Cultural and Natural Heritage. China ratified the Convention on 12 December 1985. Sites selected include cultural, natural or both—such as Mount Emei Scenic Area with its stunning monument to Buddhism (*see* page 341).

The sites and their descriptions are presented here as per the World Heritage List, courtesy of UNESCO's World Heritage Centre (WHC), and in the order of the year they were inscribed. For the list of criterion, see page 375. Additional information by this guide's authors, inset and in italics, is given for several of the sites.

Some travellers may be surprised to find a favourite Chinese treasure not listed here, but they must take heart as the selection process is of course an ongoing one. Among the many sites China has put forward for consideration by the WHC are Beijing's Beihai Park, Dali Chanshan Mountain and Erhai Lake Scenic Spot, and the entire Silk Road (Chinese section). More unique delights are sure to be added to the World Heritage List, and in so doing, will hopefully keep the gateway of understanding open.

Garden of the Master of the Nets, Suzhou.

World Heritage Sites

KAZAKHSTAN

Almaty

KYRGYZSTAN

Urumqi

Kashgar

TAJIKISTAN

▲ Muztagata

Turpan

XINJIANG

Khotan

Dunhuang
• 6

Jiayuguan

GANSU

Qinghai
Lake

QINGHAI

Xining •

Lanzho

TIBET AUTONOMOUS REGION

New Delhi
•

Shigatse
•

14 •Lhasa

8

9

SICHUAN

32

Chengdu

24
16

Gongga
Shan   Emei
▲   Shan

BHUTAN

29

INDIA

BANGLADESH

•Dacca

17

Dali •

Kunming

MYANMAR
(BURMA)

YUNNAN

Mandalay
•

BAY OF BENGAL

LAOS

THAILAND

Rangoon
•

1   Peking Man Site at Zhoukoudian
2   The Great Wall
3   Imperial Palaces of the Ming and Qing Dynasties
    in Beijing and Shenyang
4   Mausoleum of the First Qin Emperor
5   Mount Taishan
6   Mogao Caves
7   Mount Huangshan
8   Jiuzhaigou Valley Scenic and Historic Interest Area
9   Huanglong Scenic and Historic Interest Area
10 Wulingyuan Scenic and Historic Interest Area
11 Mountain Resort and its Outlying Temples, Chengde
12 Temple and Cemetery of Confucius and
    the Kong Family Mansion in Qufu
13 Ancient Building Complex in the Wudang Mountains
14 Historic Ensemble of the Potala Palace, Lhasa
15 Lushan National Park
16 Mount Emei Scenic Area, including Leshan
    Giant Buddha Scenic Area
17 Old Town of Lijiang
18 Ancient City of Pingyao
19 Classical Gardens of Suzhou
20 Summer Palace, an Imperial Garden in Beijing
21 Temple of Heaven: an Imperial Sacrificial Altar in Beijing
22 Mount Wuyi
23 Dazu Rock Carvings
24 Mount Qingcheng and the Dujiangyan Irrigation System
25 Ancient Villages in Southern Anhui–Xidi and Hongcun
26 Longmen Grottoes
27 Imperial Tombs of the Ming and Qing Dynasties
28 Yungang Grottoes
29 Three Parallel Rivers of Yunnan Protected Areas
30 Capital Cities and Tombs of the Ancient Koguryo Kingdom
31 Historic Centre of Macau
32 Sichuan Giant Panda Sanctuaries
33 Yin Xu
34 Kaiping Diaolou and Villages
35 South China Karst

© Airphoto International Ltd.

PEKING MAN SITE AT ZHOUKOUDIAN #1

Date of Inscription: 1987
Criteria: C (iii) (vi)
Fangshanxian County, **Beijing Municipality**, N39 44 E115 55; ref: **449**

Scientific work at the site, which lies 42 km southwest of Beijing, is still underway. So far, it has led to the discovery of the remains of *Sinanthropus pekinensis*, who lived in the Middle Pleistocene, along with various objects, and remains of *Homo sapiens sapiens* dating as far back as 18,000–11,000 BCE The site is not only an exceptional reminder of the prehistorical human societies of the Asian continent, but also illustrates the process of evolution.

(Above) *Five Peking Man skulls disappeared in 1941 when transported elsewhere for safekeeping. These are their replicas. [China Intercontinental Press]*
(Right) *The Great Wall wending its way across typically rugged terrain. [Anthony Cassidy]*

THE GREAT WALL #2 (SEE GREAT WALL SECTION PAGES 299–311)

Date of Inscription: 1987; **Criteria:** C (i) (ii) (iii) (iv) (vi)

Liaoning, Jilin, Hebei, Beijing, Tianjin, Shanxi, Inner Mongolia, Shaanxi, Ningxia, Gansu, Xinjiang, Shandong, Henan, Hubei, Hunan, Sichuan, Qinghai provinces, municipalities and autonomous Regions, N39 59 E117 50; ref: 438

In c. 220 BCE, under Qin Shi Huang, sections of earlier fortifications were joined together to form a united defence system against invasions from the north. Construction continued up to the Ming dynasty (1368–1644), when the Great Wall became the world's largest military structure. Its historic and strategic importance is matched only by its architectural significance.

IMPERIAL PALACES OF THE MING AND QING DYNASTIES IN BEIJING AND SHENYANG #3

Date of Inscription: 1987
Extension: 2004
Criteria: C (i) (ii) (iii) (iv) (v) (vi)
N39 54 58.8 E116 23 27.2; ref: **439bis**

Seat of supreme power for over five centuries, the Forbidden City, with its landscaped gardens and many buildings (whose nearly 10,000 rooms contain furniture and works of art), constitutes a priceless testimony to Chinese civilization during the Ming and Qing dynasties.

The Hall of Complete Harmony, Forbidden City, Beijing.

Extension: The Imperial Palace of the Qing dynasty in Shenyang consists of 114 buildings, constructed between 1625–26 and 1783. It contains an important library and testifies to the foundation of the last dynasty that ruled China, before it expanded its power to the centre of the country and moved the capital to Beijing. This palace then became auxiliary to the Imperial Palace in Beijing. This remarkable architectural edifice offers important historical testimony to the history of the Qing dynasty and to the cultural traditions of the Manchu and other tribes in the north of China.

JUSTIFICATION FOR INSCRIPTION

Criterion (i): The Imperial Palaces represent masterpieces in the development of imperial palace architecture in China.

Criterion (ii): The architecture of the Imperial Palace complexes, particularly in Shenyang, exhibits an important interchange of influences of traditional architecture and Chinese palace architecture particularly in the 17th and 18th centuries.

Criterion (iii): The Imperial Palaces bear exceptional testimony to Chinese civilisation at the time of the Ming and Qing dynasties, being true reserves of landscapes, architecture, furnishings and objects of art, as well as carrying exceptional evidence to the living traditions and the customs of Shamanism practised by the Manchu people for centuries.

Criterion (iv): The Imperial Palaces provide outstanding examples of the greatest palatial architectural ensembles in China. They illustrate the grandeur of the imperial institution from the Qing dynasty to the earlier Ming and Yuan dynasties, as well as Manchu traditions, and present evidence on the evolution of this architecture in the 17th and 18th centuries.

More than 200,000 labourers worked to build the Forbidden City between 1407 and 1420.

MAUSOLEUM OF THE FIRST QIN EMPEROR #4
Date of Inscription: 1987; **Criteria:** C (i) (iii) (iv) (vi)
Lintong County, **Shaanxi Province**, N34 23 E109 6; ref: **441**

No doubt thousands of statues still remain to be unearthed at this archaeological site, which was not discovered until 1974. Qin (d. 210 BCE), the first unifier of China, is buried, surrounded by the famous Terracotta Warriors, at the centre of a complex designed to mirror the urban plan of the capital, Xianyan. The figures are all different; with their horses, chariots and weapons, they are masterpieces of realism and also of great historical interest.

Xi'an became a hotbed of archeaological activity after the discovery of Terracotta Warriors, (above) *which were commissioned by Emperor Qin Shi Huangdi. His burial mound (preceding pages) is close by at Lintong, east of Xi'an, where his tomb remains unexplored. [Xia Juxian]*

MOUNT TAISHAN #5

Date of Inscription: 1987
Criteria: N (iii) C (i) (ii) (iii) (iv) (v) (vi)
Spanning the cities of Tai'an and Jinan in central **Shandong Province** with the main peak in the city of Tai'an, N36 16 E117 06; ref: **437**

The sacred Mount Tai ('shan' means 'mountain') was the object of an imperial cult for nearly 2,000 years, and the artistic masterpieces found there are in perfect harmony with the natural landscape. It has always been a source of inspiration for Chinese artists and scholars and symbolizes ancient Chinese civilizations and beliefs.

Taishan (Mount Tai) rises above the folded landscape of the Shandong Peninsula in northeast China. As early as the time of Confucius (551–479 BCE), it was famous as a centre for pilgrimage. As Confucius said, 'From the summit of Mount Tai the earth seems small'. Qin Shi Huangdi, the first emperor of China, climbed Mount Tai to make a sacrifice in the second century BCE, but history records that he was buffeted by storms because he lacked the necessary righteousness!

Throughout the ages, emperors regularly visited Mount Tai, leaving behind records of their visits—a few characters written in their own calligraphy, for example, set in stone at favoured scenic points. The modern traveller can join the less grand pilgrims and sightseers who throng the mountain through the spring, summer and autumn months, and enjoy the climb of 7,000 steps and an overnight stay at the simple guesthouse on the summit. (Even though the tourist influx has resulted in the installation of a cable car, walking is still the best means of experiencing the mountain.)

Mount Tai is just over 1,500 metres (5,000 feet) in height, and a fit person can usually climb to the summit in four to five hours. In order to arrive before sunset, the less fit should start the ascent early in the morning, since the steps on the last part of the climb are extremely steep and need to be negotiated in good light. The best time of year to climb the mountain is in spring, but people have climbed it in the dead of winter, when it was cloaked in snow, and have found the experience delightful—if a little chilly.

Most visitors hope for a clear morning on which to enjoy the sunrise over the sea of clouds that lies above the plain. This is best described by Mary Augusta Mullikin and Anna M. Hotchkis in their book, The Nine Sacred Mountains of China, written in the mid-1930s: 'On a clear day the view from the top is one

World Heritage Sites

The Azure Cloud Temple on the top of the mountain, the holy shrine
of the Goddess of Mount Taishan. The temple was built in the 11th century,
and has undergone repeated repairs. [China Intercontinental Press]

continuous line of interlacing mountains lying to the north and east, whereas to
the south the plain spreads out in a glory of light, as though the tawny soil had
become a golden yellow carpet'.

Chinese city dwellers come to the mountain for sightseeing holidays, and
they enjoy the **Dai Temple** at the foot of the mountain as well as the various
shrines and temples en route. But many country folk, particularly the women,
still visit the mountain as part of a pilgrimage. Taishan is dedicated to the Taoist
deity, the Jade Emperor, but the most popular shrine and temple is dedicated to
the Jade Emperor's daughter. It is called the **Princess of the Coloured Clouds
Temple**. The peasant women of Shandong visit her temple to pray for sons and
grandsons, a prayer of greater urgency in these days of one-child families, when
all parents and grandparents wish for a male heir to carry on their name. They
throw sweets, small coins and scarves as offerings to the princess.

MOGAO CAVES #6

Date of Inscription: 1987
Criteria: C (i) (ii) (iii) (iv) (v) (vi)
Dunhuang County, **Gansu Province**. At the eastern foot of Mount Mingsha, 25 kilometres southeast of the county seat. N40 08 E94 49; ref: **440**

Situated at a strategic point along the Silk Route, at the crossroads of trade as well as religious, cultural and intellectual influences, the 492 cells and cave sanctuaries in Mogao are famous for their statues and wall paintings, spanning 1,000 years of Buddhist art.

(Above) *Murals from the Mogao Grottoes, Dunhuang, span more than 45,000 metres squared. As an oasis on the Silk Road, the area brought a variety of peoples together such as Chinese, Uyghers, Tibetans amongst others. Each group of people brought with them their influences, such as the Indian Buddhist art in the earlier works. More recent artistry depicts local daily life and activities, and with a bit of homework, the lay person is said to be able to tell the works of the Tang Dynasty from those of the Song Dynasty. The 750 caves are stacked 50 metres(164 feet) high on the eastern slope of Mingsha Shan (Mount Echoing Sand). Statuary ranges from 2cm, less than an inch high, to 34.5 metres (113 feet) high. The works at Mogao span 10 dynasties. [CGS]*

MOUNT HUANGSHAN #7

Date of Inscription: 1990; **Criteria:** N (iii) (iv) C (ii)
City of Huangshan, **Anhui Province**, N30 10 E118 11; ref: 547

Huangshan, known as 'the loveliest mountain of China', was acclaimed through art and literature during a good part of Chinese history (e.g. the Shanshui 'mountain and water' style of the mid-16th century). Today it holds the same fascination for visitors, poets, painters and photographers who come on pilgrimage to the site, which is renowned for its magnificent scenery made up of many granite peaks and rocks emerging out of a sea of clouds.

> *Huangshan (Yellow Mountain) in Anhui Province was never classified as a sacred mountain, but in recent years it has become one of the most popular destinations in eastern China, largely due to its proximity to Shanghai. That should serve as a warning. The mountain is a favourite with Chinese holidaymakers, and therefore the summer months should be avoided—unless, of course, you like crowds.*

Unlike the smooth-topped Taishan, Huangshan rises in a series of craggy peaks which inspired a whole school of painting in the late Ming period. The peaks themselves have literary names which reflect the traditional reverence Chinese scholars feel for mountains—Lotus Flower Peak, Bright Summit and Heavenly Capital Peak, for example. Between Purple Cloud Peak and Peach Blossom Peak are hot spring pools which are a pleasure to bathe in after a stiff walk.

Huangshan, at just over 1,800 metres (6,000 feet), does not offer easy hiking, and a good pair of thick-soled shoes should be worn, since the granite trails are tough on the feet. Overnight guesthouses on the summits offer basic accommodation, but hikers should remember to bring warm and waterproof clothing (those swirling seas of clouds look wonderful from a distance, but walking through them can be damp and demoralizing without proper protective clothing), and some supplies of high-energy food such as chocolate and dried fruit.

Strange-looking pine trees, grotesque rocks and the sea of clouds are three fantastic scenes on Mount Huangshan. [China Intercontinental Press]

JIUZHAIGOU VALLEY SCENIC AND HISTORIC INTEREST AREA #8
Date of Inscription: 1992; **Criteria:** N (iii)
Nanping County, **Sichuan Province**, N33 05 E103 55; ref: 637

Stretching over 72,000ha in the northern part of Sichuan Province, the jagged Jiuzhaigou valley reaches a height of more than 4,800m, thus comprising a series of diverse forest ecosystems. Its superb landscapes are particularly interesting for their series of narrow conic karst land forms and spectacular waterfalls. Some 140 bird species also inhabit the valley, as well as a number of endangered plant and animal species, including the giant panda and the Sichuan takin.

(Above) *Five-coloured Pool, Jiuzhaigou. [Ingrid Morejohn]*
(Right) *Limestone pool at Huanglong Si. [Wong How Man]*

HUANGLONG SCENIC AND HISTORIC INTEREST AREA #9

Date of Inscription: 1992
Criteria: N (iii)
Songpan County, **Sichuan Province**, N32 45 15 E103 49 20; ref: **638**

Situated in the northwest of Sichuan Province, the Huanglong valley is made up of snow-capped peaks and the easternmost of all the Chinese glaciers. In addition to its mountain landscape, diverse forest ecosystems can be found, as well as spectacular limestone formations, waterfalls and hot springs. The area also has a population of endangered animals, including the giant panda and the Sichuan golden snub-nosed monkey.

WILDLIFE IN CHINA   —Martin Williams

ildlife enthusiasts hoping to spot great numbers of unusual birds and mammals while on a sightseeing tour of China are likely to be disappointed. Damage to the environment, excessive trapping and hunting, along with pressure imposed on ecosystems by the huge population, have drastically reduced wildlife in much of the country. Visitors with only a casual interest in wildlife notice that few birds are to be seen, whether around tourist sites or on journeys through the countryside.

Yet there are areas which are rich in wildlife species that are unique to China or at least rare in other countries: the panda reserves in north Sichuan, whose forests also host rare pheasants; Poyang Lake, the winter home of over 90 per cent of the world's Siberian Cranes; the tropical forests in Xishuangbanna, which harbour over 400 species of bird and over half of China's mammal species—these are among the sites which even the most well-travelled naturalists would find rewarding. Giant Pandas, Manchurian Tigers, River Dolphins, Golden Monkeys and Crested Ibises are among the endangered species which have recently received protection due to the introduction of conservation measures by the Chinese government.

Reaching the prime wildlife areas may require some effort, and some are inaccessible to foreigners or restricted to visitors on organized tours. Hence—particularly for those with money but little time—joining a specialized tour may be the best means of seeing wildlife in China.

Some localities which may be visited by independent travellers are given below. The emphasis is on birds, since bird-watchers predominate among the naturalists who have explored China in recent years. Note that the environs of some tourist sites have proved convenient for bird-watching. The Great Wall at Badaling and the Summer Palace near Beijing are examples. Buddhist temples can also be good, since they are often surrounded by woodland in areas which are otherwise deforested.

A Giant Panda appears to be playing a flute while eating its staple diet of bamboo.
[China Photo Library]

Changbaishan, Jilin Province. The slopes of this mountain have superb forests, and good numbers of birds breed here. Manchurian Tigers are occasionally reported.

Zhalong Nature Reserve, Heilongjiang (about 250 kilometres—155 miles—south of Qiqihar) is a huge wetland. Red-crowned and White-naped Cranes breed here, and four other crane species breed nearby or pass in migration. Around 500 Siberian Cranes spend April and early May in the area.

Beidaihe, Hebei Province, is a seaside resort and one of Asia's best places for observing bird migration. Around 280 species of birds migrate each year. Over 700 cranes of four species pass in early spring (20 March to 4 April is usually the best period). Early April to late May is the main spring migration period for most other birds (late April to mid-May being the best). Early September is excellent for shorebirds and Pied Harries, and the autumn migration continues until the middle of November, with cranes, geese, Oriental White Storks and Great Bustards passing in numbers around the beginning of the month. By this time, most smaller birds have headed south.

Yan Chinao Nature Reserve, Jiangsu Province, is a coastal wetland where Sanders Gulls breed, and in winter over 200 Red-crowned Cranes and several thousand ducks and shorebirds are seen on the marshes. Though the reserve is large, one bird-watcher has reported seeing 50 Red-crowned Cranes during a half-day's walk from the village of Yancheng.

Qinghai Lake, Qinghai Province. It seems that the rather sparsely populated Qinghai-Tibetan plateau is relatively rich in birds, and visits to the environs of Koko Nor (beside Qinghai Lake) have yielded some very interesting species, including several which are unique to China.

Jiuzhaigou, in Sichuan Province, is one of the areas where Giant Pandas live (wild pandas are very rarely seen). Visits to the area have produced sightings of some very rarely seen species, and pheasants may also be found.

Emeishan, in Sichuan Province, has forests which have proved very good for bird-watching. One species—the Emeishan Liocichla—is unique to the mountain.

Most peaks in Wulingyuan Scenic Area look like pilliars or awls chopped out with a knife or an ax. [China Intercontinental Press]

WULINGYUAN SCENIC AND HISTORIC INTEREST AREA #10

Date of Inscription: 1992
Criteria: N (iii)
The Wulingyuan District of the City of Dayong, **Hunan Province**, N29 20 E110 30
ref: 640

A spectacular area stretching over more than 26,000ha in China's Hunan Province, the site is dominated by more than 3,000 narrow sandstone pillars and peaks, many over 200m high. Between the peaks lie ravines and gorges with streams, pools and waterfalls, some 40 caves, and two large natural bridges. In addition to the striking beauty of the landscape, the region is also noted for the fact that it is home to a number of endangered plant and animal species.

MOUNTAIN RESORT AND ITS OUTLYING TEMPLES, CHENGDE #11

Date of Inscription: 1994; **Criteria:** C (ii) (iv)
Chengde City, **Hebei Province**, N41 E118; ref: 703

The Mountain Resort (the Qing dynasty's summer palace), in Hebei Province, was built between 1703 and 1792. It is a vast complex of palaces and administrative and ceremonial buildings. Temples of various architectural styles and imperial gardens blend harmoniously into a landscape of lakes, pastureland and forests. In addition to its aesthetic interest, the mountain resort is a rare historic vestige of the final development of feudal society in China.

(Left) *Thousand-armed Goddess of Mercy at Puning Temple, Chengde.[James Montgomery]*
(Below) *The Yanyu Pavilion is modelled after the building of the same name on the Nanhu lake in Jiaxing, Zhejiang Province. [China Intercontinental Press]*

TEMPLE AND CEMETERY OF CONFUCIUS AND THE KONG FAMILY MANSION IN QUFU #12

Date of Inscription: 1994; **Criteria:** C (i) (iv) (vi)

Qufu City, **Shandong Province**, N35 36 42 E116 58 30; ref: **704**

The temple, cemetery and family mansion of Confucius, the great philosopher, politician and educator of the 6th–5th centuries BCE, are located at Qufu, in Shandong Province. Built to commemorate him in 478 BCE, the temple has been destroyed and reconstructed over the centuries; today it comprises more than 100 buildings. The cemetery contains Confucius' tomb and the remains of more than 100,000 of his descendants. The small house of the Kong family developed into a gigantic aristocratic residence, of which 152 buildings remain. The Qufu complex of monuments has retained its outstanding artistic and historic character due to the devotion of successive Chinese emperors over more than 2,000 years.

(Above) *Flanking the pathway leading to the tomb of Confucius are animal and human figures of stone, forming a squad of guards for the sage in the nether world. [China Intercontinental Press].*

(Right) *A glimpse of the Taihe Palace on the top of Tianzhu Peak. [China Intercontinental Press]*

ANCIENT BUILDING COMPLEX IN THE WUDANG MOUNTAINS #13

Date of Inscription: 1994
Criteria: C (i) (ii) (vi)
Danjiangkou City, **Hubei Province**, N32 28 E111 00; ref: **705**

The palaces and temples which form the nucleus of this group of secular and religious buildings exemplify the architectural and artistic achievements of China's Yuan, Ming and Qing dynasties. Situated in the scenic valleys and on the slopes of the Wudang mountains in Hubei Province, the site, which was built as an organized complex during the Ming dynasty (14th–17th centuries), contains Taoist buildings from as early as the 7th century. It represents the highest standards of Chinese art and architecture for a period of nearly 1,000 years.

Bronze chime bells from the tomb of Marquis Yi of Zeng; If you go to the Wudang Mountains, you'll surely pass through Hubei's provincial capital, Wuhan—a visit to the excellent Hubei Provincial Museum there is a must. [Hubei Provincial Museum, Wuhan]

HISTORIC ENSEMBLE OF THE POTALA PALACE, LHASA #14

Date of Inscription: 1994
Extension: 2000, 2001
Criteria: C (i) (iv) (vi)
Lhasa, **Tibet Autonomous Region**, N29 39 E91 08; ref: **707ter**

The Potala Palace, winter palace of the Dalai Lama since the 7th century, symbolizes Tibetan Buddhism and its central role in the traditional administration of Tibet. The complex, comprising the White and Red Palaces with their ancillary buildings, is built on Red Mountain in the centre of Lhasa Valley, at an altitude of 3,700m. Also founded in the 7th century, the Jokhang Temple Monastery is an exceptional Buddhist religious complex. Norbulingka, the Dalai Lama's former summer palace, constructed in the 18th century, is a masterpiece of Tibetan art. The beauty and originality of the architecture of these three sites, their rich ornamentation and harmonious integration in a striking landscape, add to their historic and religious interest.

The Potala Palace, historic home of the Dalai Lamas, who are revered as living gods.
[Jeremy Tredinnick]

LUSHAN NATIONAL PARK #15
Date of Inscription: 1996; **Criteria:** C (ii) (iii) (iv) (vi)
Jiujiang City, **Jiangxi Province**, N29 26 E115 52; ref: 778

Mount Lushan, in Jiangxi, is one of the spiritual centres of Chinese civilization. Buddhist and Taoist temples, along with landmarks of Confucianism, where the most eminent masters taught, blend effortlessly into a strikingly beautiful landscape which has inspired countless artists who developed the aesthetic approach to nature found in Chinese culture.

JUSTIFICATION FOR INSCRIPTION
The Committee decided to inscribe this property on the basis of cultural criteria (ii), (iii), (iv) and (vi) as a cultural landscape of outstanding aesthetic value and its powerful associations with Chinese spiritual and cultural life.

A religious ceremony in progress in Eastern Wood Temple on Mount Lushan. [China Intercontinental Press]

Mount Emei Scenic Area, including Leshan Giant Buddha Scenic Area #16

Date of Inscription: 1996
Criteria: N (iv) C (iv) (vi)
Emeishan City, **Sichuan Province**, N29 43 55 E103 21 40; ref: 779

The first Buddhist temple in China was built here in Sichuan Province in the 1st century CE in the beautiful surroundings of the summit Mount Emei. The addition of other temples turned the site into one of Buddhism's holiest sites. Over the centuries, the cultural treasures grew in number. The most remarkable is the Giant Buddha of Leshan, carved out of a hillside in the 8th century and looking down on the confluence of three rivers. At 71m high, it is the largest Buddha in the world. Mount Emei is also notable for its exceptionally diverse vegetation, ranging from subtropical to subalpine pine forests. Some of the trees there are more than 1,000 years old.

JUSTIFICATION FOR INSCRIPTION

The Committee decided to inscribe the nominated property under cultural criteria (iv) and (vi), considering the area of Mt. Emei is of exceptional cultural significance, since it is the place where Buddhism first became established on Chinese territory and from where it spread widely throughout the East. It is also an area of natural beauty into which the human element has been integrated, and meets natural criterion (iv) for its high plant species diversity with a large number of endemic species. It also underlined the importance of the link between the tangible and intangible, the natural and the cultural.

Emeishan lies to the southwest of the city of Chengdu in Sichuan Province. It is a Buddhist mountain and represents Puxian, the Bodhisattva of Universal Kindness. As it is higher than most of China's other sacred mountains, rising to a lofty 3,000 metres (10,000 feet), Emeishan cannot be visited in less than three days—which include two overnight stops at monastic guesthouses scattered over the mountain slopes.

There is a wide choice of walking trails to be followed, but the ascent to the summit requires some steep climbing—so be prepared. Once you are up there, the view is breathtaking (assuming you are lucky enough to be there on a fine day). If all the circumstances are correct, you will not only see the sun from the summit but also the strange light effect known as 'Buddha's Halo', which appears between the clouds.

World Heritage Sites

The walks on Emeishan are truly beautiful. Unlike the trails on the northern mountains, which cut through rock and pines, those on Emeishan twist through cool bamboo thickets where countless butterflies dance in the summer sunlight. Butterflies as well as many insects flourish amidst the mountain glades. Fast-flowing streams rush past small farmsteads, and a variety of shrubs grow along the mountain paths. At the overnight stop of the **Pavilion of the Clear Singing Waters**, *two Streams—the Black and the White—meet each other in a frothing torrent (hence the name of the pavilion). Monks run the guesthouses, and their food is simple and vegetarian. Washing facilities are minimal, but on a warm afternoon you can have a bucket-bath out in the sun.*

There are said to be pandas living on the western slopes of the mountain, where there are no walking trails. However, it is unlikely that you will catch a glimpse of these shy creatures. A hike to the summit will more probably bring you face-to-face with a horde of chattering monkeys. Beware of their friendship—they are unrepentant beggars, and dislike being refused anything.

Emeishan has become a popular tourist destination in the summer months, and holiday-makers, in addition to the pilgrims, have sometimes filled all the available accommodation. You are advised to inquire about advance booking of beds in the guesthouses on Emeishan; this can be done at the office in **Baoguo Monastery** *at the foot of the mountain. Hikers who are pressed for time can take buses which make regular runs up a back road to a halfway point on the mountain. En route, the bus stops near a path that leads to* **Wannian Temple**, *which has a huge bronze statue of Puxian riding on an elephant. At the end of the road, you can ride a cable car to the summit, thereby doing hardly any hiking at all. Otherwise, start walking from the bottom, armed with a map from the office at Baoguo Monastery, or from Wannian Temple. There are two main routes to the summit, the northern (shorter and more direct) and the southern (more winding, more rugged). Whichever route you follow, be sure to travel light—the walk is strenuous—and don't forget to pack snacks, waterproof clothing, a thick jersey and a complete change of clothing in case of bad weather.*

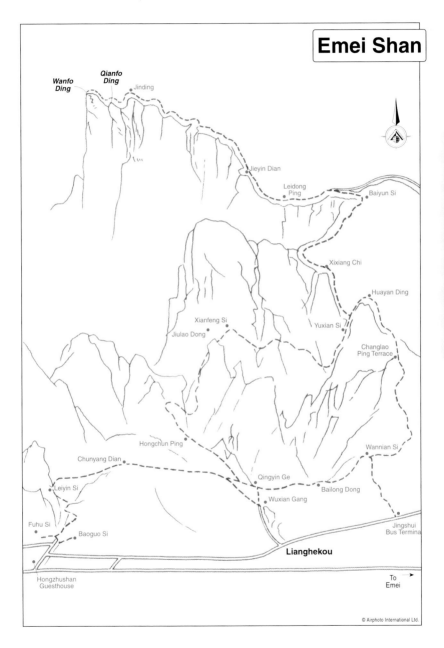

Emei Shan

© Airphoto International Ltd.

Naxi women dance in Lijiang's old Market Square. [Jeremy Tredinnick]

Dawn breaks over the rooftops of Lijiang's Old Town. [Jeremy Tredinnick]

OLD TOWN OF LIJIANG #17

Date of Inscription: 1997
Criteria: C (ii) (iv) (v)
Lijiang's old town (including the Dayan old town, Basha housing cluster and Shuhe housing cluster), N26 34 E94 12; ref: **811**

The Old Town of Lijiang, which is perfectly adapted to the uneven topography of this key commercial and strategic site, has retained a historic townscape of high quality and authenticity. Its architecture is noteworthy for the blending of elements from several cultures that have come together over many centuries. Lijiang also possesses an ancient water-supply system of great complexity and ingenuity that still functions effectively today.

JUSTIFICATION FOR INSCRIPTION

The Committee decided to inscribe this site on the basis of cultural criteria (ii), (iv) and (v). Lijiang is an exceptional ancient town set in a dramatic landscape which represents the harmonious fusion of different cultural traditions to produce an urban landscape of outstanding quality.

ANCIENT CITY OF PINGYAO #18

Date of Inscription: 1997; **Criteria:** C (ii) (iii) (iv)
Pingyao County, **Shan Xi Province**, N37 14 E112 11; ref: **812**

Pingyao is an exceptionally well-preserved example of a traditional Han Chinese city, founded in the 14th century. Its urban fabric shows the evolution of architectural styles and town planning in Imperial China over five centuries. Of special interest are the imposing buildings associated with banking, for which Pingyao was the major centre for the whole of China in the 19th and early 20th centuries.

JUSTIFICATION FOR INSCRIPTION

The Committee decided to inscribe this property on the basis of criteria (ii), (iii) and (iv), considering that the Ancient City of Pingyao is an outstanding example of a Han Chinese city of the Ming and Qing Dynasties (14th–20th centuries) that has retained all its features to an exceptional degree and in doing so provides a remarkably complete picture of cultural, social, economic, and religious development during one of the most seminal periods of Chinese history.

PINGYAO

—by *Stephen Hallett*

F or all those who bemoan the physical destruction of China's unique architectural heritage and shed tears over the wholesale dismemberment of old Beijing, a visit to Pingyao is a heartening remedy. Lying 90 kilometres south of Taiyuan, provincial capital of Shanxi, Pingyao is the most complete of the few walled cities that survive in China. A leisurely 12-hour overnight train ride from Beijing's West Station takes you to Pingyao Station, less than a kilometre from the town itself. Watch out for the hotel touts, who greet you on the platform and eagerly try and hustle you into waiting pedicabs. In this, as in other respects, a visit to Pingyao is like a journey back in time; there is a timelessness about the place that makes it rare in today's China.

The city is most remarkable for its imposing Ming dynasty walls, 6.4 kilometres in circumference and an average of ten metres high and 12 metres thick. Historical records suggest that these walls actually date from the Western Zhou period (700 BCE) when, as in other ancient Chinese towns, they were built of rammed earth. But in 1370 CE, during the reign of the Ming Emperor Hong Wu, the walls were rebuilt and brick clad, taking on the distinctive shape they have today. After years of poverty and neglect, the town began a major refurbishment during the 1990s and the crumbling walls were restored to their former glory. The main reason for this heaven-sent act of preservation was the 1997 listing of the town by UNESCO as a World Heritage site. Some acclaim may also have come courtesy of director Zhang Yimou's film *Raise the Red Lantern*, which was filmed during the 1980s in Qiaojia Dayuan (Qiao Family Mansion). It is a huge wealthy family compound about 40 kilometres north of Pingyao. Despite World Heritage status, the town has avoided becoming twee and remains authentically dusty and chaotic—although the explosion in tourism numbers is having a sad but inevitable effect, with many locals making way for entrepreneurial ventures.

While most tourists visit Pingyao on a day trip from Taiyuan, a longer stay in the town is thoroughly recommended. All of the inner town can be reached on foot and pedicabs or minibuses will take visitors to temples and other sites of interest outside the town.

Legend has it that Pingyao was laid out in the shape of a turtle, a symbol of longevity in China, and this has protected the town from flood, war and famine for many centuries. A circumparambulation of the city walls will make this idea clear: the south gate represents the turtle's head, the two wells outside the gate, its eyes; the east and west gates are the turtle's legs, while the north gate is its tail (and appropriately the point at which waste water and sewage leaves the town). It is also said that the numerous streets and alleys of the town represent the lines

*An aerial view of the ancient town. The street that cuts the town
in the middle serves as the town's axis line. [China Intercontinental Press]*

on the turtle's back, while the 3,000 battlements and 72 watchtowers symbolize the 3,000 students and 72 principle disciples of Confucius.

At the heart of Pingyao stands the elegant Ming dynasty market building, astride Nan Da Jie, now generally known as Ming-Qing Street. This paved street abounds in curiosity shops and restaurants, aimed firmly at the increasingly heavy through-flow of visitors. Of particular note is the fine local laquerware, for which Pingyao is famous. Halfway down this street is the friendly Tianyuankui Guesthouse, where visitors can spend a comfortable and inexpensive night in a traditional room, complete with *kang* (a raised brick bed) and latticed windows.

The town is rather like a miniature version of old Beijing, with its alleyways, temples and courtyard houses. Of particular note is the courtyard of the old county Yamen (Xian Ya Shu—the former magistrate's offices), which is now preserved as a museum and gives a good insight into local government and politics in imperial China. Local actors here present regular re-enactments of magisterial hearings from the Qing dynasty law books.

During the 19th century Pingyao became famous as one of China's first banking centres, making it by far the wealthiest town in this poor part of Shanxi. This development was largely the work of two local business tycoons, Li Daquan and Lei Lutai, founders of China's first investment bank. The site of their business, the Rishengchang (Sunrise Prosperity) is now a museum to the marvels of early Chinese capitalism. By the mid-19th century news of Pingyao's prosperity had spread far and wide and a saying went about that 'its appetite was insatiable, it's produce inexhaustible'.

Other sites of interest in the town include the large, religiously diverse Temple of the City God (Chenghuang Miao) which, with its medley of Buddhist, Taoist and pagan effigies, dates back at least to the late Ming dynasty (16th century); the pretty Qingxu Taoist Temple (Qingxu Guan), built during the Tang and Song dynasties; and the Tianjixiang Museum (Tian Jixiang Bowuguan), which displays further riches of Pingyao's Qing dynasty capitalists. Outside the town are several important historical and religious sites. Of particular note are the Shuanglin Temple (Shuanglin Si), five kilometres south of the town, remarkable for its extensive collection painted clay sculptures, dating back to the Song, Yuan, Ming and Qing dynasties. Twelve kilometres north of Pingyao lies the Zhengguo Temple (Zhenguo Si), which dates back to the Five Dynasties (10th century CE) and is notable as one of the few remaining wooden structures of that period. And further afield (40 kilometres north of the town) is the exquisite Qiao Family Mansion, built in 1755, former residence of a famous Qing businessman, Qiao Zhiyong, and offering a rare insight into the lives of old China's provincial elite.

Suzhou, 1978. Sadly, many of these characteristic whitewashed cottages have been demolished to make way for new developments as the city expands to keep pace with nearby Shanghai.

CLASSICAL GARDENS OF SUZHOU #19 (SEE ALSO PAGES 161–165)

Date of Inscription: 1997; **Extension:** 2000
Criteria: C (i) (ii) (iii) (iv) (v)
Suzhou City, **Jiangsu Province**, N31 19 36.2 E120 37 32.3; ref: **813bis**

Classical Chinese garden design, which seeks to recreate natural landscapes in miniature, is nowhere better illustrated than in the nine gardens in the historic city of Suzhou. They are generally acknowledged to be masterpieces of the genre. Dating from the 11th-19th century, the gardens reflect the profound metaphysical importance of natural beauty in Chinese culture in their meticulous design.

JUSTIFICATION FOR INSCRIPTION
The Committee decided to inscribe this property on the basis of criteria (i), (ii), (iii), (iv) and (v), considering that the four classical gardens of Suzhou are masterpieces of Chinese landscape garden design in which art, nature, and ideas are integrated perfectly to create ensembles of great beauty and peaceful harmony, and four gardens are integral to the entire historic urban plan.

(Left) *Lingering Garden, a pool of inspiration in Suzhou;* (above) *Suzhou's gardens are the finest in the land.*

World Heritage Sites

SUMMER PALACE, AN IMPERIAL GARDEN IN BEIJING #20

Date of Inscription: 1998; **Criteria:** C (i) (ii) (iii)
Beijing, N39 59 51 E116 16 08; ref: **880**

The Summer Palace in Beijing—first built in 1750, largely destroyed in the war of 1860 and restored on its original foundations in 1886—is a masterpiece of Chinese landscape garden design. The natural landscape of hills and open water is combined with man-made features such as pavilions, halls, palaces, temples and bridges to form a harmonious ensemble of outstanding aesthetic value.

JUSTIFICATION FOR INSCRIPTION

Criterion (i): The Summer Palace in Beijing is an outstanding expression of the creative art of Chinese landscape garden design, incorporating the works of humankind and nature in a harmonious whole.

Criterion (ii): The Summer Palace epitomizes the philosophy and practice of Chinese garden design, which played a key role in the development of this cultural form throughout the East.

Criterion (iii): The imperial Chinese garden, illustrated by the Summer Palace, is a potent symbol of one of the major world civilizations.

Qianlong's Bronze Ox, just a stone's throw from the Summer Palace's Seventeen-arch Bridge, with Longevity Hill on the horizon.

TEMPLE OF HEAVEN: AN IMPERIAL SACRIFICIAL ALTAR IN BEIJING #21

Date of Inscription: 1998; **Criteria:** C (i) (ii) (iii)
Tiantan Park, **Beijing**, N39 52 56.1 E116 24 23.7; ref: **881**

The Temple of Heaven, founded in the first half of the 15th century, is a dignified complex of fine religious buildings set in gardens and surrounded by historic pine woods. In its overall layout and that of its individual buildings, it symbolizes the relationship between earth and heaven—the human world and God's world—which stands at the heart of Chinese cosmogony, and also the special role played by the emperors within that relationship.

JUSTIFICATION FOR INSCRIPTION

Criterion (i): The Temple of Heaven is a masterpiece of architecture and landscape design which simply and graphically illustrates a cosmogony of great importance for the evolution of one of the world's great civilizations.

Criterion (ii): The symbolic layout and design of the Temple of Heaven had a profound influence on architecture and planning in the Far East over many centuries.

Criterion (iii): For more than 2,000 years China was ruled by a series of feudal dynasties, the legitimacy of which is symbolized by the design and layout of the Temple of Heaven.

The Hall of Prayer for Good Harvest has been an iconic symbol of China for centuries, and is one of Beijing's top tourist destinations. [Peter Danford]

THE TRAPPINGS OF POWER

Every time I went to my schoolroom to study, or visited the High Consorts to pay my respects, or went for a stroll in the garden I was always followed by a large retinue. Every trip I made to the Summer Palace must have cost thousands of Mexican dollars: the Republic's police had to be asked to line the roads to protect me and I was accompanied by a motorcade consisting of dozens of vehicles.

Whenever I went for a stroll in the garden a procession had to be organized. In front went a eunuch from the Administrative Bureau whose function was roughly that of a motor horn: he walked twenty or thirty yards ahead of the rest of the party intoning the sound "chir . . . chir . . ." as a warning to anyone who might be in the vicinity to go away at once. Next came two chief eunuchs advancing crabwise on either side of the path; ten paces behind them came the centre of the procession—the Empress Dowager or myself. If I was being carried in a chair there would be two junior eunuchs walking beside me to attend to my wants at any moment; if I was walking they would be supporting me. Next came a eunuch with a large silk canopy followed by a large group of eunuchs of whom some were empty-handed and others were holding all sorts of things: a seat in case I wanted to rest, changes of clothing, umbrellas and parasols. After these eunuchs of the imperial presence came eunuchs of the imperial tea bureau with boxes of various kinds of cakes and delicacies, and, of course, jugs of hot water and a tea service; they were followed by eunuchs of the imperial dispensary bearing cases of medicine and first-aid equipment suspended from carrying poles. The medicines carried always included potions prepared from lampwick sedge, chrysanthemums, the roots of reeds, bamboo leaves, and bamboo skins; in summer there were always Essence of Betony Pills for Rectifying the Vapour, Six Harmony Pills for Stabilizing the Centre, Gold Coated Heat-Dispersing Cinnabar, Fragrant Herb Pills, Omnipurpose Bars, colic medicine and anti-plague powder; and through-out all four seasons there would be the Three Immortals Beverage to aid the digestion, as well as many other medicaments. At the end of the procession came the eunuchs who carried commodes and chamber-pots. If I was walking a sedanchair, open or covered according to the season, would bring up the rear. This motley procession of several dozen people would proceed in perfect silence and order.

But I would often throw it into confusion. When I was young I liked to run around when I was in high spirits just as any child does. At first they would all scuttle along after me puffing and panting with their procession reduced to chaos. When I grew a little older and knew how to give orders I would tell them to stand and wait for me; then apart from the junior eunuchs of the imperial presence who came with me they would all stand there waiting in silence with their loads. After I had finished running around they would form up again behind me. When I learnt to ride a bicycle and ordered the removal of all the upright wooden thresholds in the palace so that I could ride around without obstruction the procession was no longer able to follow me and so it had to be temporarily abolished. But when I went to pay my respects to the High Consorts or to my schoolroom I still had to have something of a retinue, and without it I would have felt rather odd. When I heard people telling the story of the last emperor of the Ming Dynasty who had only one eunuch left with him at the end I felt very uncomfortable.

Pu Yi, From Emperor to Citizen, translated by W J F Jenner

Aisin-Gioro Pu Yi, *From emperor to citizen: the autobiography of Aisin-Gioro Pu Yi*. Foreign Language Press, 2002. Henry Pu Yi (1906–1967), the last emperor of China, was a member of the Ch'ing (or Qing) Dynasty and a Manchu. He describes in vivid detail the events of the 50 years between his ascension to the throne and the last, decadent days of the Qing Dynasty through to the final period of his life as a retiring scholar, citizen of the People's Republic of China and quiet-living resident of Beijing.

Literary Excerpt

MOUNT WUYI #22

Date of Inscription: 1999
Criteria: N (iii) (iv) C (iii) (vi)
Wuyishan City, **Fujian Province**, N27 43 E117 41; ref: **911**

Mount Wuyi is the most outstanding area for biodiversity conservation in southeast China and a refuge for a large number of ancient, relict species, many of them endemic to China. The serene beauty of the dramatic gorges of the Nine Bend River, with its numerous temples and monasteries, many now in ruins, provided the setting for the development and spread of neo-Confucianism, which has been influential in the cultures of East Asia since the 11th century. In the 1st century BCE a large administrative capital was built at nearby Chengcun by the Han dynasty rulers. Its massive walls enclose an archaeological site of great significance.

JUSTIFICATION FOR INSCRIPTION

Natural criteria (iii) and (iv): Mount Wuyi is one of the most outstanding subtropical forests in the world. It is the largest, most representative example of a largely intact forest encompassing the diversity of the Chinese Subtropical Forest and the South Chinese Rainforest. It acts as a refuge for a large number of ancient, relict plant species, many of them endemic to China and contains large numbers of reptile, amphibian and insect species. The riverine landscape of Nine-Bend Stream (lower gorge) is also of exceptional scenic quality in its juxtaposition of smooth rock cliffs with clear, deep water. Cultural criteria (iii) and (vi); Criterion (iii): Mount Wuyi is a landscape of great beauty that has been protected for more than twelve centuries. It contains a series of exceptional archaeological sites, including the Han City established in the 1st century BCE and a number of temples and study centres associated with the birth of Neo-Confucianism in the 11th century CE. Criterion (vi): Mount Wuyi was the cradle of Neo-Confucianism, a doctrine that played a dominant role in the countries of East and Southeast Asia for many centuries, and influenced philosophy and government over much of the world.

> *Finally, in the northwest of the province, is the marvellous resort area of the Wuyi Mountains, popular since the second century BCE. A trip to these mountains takes you through scenery as evocative as the landscapes of Guilin. Most visitors enjoy a trip on the **Nine-Twist Stream** (Jiuqu Xi), punting past sheer cliffs, strange rock formations and flowery river banks. Many famous visitors have come here over the centuries, and the various stone inscriptions by the side of the river have been carved in the calligraphy*

of well-known painters, poets and scholars. Of special interest is the exhibition of 3,000-year-old boat-shaped coffins which were found on ledges high up on the river cliffs. Horticulture enthusiasts and bird-watchers will wish to make an expedition to the **Wuyi Nature Reserve**, filled with a subtropical virgin forest and a variety of flora which excited European botanists in the 19th century. In addition, tea is cultivated by the 3,000 villagers who live in the area. The reserve is also a migratory stopping place for birds.

(Above) *Fujian Province, early 1900s [Museum of History]*; (following pages) *The red sandstone peaks of Longhu Shan, near the town of Yingtan in Jiangxi Province. These oddly shaped peaks are an extension of the Wuyi mountain range of Fujian. [Kevin Bishop]*

DAZU ROCK CARVINGS #23

Date of Inscription: 1999; **Criteria:** C (i) (ii) (iii)
Dazu County, **Chongqing Municipality**, N29 42 04 E105 42 18; ref: **912**

The steep hillsides of the Dazu area contain an exceptional series of rock carvings dating from the 9th to the 13th century. They are remarkable for their aesthetic quality, their rich diversity of subject matter, both secular and religious, and the light that they shed on everyday life in China during this period. They provide outstanding evidence of the harmonious synthesis of Buddhism, Taoism and Confucianism.

JUSTIFICATION FOR INSCRIPTION

Criterion (i): The Dazu carvings represent the pinnacle of Chinese rock art for their high aesthetic quality and their diversity of style and subject matter.

Criterion (ii): Tantric Buddhism from India and the Chinese Taoist and Confucian beliefs came together at Dazu to create a highly original and influential manifestation of spiritual harmony.

Criterion (iii): The eclectic nature of religious belief in later Imperial China is given material expression in the exceptional artistic heritage of the Dazu rock art.

Rock sculpture at Dazu Buddhist Grottoes, the 'Revolving Wheel', Beishan. [Ingrid Morejohn]

MOUNT QINGCHENG AND THE DUJIANGYAN IRRIGATION SYSTEM #24

Date of Inscription: 2000; **Criteria:** C (ii) (iv) (vi)

Dujiangyan City, **Sichuan Province**, N31 00 06 E103 36 19; ref: **1001**

Construction of the Dujiangyan irrigation system began in the 3rd century BCE. This system still controls the waters of the Minjiang River and distributes it to the fertile farmland of the Chengdu plains. Mount Qingcheng was the birthplace of Taoism, which is celebrated in a series of ancient temples.

JUSTIFICATION FOR INSCRIPTION

Criterion (ii): The Dujiangyan Irrigation System, begun in the 2nd century BCE, is a major landmark in the development of water management and technology, and is still discharging its functions perfectly.

Criterion (iv): The immense advances in science and technology achieved in ancient China are graphically illustrated by the Dujiangyan Irrigation System.

Criterion (vi): The temples of Mount Qingcheng are closely associated with the foundation of Taoism, one of the most influential religions of East Asia over a long period of history.

World Heritage Sites

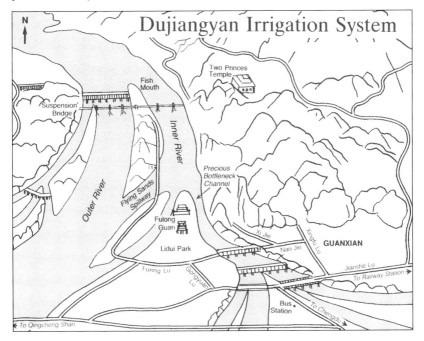

[Professor Bai Yiliang]

ANCIENT VILLAGES IN SOUTHERN ANHUI–XIDI AND HONGCUN #25

Date of Inscription: 2000; **Criteria:** C (iii) (iv) (v)
Yi County, Huangshan City, **Anhui Province**, N29 54 16 E117 59 15; ref: **1002**

The two traditional villages of Xidi and Hongcun preserve to a remarkable extent the appearance of non-urban settlements of a type that largely disappeared or was transformed during the last century. Their street plan, their architecture and decoration, and the integration of houses with comprehensive water systems are unique surviving examples.

JUSTIFICATION FOR INSCRIPTION

Criterion (iii): The villages of Xidi and Hongcun are graphic illustrations of a type of human settlement created during a feudal period and based on a prosperous trading economy.

Criterion (v): The traditional non-urban settlements of China, which have to a very large extent disappeared during the past century, are exceptionally well preserved in the villages of Xidi and Hongcun.

The rare vernacular architecture of Hongcun surrounds the semilunar pond in the centre of the village. [China Intercontinental Press]

Just one scene from the 1,352 caves in itself is opulent with detail. [CGS]

LONGMEN GROTTOES #26

Date of Inscription: 2000; **Criteria:** C (i) (ii) (iii)
Luoyang City, **Henan Province**, N34 28 0 E112 28 0; ref: **1003**

The grottoes and niches of Longmen contain the largest and most impressive collection of Chinese art of the late Northern Wei and Tang dynasties (316–907). These works, entirely devoted to the Buddhist religion, represent the high point of Chinese stone carving.

JUSTIFICATION FOR INSCRIPTION

Criterion (i): The sculptures of the Longmen Grottoes are an outstanding manifestation of human artistic creativity.

Criterion (ii): The Longmen Grottoes illustrate the perfection of a long-established art form which was to play a highly significant role in the cultural evolution of this region of Asia.

Criterion (iii): The high cultural level and sophisticated society of Tang dynasty China is encapsulated in the exceptional stone carvings of the Longmen Grottoes.

IMPERIAL TOMBS OF THE MING AND QING DYNASTIES #27

Date of Inscription: 2000
Extension: 2003,2004
Criteria: C (i) (ii) (iii) (iv) (vi)
Nanjing City, **Jiangsu Province** (Xiaoling Tomb); Changping District, **Beijing** (Ming Tombs), N41 11 E178 38; ref: **1004bis**

The Imperial Tombs of the Ming and Qing dynasties are four groups of tombs in four provinces of eastern China. The tombs, designed in keeping with the Chinese principles of geomancy (fengshui), provide outstanding evidence of Chinese beliefs and traditions from the 14th century onwards and are significant examples of architecture and applied arts from that period.

JUSTIFICATION FOR INSCRIPTION

Criterion (i): The harmonious integration of remarkable architectural groups in a natural environment chosen to meet the criteria of geomancy (fengshui) makes the Ming and Qing Imperial Tombs masterpieces of human creative genius.

Criteria (ii), (iii) and (iv): The imperial mausolea are outstanding testimony to a cultural and architectural tradition that for over five hundred years dominated this part of the world; by reason of their integration into the natural environment, they make up a unique ensemble of cultural landscapes.

Criterion (vi): The Ming and Qing tombs are dazzling illustrations of the beliefs, world view, and geomantic theories of fengshui prevalent in feudal China. They have served as burial edifices for illustrious personages and as the theatre for significant events that have marked the history of China.

The 1,800-metre-long winding Sacred Way has six kinds of animals in 12 pairs to guard the Ming Emperor's Tomb in Nanjing. This path originally started in Sifangchang (Rectangular City) at a pavilion bearing a carved stone stele commemorating Emperor Zhu Yuanzhang (Emperor Ming Taizu), though this pavilion is no longer intact. At the end of the Sacred Way are two columns, Huabiao, and four pairs of ministers and generals to guard the emperor. The mausoleum, the clay vault, which is 400 metres in diameter and where the emperor and his queen were buried, lies at the northern base of Mount Zijin (Mount Purple Gold). Its construction commenced in 1381 and was completed in 1405 by about 100,000 labourers. It is rare to find the Sacred Way as empty as depicted here, circa 1980, as burgeoning tourism now finds it often brimming with sightseers. [Caroline Courtauld]

YUNGANG GROTTOES #28

Date of Inscription: 2001; **Criteria:** C (i) (ii) (iii) (iv)
Datong City, **Shanxi Province**, N40 6 35 E113 7 20; ref: **1039**

The Yungang Grottoes, in Datong City, Shanxi Province, with their 252 caves and 51,000 statues, represent the outstanding achievement of Buddhist cave art in China in the 5th and 6th centuries. The Five Caves created by Tan Yao, with their strict unity of layout and design, constitute a classical masterpiece of the first peak of Chinese Buddhist art.

JUSTIFICATION FOR INSCRIPTION

Criterion (i): The assemblage of statuary of the Yungang Grottoes is a masterpiece of early Chinese Buddhist cave art.

Criterion (ii): The Yungang cave art represent the successful fusion of Buddhist religious symbolic art from south and central Asia with Chinese cultural traditions, starting in the 5th century CE under Imperial auspices.

Criterion (iii): The power and endurance of Buddhist belief in China are vividly illustrated by the Yungang Grottoes.

Criterion (iv): The Buddhist tradition of religious cave art achieved its first major impact at Yungang, where it developed its own distinct character and artistic power.

Maitreya from Cave 13, Yungang. [China Intercontinental Press]

THREE PARALLEL RIVERS OF YUNNAN PROTECTED AREAS #29
Date of Inscription: 2003; Criteria: N (i) (ii) (iii) (iv)
Lijiang Prefecture, Diqing Tibetan Autonomous Prefecture and Nujiang Lisu Autonomous Prefecture, **Yunnan Province**, N27 53 42 E98 24 23; ref: 1083

Consisting of eight geographical clusters of protected areas within the boundaries of the Three Parallel Rivers National Park, in the mountainous northwest of Yunnan Province, the 1.7 million hectare site features sections of the upper reaches of three of the great rivers of Asia: the Yangtze (Jinsha), Mekong and Salween run roughly parallel, north to south, through steep gorges which, in places, are 3,000m deep and are bordered by glaciated peaks more than 6,000m high. The site is an epicentre of Chinese biodiversity. It is also one of the richest temperate regions of the world in terms of biodiversity.

JUSTIFICATION FOR INSCRIPTION

Criterion (i): The property is of outstanding value for displaying the geological history of the last 50 million years associated with the collision of the Indian Plate with the Eurasian Plate, the closure of the ancient Tethys Sea, and the uplifting of the Himalaya Range and the Tibetan Plateau. These were major geological events in the evolution of the land surface of Asia and they are on-going. The diverse rock types within the site record this history and, in addition, the range of karst, granite monolith, and Danxia sandstone landforms in the alpine zone include some of the best of their type in the mountains of the world.

Criterion (ii): The dramatic expression of ecological processes in the Three Parallel Rivers site has resulted from a mix of geological, climatic and topographical effects. First, the location of the area within an active orographic belt has resulted in a wide range of rock substrates from igneous (four types) through to various sedimentary types including limestones, sandstones and conglomerates. An exceptional range of topographical features—from gorges to karst to glaciated peaks—is associated with the site being at a "collision point" of tectonic plates. Add the fact that the area was a Pleistocene refugium and is located at a biogeographical convergence zone (i.e. with temperate and tropical elements) and the physical foundations for evolution of its high biodiversity are all present. Along with the landscape diversity with a steep gradient of almost 6,000m vertical, a monsoon climate affects most of the area and provides another favourable ecological stimulus that has allowed the full range of temperate Palearctic biomes to develop.

(Following pages) *The Jinsha Jiang (River of Golden Sands), the first great bend on the Yangzi, at Shigu. [China Intercontinental Press]*

World Heritage Sites

Criterion (iii): Superlative natural phenomena or natural beauty and aesthetic importance The deep, parallel gorges of the Jinsha, Lancang and Nu Jiang are the outstanding natural feature of the site; while large sections of the three rivers lie just outside the site boundaries, the river gorges are nevertheless the dominant scenic element in the area. High mountains are everywhere, with the glaciated peaks of the Meili, Baima and Haba Snow Mountains providing a spectacular scenic skyline. The Mingyongqia Glacier is a notable natural phemonenon, descending to 2700m altitude from Mt Kawagebo (6740m)—claimed to be the lowest altitude for a glacier at such a low latitude (28° N) in the northern hemisphere. Other outstanding scenic landforms are the alpine karst (especially the 'stone moon' in the Moon Mountain Scenic Area above the Nu Jiang Gorge) and the 'tortoise shell' weathering of the alpine Danxia.

Criterion (iv): Biodiversity and threatened species. Northwest Yunnan is the area of richest biodiversity in China and may be the most biologically diverse temperate region on earth. The site encompasses most of the natural habitats in the Hengduan Mountains, one of the world's most important remaining areas for the conservation of the earth's biodiversity. The outstanding topographic and climatic diversity of the site, coupled with its location at the juncture of the East Asia, Southeast Asia, and Tibetan Plateau biogeographical realms and its function as a N-S corridor for the movement of plants and animals (especially during the ice ages), marks it as a truly unique landscape, which still retains a high degree of natural character despite thousands of years of human habitation. As the last remaining stronghold for an extensive suite of rare and endangered plants and animals, the site is of outstanding universal value.

CAPITAL CITIES AND TOMBS OF THE ANCIENT KOGURYO KINGDOM #30

Date of Inscription: 2004
Criteria: C (i) (ii) (iii) (iv) (v); ref: **1135**
Huanren County, **Liaoning Province** and Ji'an, **Jilin Province**, N41 09 25 E126 11 14

The site includes archaeological remains of three cities and 40 tombs: Wunu Mountain City, Guonei City and Wandu Mountain City: 14 tombs are imperial, 26 of nobles. All belong to the Koguryo culture, named after the dynasty that ruled over parts of northern China and the northern half of the Korean Peninsula from 37 BCE to 668 CE. Wunu Mountain City is only partly excavated. Guonei City, within the modern city of Ji'an, played the role of a supporting capital after the main Koguryo capital moved to Pyongyang. Wandu Mountain City, one of the capitals of the Koguryo Kingdom, contains many vestiges, including a large palace and 37 tombs. Some of the tombs have elaborate ceilings, designed to roof wide spaces without columns and carry the heavy load of a stone or earth tumulus (mound) which was placed above them.

JUSTIFICATION FOR INSCRIPTION

Criterion (i): The tombs represent a masterpiece of the human creative genius in their wall paintings and structures.

Criterion (ii): The capital cities of the Koguryo Kingdom are an early example of mountain cities, later imitated by neighbouring cultures. The tombs, particularly the important stele and a long inscription in one of the tombs, show the impact of Chinese culture on the Koguryo (who did not develop their own writing). The paintings in the tombs, while showing artistic skills and specific style, are also an example of the strong impact from other cultures.

Criterion (iii): The Capital Cities and Tombs of the Ancient Koguryo Kingdom represent exceptional testimony to the vanished Koguryo civilization.

Criterion (iv): The system of capital cities represented by Guonei City and Wandu Mountain City also influenced the construction of later capitals built by the Koguryo regime; the Koguryo tombs provide outstanding examples of the evolution of piled-stone and earthen tomb construction.

Criterion (v): The capital cities of the Koguryo Kingdom represent a perfect blending of human creation and nature whether with the rocks or with forests and rivers.

HISTORIC CENTRE OF MACAO #31 (SEE PAGE 298)

Date of Inscription: 2005; **Criteria:** C (ii) (iii) (iv) (vi)
Macao Special Administrative Region, N22 11 52.0 E113 32 47.0; ref: **1110**

Macao, a lucrative port of strategic importance in the development of international trade, was under Portuguese administration from the mid-16th century until 1999, when it came under Chinese sovereignty. With its historic street, residential, religious and public Portuguese and Chinese buildings, the historic centre of Macao provides a unique testimony to the meeting of aesthetic, cultural, architectural and technological influences from East and West. The site also contains a fortress and a lighthouse, which is the oldest in China. The site bears testimony to one of the earliest and longest-lasting encounters between China and the West based on the vibrancy of international trade.

At night the alleys leading off Senado Square are tastefully lit. [Jeremy Tredinnick]

World Heritage Sites

SICHUAN GIANT PANDA SANCTUARIES #32

Date of inscription: 2006; **Criteria:** (x)
Qionglai and Jiajin Mountains, **Sichuan Province**, N30 50 E103 00; ref: **1213**

The Sichuan Giant Panda Sanctuaries are home to more than 30 percent of the world's pandas, which are classed as highly endangered, and cover 924,500 hectares comprising seven nature reserves and nine scenic parks. The sanctuaries constitute the largest remaining contiguous habitat of the giant panda, a relict from the paleotropic forests of the Tertiary Era. This is also the species' most important site for captive breeding. The sanctuaries are home to other globally endangered animals such as the red panda, the snow leopard and clouded leopard. They are among the botanically richest sites of any region in the world outside the tropical rainforests, with between 5,000 and 6,000 species of flora in over 1,000 genera.

Pandas in a display of rough-and-tumble. [Martin Williams]

YIN XU #33

Date of inscription: 2006; **Criteria**: (ii) (iii) (iv) (vi)
Near to Anyang City, **Henan Province**, N36 07 E114 18; ref: **1114**

The archaeological site of Yin Xu, some 500 kilometres south of Beijing, is an ancient capital city of the late Shang Dynasty (1300–1046 BCE). It testifies to the golden age of early Chinese culture, crafts and sciences, a time of great prosperity of the Chinese Bronze Age. A number of royal tombs and palaces, prototypes of later Chinese architecture, have been unearthed on the site, including the Palace and Royal Ancestral Shrines Area, with more than 80 house foundations, and the only tomb of a member of the royal family of the Shang Dynasty to have remained intact, the Tomb of Fu Hao. The large number and superb craftsmanship of the burial accessories found there bear testimony to the advanced level of Shang crafts industry. Inscriptions on oracle bones found in Yin Xu bear invaluable testimony to the development of one of the world's oldest writing systems, ancient beliefs and social systems.

KAIPING DIAOLOU AND VILLAGES #34

Date of Inscription: 2007
Criteria: (ii) (iii) (iv)
Among the villages of Chican, Tangkou, Baihe and Xiangang, **Guangdong Province**, N22 17 E112 33; ref: **1112**

Kaiping Diaolou and Villages feature the Diaolou, multi-storeyed defensive village houses in Kaiping, which display a complex and flamboyant fusion of Chinese and Western structural and decorative forms. They reflect the significant role of émigré Kaiping people in the development of several countries in South Asia, Australasia and

North America, during the late 19th and early 20th centuries. There are four groups of Diaolou and 20 of the most symbolic ones are inscribed on the List. These buildings take three forms: communal towers built by several families and used as temporary refuge; residential towers built by individual rich families and used as fortified residences, and watchtowers. Built of stone, *pise*, brick or concrete, these buildings represent a complex and confident fusion between Chinese and Western architectural styles. Retaining a harmonious relationship with the surrounding landscape, the Diaolou testify to the final flowering of local building traditions that started in the Ming period in response to local banditry.

Differing architectural styles come together in this region of Guangdong Province.

South China Karst #35 (see pages 236–7)

Date of Inscription: 2007
Criteria: (vii) (viii)
Various locations in Shilin Yi County, Libo County, Wulong County, **Yunnan, Guizhou and Guangxi provinces**, N25 13 15 E107 58 30; ref: **1248**

The South China Karst region extends over a surface of half a million square kilometres lying mainly in Yunnan, Guizhou and Guangxi provinces. It represents one of the world's most spectacular examples of humid tropical to subtropical karst landscapes. The stone forests of Shilin are considered superlative natural phenomena and a world reference with a wider range of pinnacle shapes than other karst landscapes with pinnacles, and a higher diversity of shapes and changing colours. The cone and tower karsts of Libo, also considered the world reference site for these types of karst, form a distinctive and beautiful landscape. Wulong Karst has been inscribed for its giant dolines (sinkholes), natural bridges and caves.

WORLD HERITAGE SITE CRITERION

To receive World Heritage status, a site must have "outstanding universal value", must also meet "conditions of integrity and/or authenticity", and it must have "an adequate protection and management system to ensure its safeguarding". To be nominated, a site must meet either one or more of various cultural or natural criterion (for more information on the selection process, see http://whc.unesco.org/en/guidelines):

(i) represent a masterpiece of human creative genius;

(ii) exhibit an important interchange of human values, over a span of time or within a cultural area of the world, on developments in architecture or technology, monumental arts, town-planning or landscape design;

(iii) bear a unique or at least exceptional testimony to a cultural tradition or to a civilization which is living or which has disappeared;

(iv) be an outstanding example of a type of building, architectural or technological ensemble or landscape which illustrates (a) significant stage(s) in human history;

(v) be an outstanding example of a traditional human settlement, land-use, or sea-use which is representative of a culture (or cultures), or human interaction with the environment, especially when it has become vulnerable under the impact of irreversible change;

(vi) be directly or tangibly associated with events or living traditions, with ideas, or with beliefs, with artistic and literary works of outstanding universal significance. (The Committee considers that this criterion should preferably be used in conjunction with other criteria);

(vii) contain superlative natural phenomena or areas of exceptional natural beauty and aesthetic importance;

(viii) be outstanding examples representing major stages of Earth's history, including the record of life, significant ongoing geological processes in the development of landforms, or significant geomorphic or physiographic features;

(ix) be outstanding examples representing significant ongoing ecological and biological processes in the evolution and development of terrestrial, fresh water, coastal and marine ecosystems and communities of plants and animals;

(x) contain the most important and significant natural habitats for in-situ conservation of biological diversity, including those containing threatened species of outstanding universal value from the point of view of science or conservation.

The intricate design and meticulous care needed in the restoration of classical Chinese architecture is apparent in this example to be seen in the Summer Palace, Beijing something that is sadly lacking in many recent restorations of historical buildings in China. [Kevin Bishop]

World Heritage Sites

CHINESE CALLIGRAPHY

C hinese people have a special reverence for the arts of calligraphy and painting. In traditional China, the scholar class considered the practice of calligraphy, painting and poetry to be the highest skills an educated man could acquire. Scholars who took the imperial examination were often judged by the quality of their handwriting, and even the best essay, if written in a poor hand, could result in failure for a candidate. How a man wielded his brush was believed to indicate his character and qualities. Even today, when most students use pens rather than brushes to write their university exam papers, a good hand is still admired.

Calligraphy is an art form in China because of the special nature of the Chinese language. Writing Chinese characters involves making a variety of strokes which need to exhibit emphasis, fluidity, lightness and balance, and the discipline lends itself to creative interpretation. The earliest Chinese characters were cut on the shells of tortoises or the bones of animals, and later they were inscribed on bronze vessels. Their shape was clearly influenced by the fact that a sharp implement was used to etch the words on a hard surface. In the earliest style of Chinese calligraphy, known as *Zhuan Shu* (Seal Script), the strokes of the characters are curved and pictorial in style, reflecting the representational quality of the early characters. To this day, calligraphers still practise the writing of Seal Script and—as its name suggests—it is most commonly used in the carving of seals.

During the Qin dynasty, a regular script was formulated under the rule of Qin Shi Huangdi. This script is known as *Li Shu* (Official Script). The strokes of the characters were made more regular and compact. During the Han dynasty, the invention of paper and the development of writing by brush led to a greater expressiveness in calligraphy. Two styles emerged. One of these was the *Kai Shu* (Regular Script), in which the characters were invested with an even greater regularity of form. There is a more geometric and angular shape to the characters; they are written as if placed in the centre of an imaginary square. During this period another script was developed, more cursive and free in form, which is called *Cao Shu* (Grass Script). Grass Script and the later script of *Xing Shu* (Running Script) both allow the writer a greater freedom of expression. Yet the strong and irregular strokes of the two scripts do have their conventions, which prevent the deforming of the characters. The brush may seem to dip and dash across the surface in a kind of shorthand Chinese, but the structural elements of the characters are still respected.

These five scripts of Chinese calligraphy—Seal, Official, Regular, Grass and Running—allow for great variety and experimentation of style within given, understood conventions. Chinese scholars who spend a lifetime perfecting their brushwork often try to master more than one style, using different scripts for different occasions. It is common to see the Grass and Running Scripts used for writing poetry at the side of paintings, while the more formal styles of Seal, Official and Regular Scripts are used for official inscriptions, letters and the scroll hangings, with their two-line quotations from a poem or homily, which used to hang in most people's houses.

Because of the value that Chinese people have traditionally placed on the words of their language, a character written out in good calligraphy was believed to have a good effect. Shops and restaurants in traditional China always paid large amounts of money to have their sign boards and advertisements written out in fine calligraphy, so as to attract business. And even a poor household, where nobody could read and write, would buy auspicious New Year couplets in good calligraphy, to hang on either side of their doors. The poorest peasant would often have the character *man*, meaning 'full', written out on his rice bucket as a good luck charm. Words were believed to possess the power of their meaning, and the writing of words was a revered art.

The appreciation of such an art form is difficult for those who cannot read Chinese, so it is doubly important to find out what you are looking at if you visit an exhibition of calligraphy. If you have a guide nearby, ask for a translation of the characters and an explanation of which style you are viewing. Then it is up to you to look at the balance of space and characters on the page, the ease or the tension, the regularity or irregularity of the script. Look for the way the brush has been used on the paper. Is the manner firm and tense, or fluid and rhythmic? Are the characters written out in bold isolated units or do they run together like a flowing stream? Answers to these questions will give you some idea of the calligrapher's intentions.

Special Topic

PRACTICAL INFORMATION

In today's world of web-based connectivity, the role of printed guidebooks has had to change considerably when it comes to the practicalities of travel, the nuts and bolts of getting to a destination, finding accommodation, eating and moving around within the region. The fact is that no matter how fast a guidebook is published, in this regard it will always be out of date when compared to the more frequently updated information available on the internet.

This is especially true of China, where leaps forward in recent years have been prodigious and frequent. (As an example, Beijing saw the launch of at least three new international-brand five-star hotels in a three-month period over the 2007–2008 winter season.) The developed world's interest in all things Chinese, as well as Beijing's hosting of the 2008 Olympics and Shanghai's preparations for World Expo 2010 has resulted in an explosion of internet sites dedicated to almost every facet of China, its emerging markets and tourism potential. Marry this situation with almost ubiquitous internet access throughout the developed—and much of the developing—world, and it is clear that the overwhelming majority of business or leisure-oriented travellers *can* and *will* find the best practical information about China by surfing the World Wide Web.

Therefore, rather than listing individual hotels, restaurants and trying to give pertinent topical travel advice, the following section will present a comprehensive (but by no means complete) rundown of the best China-related websites currently to be found on the Net. Used intelligently, this is your best way to find the best prices, special offers and newest attractions available in the modern-day Middle Kingdom.

If you are one of the remaining few who staunchly resist the tide of technology engulfing us, we apologise and sympathise, but submit that we must move with prevailing currents and offer our readers the most up-to-date and easily accessible source of information. For better or worse, that is now to be found in cyberspace. Look at it this way: you now have a whole new virtual world to travel in.

Of course, the usual caveat applies to the cyberworld too—websites come and go all the time, so we cannot guarantee that all the following will be up and running when you hit the button.

ACCOMMODATION

Banyan Tree: www.banyantree.com

Crowne Plaza and Holiday Inn Hotels: www.ichotelsgroup.com

Four Seasons Hotels & Resorts: www.fourseasons.com

Grand Hyatt and Hyatt Regency Hotels: www.hyatt.com

Hilton Hotels: www.hilton.com

Howard Johnson: www.hojo.com

InterContinental Hotels & Resorts: www.intercontinental.com

Jin Jiang Hotels: www.jinjianghotels.com

Kempinski Hotels: www.kempinski.com

Mandarin Oriental: www.mandarin-oriental.com

Marriott, JW Marriott and Renaissance Hotels: www.marriott.com

Meritus and JC Mandarin Hotels: www.meritus-hotels.com

Okura Hotels & Resorts: http://home.okura.com

The Peninsula Hotels: www.peninsula.com

Park Hyatt: www.parkhyatt.com

Radisson Hotels & Resorts: www.radisson.com

Raffles Hotels & Resorts: www.beijing.raffles.com

Ramada Hotels: www.ramada.com

The Ritz-Carlton: www.ritzcarlton.com

Shangri-La Hotels and Resorts: www.shangri-la.com

Sheraton, St. Regis, Le Meridien, Westin and W Hotels: www.starwoodhotels.com

Silk Road Hotel Management Company: www.the-silk-road.com

Sofitel, Pullman, Novotel, Mercure and Ibis Hotels: www.accor.com

Swissotel Hotels and Resorts: www.swissotel.com

Other than the international options above, there are of course many private and boutique hotels of excellent quality—usually highlighting the traditional architecture and décor of a specific region—available throughout the country, for example the Fuchun Resort near Hangzhou (**www.fuchunresort.com**) and the Hotel of Modern Art near Guilin (**www.homarc.com**). To find out about these and other more affordable accommodation, the following general accommodation websites are invaluable:

www.asiahotels.com   www.hotelclub.net   www.sinohotel.com

TOUR & TRAVEL ORGANIZATIONS AND COMPANIES

www.cnta.com: The domain of the China National Tourism Authority, with basic information on practicalities, hotels, restaurants, shopping, attractions and festivals.

www.cnto.org: The official site of the China National Tourism Office—based in the US.

www.abercrombiekent.com: Abercrombie & Kent offers luxury tours throughout the country.

www.audleytravel.com: UK-based, offering tailor-made tours to Tibet, Silk Road and the Yangzi River.

www.helenwongstours.com: Helen Wong's Tours, based in Australia.

www.geoex.com: Geographic Expeditions, based in the US.

www.goldenbridge.net: Golden Bridge International, based in Hong Kong.

www.mircorp.com: Mir Corporation, based in the US.

www.sundownerstravel.com: Sundowners Overland, with offices in London and Melbourne.

www.tcs-expeditions.com: US-based, TCS offers extensive trips throughout China.

www.steppestravel.co.uk: UK-based, Steppes Travel offers tailor-made itineraries.

www.seexj.com.cn: CYTS Xinjiang International Tour Company website, specializing in Xinjiang and Silk Road trips.

www.chinahighlights.com: CITS Guilin travel site with plenty of general information.

www.tangula.com.cn: Tangula Luxury Trains, offering five-star trips from Beijing to Lhasa via Xi'an, and to Lijiang via Guilin, Kunming and Dali.

www.cyclechina.com: Two-wheeled adventure tours throughout China, from city tours to major cross-country trips.

www.wildfrontiers.co.uk: UK-based, offering Yunnan, Silk Road and Central Asian frontier tours.

www.wildchina.com: Beijing-based company offering interesting tours to off-the-beaten-track destinations.

For Three Gorges cruises from specialist companies, try:

www.regalchinacruises.net

www.orientcruisetravel.com

www.victoriacruises.com

The following general online agencies combine updated current travel information with airline, hotel and tour booking facilities:

www.tripadvisor.com   http://english.ctrip.com

www.travelchinaguide.com   www.smarttravel.com

www.zuji.com.hk   www.orientaltravel.com

www.chinaplanner.com

Beijing

www.ebeijing.gov.cn: A basic introduction to the city from the Beijing Municipal Government.

www.wildwall.com: The best site for the Great Wall and how to visit, with an emphasis on conservation.

www.bjreview.com.cn: Comment and features from the long-established monthly *Beijing Review*.

www.visitbeijing.com: Domain of the Beijing Tourism Administration and the Beijing Tourism Industry Bureau featuring nation-wide travel news, shopping guides and bizarre travel tips.

www.thebeijingguide.com: A well-designed site, steeped in cultural delights, with traditional music, 360° vistas, videos and more including practical information.

www.cbw.com/btm: Home of the government monthly travel journal—*Beijing This Month*.

www.crienglish.com: Beijing-based China Radio International provides recorded news, features and music as well as a text magazine covering many aspects of modern China.

www.beijingpage.com: Comprehensive Web directory related to Beijing.

www.btmbeijing.com: Beijing This Month e-zine.

www.beijingtraveltips.com

www.thatsbeijing.com

www.thebeijinger.com

Shanghai

www.theshanghaiguide.com: The online China Guide's Shanghai pages.

www.shanghaidaily.com: News from *The Shanghai Daily* newspaper.

http://english.pudong.gov.cn: News and information from the Pudong government.

www.expatsh.com: Useful information if you are planning a move to Shanghai.

www.gingergriffin.com: Sketches of old Shanghai and historical tours of the city.

www.movius.us: Interesting views on Shanghai from US-born local Lisa Movius.

www.shanghai.gov.cn: Practical information from the Shanghai Municipal Government.

http://app1.chinadaily.com.cn/star/index.html: News from *The Shanghai Star* paper.

http://lyw.sh.gov.cn/en/info/list.html: Site of the Shanghai Tourist Information and Service Centre.

www.webguideshanghai.com: American initiated web directory for Shanghai.

www.wangjianshuo.com: Highly-successful blog with useful visitor information.

www.expo2010china.com: The 2010 Shanghai World Expo news site.

www.xintiandi.com: All about Shanghai's most chic entertainment district.

www.shanghai-eats.com: Listings and fair reviews of Shanghai's plethora of eating establishments.

OTHER CITIES & PROVINCES

www.cityofsailing.com: website for Qingdao.

www.cq.gov.cn: Chongqing Municipal Government.

www.dalianxpat.com: Guide and forums related to Dalian.

www.discoverhongkong.com: Official site of the Hong Kong Tourism Board.

www.gansu.gov.cn: Gansu Provincial People's Government website.

www.gokunming.com: Comprehensive city guide to Kunming.

www.guilinchina.net: Guilin travel site.

www.hangzhouexpat.com: Online community site for Hangzhou.

www.ihotpot.com: Sichuan Travel Guide.

www.liaoning-gateway.com: Information guide for Liaoning Province, including Dalian, Shenyang, etc.

www.macauzhuhai.com: Travel and general information about Macau and Zhuhai.

www.mychinastart.com: Offers a vast number of links to all major regions and cities in China.

www.myredstar.com: Guide to Qingdao and Shandong Province.

www.ningboguide.com: Web guide to Ningbo.

http://suzhou.ixpat.com: Community website for Suzhou.

www.thatsguangzhou.com: Guangzhou AsiaXpat site.

www.tianjinexpats.net: City information for and by expatriate residents.

www.visithangzhou.com: Hangzhou travel site.

www.whatsonxiamen.com: Entertainment, culture and travel info for Xiamen.

http://english.xm.gov.cn: The Xiamen Municipal Government's official website.

www.wuhan.com: Business and tourism site for Wuhan.

www.wuhantime.com: Expat web portal for Wuhan.

www.wuhantour.gov.cn: Wuhan Tourism Administration.

www.thexianguide.com: The online China Guide's Xian pages.

www.yangers.com: Yangshuo travel site.

www.yichang.gov.cn: Yichang Municipal Government.

www.yunnantourism.net: Yunnan Provincial Tourism Information Centre.

HEALTH & SAFETY

www.healthinchina.com: Medical advice and contacts for travellers.

www.cdc.gov/travel/destinationchina.aspx: US Center for Contagious Diseases website, giving up-to-date information on potential health hazards in China.

www.who.int/countries/chn/en: World Health Organization.

GENERAL

www.odysseypublications.com: Information on Odyssey's wide range of regional historical and cultural guides.

www.embassiesinchina.com: Embassy and consulate addresses throughout China.

www.fmprc.gov.cn/eng: Official foreign-policy information and news.

www.china-embassy.org/eng: Chinese Government site for visa information.

www.chinatt.org: An invaluable English-language Chinese Railway Timetable available to buy online (pdf electronic format US$10, A4 printed size US$20).

http://wikitravel.org: A constantly updated and enlarged database of info on all aspects of tourist travel.

www.thatsmagazines.com: AsiaXpat site with links to pages related to living in Beijing, Shanghai and Guangzhou.

www.cityweekend.com.cn: Listings and reviews of entertainment options in Beijing, Shanghai and Guangzhou.

www.xianzai.com: E-zines for Beijing, Shanghai, Guangdong and Dalian.

www.chinaexpat.com: Offers a huge amount of information on cities and regions throughout the country, including a China's 50 Best Websites page.

www.lonelyplanet.com: Its Thorn Tree Travel Forum can be a good source of up-to-the-minute travel information.

www.chinatoday.com: Huge amounts of information collated from global sources by InfoPacific Development Inc.

ART & CULTURE

www.chinapages.com: Focus on art, literature and history including clips of Beijing opera-as well as an online Chinese dictionary.

www.answers.com: A cornucopia of fascinating information from Peking Man to China's space programme.

www.chinavista.com: A culture and travel portal with information on destinations, entertainment, art and culture, and links to many associated sites.

www.china-window.com: Business-based, but very informative on arts, culture, history, cuisine and destinations.

www.chineseculture.about.com: Informative and comprehensive guide to the arts, culture and history of China.

www.ibiblio.org/chinese-music: An online jukebox featuring a range of Chinese music from revolutionary to folk and opera.

www.qi-journal.com: An interesting online magazine related to Chinese culture, philosophy and health. Includes sections on traditional Chinese medicine, tai chi, Qigong and feng shui as well as Chinese history, language and astrology.

LANGUAGE

www.mandarintools.com: An advanced site for serious learners, with Chinese software downloads and an online dictionary.

www.chinese-outpost.com: An introduction to the basics of the Chinese language.

www.zhongwen.com: Learn Chinese online and get an instant translation of your name and its associated meaning.

www.chinesepod.com: Learn Mandarin through podcasts.

NEWS SITES

www.chinadaily.com.cn: Online version of China's only English daily national newspaper. Features national and business news, as well as weather and sport.

www.china.org.cn/english: Authorized state portal with daily updates of general and business news. Contains topical features and a travel guide section.

www.cnd.org: Topical news and an extensive historical archive, from 1644 to the present, with an extensive photo library covering most places you are likely to visit.

http://english.peopledaily.com.cn: English version of the main Communist Party daily with official views on the economy and politics as well as current headlines, topical features and city weather.

www.einnews.com/china: Part of the European Internet News global network. Extensive general and business news, with links to travel-related sites.

www.sinolinx.com: A collection of China-related headlines culled from the Net.

www.chinaview.cn: News from China's official news agency, Xinhua, in English.

BUSINESS-RELATED SITES

www.ccpit.org: Trade and associated matters from the China Council for the Promotion of International Trade.

www.china1laws.com: Useful information on doing business with legal perspectives. (site becomes—www.1488.com)

www.chinabiz.org : Comprehensive online daily full of business oriented news, with numerous links to news and entertainment sites.

www.chinabusiness-press.com: Government-approved China business magazine, with links to numerous Chinese companies.

www.chinapages.com: Up-to-date business news and information on Chinese companies.

http://english.mofcom.gov.cn/: Topical business information from the Ministry of Commerce.

www.sinofile.net: Multi-sector business news based on a wide range of Chinese press reports—and special business features.

www.sinonews.com: Highlights news on business and investment opportunities.

www.stats.gov.cn/english: Official statistics from the National Bureau of Statistics on all aspects of the economy and society.

Note: *Some of these sites may not be accessible in China, so it is best to check these sites before you arrive in the country.*

AIRLINES

Most good hotels have travel agents on their premises or can direct you to one nearby; prices will vary depending upon the season and even the time of day. Below is a list of websites for the main Chinese airlines and a selection of offshore airlines serving China, in alphabetical order:

Aeroflot: **www.aeroflot.com**

Air China: **www.airchina.com.cn**

Air France: **www.airfrance.com**

American Airlines: **www.aa.com**

British Airways: **www.britishairways.com**

Bangkok Airways: **www.bangkokair.com**

Cathay Pacific: **www.cathaypacific.com**

China Eastern Airlines: **www.ce-air.com**

China Southern Airlines: **www.csair.com**

China Xinjiang Airlines: **www.cxa.web.ur.ru**

Dragon Air: **www.dragonair.com**

Hong Kong Express Airways: **www.hongkongexpress.com**

Hainan Airlines: **www.hnair.com**

Lufthansa: **www.lufthansa.de**

Northwest Airlines: **www.nwa.com**

Qantas: **www.qantas.com.au**

Shanghai Airlines: **www.shanghai-air.com**

Singapore Airlines: **www.singaporeair.com**

Thai Airways International: **www.thaiairways.com**

United Airlines: **www.united.com**

Virgin Atlantic Airways: **www.virgin-atlantic.com**

A BRIEF GUIDE TO THE CHINESE LANGUAGE

Mandarin (*Putonghua* or common speech), designated as the official Chinese language by the Guomindang government in 1912, is historically a dialect of the Beijing area. The Beijing dialect is one of five main dialect groups—another one being Wu that is spoken in the Shanghai region. The differences between the Shanghai and Beijing dialects can be compared to the differences between the English and French languages.

Regardless of the differences in the spoken language it is consoling to find that the written script is uniform throughout China. The only quandary presented is that over 50,000 characters are entered in the largest dictionary. In practice, however, educated people ordinarily use just 4,000 to 5,000 characters. The mammoth 900,000 character *Selected Works of Chairman Mao* is based on a glossary of just over 3,000 different characters.

Each character is a syllable, many of which can stand alone as words. In fact words with one or two syllables account for more than nine out of 10 of those found in the Chinese language. Characters based on pictures formed the basis for the development of the Chinese script. For instance the character for a person (人) is based on a side view of a human being, the character for big or large (大) resembles a man standing legs apart and arms widespread, whilst the character for a tree (木) depicts a tree with roots and branches. Whilst there are only a few hundred such pictographic characters there are many more which build upon them, though an association or indication to form other words. For example, one person behind another person (从) means to come from or follow and one person above two others (众) means a crowd.

The Chinese government introduced the pinyin system in 1958 allowing an approach to the spoken language through the 26 characters of the Roman alphabet and its associated numerals. Around the same time, the written script was 'simplified' with many characters being rewritten in a less complicated arrangement so as to make them easier to learn. The pinyin system enables foreigners to achieve a reasonable level of spoken Chinese without any knowledge of the characters. This approach is also used in primary education as an aid to basic character recognition.

You will encounter pinyin on road signs, some maps and store fronts and in the Western media. You will initially meet with some difficulty in pronouncing Romanized Chinese words, despite the fact that most sounds correspond to usual pronunciation of the letters in English. The exceptions are:

Chinese Language

Initials

c   is like the *ts* in 'i*ts*'

q   is like the *ch* in '*cheese*'

x   has no English equivalent, and can best be described as a hissing consonant that lies somewhere between *sh* and *s*. The sound was rendered as *hs* under an earlier transcription system.

z   is like the *ds* in 'fa*ds*'

zh   is unaspirated, and sounds like the *j* in 'jug'.

Finals

a   sounds like '*ah*'

e   is pronounced as in '*her*'

i   is pronounced as in 'ski' (written as *yi* when not preceded by an initial consonant). However, in *ci, chi, ri, shi, zi* and *zhi*, the sound represented by the final is quite different and is similar to the *ir* in 'si*r*' but without much stressing of the *r* sound

o   sounds like the *aw* in 'law'

u   sounds like the *oo* in '*ooze*'

ü   is pronounced as the German *ü* (written as *yu* when not preceded by an initial consonant). The last two finals are usually written simply as *e* and *u*.

Finals in Combination

When two or more finals are combined, such as in *hao, jiao* and *liu*, each letter retains its sound value as indicated in the list above, but note the following:

ai   is like the *ie* in 'tie'

ei   is like the *ay* in 'bay'

ian   is like the *ien* in 'Vienna'

ie   similar to '*ear*'

ou   is like the *o* in 'code'

uai sounds like 'why'

uan is like the *uan* in 'iguana' (except when proceeded by *j*, *q*, *x* and *y*; in these cases a *u* following any of these four consonants is in fact *ü* and *uan* is similar to *uen*.)

ue   is like the *ue* in 'duet'

ui   sounds like 'way'

Tones

A Chinese syllable consists of not only an initial and a final or finals, but also as tone or pitch of the voice when the words are spoken. In *Pinyin* the four basic tones are marked ¯, ´, and `. These marks are almost never shown in printed form except in language text.

RECOMMENDED READING

For more detailed cultural and practical guidance to many of China's cities, provinces and thematic journeys of China, look for other Odyssey titles which now include: *Beijing & Shanghai; Xi'an; Guizhou; The Silk Road;* and *The Yangzi River.*

China: A Short Cultural History by C. P. Fitzgerald (Cresset Press, London 1961) is an excellent chronological introduction to Chinese civilization. An anthology, edited by R. Dawson, entitled *The Legacy of China* (Oxford University Press 1964) covers, section by section, the philosophy, literature, arts, science and politics of China. Jonathan Spence's *Gate of Heavenly Peace* (Viking Press 1981) is a well-written survey of recent Chinese history. His *Search for Modern China* (Hutchinson 1990) is an epic narrative from around 1600 to the present.

The Story of the Stone by Cao Xueqin, translated by David Hawkes and John Minford in five volumes (Penguin 1973–88), is that great 18th-century novel of manners better known as *The Dream of the Red Chamber.* There are other excellent translations of Chinese literature. *The Romance of the Three Kingdoms* is available in various translations. The poems of the two Tang masters, Li Bai (Li Po) and Du Fu (Tu Fu), have been translated by Arthur Cooper in the collection *Li Po and Tu Fu* (Penguin 1973).

Chinese archaeology has attracted world attention in recent years. *China: Ancient Culture, Modern Land* (University of Oklahoma Press 1994) is a highly informative and well-illustrated tome. *Style in the Arts of China* by William Watson (Penguin 1974) is an interesting handbook, analyzing the forms of Chinese art in terms of style. Mary Tregear's *Chinese Art* (Thames and Hudson 1980) is a good short introduction to a vast subject. *Chinese Monumental Art* by P. C. Swann (Thames & Hudson 1963) covers a number of topics, including the four principal Buddhist cave sites and the Great Wall. *The Nine Sacred Mountains of China* by M. A. Mullikin and A. M. Hotchkis (Hong Kong 1973) describes the five Taoist peaks and the four Buddhist mountains, as does *Travels through Sacred China* by Martin Palmer (Thorsons 1994).

Sven Hedin, the great Swedish explorer of the early 20th century, produced some very exciting material on Xinjiang and Tibet. He wrote *The Silk Road* (Routledge & Sons, London 1938) and *Trans-Himalaya: Discoveries and Adventures in Tibet* (Macmillan 1909). A more recent publication about early travellers in Central Asia is *Foreign Devils on the Silk Road* by P. Hopkirk (Oxford University Press 1986). For those interested in both exploration and botany, *Plant Hunting in China* by E.H.M. Cox (Oxford University Press 1986) is recommended.

Recommended Reading

There are many books attempting to interpret the Chinese revolution. *Red Star Over China* by E. Snow (Gollancz 1938) is the classic report on the communists at the beginning of the anti-Japanese war, illuminated by the author-journalist's long conversations with Mao Zedong. *Fanshen: A Documentary of Revolution in a Chinese Village* by W. Hinton (Vintage Books 1966) describes in detail the dynamics of revolution in a peasant society, while *Life and Death in Shanghai* (Grafton Books, London 1986) is an autobiographical work by Nien Cheng about her seven-year imprisonment during the Cultural Revolution. For a taste of contemporary travel off the beaten track, *Alone on the Great Wall* by William Lindesay (Hodder 1989/Fulcrum 1991) is a thrilling account of an Englishman's journey on foot along the Great Wall. Other epic journeys can be relived by reading William Lindesay's *Marching with Mao: A Biographical Journey* (Hodder 1993), retracing the route of the Long March and Kevin Bishop's *China's Imperial Way* (Odyssey 1997), following the ancient trade route between Beijing and Hong Kong. The delightful *River Town—Two Years On The Yangtse*, by Peter Hessler is also a must read before your China travel.

While not specifically relating to China, reading C.J. Moore's *In Other Words: A Language Lover's Guide to the Most Intriguing Words Around the World* (Oxford University Press 2006) surely aids raising cultural tolerance levels. Religious tolerance within the Middle Kingdom has a long and varied history as do *The Jews in China* (China Intercontinental Press 2001), a fascinating, graphically illustrated story. History is also served up in lavish images in *World Heritage Sites in China* (China Intercontinental Press 2003) while further studies in Sino-heritage can be found in Joanna Capon's *Guide to Museums in China* (Orientations Magazine Ltd 2002).

Squeezing in a few more good books is simply irresistible; to further burden your bookshelf with rewarding reads: *Xuanzang: A Buddhist Pilgrim on the Silk Road* by Sally Hovey Wriggins (Westview Press, 1997); *Ten Thousand Miles Without a Cloud* by Sun Shuyin (Perennial 2004); *The Chinese* by Jasper Becker (John Murray 2003); *A Traveller's History of China* by Stephen G Haw (Interlink Publishing Group 2003), described by one sinophile as "an indispensable little volume, well worth having in your kit-bag!"; *Treason by the Book: Traitors, Conspirators and Guardians of an Emperor* by Jonathan Spence (Penguin Books 2002); *Old Shanghai—Gangsters in Paradise* by Lynn Pann (Heinemann Asia 1984); *A Bend in the Yellow River* by Justin Hill (Weidenfeld Nicolson Illustrated 1998); *The River at the Centre of the World* by Simon Winchester (Penguin Books 1998); *Life Along the Silk Road* by Susan Whitfield (John Murray 2004); and *South of the Clouds: Tales from Yunnan* by Lucien Miller (University of Washington Press 2005).

INDEX

Compiled by Don Brech Records Management International Ltd., Hong Kong

Indext

Index